The Tankship Tromedy

The Impending Disasters in Tankers

Jack Devanney

Sisyphus Beach

Tavernier, Florida

2006

Published by The CTX Press
212 Tarpon Street
Tavernier, FL 33070

    Publishers's Cataloging-in-Publication Data
    Devanney, Jack

    The tankship tromedy: the impending disasters in tankers / Jack Devanney — Tavernier, Fla :
    The CTX Press, 2006

    p. : cm.
    ISBN: 0-9776479-0-0
    ISBN 13: 978-0-9776479-0-3

    1. Tankers – Design and Construction. 2. Tankers – Casualties. 3. Tankers – History. I. Devanney, Jack. II. Title

VM455.D38 2005
387.2/45—dc22   2005938363

Printed in the United States of America
10 09 08 07 06 • 5 4 3 2 1

Contents

List of Tables

List of Figures

Preface

Tanker design, construction and operation has been controlled by a weird form of self-regulation called the Classification Society, combined with sporadic, emotional intervention by outsiders in the aftermath of a big oil spill. The Classification Societies — and their partners the Flag States — compete for and are financially dependent on the entities that they are supposed to regulate: the shipyards that build the tankers and the shipowners that operate them. This incestuous relationship has produced a steady deterioration in tankship standards since World War II. The well-meaning but technically ignorant outside intervention has not only not been directed at the core problems facing tankers; but in several critical areas has exacerbated those problems. The result is a mess.

The tanker being built today is flimsy, highly unreliable, unmaneuverable, and nearly impossible to maintain. And the situation is becoming progressively worse. As a result, we will have gargantuan spills in the future that need not have happened. This book outlines the sad history of tanker regulation and calls for fundamental changes in both tanker design and the regulatory system. The main body of the book assumes no prior knowledge of tankers. All the technical detail has been banished to appendices.

With respect to the ship itself, I argue that we must:

- Substantially upgrade our hull structural standards, and adopt a far more conservative machinery design philosophy. The ships need at least 15% more steel. Otherwise we are guaranteed massive structural failure spills.
- Require much better cargo sub-division, going back to lots of smaller tanks, regularly arranged.
- Put a blanket of inert gas in all double hull ballast spaces. The book documents that cargo leaking into ballast tanks is the single most important cause of both tanker spillage and tankerman deaths. The book describes how two classes of double hull tankers built in Korea in 2001-2003 had their ballast tanks successfully inerted. The book

demonstrates that ballast tank inerting is critical to tanker safety not only by preventing an explosion should a leak occur, but even more importantly by preventing the leak in the first place by drastically reducing corrosion in way of coating breakdown. Some of this material is being made public for the first time.

- Mandate twin screw in the form of two fully independent engine rooms. Under the current system, 99.6% of all tankers, however large, are single screw. These ships are always a single failure away from being helplessly adrift. The book presents evidence, never before public, that there are at least ten total loss of power incidents on tankers every day. Twin screw, properly implemented, would reduce this failure rate by more than a factor of one thousand. Twin screw would also drastically improve tanker low speed maneuverability which is implicated in a number of big spills including the Aegean Sea shown on the cover.

The combined cost of these reforms will be about the same as the cost of imposing double hulls.

With respect to the tanker regulatory system,

- We must require that ship builders take responsibility for the tankers they build both in the form of a meaningful guarantee and liability for imprudent design and construction. Under the current system, the ship building warranty is a joke — you will get a better guarantee with a toaster — and the shipyards are explicitly absolved from any real liability for their products.

- We must break through the layers of secrecy fostered by the Classification Society system which prevents us from learning from our mistakes.

- We must replace the current, shipowner controlled, Flag State/Classification Society system. It is not regulation; it's an auction. The book argues for an expanded form of port state control in which the port state inspectors go into the tanks. And these inspectors must be guided by a philosophy which is entirely different from current Classification Society surveys.

The Center for Tankship eXcellence (CTX) is an organization devoted to achieving these reforms. It is my hope that those who feel as I do will contact the CTX and offer to help. The website is `www.c4tx.org` and the email address is `ctx@c4tx.org`. In particular, I appeal to tankermen — all of whom already know that the argument outlined above is essentially correct — to come forward with facts and anecdotes supporting the cause.

We have made the mess. We must clean it up.

Acknowledgments

Where do you stop? Do you thank the mentors: John Dunn, John Ferguson, Kim Hochung, Angelo Lengadas, Don Liu, Erling Naess and the scores of tankermen who taught you whatever you know about tankers? Do you thank the shipowners and investors: Basil Papachristidis, J. P. Roed, and Jim Tisch, who were crazy enough to bet on an academic armed only with a computer program? How about partners in crime like Spiros Alamanis, Greg Doyle, Mike Kennedy, Kostas Liopiris and Peter Tsevas? Do you thank your kid brother for conning you into leaving the faculty at MIT to seek your fortune in the tanker market? Definitely not on the latter.

Best to stick with the book itself. Pat Doyle set up the CTX Casualty Database. Kieran Devanney programmed many of the drawings in the appendices. AMSA, CEDRE, Roy Hann, Long Island Maritime Museum, Tony Richardson, Auke Visser, and the Shiplaw program at the University of Capetown contributed pictures. Deborah Ansell at the ITOPF library was a patient, invaluable resource. Reviewers Dave Devanney, Leo Fitzpatrick, Mike Kennedy, Peter MacKenzie made many improvements and caught some of the mistakes. These cowards wish to disassociate themselves from the remaining errors and all the scurrilous remarks. Molly put up with a retirement that became more obsession than vacation with her usual easy going good humor.

Thanks to all.[1]

---

[1] This book was prepared with free, Open Source software, principally the Vim editor, the GIMP image processor, and the Latex text formatter, on the GNU/Linux operating system. Without the Open Source community, this book would not have happened.

Chapter 1

Introduction

1.1 A Bit Player in the Tromedy

Big tankers have been my professional life. Over the last thirty years, my partners and I have bought, and operated for periods up to 18 years, nine very large tankers. We ordered, built, operated and sold the four largest tankers constructed in the last 25 years. We ordered, built and sold prior to delivery four more very large tankers. We owned a tanker brokerage firm in Connecticut, a tanker agency in the Caymans, and a tanker software firm in the Keys. I have inspected over 100 big tankers, been responsible for a score of major dry dockings, managed two massive newbuilding projects, and even spent a stint as the world's worst tanker broker.

Throughout this period, I have continually been bemused and occasionally angered by the inefficiency, the sheer wastefulness, and in some cases the counter-productive stupidity of our attempts to regulate this industry. Sometimes it would me make laugh; sometimes make me cry. It's a *tromedy*. Occasionally, I would get so fed up, I'd tell myself, if you get a chance, you shall write a book on how not to regulate an industry using tankers as an example. Well, in my dotage, I have that chance.

But there is more to this book than an old man's pique. One of the major themes of this story is that things are getting worse, not better. I will argue that tankship standards have deteriorated drastically in the last 30 years. Over this period, tankers have become weaker, less reliable, and far more difficult to maintain. This is an astonishing result given that over the same period the perception of a major oil spill has gone from a godawful mess to an environmental catastrophe with the potential for multi-billion dollar claims. I will further argue that under the current system, things

1

will continue to get worse, both with respect to the quality of the ship and the quality of tanker maintenance. Surely such a strange paradox needs explaining.

The operative word here is explain, not blame. Don't get me wrong, I'm happy to play the blame game. Problem is I don't have enough medals to hand out to all the applicants. Deserving culprits abound: grasping, short-sighted, uncaring owners; parsimonious, perception petrified charterers; conflicted, round-heeled Classification Societies; rule beating, liability ducking shipyards; bigoted, better-than-thou environmentalists; hyperbole wielding, rating obsessed, media vultures; and manipulative, technically ignorant politicians. We will meet them all; and not have a great deal of good to say about any of them. But these are just ordinary people being ordinary people. The regulatory system has to understand that, if you encourage and protect bad behavior, you will get bad and increasingly worse behavior.

Unfortunately, this is what the *Tromedy* does. The Tromedy is my name for the web of relationships by which we regulate the tanker industry. I will try to explain the Tromedy as it is, and how it came to be, mainly in Chapter 2. This chapter will also serve to introduce the reasonably few technical terms we will need the rest of the way.[1]

Chapters 3 thru 5 complete this background. Chapters 3 and 4 study tanker spills and their real cause, which is never grounding, collision or explosion. To progress, we need to know what caused the grounding, collision or explosion. Chapter 5 describes how the Tromedy designs and builds tankers.

Chapters 6 and 7 argue for specific changes in the Tromedy which I believe would restore some measure of sanity to the way we regulate tankers. Chapter 6 focuses on the technical aspects of tanker design and construction. Chapter 7 concentrates on the regulatory structure itself.

There are a couple of issues that this book is not about. I will not talk about the biological or economic impacts of oil spills. I'm not qualified. Nor will I spend much time on oil containment and collection. Other than to point out that, at least in open water, it is a pointless waste of resources. As soon as oil is released into the water, the Tromedy has already failed. What happens after that is outside the ken of this book.

Perhaps more surprisingly, I will spend very little time discussing the merits of double bottoms versus single bottoms or double sides versus single sides. I, who built the four biggest double bottom ships ever, am on record as believing that double bottoms are a really dumb idea. But number of

---

[1] These terms will be italicized on first use, and the definition repeated in the Glossary.

skins is not central to the thesis of this book. In fact, I will argue that one of the reasons why tanker regulation is so screwed up is that it has become obsessed with twin skins to the detriment of far more important issues. I don't intend to repeat the same mistake here.

However, from time to time, this book does need to refer to the physics of how a tank spills oil. This straightforward subject has become hopelessly politicized. Many documents discussing this issue are misleading, or simply incorrect. I know of no reasonably complete, accurate reference. So I have included Appendix C which outlines the simple, if sometimes surprising, physics of tanker oil spillage.

Appendix C is considerably more technical than the rest of the book. It is primarily aimed at tanker operators, spill responders, and tanker designers. Nobody else needs to read it. What happens after a tanker strands or collides is completely peripheral to the core problems in tanker regulation. Nor, it turns out, does it make much difference in terms of overall tanker spillage.[2]

---

[2] I also could not resist casting a few stones at the Tromedy's method for evaluating tanker designs from a spillage point of view in Appendix D. This is tromedic trivia which all but the most voyeuristic should ignore.

1.2   Dedication

This is a book about tankers, mostly big tankers. It has some terrible things to say about the system that has evolved to regulate the tanker industry. I am painfully aware that these statements will be lifted out of context and misused by people with parochial agendas. One target of this misuse will be tanker crews.

So let me make my bias clear. I have found tankermen as a group to be more hardworking, responsible, honest, caring and funny than shoreside people. My guess is that this is a product of three things:

- What they are doing is both important, and tangible. When thirty men move 300,000 tons of oil – more than 10% of all the oil that will be consumed in the United States on the day of arrival – 12,000 miles in five weeks, those guys have indeed accomplished a magnificent task. And they know it and, while they would never admit it, it's a source of pride and responsibility. How much of your nation's need for anything have you supplied in the last five weeks?

- Yet big tankermen have no choice but to be humble. They are dwarfed by their ship, the largest movable structure ever built by man. If you want to feel puny, go down in the engine room and stand next to the main engine. It's longer than a tennis court and four stories high. But the main engine occupies only a small portion of the engine room. Look up; the engine room is taller than a fifteen story building.

  And the engine room occupies only a tiny portion (about 6%) of the ship. A single tank can be longer, wider, *and taller* than St. Patrick's Cathedral and there are twenty plus tanks on-board. No one can wander around a big tanker without feeling like a small cog in a big machine.

- Far more importantly, their enormous ship is a speck on God's ocean. Tankermen are first and foremost seamen. Like all seamen they respect nature; respect in this context is just a polite word for fear. Like all seaman (and aviators) they are always talking about the weather. And it's not to make small talk. If the weather is good, they ask how long will it last? If the weather is bad, they ask will it get worse?

  But they are a special breed of seamen. A crewman on a big tanker may round the Cape of Good Hope five or more times a year. Many seaman these days have never seen the Southern Ocean. They have all run into storms in which their giant ship's speed first dwindles and then goes negative as a 34,000 kilowatt tanker is blown backwards. Off the Cape they have watched in awe as greenwater completely covers the deck and rolls back to the accommodations 300 meters from the bow carrying away 5 ton lifeboats in davits 20 meters above the water. The idea that a tankerman thinks his mighty ship has conquered the ocean is so absurd, that you probably won't even get a smile if you try this concept on one.

Such an environment breeds perspective. Perspective is what big tanker crews have and the Tromedy does not. This book is an attempt to change the latter. It is dedicated to the former.

1.3   Blame the Crew

You can't delve very deeply into tanker issues before you will run across a statement like "IMO estimates that over 90 percent of all marine pollution incidents are due to human error."[29, p 132] IMO is the International Maritime Organization whose official casualty synopsis has a section called "Human Factors" which apparently must be filled in. It is often the longest section in the casualty description.

On one level, blaming spills or other tanker problems on "human error" is a barren truism. Tankers are created and operated by humans. Any problem with any man made system is ultimately a human error. "Human error" tells us nothing.

Much worse, "human error" is usually a code phrase for "blame the crew". As we shall see, in many tanker casualties, the crew made one or more mistakes. Most investigations focus on these mistakes. There are a number of reasons for this:

1. Crew errors are usually easy to recognize. Lousy design, lousy maintenance, lousy enforcement of the construction rules, and flaws in the rules themselves tend to be much harder to identify, often requiring specialized technical knowledge. But we are all experts on human nature, especially when it comes to pointing out somebody else's mistakes.

2. The writ of many investigating organizations is to identify only the most proximate causes. Most of the investigators themselves are or were operators. Operators are conditioned to accept the system as it is and deal with it as best they can. They naturally focus on operational problems.

3. But by far the most important reason to blame the crew is that it is an easy out. A crew screw-up means we don't have to look into the culpability of the owner that provided the under-sized crew with a lousy, poorly maintained ship. We don't have to look into the culpability of the yard that built the lousy ship. We don't have to look into the culpability of the regulatory system which approved the lousy design and overlooked the lousy maintenance.

Many of the so-called investigation reports are written by people who have a big stake in blaming the crew. A Classification Society report will almost always exonerate the Classification Society. A Flag State report will invariably exonerate the Flag State. Neither want to upset their customers: the shipyards and the shipowners. That leaves the crew, who have little means for defending themselves.[3]

One result of all this is that there is no section on "Systemic Factors" in the IMO synopsis. It probably never occurred to the IMO bureaucrats to put one in.

This book takes the opposite view. From my thirty years around tankers, I am convinced that the fundamental problem is not the crew, but the system, the Tromedy. In fact, I've been continually amazed at the ability of crews to cope with difficult to near-impossible conditions. And when they are unable to cope, we call it human error. So while this book will not ignore a proximate crew mistake, it will focus on the ship, its condition, and its design; and the system that generated that ship and condition.

---

[3] The 1980 loss of the OBO DERBYSHIRE with all 44 souls on-board is the exception that proves the rule. The Tromedy produced the usual slew of self-exonerating reports. The unusual aspect of the DERBYSHIRE was the crew were all British and Peter Ridyard, the father of of one of the crew, was a Tromedy insider. Ridyard, a ship surveyor, understood the Tromedy. The relatives of the crew rallied around Ridyard; and, through an extraordinary 20 year effort, were eventually able to show that the Tromedy had produced a ship which could not be expected to survive even a moderately bad Pacific storm.[28, 64]

1.4   The CTX Casualty Database

This book is designed to be used in conjunction with the Center for Tankship eXcellence (CTX) website, `www.c4tx.org`.[4] In particular, the book will often refer to the database of tanker casualties at this website.

You may be surprised to learn — as I was — that tanker regulation has been based on proprietary casualty databases, databases that are not only not subject to public scrutiny but are subject to strict rules against disclosure. The data on which this regulation is based cannot be reviewed or checked for errors, omissions, or bias. The CTX database is totally public, free, and welcomes corrections and additions.[5]

To access this database, point your browser at `www.c4tx.org`, select SPILLS, and then search for the spill or casualty you want. You can do this by date or ship name or ship *IMO number*.[6]

For example, if you want to learn more about the loss of the DERBYSHIRE mentioned in the last section, simply search for "Derbyshire". This will bring up a brief summary of the casualty and links to a Precis file and a Tanker Data file. The Tanker Data link displays data on the ship. The Precis file contains text descriptions of the spill from a variety of sources or links to those sources or both.[7] Sometimes these links will have very instructive photographs which are not replicated in this book. The fact that the vessel name is set in SMALL CAPS like this is a reminder that this casualty is in the CTX database. Feel free to check-out all the information collected there and see if you agree with my take on the spill.[8]

You can also search on the ship's IMO number once you pick it up from one of the ship's casualties to see all the casualties in the database that that ship was involved in.

---

[4] The Center for Tankship eXcellence is a non-profit devoted to improving tanker design and operation, and keeping me off my windsurfer.

[5] The CTX database does not include war related tanker casualties.

[6] Ship names change. Few tankers keep the same name for their whole career. And the same name is used over and over again. Ship name is not a reliable way of identifying a ship. The International Maritime Organization (IMO) has decreed that each large ship be assigned a number. This seven digit number is unique and stays with the ship for her whole life. Most ship databases uses this *IMO number* as the ship key. Unfortunately, few spill sources report the ship's IMO number.

The ship name used in the CTX database is the name at the time of the casualty. Thus, the same ship can show up under more than one name.

[7] The CTX purposely does no screening of these sources. Caveat lector.

[8] To keep the bibliography down to a semi-manageable size, I will not repeat the citations contained in the Precis files.

Chapter 2

A Brief History of Tanker Regulation

2.1   The Rise of the Classification Society

The first successful, sea-going, bulk tanker, the Glückauf, wasn't built until 1886. By that time, a well developed system for regulating the design and construction of ships in international trade was already in place. Intriguingly, this system was almost entirely non-governmental. The fact is that national governments could not effectively regulate ships in international trade if they wanted to. Their writ stopped a mile or two off their own coast. In most cases, their interest stopped about the same distance off-shore, as long as their own nationals were not at risk.

But there was one group that had a strong self-interest in the condition of a ship. And that was the *underwriters*. Given the inherent risks in international maritime trade, especially in the 19th century and earlier, the development of a mechanism for sharing those risks was inevitable. In the 17th century Great Britain began to rule the seas. British ships started trading to all parts of the world. London was the center of this activity.

London merchants, shipowners, and captains took to hanging around Edward Lloyds coffee house to share gossip and make deals including sharing the risks and rewards of individual voyages. This became known as *underwriting* after the practice of signing ones name to the bottom of a document pledging to make good a portion of the losses if the ship didn't make it in return for a portion of the profits.

It did not take long to realize that the underwriters needed a way of assessing the quality of the ships that they were being asked to insure. In

1760, the Register Society was formed to publish an annual register of ships. This publication attempted to classify the condition of the ship's hull and equipment. The hull was rated "A", "E", "I", "O", or "U". (I have no idea why vowels were used.) The equipment was rated "1", "2",or "3", whence the expression "A1" for first or highest class.

The purpose of this system was not to create safe, reliable ships. It was to evaluate risk. Despite the commercials, insurance companies are not in the business of reducing risk. A zero risk world would put them out of business. They love risk; they just want to be sure of the odds, so they can set the premia profitably. Indirectly, the system can put upward pressures on ship standards since on average a better ship will pay a lower premium. But that's a by-product, not the purpose.

In fact, the safety standards on-board ships stayed appallingly low. In was not until 1876 that Samuel Plimsoll's book "Our Seamen" shocked the British into passing the Unseaworthy Ships Bill which mandated minimal loading restrictions. Plimsoll was rewarded with numerous law-suits from outraged shipowners.[1] Plimsoll himself pointed out the obvious downside of

---

[1] Here's an admiring portrait of Plimsoll from Vanity Fair, 1873, in the wonderfully fulsome prose of the time.

> He is not a clever man, he is a poor speaker and a feeble writer, but he has a big good heart, and with the untutored utterings of that he has stirred even the most indifferent. He has taken up a cause, not a popular cause nor a powerful one — only the cause of the British sailor who is sent to sea in rotten vessels in order that ship-owners may thrive. He has written a book about it — a book jumbled together in the fashion of an insane farrago, written without method and without art, but powerful and eloquent beyond any work that has appeared for years because it is the simple honest cry of a simple honest man. Also a man who is bold enough to tell what he believes to be the truth, and it is still pleasing to many people in these Islands to find that in any accessible form.

> He has his reward. Any number of actions for libel have been commenced against him, he has been forced to apologize in the House of Commons, and were it not that he has found strong and passionate support among the public, he would be a lost man. His crime indeed is great. He has declared that there are men among the Merchants of England who prefer their own profits to the lives of their servants, and who habitually sacrifice their men to their money. He has moreover averred that the labouring classes are the more part a brave, high-souled, generous race who merit better treatment than to have their highest qualities made the instruments of their destruction. He tells of men who go to certain death rather than have their courage impugned, of men who freely share their meager crust with companions in poverty, and he claims sympathy and admiration for them although it is well-known that they are ill-washed, uncouth and rude of speech. Manifestly such a proceeding could only be the offspring of a distempered brain, and so it

insurance.

> The ability of shipowners to insure themselves against the risks
> they take not only with their property, but with other peoples'
> lives, is itself the greatest threat to the safe operation of ships.[13,
> p 165]

Plimsoll may have been crazy; but he was no dummy. In most of the casualties we will study in this book, the owners only loss was a small deductible.
In many cases, the ship was insured for more than her market value. The
owner came out ahead.

Anyway in order to rate ships, you needed inspections or *surveys*. This
process gradually became more systematic. In 1834, the Register Society
published the first Rules for the survey and classification of vessels, and
changed its name to Lloyds Register of Shipping. A full time bureaucracy
of *surveyors* (inspectors) and support people was put in place. Similar
developments were taking place in the other major maritime nations.

In a uniquely American development, there were two competing registers
in the USA in the 1850's. One of these outfits eventually became dominant
and is now called the American Bureau of Shipping. And herein lies the
problem. **Somebody has to pay for the inspections.** Early on the
inspection services used the proceeds from the sales of the annual register
for this purpose. They were in essence publishers. Since the purchasers of
the registers were underwriters and *shippers* (merchants who require ships),
whose only interest was in the true condition of the ship, this was a sound
system.[2] If an inspection service published an unreliable register, it lost its
customers.

But over time things changed. As the inspection process became more
comprehensive and more bureaucratic, the cost of the inspections escalated
rapidly. The market for the registers was very limited. If the publishers

---

has gone forth that the sailors' champion is "mad on this question."

Moreover he is very fond of his wife, and continually mentions her as having
assisted in his work, which is another proof of madness. Whereupon it is clear
that no great attention need be paid to Plimsoll. He has secured the inquiry
he asked for however, and in due course of time we shall learn from it that
there never was a country where the humble capitalist was so enslaved by
the arrogant labourer as this, nor a trade in which the labourer's arrogance
was so strongly marked as in that which has to do with ships.

[2] Shippers are not shipowners. Shippers are the shipowner's customers. In the tanker
market, shippers are usually called *charterers*.

attempted to raise the price of the registers to the required level, then readers would group together and buy a single copy reducing the sales still further.

This is the point where the underwriters could in theory have stepped in, paid for the inspections, and added the cost of the surveys to the insurance premia. But this is not what happened. The register publishers hit on the idea of charging the shipowner for the inspections. The shipowner needed the rating to obtain insurance and shippers. It seemed only fair that each shipowner pay the cost of inspecting his ships. He was the obvious source of revenue. At this point the register publishers became *Classification Societies*, classifying ships for the shipowners as a service.

Despite the conflict inherent in the regulatee paying the regulator, this system held up marginally well for a hundred years or so. In each major maritime nation, a single Classification Society emerged. The practices of each national insurance market pretty much limited shipowners to that Flag's Classification Society. This did not give the owners a lot of wiggle room. Each Classification Society or *Class* had a practical monopoly on ships of its Flag.[3] But as we shall see, the Class system broke down after World War II with the rise of Flags of Convenience and the concomitant practice of shopping for a Classification Society.

In the late 1800's, the Classification Societies extended their services to new construction. By this time, the practice of financing ships via bank mortgages had developed, and the banks needed some sort of assurance with respect to the quality of their collateral. Each Society gradually developed its standards of good shipbuilding practice into its *Class Rules* for construction and offered their services in the inspection of ships under construction. Interestingly, the shipyards, not the shipowners, are charged for the pre-delivery surveys and inspections, extending the vendor/client relationship between regulator and regulatee to the ship's pre-delivery life.

The Glückauf inherited the Class system. In fact, through 1967, there was almost no difference between tanker regulation and the regulation of any other ships.[4]

---

[3] The term "Classification Society" has far too many syllables so I will follow common practice in the industry and just say "Class". The weird capitalization is supposed to remind you that I am not using the word in the normal sense. For the same reason, I will capitalize "Flag" when I am talking about the country where the ship is registered, the "Flag State".

[4] Tankers had their own chapter in the Class Rules, but so did every other specialized ship.

Figure 2.1: Glückauf stranded on Fire Island, 1893. No modern tanker would still be intact in this situation. Source: Long Island Maritime Museum.

2.2   Pre-World War I

Prior to World War I, the tanker industry was the province of the oil companies. Almost all tankers were built by an oil company to move its own oil. In the 1880's, outside of Russia, there was only one oil company that counted and that was the Standard Oil Trust. Standard was moving kerosene from the US East Coast to Europe and to Asia. Most of this oil was moving in barrels and tins, but there were some experiments with carrying oil in bulk, mainly by Standard's European subsidiaries. Most of these ships, usually hybrid sailing ships, or conversions of conventional ships, were failures. But in 1886, the German subsidiary of Standard, bought a Swan designed, Newcastle built ship, and called it the Glückauf.[57][p 24-25] The Glückauf was the first successful seagoing tankship. She could carry almost 3000 tons of kerosene in 16 tanks arranged in two columns in the hull. Her machinery was aft. Except for the fact that she was coal fired, she was quite modern in concept. But Standard really didn't follow up on the Glückauf. Surprisingly Rockefeller who gained control of the American oil industry by monopolizing distribution from the Pennsylvania oil fields did not focus on ocean transportation.

This opened the door for Marcus Samuels. In 1883, the Rothchilds had a problem. They had built a railroad from the prolific oil fields around Baku on the Caspian to Batum on the Black Sea. They had the oil, they had the railroad, and, thanks to Standard, they had no customers.

Through a ship broker in London named Fred Lane, they were put in touch with Marcus Samuels. Samuel's father had been a shell merchant on the London docks, buying curios from returning sailors including sea shells and turning them into knickknacks which he sold to English ladies. He built this slender trade into a thriving export/import business between Asia and England. Marcus and his brother Samuel further expanded this operation in cooperation with the big British Far East trading houses.

Lane told Samuels about the Rothchild's problem. Lane knew the only possible outlet was Asia, and Samuels knew Asia. Together they made a trip to the Caspian where Samuels saw a bulk tanker. These ships were developed by Ludwig Nobel, the oil king of Baku, to move oil from Baku to Astrakhan, at the mouth of the Volga.[5] Samuels knew how he was going to take on Standard Oil.

Standard Oil was supplying the Asian kerosene market with five gallon

---

[5] The Nobel ships, built in Sweden, also undoubtedly influenced the design of the Glückauf.

blue tins shipped from the US East Coast around the Cape of Good Hope in sailing ships. Bulk tankers were barred from the Suez Canal for safety reasons. (Of course, at the time, the few ocean going tankships that existed were all owned by Standard Oil or its fronts.) And there were not enough coal bunkering stations on the Cape route to support steam tankers.

Samuels turned to a marine engineer named Fortescue Flannery. Flannery came up with a tanker with carrying capacity or *deadweight* of 5010 tons.[6] She had ten cargo tanks arranged in a 2 by 5 pattern. The tanks were fitted with a steam cleaning system, so she could load grain and sugar for the return trip. Her machinery was aft and, like the Nobel ships, she could burn oil. She also had separate non-cargo tanks that could be filled with sea water. The idea was that these tanks would be filled prior to transiting the Suez Canal and, if the ship grounded, these tanks would be pumped out, and the ship would refloat itself. (This is the exact opposite of the current use of double bottoms.) Samuels decided to name all his ships after sea shells. This first ship, launched in 1892, was called the Murex.

The Suez Canal Authority approved the Murex and her sisters. This was probably more the result of the British government's favoring an English enterprise than the technical merits of the Murex. But the Murex class proved to be good ships. The Murex herself was lost in World War I, torpedoed by a U-boat in 1916.

Samuels ploy was successful. Standard could not compete with the combination of the new transportation technology and being barred from the Canal. Very quickly Samuel's shiny red tins (made in Asia) supplanted Standard's rusty blue ones. Samuels named his operation Shell Transport and Trading Company.

Immediately, Standard started building tankships similar to the Murex. By 1900, Standard owned some 60 tankers mainly involved in the trans-Atlantic trade and Shell owned 15 deep sea tankers mostly trading Black Sea to Asia.

In the first decade of the 20th century, Royal Dutch (Indonesian oil) and Eagle (Mexican oil) joined Standard and Shell in building tankships. Isherwood developed the longitudinal framing system which allowed much larger ships and a simpler construction process. Eagle in particular was at the forefront in taking advantage of this technology, building a 20 ship fleet of of 9,000 and 15,000 tonners just before World War I. And with the advent

---

[6] To be distinguished from the weight of the ship when empty which is called the *lightweight*. The Murex had a lightweight of about 2500 tons. The lightweight is a very important measure of how much steel the ship has. But henceforth when I refer to a ship as a 12,345 tonner, I mean the ship has a carrying capacity of 12,345 tons.

of electricity, the main cargo changed from kerosene to gasoline and fuel oil.

The regulatory structure was simple. The oil companies built tankers for their own use, fully expecting to own them their whole lives. They wanted reasonably reliable, safe transportation service. Tankers were like refineries, just another investment. You would be stupid to build an unsafe or short-lived one.[7] The oil companies quickly amassed tankship experience, quietly corrected their mistakes, and moved oil. The Classification Societies played a negligible role. The oil companies did not need customers for their tankers, nor did they really need insurance. They knew far more about tankships than the Class surveyors. They did not need the Classification Societies.

---

[7] I find the longevity of the pre-World War I tankers fascinating. We have pretty good data on the pre-WWI Standard Oil fleet.[52][pages 19-33] Throwing out ships that were lost at sea or sunk during World War I, we end up with 27 tankers. The average life of these ships was 36 years. Nine lived to be over 40; one lived to 50. The last of these ships was scrapped in 1962. The numbers would have been better if five of these pre-World War I ships had not been sunk in World War II.

2.3 World War I thru World War II

The period between the wars saw the emergence of the *independent* tanker owner. An independent tanker owner has no oil of his own to move. Rather he relies on renting or *chartering* his ship to an oil company or oil trader which requires tankship services. The oil company who rents the ship is called the *charterer*.

Even before World War I, the nearly monolithic nature of the oil business was changing rapidly. It wasn't just the break up of Standard Oil in 1911 into a pride of operationally different companies. More important was the emergence of the Texas and Oklahoma oil fields. Standard was slow to exploit this new production and new companies like Gulf Oil and Texaco were not. The main advantage that the newcomers had was that it was cheaper to transport this oil by tanker to the East Coast than by the spidery pipeline network that Standard was pushing thru the Midwest. Tanker demand further blossomed with the development of Mexican and then Venezuelan production.

In such a rapidly changing situation, it was inevitable that from time to time an oil company would find itself short of transportation capacity. Prior to World War I, such a company would either have to make a deal with an unhelpful competitor or put the excess cargo on general cargo ship in tins, an extremely expensive alternative.

Naturally, there were some sharp eyed individuals ready to exploit this situation. As early as 1913, Wilhemsen, a Norwegian shipowner, started building tankers. By the end of WWI, Wilhemsen had ten tankships. Since tankers were in very short supply during the war, it was an extremely lucrative investment.

It was The Great War that really put the independent tanker owner in business. In 1917, England and France came perilously close to running out of oil. The resumption of the unrestricted submarine campaign by Germany on February 1st was a strategic blunder. It brought the US into the war on April 6th. But it was a tactical success. And the primary target was tankers. By May 1917, the Admiralty was down to a three month's supply of fuel. In July 1917, the American ambassador wrote Washington "The Germans are succeeding. They have lately sunk so many fuel oil ships, that this country may very soon be in a perilous condition — even the Grand Fleet may not have enough fuel." On December 15th, Clemenceau begged Wilson for more tankers pointing out the obvious "gasoline is as vital as blood in the coming battles... a failure in the supply of gasoline would cause the immediate paralysis of our armies."[82]

Wilson responded most vigorously. The War Shipping Board was set up with draconian powers and the unheard amount of 1.3 billion dollars. The board commandeered all American ships, and all ships under construction regardless of nationality. It took over all the US yards and built from scratch the largest yard in the world at Hog Island, Philadelphia (now the site of the Philly airport). In 1918, the Shipping Board built 533 ships totally 3.3 million tons. This monster could not be turned off overnight. In 1919 the Shipping Board churned out 1180 ships totaling 6.4 million tons, *despite the fact that the war had ended in November, 1918*. From 1916 to 1921, American yards produced 316 tankers totally 3.2 million deadweight tons. At the beginning of the war, the entire world tanker fleet was just over 2 million tons.[67, page 70-71]

To put it politely, there was a great deal of waste. Almost everybody involved in this effort was well compensated. Even Hurley the head of the Shipping Board during most of this period admits the average cost of these vessels, nearly a million dollars, was three to four times as much as the pre-war numbers.[33] Since many of the ships were quite small, this is certainly conservative. Charges of corruption abounded but nothing ever came of them.

Tanker demand held up for a year or so after the war, but then a massive surplus developed. In 1923 some 800,000 tons of War Shipping Board tankers were laid up. These ships combined with a pliant bureaucracy were inviting targets for speculators. Consider the case of Daniel Ludwig, a young ex-rum runner and small time tug boat operator. In 1921, Ludwig got a hold of an old Standard Oil tanker called the Wico for $25,000 ($5,000 down). But he did not have five thousand dollars. So he found a guy named Tomlinson, to whom he sold 51% of the deal for the $5,000. Later he sold out to Tomlinson for $40,000.[68] The most successful independent tanker owner ever was on his way.

Here's a little story about Ludwig to which we will refer later. In 1925, Ludwig picked up the 7400 ton Phoenix for $57,000 ($14,000 of his own money, bank loan for the rest) from the War Shipping Board. The Phoenix was a dry cargo ship converted to a tanker by putting vertical cylindrical tanks in each hold. In other words, she was a double hull. One day in Boston with the ship loaded with gasoline, the tanks which were riveted started leaking. Two crew working in the double hull space were overcome by the fumes. Ludwig, who was a hands on guy, started to go down to investigate. As he did the space exploded. Ludwig was blown thru one deck and badly injured his back. The two crew men were killed. Ludwig became a firm believer in welding.

If you knew the right people, the Shipping Board's terms could be extremely generous. You could buy a mothballed ship for $50,000 and the promise to spend say $100,000 on renovation. And to sweeten the deal you only had to pay 10% or $15,000 up front. And the Shipping Board's Construction Loan Committee would loan you as much as 75% of the renovation funds. This was not the kind of game that the oil companies were interested in playing. They had better things to do than small time manipulation of Shipping Board bureaucrats. So most of the surplus tonnage ended up in the hands of individuals.

The second major impetus to independent tanker ownership was off-the-books financing. In the 1920's the oil business was booming. The oil companies needed capital to develop their discoveries, their refineries, and their retail distribution systems. They wanted to borrow as much money as possible as cheaply as possible. A key to this was the company's bond rating. The bond rating in turn was strongly influenced by the firm's debt/equity ratio. Oil company accountants discovered that, if instead of borrowing money to build their own ships, they gave an independent shipowner a 7 or 8 year lease, the independent could take that lease (known as a *long term charter*) to a bank, and borrow the money to build the ship against the charter. Under the accounting rules of the day, the oil company's obligation to pay the charter hire was not recognized as debt, so the company's bond rating was unaffected.[8]

Between the independents scooping up surplus tonnage, and long term charters, by the beginning of World War II, 39% of the world's tanker fleet was owned by independents. A full fledged market, centered in London, for exchanging tank ship services between oil companies and independents had developed. But the oil companies were still very much in control.

From a regulatory point of view, the most important development of this period was the invention of the *Flag of Convenience* (FOC). When World War II started in Europe in 1939, Roosevelt was in a bind. FDR needed to supply England with the goods without which it would starve. The British Flag fleet was being decimated by the U-boats. But FDR could not use American Flag ships because in 1935 he had pushed through the Shipping Neutrality Act which forbade American Flag ships from trading with belligerents. He had done this in a failed attempt to dissuade Mussolini from invading Ethiopia. He couldn't repeal the Shipping Neutrality Act.

---

[8] This was true despite the fact that the oil company often co-signed the mortgage, and usually paid the charter hire directly to the bank. Auditors depend on the companies they regulate in much the same manner as Classification Societies depend on ship owners.

That would bring the isolationists down on him big time. The solution was to quietly allow American Flag owners to reflag their ships to Panama.[9]

The carrot was freedom from US regulation and most importantly US crew costs, which had become more than double European.[55, page 94] By 1939, 52 tankers totaling 700,000 tons were registered in Panama.[57, page 107] A very important door had been opened.

---

[9] The FOC ploy had been used before. In 1922, the United American Line was allowed to switch its passenger liners to Panamanian Flag to avoid the ban on alcohol. In 1935, Esso transferred its Dantzig Flag (already a sort of FOC) fleet to Panama to avoid German appropriation. Much earlier, slavers had switched Flags to avoid anti-slavery laws. In fact, ships have been changing Flags for momentary convenience since the dawn of maritime history. But this development was totally different in terms of scale, organization, and, as we shall see, impact on shipping regulation.

2.4 Flags of Convenience

World War II changed everything. Few industries were affected more drastically by World War II than the tanker business. As soon as the war ended a whole series of massive changes began.

The oil companies' tanker fleets had been commandeered and decimated. But the companies weren't worried. The conventional wisdom held that there would be a worldwide slump after the war. With all the ships built during the war, a massive glut was inevitable. And indeed in 1946 a large number of tankers were laid up and mothballed. You could buy a two year old 18,000 ton tanker for less than a million dollars. By this time the disgraced Shipping Board had been replaced by the US Maritime Commission. But it was just a new name for the same game.

A few individuals saw this as an opportunity. Onassis, Niarchos, and others snapped up the surplus tankers and waited. They did not have to wait long. The world did not go into a slump after the war. Europe with the help of the Marshall Plan rebuilt rapidly. Europe needed oil and the only available oil was across the Atlantic in Texas and Venezuela. In 1947, a shortage of in-service tankers developed. The oil companies were forced to deal with the independents. Tanker rates tripled almost overnight. The speculators recouped their investment and more in a single voyage.

Daniel Ludwig, that remarkable combination of vision and street smarts, had a different idea. He had turned a nothing shipyard in Norfolk into a goldmine with lucrative wartime contracts. His concept was to take the block construction method developed in the USA during the war to the intact but empty yards in Japan and blow away the Europeans and the rest of the world with production and operating economies. The economies of size were obvious to Ludwig. He immediately started building 30,000 ton ships. Others followed and the race was on.

With the oil companies in charge, tankship size had changed little since World War I. Esso built a couple of 22,000 tonners in 1921. These remained the largest tankers ever built for over 25 years. The workhorse tankers of World War II, the T-2 and T-3, had a deadweight of 16,000 and 18,000 tons respectively. But in 1948, Ludwig launched the first of the ill-fated, 30,000 ton Bulkpetrol class.[10] In 1952, he delivered his first ship from the old Impe-

---

[10] Five of this class were built. Only the Bulkpetrol herself survived long enough to be scrapped. Three (AMPHIALOS, KEO, and PACOCEAN) broke in two in heavy weather killing at least 32 crew men and spilling about 90,000 tons in total. One, the GOLDEN DRAKE was lost to an explosion, probably structurally related. A disastrous record which has never been properly investigated. Best guess is that Ludwig's ambitions had run ahead of

rial Navy yard in Kure; the Petrokure was a 38,000 tonner. Onassis followed with a 45,000 tonner in the same year. Ludwig up the ante to 56,000 tons in 1955 with the strange, innovative, and short-lived SINCLAIR PETROLORE.[11] The 85,000 ton Universe Leader followed in 1956, just in time for the first Suez Canal closure. In ten years, tanker size had quadrupled.

And it just kept going. In 1958, Ludwig breached the 100,000 ton barrier with the Universe Apollo. In 1964, a 63,000 ton tanker built in 1959 was jumboized — expanded by inserting a new middle section — to a 120,000 tonner. Her name was the Torrey Canyon. In 1966, the 206,000 ton Idemitsu Maru was delivered. In twenty years, the independents had increased tanker size by a factor of ten.

The independents brought more than a willingness to take risks, both market and technical. They brought an ability to think outside the box. Ludwig was unhappy with the cost and quality of American crews. In the Cayman Islands, he found what he wanted: terrific seamen, dirt cheap. The independents were footloose and they weren't particularly interested in paying taxes. That included the tonnage taxes and other fees charged by the traditional maritime powers. They jumped on FDR's Flag of Convenience, basically setting up their own Flags, first in Panama, and then in Liberia and elsewhere.[12] It is important to note that the Panamanian and Liberian Flags had the support of the US Government. The US military was convinced that it had to have an American merchant marine for support in time of war. But strongly unionized, featherbedding American crews cost two or three times that of hardworking non-American crews. It was obvious that American Flag ships could not compete with foreign Flag. The solution of allowing non-American crew was rejected by the unions. So the US government opted for quiet but strong support for FOC's which were deemed to be under effective US control.

It wasn't just the independents that used these Flags. After World War II, almost all the major American oil companies' tankers were registered in Panama or Liberia. Not only did this allow them access to better, much cheaper crews, but there was no US tax until the foreign shipowning sub-

---

his grasp of welding technology.

[11] The SINCLAIR PETROLORE, Figure 2.2, was truly unique; not only the biggest ship in the world but a self-unloading ore/oiler. The world has never seen anything like her before or since. In 1960, she exploded off Brazil spilling 60 million liters. This was the largest oil spill ever at the time by at least a factor of two. Most likely cause was cargo leaking into the double bottom.

[12] Much later I made my own small contribution to meaningless fabric on the jackstaff by initiating the Marshall Islands Flag in a failed attempt to obtain US Navy protection for our American owned ships in the Persian Gulf during the Iran-Iraq War.

sidiary dividended profits back to the parent.

For our purposes, by far the most important feature of these Flags of Convenience is that **essentially all of the Flag State inspection duties were turned over to the Classification Societies**. The Flag State appoints the ship's Class as its agent for inspection. At the same time, the link between a major maritime Flag and a Classification Society was broken. A UK ship was Classed by Lloyds Register (LR). An American Flag ship was Classed by American Bureau of Shipping (ABS). A Norwegian ship was Classed by Det Norske Veritas (DNV). And so on. That was understood. But if your ship is Liberian, which Class do you hire? The answer is: you shop for the best deal. **Now the Classification Societies had to compete with each other for business.** If a Class surveyor proved unreasonably inflexible, you complained to his boss; and, if that didn't work, you switched Class.

The oil companies simply couldn't compete with these pirates. They were smarter, quicker, nimbler; and they didn't have to follow the same rules. In those days, the oil companies used to say their policy was to own 50% of their own requirements to move oil, lease another 30% of their tanker requirements on a 3 to 7 year basis (known as a term charter), and depend on *spot charters* (the rental of a tanker for an individual voyage) for the remaining 20%. But by 1959, less than one-third of all tanker tonnage was owned by oil companies.[83][page 62]

The tanker market is extremely cyclic. The basic pattern is longish periods of slumps interspersed with short lived spikes during which the spot tanker rate can go through the roof. Every time the tanker market started to tighten up, the independents would get their orders for new ships in first. By the time a major oil company had approved a newbuilding program, the market would be back in slump and the oil company program would be cut back or canceled. By the mid 1960's three quarters of the world's tanker fleet were owned by independents.

Figure 2.2: Sinclair Petrolore: Self-Unloading Ore-Oil Carrier. Source: www.solentwaters.co.uk

2.5 Torrey Canyon and IMO

The halcyon days for the pirates started to come to an end on the morning of March 18th, 1967. On making landfall at the Scilly Isles off Lands End, England, the recently jumboized TORREY CANYON, bound for Milford Haven in Wales, found herself 20 miles east of her intended course. The ship was fully loaded with 120,000 tons of cargo. The Captain needed to make the tide at Milford Haven. To save a little time, he decided to go through the gap between the Scillies and Seven Stones Reef, a senseless decision given his options. The tide was setting them to the east. They made a plotting error. In extremis, the autopilot was temporarily disengaged, delaying the final turn. By the time the Captain realized he was too close to Seven Stones on his starboard side, it was too late given the sluggish maneuverability of the ship. The ship and cargo were lost, and the world was awakened to the damage that could be caused by a large oil spill.

The TORREY CANYON generated a great deal of regulation. The 1969 CLC Convention produced a much stricter definition of the shipowner's spill liability and set up a system for compensating victims of pollution damage. The musically named Intervention Convention allowed coastal states to take early action against vessels which pose a threat to their shorelines. But from the point of view of the tankers themselves, the most important result of the The TORREY CANYON was the International Convention for the Prevention of Pollution from Ships, 1973, usually called MARPOL/73.

MARPOL/73 itself was nearly toothless. The only concrete regulation in MARPOL/73 was an intelligent limitation on tank size, which did not come into effect until 1977. Besides that MARPOL/73 doesn't say much, other than spills should be investigated and reported on by the Flag State.[13] But a non-Class mechanism for the international regulation of tankers had been created.

MARPOL/73 was agreed to under the auspices of the International Maritime Organization or IMO. IMO is an offshoot of the United Nations. It is important to recognize that IMO itself has no regulatory power. It was created in 1948 "to provide machinery for the cooperation among governments" on maritime trade. The original name, Inter-Governmental Maritime Consultative Organization, says it all. IMO actually does little more than sched-

---

[13] Flag State compliance with this requirement is spotty. Worse, most of the reports are kept secret. Only an IMO priesthood has the right to see the full reports. They are not subject to public review. An IMO sub-committee prepares a "public" summary of the reports, but even these summaries are kept on a password locked web page. Welcome to the strange, secretive world of IMO.

Figure 2.3: Tugs abandoning attempt to refloat Torrey Canyon as weather starts to deteriorate. Ship still intact at this point. Source: Royal Navy

ule meetings in which representatives of the various national governments, the *member states*, thrash out potential regulation.[14] This draft regulation is then voted on by each member state, and, when a sufficient number of the member states ratify the regulation, it is supposed to be enforced by all the member states. But a member state can opt out, as the USA chose to do in 1992 because it was unhappy with the IMO double hull rules. Or simply ignore the regulation. Under an amendment ratified in 1978 member states were supposed to provide dirty ballast reception facilities at many tanker load ports. Most did not. IMO has no enforcement power.

Much worse, IMO is built around the concept of the *Flag State*. A member country is a member of IMO by virtue of the ships that are registered under its Flag. Voting is based on the size of each country's fleet. This means the Marshall Islands has three times more voting power than the USA. **By the time IMO became real, the Flag State had become a charade.**

Nonetheless, any regulation that IMO adopts is effectively law for tanker owners. All it takes is one or two major *Port States* to enforce the regulation, and the tanker owners must comply.[15] Otherwise, their ships are commercially crippled. The Port States are the real power in tanker regulation as we shall see when the USA unilaterally passed double hull regulation in 1990.

In short, the TORREY CANYON had no immediate impact on tanker design or operation. But the world had finally been alerted to the danger of a big spill, and a non-Class regulatory mechanism, albeit badly flawed, had been set up.

---

[14] This is done through a series of IMO committees, made up of a disparate collection of Flag State appointed "experts". In many cases, the committee chair, the key drafter of the regulation, is — you guessed it — a Classification Society employee.

[15] The Port State is the country where a ship loads or discharges.

2.6   VLCC's and Inerting

As far as tanker owners were concerned, the important development of 1967 was not the TORREY CANYON, but the second closing of the Suez Canal in June as a result of the Six-Day War. This sent the tanker market into a three year boom. The owners were becoming very rich, and building bigger and bigger ships. In 1966, the first ship over 200,000 tons deadweight was delivered. Since the press had started calling the 60,000 and 80,000 tonners built in the early 1960's "supertankers". No one knew what to call these new ships. For want of imagination, they became known as *VLCC*'s (Very Large Crude Carriers)

These big ships had an unanticipated but critical problem. In the space of three weeks in December, 1969, three nearly new VLCC's had massive cargo tank explosions. In all three cases the ships were cleaning empty cargo tanks. Something was terribly wrong.

Cargo tank cleaning is accomplished by machines that look like and work like enormous lawn sprinklers. These gadgets shoot a revolving high pressure jet of sea water around the tank, in theory blasting the surfaces clean of oil. Two of the tankers involved, the MARPESSA and the MACTRA were Shell ships. The third was the brand new KONG HAAKON VII. The MARPESSA, on her maiden ballast leg, sank killing two crewmen. The MACTRA, Figure 2.4, and the KONG HAAKON VII, Figure 2.5, had a large portion of their main decks blown away but survived.

Shell instituted a crash research program and came to the conclusion that the high speed jets of water impinging on the steel surface of the tank were creating static electricity, in somewhat the same way that rain drops in a thunderstorm do. When enough static electric builds up, it produces a spark in space that is full of hydrocarbon vapor. The process is tank sized dependent and didn't really make itself obvious until tanks grew to VLCC size.

It was clear that the old way would no longer work. The solution was *cargo tank inerting*. The exhaust or stack gas from a properly operated boiler contains 2 to 5% oxygen, as opposed to about 21% for normal air. If the tank atmosphere contains less than about 11% O_2, then the mixture will not support combustion regardless of the hydrocarbon content. The idea was to take the boiler stack gas, run it through a scrubber, which is an oversized shower which cools the gas and removes most of the sulfur, and pipe this *inert gas* into the tanks.

Figure 2.4: Mactra deck after tank cleaning explosion. Two killed.
Source: Auke Visser, supertankers.topcities.com

Figure 2.5: Kong Haakon deck after tank cleaning explosion. Obvious similarity to Mactra. Source: Auke Visser, supertankers.topcities.com

**Inerting was a tremendous step forward in tankship safety —
the single most important step of all time.** Not only were cargo tank
cleaning explosions eliminated on properly inerted tankers, but all sorts
of other explosions as well. When a tanker loads petroleum or ballasts a
cargo tank, the vapors in the tank are pushed out onto the area above the
deck. If the tank is inerted, the mixture emerging from the tank is non-
combustible and by the time the ambient air has increased the O_2 level to
a combustible level, the hydrocarbons will almost always be diluted to less
than the flammable level. If the tank is not inerted, then you have a real
chance of an explosion such as the fire on the SANSINENA that killed nine
people in Los Angeles in 1976.

If an inerted tank is breached, there is a better chance of avoiding a
fire than in a non-inerted tank, and a far better chance of confining any
fire to the damaged tank. In 1979, the horribly corroded structure of the
Total tanker, BETELGEUSE, failed as she was discharging at Bantry Bay
in Ireland.[60] She immediately exploded; 50 people were murdered.[16] In-
excusably, ten years after the MARPESSA, this 121,000 ton tanker was not
inerted. Eight months later, the VLCC ENERGY CONCENTRATION broke in
two discharging at Rotterdam. She still had 115,000 tons of cargo on-board.
But there was no fire and no casualties. The ENERGY CONCENTRATION was
inerted.

Inerting saved many tankermen lives during the Iran-Iraq War. Here's
a particularly dramatic example from Newton.[57, page 118]

> A typical [sic] attack on a tanker is recounted by Captain Bruce Ewen,
> master at the time of the 412,000 dwt World Petrobras which was
> bombed by Iraqi jets on 22 December 1987. At the time the tanker
> was providing floating storage off Iran's Larak Island in the northern
> part of the Strait of Hormuz. Two Russian made 500 lb bombs with
> parachute drogues attached dropped onto the maindeck during the
> attack by Mirage jets, which also hit two other tankers off the island.
>
> World Petrobras was at the time transferring oil from one tanker, Free
> Enterprise, into another, British Respect. "When the bombs struck,"
> Ewen recalls, "the rubber hoses attaching us to the British Respect
> were set afire and a large amount of shrapnel from our deck fittings
> blew through the side of the British Respect. Since we were both
> inerted and had our inert gas plants running, an explosion was avoided.

---

[16] Total is a big French oil company, largely government owned. Can't blame the pirates
for this one. The Irish investigation revealed that Total and the ship's Classification Society, Bureau Veritas, knew the ballast tanks were in despicable condition, but consciously
decided not to do anything about it because Total intended to sell the ship. The word
murdered is not used lightly.

> However, we needed to get British Respect away from us so we could get firefighting tugs alongside."

> "We cut her aft ropes and her master went ahead on the engines and ran the forward ropes off the reels. When she parted the hoses, a large amount of oil was dumped into the water which caused a large fire and set the rubber fenders ablaze. Although this rendered our lifeboat and the liferaft on the port side beyond use, the current was fairly quick so the danger passed in a fairly short time."

The World Petrobras resumed operations 42 hours later.

Not all tankermen were so fortunate. 62 tankers and 250 tankermen were lost in The Tanker War. But there were over 500 attacks on defenceless tankers in the Iran-Iraq War. Without inerting, the toll would have been far higher.

Finally, inert gas dramatically reduces steel corrosion rates in the cargo tanks. Corrosion is an oxidation process and proceeds much more slowly in an oxygen depleted environment. This is explored in detail in Section 6.4.

Under strong pressure from most major oil companies, cargo tank inerting was quickly adopted by most owners of big tankers. By the late 1970's nearly all tankers larger than 100,000 tons were fitted with inert gas systems. (The BETELGEUSE was an unforgivable exception.) However, progress on smaller ships was indefensibly slow. It wasn't until May, 1985 that IMO finally required inert gas systems on (almost) all tankers over 20,000 tons. In the late 70's and early 80's, one can make a strong argument that at least 88 lives were unnecessarily lost on non-inerted tankers. See Section 3.7. The Tromedy let us down big time here.

It was soon realized that seawater does not do a good job of cleaning oil, something any housewife could have told us. In most cases, you will get a much cleaner tank if instead of seawater you use high pressure jets of the crude oil itself. This is known as Crude Oil Washing or *cow-ing*, a process that was pioneered by BP. Cow-ing has three big advantages over sea water washing:

1. The tank almost always ends up cleaner.
2. You don't introduce corrosive salt water into the tank.
3. You don't have oily water to dispose of after the cleaning.

Most tanker owners now only use seawater washing when a tank needs to be cleaned for inspection. On our ships, we found that even this was unnecessary and unproductive, and seawater washing was eliminated entirely.

Figure 2.6: The Betelgeuse at Whiddy Island. Horribly corroded segregated ballast tanks. Uninerted. Fully Class Approved. 50 dead. Source: Auke Visser, supertankers.topcities.com

2.7   Boom, Bust, and the Argo Merchant

The early 1970's were heady years for tanker owners. Although the tanker fleet was expanding at 12-13% per year in the late 60's and very early 70's, tanker supply could not keep up with ton-mile demand growth. In 1973, VLCC rates skyrocketed. At the height of the boom, the Kong Haakon VII, refitted with a new deck, netted nine million dollars for a single 2.5 month voyage from the Persian Gulf to Northern Europe. That is, approximately one-half what it cost to build her four years earlier.

The 1973 boom produced an ordering frenzy. In one quarter, 75 million tons of new tankers were ordered. At the time, the entire tanker fleet afloat was about 150 million tons. The principle orderers were the major oil companies. They had watched the independents become fabulously rich with their aggressive newbuilding programs. This time, despite new tanker prices doubling and tripling, they were not going to be left out. Esso, Shell, Chevron each had forty or more very big tankers on order.

Many of these ships were much larger than a VLCC, as much as twice as large. The tanker industry's limited vocabulary had been exhausted. Tankers above about 350,000 tons became known as *Ultra Large Crude Carriers* or ULCC's.

Alas, on Yom Kippur, October, 10th, 1973, it all came to a crashing halt. The Yom Kippur War combined with a partial embargo, cut tanker demand at the same time that a flood of tonnage was coming out of the yards. Oil prices tripled to the unheard level of $10 per barrel, depressing oil consumption growth. Tanker rates plummeted to levels which would barely pay the fuel cost of a voyage. Eighty million dollar ships went straight from the newbuilding yards to lay up.

And it just kept getting worse. In 1975, the Suez Canal reopened. In 1979 just as the market was starting to recover, the Iranian Revolution pushed oil prices to $30 sending the world economy into depression. Oil consumption actually contracted. It wasn't until the late 1980's that tankers became profitable again. The oil companies' massive investment in big tankers in 1973 turned out to be a colossal blunder.[17]

The mid-70's were a quiet period in tanker regulation. But in hindsight there was one important development. On 15 December 1976, the 28,000 ton tanker ARGO MERCHANT stranded on Nantucket Shoals 29 miles SE

---

[17] In the early/mid 1980's, my partners and I bought eight of these ships. We paid a total of 45 million dollars for ships that 7 or 8 years earlier had cost the oil companies over 500 million dollars. Four, built in Japan, were good tankers. Two were at best mediocre. Two were lemons. These last four were built in Europe.

of Nantucket. The ship was fully loaded with fuel oil, eventually broke up, and generated a 29 million liter spill. The navigational practices onboard were deplorable; the ship was under-manned; and the owner had failed to supply the ship with proper charts or maintain the navigational and other equipment.[13][page 8] This was one putrid tanker. But the oil stayed offshore and the spill had little impact outside the United States.

The regulatory significance of the ARGO MERCHANT was that the US Coast Guard boarded the ship and took control of the salvage attempt despite the fact that the ship was in international waters. This was the first test of the Intervention Convention. Prior to the Intervention Convention which came into force in 1975, a port state official could only inspect a ship certificates – not the ship itself – and then only in port state waters. The ARGO MERCHANT was the first real crack in the Flag States' (really Classification Societies') monopoly of tanker regulation.

2.8   The Amoco Cadiz and Marpol/78

During the early 1970's the volume of tanker trade rose dramatically. And we also had a massive increase in tanker spill volume. As Figure 2.7 shows total spill volume which had been averaging less than a 100 million liters per year in the late 60's and early 70's, climbed to around 300 million liters annually in 1975 and 1976. But for one reason or another, none of these spills received the attention of the TORREY CANYON. This changed big time on March 16, 1978.

The AMOCO CADIZ, a single screw, single rudder, VLCC was proceeding north off the coast of Brittany, when in heavy weather, her under-designed, Class approved, hydraulic steering gear failed. Five of the six studs holding one of the high pressure flanges failed, hydraulic fluid spurted out, air entered the system, and the rudder was free to swing violently back and forth, progressively destroying the system.[18] With no rudder and only one propeller, the fully loaded ship was helpless. The crew were unable to fix the leak in part because all the hydraulic fluid sloshing around on the deck

---

[18] During the trial, it came out that the the ABS approved steering gears on this class of ship had a long history of problems. They were under-speced and then not built to spec. In particular, they were built with hard cast iron bushings rather than bronze as they should have been per design. These hard bushings plowed grooves into the rams. As a result, the steering gear on the AMOCO CADIZ was leaking seven to twelve liters of fluid per day. Normally, these rams should leak only a few drops per day. Amoco was aware of the problem and had in fact replaced the iron bushes with bronze on two of the four sister ships. But not on the AMOCO CADIZ nor the Amoco Milford Haven. The difference? The Cadiz and Milford Haven were on time charter to Shell at $28,000 per day, a highly lucrative rate. The other two ships were in the spot market where the rates barely paid fuel costs, so there was little commercial cost in taking these ships out of service to replace the bushes. When the Cadiz went ashore, she had a set of bronze bushes on-board as spares. The ship's Classification Society, ABS, was aware of all this, had surveyed the steering gear on three occasions, and each time pronounced it seaworthy.[50]

The French sued ABS, but the Classification Societies have always maintained that they have no responsibility for what happens to the ships that they have Classed. All they do is issue a certificate. Here's how the International Association of Classification Societies puts it.

> Such a certificate does not imply, and should not be construed as an express warranty of safety, fitness for purpose or seaworthiness of the ship. It is an attestation only that the vessel is in compliance with the standards that have been developed and published by the society issuing the classification certificate.[34]

Every contract between Class and owner has a strong clause absolving Class of any liability for its approvals.

ABS and the French settled out of court, so I don't know how stoutly ABS defended this position that Class are not regulators at all.

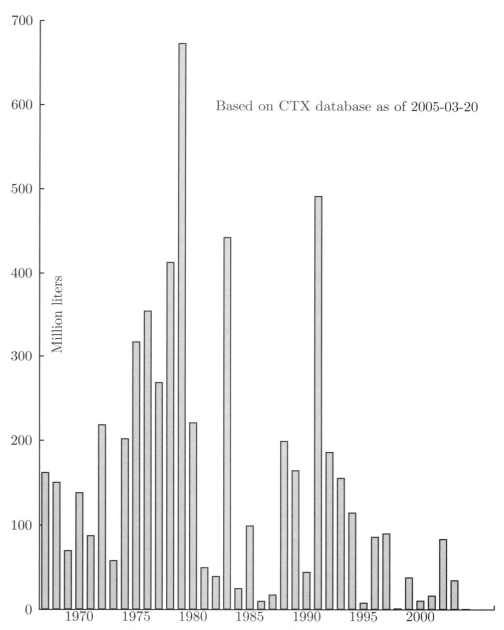

Figure 2.7: Total Tanker Spill Volume by Year

around the steering gear made for impossible footing as the ship rolled and pitched. Despite a belated attempt to take the ship under tow, the ship drifted ashore, eventually broke up, spilling 267 million liters of crude oil on the French coast. Beaches were oiled from Brest to the Channel Islands.

Enormous outrage. Another IMO conclave was immediately convened and the resulting regulations, usually called MARPOL/78, were far from toothless. But the dynamics of IMO deliberations can be weird. Even though it had nothing to do with the AMOCO CADIZ, nor even oil spills in general, the framers of MARPOL/78 focused on oily ballast water.

Oil transport is essentially a one-way trade. Tankers take oil from places that have it to places that don't. They are too specialized to carry anything back.[19] But they can't go back empty. The propeller would be out of the water, the bow subject to slamming, and the ship nearly unmaneuverable. Therefore, tankers use sea water as *ballast*. Ballast is both a noun and a verb, and can be used as an adjective. The process of taking on ballast is known as *ballasting* and pumping the ballast back into the sea at the load port as *deballasting*. The portion of the voyage in which the ship doesn't have cargo on-board is called the *ballast leg*. The revenue earning portion of the trip is the *loaded leg*.

Prior to MARPOL/78, almost all tankers employed a system in which about a third of the cargo tanks were also used as ballast tanks. This meant that every time the ship deballasted she was also pumping some residual oil into the sea. By careful tank cleaning and decanting, the amount of oil in the discharged ballast water can be limited to a few hundred liters a trip. But not all ships did a good job of handling ballast water, and even a few hundred liters per trip is a sizable volume in total. MARPOL/78 introduced three major new requirements:

1. Protectively located, segregated ballast tanks on all ships built after 1980.
2. A limit of 15 ppm oil in any ballast water discharged from existing ships and measures to attempt to enforce this.
3. No discharge of any oily ballast in certain areas such as the Mediterranean combined with a requirement that tanker load ports in these areas provide ballast reception facilities. (This provision was mostly ignored by the load port states.)

In a tanker employing *segregated ballast*, a tank is either cargo or ballast but not both. Also the ballast piping and the cargo piping system are completely

---

[19] Like many statements in this brief history, this a slight over-simplification. Where necessary, we will get into the exceptions and qualifications later in the book.

separate. Segregated ballast eliminates the great bulk of tanker oily ballast water discharges. MARPOL/78 also required that the pure ballast tanks be located along the side of the ship where they would offer some protection against collisions. The rule is that 30% of the side shell in way of the tanks had to be non-cargo.

Following common practice, I will use the term *Marpol tanker* to refer to the tankers that were built to the MARPOL/78 rules. These were single hull, segregated ballast tankers, almost all built between 1980 and the very early 1990's. In the early 90's, the industry switched to double hulls which also use segregated ballast. And I will call the ships built before MARPOL/78, *pre-Marpol tankers*.

The requirement for segregated ballast had a number of critically important impacts on tanker design.

1. Tanker designers had to find more tank volume to make up for the fact they could not use the same volume for both ballast and cargo. They did this by making the tanks taller. The tank height of a Marpol tanker will be 10 to 20% larger than that of a pre-Marpol of the same length.[7, p 11] This has surprisingly important implications for the amount of outflow in a grounding. See Section C.3. In 1973, the USCG, arguing against segregated ballast, pointed out that the expected outflow in groundings increases by up to 90% relative to a pre-Marpol tanker.[16, p 43] The Coast Guard was right. Because the nearly new EXXON VALDEZ was a Marpol tanker, she spilled about 10 million liters more oil than if she had been an older pre-Marpol ship.

2. Wing tanks became narrower and longer. This was the cheap way to meet the 30% rule. Center tanks became extremely large. The number of cargo tanks decreased. A standard 250,000 ton pre-marpol VLCC would typically have 24 cargo tanks. A standard Marpol 250,000 tonner would have 11 cargo tanks plus two small *slop tanks*.[20] The growth

---

[20] Slop tanks are a key element in ballast water handling. They are small cargo tanks with extra piping for heating the liquid in the tank and decanting water from the bottom of the tank. Oily ballast is fed into these tanks, heated, and allowed to separate, oil on top, water beneath. A portion of the water is then decanted and discharged overboard thru an Overboard Discharge Monitor (ODM). The ODM generates a permanent record of the oil concentration in the water and is set to alarm and shut down at 15 ppm. The remaining oil-water mixture, called slops, is mostly oil. It is kept on-board and mixed in with the next cargo, a process called Load on Top.

ODM's are hard to tamper with, but they don't always work, and can be easily bypassed by an owner who is willing to take the risk. The risks are two-fold: (a) a port state inspector may find either physical evidence of the tampering or inconsistencies in

in tank size increased spillage if one of these tanks was breached. This was only partly balanced by the fact that the segregated ballast tanks were required to be located on the side shell. Overall a Marpol tanker spills about twice as much oil as a good pre-Marpol tanker in IMO's standard casualty scenario. See Section 5.7 for the disturbing numbers.

3. None of the ballast tanks on Marpol tankers are protected by cargo tank inerting. On a pre-Marpol ship, most of the ballast tanks are also cargo tanks. These ships have only two or three non-cargo ballast tanks. Therefore, in order to inert the cargo tanks, you also had to inert just about all the ballast tanks. The exceptions were generally one or two tanks near the middle of the ship and the forepeak tank. ***These two or three segregated ballast tanks have been the source of most of the pre-Marpol structural failures due to corrosion.*** See Section 3.3 for the gory details.[21]

4. The amount of segregated ballast tank painted area increased by a factor of more than three. A 250,000 ton pre-Marpol tanker will have about 25,000 square meters of segregated ballast tank coated area. A 250,000 ton Marpol tanker will have about 80,000 square meters of segregated ballast tank coated area. This is important because protecting the steel in sea-water only ballast tanks is one of the most difficult jobs tanker crews face. We will return to this subject in Section 6.4.

The MARPOL/78 rules actually came into force in the mid-early 1980's. But before that there was a remarkable development in spill volume. As Figure 2.7 shows total spill volume dropped abruptly in 1980 and throughout the 80's averaged about 130 million liters, a three fold reduction relative to the second half of the 70's. The MARPOL/78 rules can't be credited for this. They not only were not yet in force, but also these rules for the most part aren't even aimed at spillage as opposed to intentional ballast discharge. There is nothing in Figure 2.7 that indicates that MARPOL/78 had any impact on spillage at all.

Prior to the AMOCO CADIZ spill, the standard life cycle for a tanker was that it was built by an oil company or *first tier* owner (often against a time charter from an oil company), and then after ten or so years of operation,

---

the ODM records, (b) he could be turned in by a whistleblowing crew member.

[21] On a pre-Marpol tanker, the segregated ballast tanks were not an environmental requirement. They existed simply to put buoyancy where it was needed when the ship was fully loaded. In fact, they were not even called segregated ballast tanks. The term was *permanent* ballast tank. But in this context, the words are synonyms.

the ship would be sold to a *second tier* owner, who operated the ship just as cheaply as he possibly could. *First tier* and *second tier* in this context are euphemisms. The first tier owners ranged from fairly professional (the minority) to at best marginally competent (the majority). The standard was "can you get a bank to loan you money?" The second tier owners ranged from inept down to indescribable cretins.

The Cadiz spill made it obvious to oil company boards that a big spill with which they had any connection, either as owner or charterer, was a public relations disaster. And there were liability implications. The court cases engendered by this spill left the corporate veil in tatters. The word came down to the oil company marine departments that spillage on owned or chartered in tonnage would not be tolerated. Up to that time, the oil companies through subsidiaries had simply taken the cheapest ship offered. In the short run, the most profitable owner was the the owner who ran his ships the cheapest. A sort of Gresham's Law applied. Increasingly atrocious operation was the norm among the second tier tanker owners. See the ARGO MERCHANT, ARROW, ZOE COLOCOTRONIS spills for egregious examples.

At the same time, the tanker market went into a 15 year long slump in 1975. This made it cheap for the oil companies to be choosy. In the VLCC market, there were typically 30 or 40 ships waiting outside the Persian Gulf for a cargo. If an oil company had a cargo, a dozen or more ships would bid for the business, all at about the same very low rate. The oil company could take what it thought was the highest quality ship at almost the same price as the lowest quality. Owners either had to clean up their act, or quickly go broke. The truly awful operators mostly disappeared. The result was a three fold reduction in spillage overnight with an almost unnoticeably small increase in tanker operating costs. That is effective, efficient regulation.[22]

The slump of the 1980's had another far less beneficial effect. For nearly 100 years, the major oil companies had supported large marine departments to manage their tanker fleets. For the most part, they were well funded and technically competent. They had a wide range of experience from operating 50 and 100 ship fleets. They could effectively react to problems as Shell did in the tank cleaning explosions. And as BP did in developing crude oil washing. The oil company marine departments were the core of technical professionalism in the tanker industry. Through organizations such as

---

[22] This process did not happen on the dry bulk side. In a bulk carrier casualty, the only losers are the crew and the insurers. Nobody gives a damn about the crews and the underwriters figure it is much easier to raise premiums then standards. Since the AMOCO CADIZ, dry bulk ships have had a far worse record than tankers.

OCIMF, BSRA, and TSCF, some of their experience and knowledge trickled to the rest of the industry.

But the AMOCO CADIZ taught the oil company boards maybe they shouldn't be in the tanker business. In any event, the big investment in tankers in the mid-70's was an economic disaster for the shareholders. The marine departments lost credibility and political influence within the companies. In the long slump of the 1980's, the oil company fleets were sold off and the marine departments allowed to atrophy. The remaining organizations were mere shadows of themselves, little better than the independents with whom they had to compete for oil company dollars. In the 1980's, the main pillar of tanker standards crumbled and pretty much disappeared.

The AMOCO CADIZ had one final, little noted effect. In 1978, the major European countries had issued something called the Hague Agreement calling for inspection of foreign ships to improve crew living conditions (and preserve European seagoing jobs). But it was just a piece of paper to keep the unions happy. After the Cadiz, the Hague Agreement was expanded to include safety and pollution prevention. In 1982, 14 European ministers signed the Paris Memorandum of Understanding on Port State Control (Paris MOU). I guess it sounds better in French. Under this agreement, each of the signatories pledged to inspect 25% of the foreign ships visiting its ports and develop common inspection standards. But the Paris MOU was pretty much ignored for ten years. Few tankers were actually inspected. The few inspections that did take place concentrated on crew living conditions. During this period, our ships must have loaded/discharged at European ports several hundred times. At the time, I didn't even know the Paris MOU existed.

2.9 The Exxon Valdez and Double Hull

2.9.1 1980 Class Rules Weakening

Most of the 1980's was a quiet period on the tanker regulation front. The market was in a prolonged slump. Not many new ships were built. Overall spillage by the dubious standards of the 1970's was low. More importantly, there were no spills that caught the media's attention. A number of major structural failures, usually involving a segregated ballast tank — including the loss of the fully loaded VLCC, CASTILLO DE BELLVER[23] — and an epidemic of hull cracking went unnoticed by the public and apparently by the regulators.

In fact, over this period there was a significant weakening of the Class Rules. Most of this backsliding took place in the late 1970's and very early 1980's, when the owners, yards and Class were under severe economic pressure. In 1981, Exxon did an extensive survey of their VLCC fleet. In one case they figured that a 1970 built VLCC would need 1130 tons of new steel to be brought back to the required strength. But "Following discussions with Class, it was agreed that Rules changes since construction of these vessels would allow reduced *scantlings* under today's Rules.[24] Steel renewal estimates for the vessel were reduced to about 450 tonnes."[72] BP found that the longitudinal strength of a VLCC built to 1974 Rules would be about 6.5% greater than would be required by 1989 Rules.[51]

I found out about this deterioration in the Rules via CAPS. *CAPS* stands for Condition Assessment Program Survey. By the early 1990's, the major oil companies had figured out that the normal Class surveys were worthless. So they decided that, in order for an older tanker to be acceptable for chartering, it must be put through a much more detailed structural survey. This was called a CAPS inspection. CAPS involved taking something like 10,000 steel thickness measurements, and then putting the resulting as-measured hull thru Class's normal design evaluation program to see if it still met the Rules' strength requirements. The overall result was a CAPS rating: 1 (Good), 2 (OK), 3 (Marginal). In a way, it was a return to the original Register ratings. But, in a weak market, the charterers would only take CAPS 1 ships.

But the Class Rules CAPS used were the current circa 1992 Rules. When our 1975/1976 built ships were put thru this process, I was startled to find out that their as-built scantlings were 7 to 20% thicker than would be re-

---

[23] Third largest spill of all time. See Section 3.3 for a bunch of other examples.

[24] *Scantlings* is jargon for the size of the structural members. Think thickness.

Table 2.1: Results of Hellespont Embassy CAPS Surveys

	Section Modulus m^3					
	Required		Frame 83		Frame 71	
	1976	1992	Built	Gauged	Built	Gauged
1996-06 Deck	108.1	97.3	115.7	111.4	115.7	111.6
1996-06 Bottom	108.1	97.3	129.1	125.1	129.1	123.0
2001-05 Deck	108.1	97.3	115.2	111.5	115.2	111.6
2001-05 Bottom	108.1	97.3	129.1	123.9	129.1	122.2

quired of a new ship. Since the wastage on average was 2-4%, these 20 year old ships had scantlings well in excess of that of a brand new ship. CAPS revealed that the de facto stress levels in tanker structure had climbed roughly 10% between the early 1970's and mid 1980's.

Table 2.1 summarizes the results of two CAPS surveys of the Hellespont Embassy, the first in June, 1996, the second in May, 2001. The Hellespont Embassy was a 413,000 ton ULCC built by Mitsubishi Heavy Industries (MHI) in 1976 under the Class rules that existed in the early 1970's. This little table offers a number of interesting insights. The numbers shown are the deck section modulus (4th last and 2nd last rows) and the bottom section modulus (3rd last and last row). The deck section modulus is the single most important measure of the hull's strength against hogging moment (being pushed up in the the middle). The bottom section modulus is the corresponding measure of the hull's strength against sagging moment (being pushed down in the the middle). The second and third columns show the deterioration in the Class rules between 1976 and 1992. The required strength has dropped by 10%. The fourth and sixth columns show that Mitsubishi "over-built" the ship. As built the the ship had about 5% more deck section modulus and almost 20% more bottom section modulus than required at that time. By 1992 Class rules, the Embassy was 19% and 33% "over-built". The fifth and seventh columns show the result of the thickness measurements. In 1996 at age 20 the Embassy has an average wastage of 3 to 4%. She was still far stronger than a brand new ship built to 1992 Rules. Notice that the 1996 and 2001 readings are essentially the same. In those five years, the Embassy suffered nil wastage. This was due to the strict anoding and inerting policy that Hellespont instituted in the second part of the ship's life. See Appendix A for details. We will return to Table 2.1 several times. For now, the point is that the Class Rules on hull strength deteriorated by about 10% between the early 1970's and the early 1980's.

CAPS did not last long. It fell afoul of the same old vendor/client problem. The thickness measurers were hired by the Owner. The CAPS surveys were expensive. There was no requirement that the ship's normal Classification Society had to do the CAPS survey. The Classification Societies competed aggressively for the fees. It soon became known that it was easier to get a CAPS 1 from ABS than either Lloyds or DNV. Although LR and DNV scrambled to keep up, — we induced LR to re-rate a ship that had originally been given a CAPS 2 (unfairly, of course) to CAPS 1 under the threat of going to ABS — ABS got the lion's share of the business. The owners had to have CAPS 1. So the issue to be negotiated was: what do I have to do to get CAPS 1? The results were predictable. I've inspected plenty of CAPS 1 tankers which I would not wish on my worst enemy.[25] It took the Class Survey system about 100 years to become meaningless. It took the CAPS system about five. By the late 1990's, the charterers were taking CAPS 1 for granted, knowing that it was nothing more than a fig leaf in the event the ship got in trouble.

2.9.2 The Exxon Valdez Spill

But I'm getting ahead of myself. In early 1989, the Tromedy received a severe shock. On the night of March 24, the nearly new Marpol VLCC, EXXON VALDEZ, outbound from Valdez, Alaska ran aground as a result of a navigation error by a tired third mate, strongly abetted by the inexplicable failure of the master, the only rested member of a criminally small crew, to be on the bridge during a dicey portion of the voyage.[8] Eight of the eleven tall cargo tanks were breached. To make matters much worse, the ship grounded at high tide. The 3 meter loss in external sea water pressure when the tide went out drastically increased the outflow.[26] In all about 20% of the 200,000 ton cargo were lost. This was less than one-seventh the size of the CASTILLO DE BELLVER spill.

---

[25] In 1995 in a bar in Dubai, a Livanos superintendent told me this story. Livanos had a ULCC called the Tina, a 350,000 tonner built at Kockums in Sweden. These lightly built ships were well-known for cracking where the side shell longitudinals hit the web frames. Livanos had ABS on-board the Tina to do CAPS despite the fact that the Tina was a Lloyds ship. From experience with the Kockums 350's, the ABS surveyor knew that the ship almost certainly had cracks in the standard area. But he was told by his boss that that was none of CAPS business and not to examine the area. The superintendent subsequently checked the area, found bad cracks which was why the ship was in Dubai being repaired.

[26] See Section C.9.2.

But what a mess. Oil was found on beaches as far away as 400 miles from the spill. Hundreds of thousands of birds were killed as well as something like 4000 lovable otters and 350 seals. Pictures of badly soiled workers ineffectually cleaning badly oiled shorelines were in the newspapers for months. The drama was heightened by the Captain's drinking problem. And the tanker owner was the biggest, richest oil company in the world. Exxon ended up spending 2.5 billion dollars in clean-up costs, paying the US government and the state of Alaska 900 million dollars in natural resource damage costs, and another 100 million in fines.[41]

The 560 naval architects of the US Congress reacted quickly to the outcry and passed the Oil Pollution Act of 1990 (OPA). OPA was a sweeping piece of legislation which among other things introduced a whole new concept of liability. But the single most important provision was the phasing out of single hull tankers in US waters between 1997 and 2000 in favor of double hull ships.[27]

In a double hull tanker, the segregated ballast volume is wrapped around the cargo tanks in a sort of U. The width of the double side and double bottom is 2 to 3 meters. As long as a collision or grounding damage does not penetrate more than this width, there will be no spill. The double hull is an effective way of turning certain small spills into no spill. Much more importantly, double sides can be a very effective oil containment device as long as the damage is entirely below the waterline. See Section C.8.

On the down side,

- Any cargo tank leak will not be into the sea where it will be both dissipated and quickly spotted, but into the ballast tanks where over time an explosive concentration of hydrocarbon vapor can build up. For the pre-Marpol ships this was the case only for those cargo tanks which were contiguous to the two or three segregated ballast tanks. Yet, as we shall see in Chapter 3, this kind of leak was the single most important cause of tanker deaths and spill volumes on these ships.
- Segregated ballast tank coated area is more than eight times that of a pre-Marpol tanker of the same carrying capacity as Table 2.2 shows. Ballast tank steel maintenance has become an order of magnitude bigger job. Yet as we shall see, failure to maintain ballast tank steel has put far more oil on the water than any other cause.

We will return to these issues after studying past tanker casualties in Chapter 3.

---

[27] An important exception was made for ships discharging offshore. These could be single hull until 2015.

Table 2.2: Comparison of Segregated Ballast Tank Coated Areas
260,000 ton VLCC

HULL TYPE	Square Meters
pre-Marpol	25,000
Marpol	80,000
Double Hull	225,000

IMO moved much more slowly before coming up with amendments to MARPOL/78 in 1992 which

- mandated double hull or the functional equivalent for all tankers contracted after 6 July 1993;
- required hydrostatically balanced loading (see Appendix C) or protectively located segregated ballast tanks after age 25 for pre-Marpol ships.

The USA opted out of the 1992 amendments since they weren't synced with the OPA 1990 double hull implementation schedule, although as a practical matter there wasn't all that much difference.

But for tanker owners the most important response was that of their customers, the oil companies. The oil company boards now realized that a big spill was not just a public relations nightmare but could be a multi-billion dollar expense, even before any lost revenue due to consumer backlash. This time the word came down emphatically. The oil companies, at considerable expense, instituted on-board tanker *vetting* programs. In most cases, a tanker had to be successfully inspected by an oil company representative within a year for a ship to be even considered for chartering. Many of these inspectors were experienced tankermen.

At about the same time the US Coast Guard started the Tank Vessel Evaluation (TVE) program. Every tanker trading to the USA had to undergo an inspection from the USCG within the last 12 months. The USCG inspectors do not go into tanks. They focus almost exclusively on paperwork, and safety and environmental protection gear. But unless what they did inspect worked, the ship didn't discharge. And that meant a very unhappy charterer.

Not to be outdone, the Europeans resurrected the moribund Paris MOU. The number of actual ship inspections under the MOU jumped dramatically. By 1991, the Europeans were doing 15,000 port state inspections annually. The Paris MOU inspections cover all sorts of non-European ships. Only about 10% of these inspections are tankers. The inspections concentrate on paperwork, safety equipment, crew living conditions, and what can be seen in a walk through. The Paris MOU inspectors don't go in the tanks. Even so, about 10% of the tankers inspected had deficiencies warranting detention, an expensive wake-up call for the owners.

The cocoon had been broken. ***For the first time since the invention of the Flag of Convenience, fifty years earlier, there was a non-Classification Society inspector on-board.***[28] Up to the 1990's, the only time an allegedly third party inspector came on-board was during the annual Classification Society survey. This was limited to a check of the safety equipment and paperwork. More importantly, this friendly visit was scheduled and paid for by the owner.

Under Class Rules, a Class Surveyor cannot go aboard a ship unless he is explicitly invited to do so by the owner. Of course, if the owner doesn't schedule a survey during the flexible timeframe called for in the Class Rules, then Class will list that survey as *overdue*. Too many overdue Surveys and Class will threaten to *delist* the ship, that is, withdraw the ship's Class rating. But even here there is a great deal of flexibility. It is possible to get an extension. For major dry-dockings an extension of up to six months is almost automatic, more than that will take some pressure. Then there's the completion game. An owner will purposely leave a small portion of a major survey undone. Class will be mollified for a while. Only when this last portion is actually done, and the survey is complete will the clock start ticking for the next such survey.

Most machinery items are under *continuous* survey. This means the actual survey is delegated to the ship's Chief Engineer. The Chief sends the same information to Class that the Class surveyor would have; and everybody's happy. The only subsequent check that Class has that this information is accurate is that the ship's paperwork is consistent with that which the ship sent to Class. Self-regulation in its purest form.

If a Class surveyor finds something really wrong, then he writes up a *Condition of Class*. The wording is subject to negotiation between the surveyor and the owner's superintendent. The strongest wording I've ever seen is something like "such and such must be fixed and re-inspected at the next convenient port." The surveyor has no authority to keep the ship from sailing, nor can he *de-list* the ship. In fact, the Condition of Class he writes up is only a recommendation to Class headquarters. The owner can

---

[28] Port states would send an occasional custom inspector on-board, but it had nothing to do with the ship. His job was check for drugs and, in the Arab ports, porn. In many tanker loading ports, he was there mainly to cadge a carton of cigarettes.

sometimes get the wording softened before the recommendation is approved. After all, he is — to use Class' own terminology — the Client.

But now with charterer vetting, TVE's, and the Paris MOU people on-board, there was real adversarial pressures behind the inspections. The result was another substantial improvement in overall spillage. Between 1995 and 2004 inclusive, we averaged about 42,000 tons per year, down almost a factor of ten from the late 70's numbers. One has to be careful with such numbers. We could have one really big spill tomorrow, that would double a decade average overnight. But there is no doubt that true third party inspection has had a big impact.[29] Unfortunately, there was one crippling problem with these inspections. **The non-Class inspectors almost never went in the tanks.**

---

[29] During this period, double hull tonnage grew quickly, but for most of this period double hulls were still a minority. In 1995, about 9% of all tankers over 50,000 dwt were double hull. In 1998, this number had grown to 20%. In 2001, the percentage of double hulls was about 42%. In 2004, the percentage of double hulls was about 61%. It's hard to see much effect of this change in Figure 2.7. Slightly more oil was spilled in 2000-2003 than in 1995-1998. But to be more definitive we need to look at the individual casualties in Chapter 3.

2.10   Isoism and the Rise of the Hirelings

Between the EXXON VALDEZ and 1999, there were no spills which really caught the public's attention. This surprises me since in the BRAER[30] (1993) and the SEA EMPRESS[31] (1996), we have two dramatic casualties, both much larger than the Valdez, and both in the UK. After OPA 1990 and the 1992 amendments to MARPOL, tanker regulation entered what I call the *isoism* era.

It started with the ISO 9000 craze. The watchword was Quality Assurance. Quality was to be assured by extensive documentation of just about all operating procedures, numerous checklists, and detailed procedures to ensure that that all this paperwork was properly maintained and changed only by properly documented procedure changing procedures. Regular audits of all these procedures were required. If you jumped thru enough paperwork hoops, you were awarded a badge that said ISO 9000 approved. A cottage industry arose to administer this process. Our old friends, the Classification Societies, were the prime providers of ISO 9000 advice and audit, for a fee of course.[32]

ISO 9000 was in theory voluntary but many charterers preferred ISO 9000 ships mainly because it gave them another document to hide behind if the ship got into trouble, However, ISO style quality assurance became mandatory with the imposition in July 1998 of the International Management Code for the Safe Operation of Ships and Pollution Protection. Somehow this awkward name — most quality assurance literature reads like this — was given the acronym, ISM. Hence the medical name for this paperwork plague, *isoism*.

Some parts of isoism were obvious common sense: important procedures

---

[30] Lost power, drifted ashore in the Shetlands, broke up, and sank.

[31] Pilot misjudged tidal set entering Milford Haven.

[32] By this time the Classification Societies had expanded into all sorts of non-vessel inspection lines. One Class executive called this "growing the business". Class has whole departments devoted to specialized technical services. DNV was peddling their own vessel designs, mostly stolen from Clients' submittals. Most Classes offer a range of software. ABS bought an existing ship management software company for this purpose. The not-always-unspoken understanding is clear: use our software and it will be easier for you to jump thru all the regulatory hurdles we control. There are egregious conflicts of interest. But the main result is to give the owners more weapons with which to reward a compliant Class and admonish an obstinate one. As in the case of CAPS, a well behaved Class will get some of the owner's software, ISO, etc business; an inflexible one certainly will not.

In a way, the most interesting of these non-inspection based ventures is Lloyds Register's return to publishing. Over time LR has acquired the leading shipping weekly Fairplay and a monthly called Safety at Sea. Don't expect these two magazines to be critical of the Tromedy. In fact, they are proponents of the blame-the-crew school. See Section 3.6.1. The Tromedy is well aware of the importance of controlling the media.

should be documented. But most of it was just plain silly, a triumph of process over substance. Although it was a major nuisance and major expense, many tanker owners and all the *hirelings* welcomed isoism.

The hirelings, ship management firms, have been with us since the 1970's. The idea is to split tanker owning from tanker operation. Instead of each owner setting up his own organization to hire crew, supervise drydocking and do all the myriad day to day tasks required in running a ship, a specialized, third party firm will do it for you. This is supposed to generate economies of scale in purchasing and the like. And it allows a speculative investor to fairly easily enter and leave an extremely cyclic market based on his guess at what the tanker market is going to do next. Third party tanker management became more and more prevalent in the 1980's and 1990's with the demise of the major oil company fleets, and the death of the first generation of independents. Neither the oil companies nor the pioneering giants of independent tanker ownership would trust their ships to hirelings.

My own experience with third party managed tankers has been uniformly bad. There are two problems:

- The link between ship and crewman is broken.
- The ship manager must concentrate on short-run cost minimization.

The Ship/Crew Link Ships have this strange way of getting to crew members. When you are on a ship for 24 hours a day for months at a time, there is this natural tendency to regard it as your ship. And if you are assigned to the same ship semi-permanently, in a very real sense it becomes your ship. You take pride in her, you want her to look good, you fight for her with the owner and the superintendents. And on a more prosaic level, if something is wrong, you realize you'd better fix it and fix it right. Otherwise you will probably be faced with the same problem or worse on the next rotation. It is hard to over-emphasize the importance of this link between ship and crew. It is what makes the whole lousy system work.

The third party manager breaks this link. Crewmen are shifted willy nilly from ship to ship and owner to owner. It is hard to develop any allegiance to a ship when you don't even know who the owner is. Anyway you will probably never see the ship again. In this environment, the natural tendency to do the minimum takes over. Problems are covered up, left to the next guy, rather than fixed. Reports are sanitized. Only good news is reported. Get paid, and get off before something really bad happens.

OPEX is King Ship managers compete with each other on the basis of OPEX. Tanker owners divide their costs into three categories:

VOYEX VOYEX are expenses that depend on the ship's route and speed, where the ship goes. Basically, VOYEX consists of the fuel bill and port charges.

CAPEX Capitol costs include the initial cost of the ship and usually the cost of major dry dockings.

OPEX OPEX, operating expense, is everything else. OPEX comprises the cost of the crew, the cost of feeding the crew, insurance, and the cost of on-board maintenance.

When a ship manager courts a shipowner, he does so on the basis of OPEX. Ship manager A will say, I can run your ships with an OPEX of $5422 dollars per day. Ship manager B says I will do it for $5319 dollars. The owner takes that figure back to Shipmanager A who says OK I will do it for $5305, and gets the contract.

There are only three ways that a ship manager can meet his OPEX budget: skimp on crew, skimp on victualing, and skimp on maintenance. All three are employed. Big ship managers scour the world for the cheapest crew and, if a new source, say Russia, becomes cheaper, they immediately switch to that source.[33] Crew size is reduced to the absolute minimum required to drive the ship. This ensures an exhausted crew toward the end of a load or discharge. Despite the fact meal time is the only social event in a tanker day, they will save

---

[33] It gets worse. There is yet another level called the *manning agent*. In most cases, the ship manager does not hire the crew himself but does so through a manning agent in the crew's home country. In many countries, this is a nasty business. The manning agents don't charge the ship managers much. They make their money by exacting kickbacks from the crew for getting them a job. Often a crew is expected to pay a month's or more salary for an 8 month contract. In any event, the crew who pays the most, gets the job. Not a good way of assuring quality.

The manning agents also suborn the local government bureaucrats, who in theory are responsible for crew welfare, and are in charge of issuing manning agent licenses. The agents are almost always politically connected and well able to fend off any attempt by an owner to go around the system. The isoism paperwork is just another form of protection for these "established" agents. We were able to set up our own manning agent in Manila only because a close relative of our Managing Director was a celebrated hero of the Flower Revolution. He was able to get Cory Acquino to intercede directly in our behalf.

After we did so, one of our big headaches was keeping the crew from giving the office help "presents". It took them a long time before they realized they didn't have to pay for the job.

50 cents a man-day on food even if it's the difference — as it often is — between a decent meal and a lousy one. And worst of all, there is nil non-cosmetic maintenance. Ship managers know that looks are important. So they do enough chipping and painting to induce the casual inspector to conclude that the ship is well-maintained. This also allows them to send pretty pictures back to the owners showing what a good job they are doing. But real maintenance, especially on stuff that is not easily visible, is almost non-existent.

The owner who uses a ship manager has assumed that the way to maximize profits is to minimize OPEX. This is true only in the shortest of short-runs. Actually, putting maintenance off, especially steel and machinery maintenance, is extremely expensive. A few dollars spent on in-tank maintenance by a motivated crew will save thousands of dollars later in steel renewal. A properly operated engine room will have a fuel consumption at least 5% less than a poorly operated one. On a VLCC, this equates to a saving of a thousand dollars per day or more. The ship will last far longer. Scheduled and unscheduled downtime will be greatly reduced, increasing revenues. And the ship will be far safer.

The original pioneers, Ludwig, Onassis, Niarchos, Reksten, etc understood this. They were not spendthrifts by any means.[34] But they all used big in-house crews and made sure that their wages were at the top end of the market they were recruiting from. They fired the guys who didn't measure up, and made certain they retained the ones who did. In the long run, it is the high OPEX owner who is the most profitable; as well as the least likely to have a big casualty.

The reason why isoism was welcomed by tanker owner and hireling alike, is that it provides a substantial barrier to new entry. The buzz in the tanker watering holes was "what a crock, but at least it will get rid of the ma and pa's". No longer could an outside investor simply buy a ship, hire a crew, and start trading. Isoism requires that you have an operating record, an impossibility for a newcomer. Of course, you could buy a ship and hire an existing ship management firm. But intelligent investors would recognize that meant entrusting your ship to an operator who has no stake in the ship and over which you had limited control. If the would-be shipowner was dissuaded, the existing owners were happy. If he chose to go the ship management route, the hirelings were happy. Isoism was an excellent way of protecting the established operators, regardless of their level of competence. Most importantly, **isoism assures that more and more tankers will be operated by the hirelings**.

---

[34] Ludwig's parsimony was legendary.

2.11   Kirki to Erika

In the 80's and 90's, we began seeing more and more structural failures. It started with a rash of tank explosions and fires including the ABT SUMMER,[35] and the KHARK 5. These were all pre-Marpol tankers. In all these casualties the cause or most likely cause was cargo leaking into a non-inerted midships segregated ballast tank, and then igniting.

Figure 2.8: World Horizon after "freak wave" removed forepeak tank. This wave was able to excise only the forepeak tank with almost surgical precision. The true cause was that this segregated ballast tank was very badly corroded. The surrounding spaces were not. Spill was about 850 kiloliters. Source: University of Capetown.

We also started seeing big failures in the forepeak tank, the other segregated ballast tank in a pre-Marpol tanker. In several of these cases, the forepeak tank simply fell off. Examples include the WORLD HORIZON, Figure 2.8, the GALP FUNCHAL, the TOCHAL, Figure 2.9 and the ENERGY ENDURANCE

---

[35] Second largest spill of all time. See also the ANDROS PATRIA and the CASTILLO DE BELLVER.

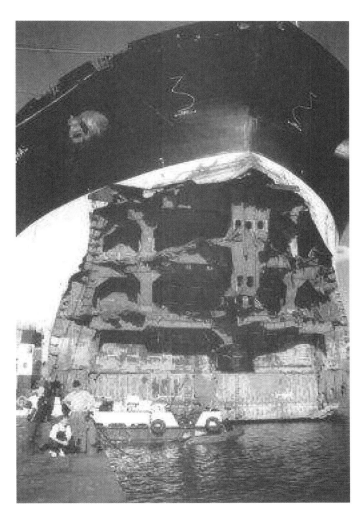

Figure 2.9: Tochal sans forepeak tank. The cut is not quite as clean as the World Horizon, but the boundaries of the forepeak tank are clearly delineated. And this picture gives a better view of the forepeak tank corrosion. The ship was towed stern first into False Bay and lightered. About two hundred kiloliters of fuel oil was spilled from the forward bunker tank. Without a port of refuge, this could easily have been a 300 million liter spill. The Tochal was fully approved by her Classification Society. Source: University of Capetown.

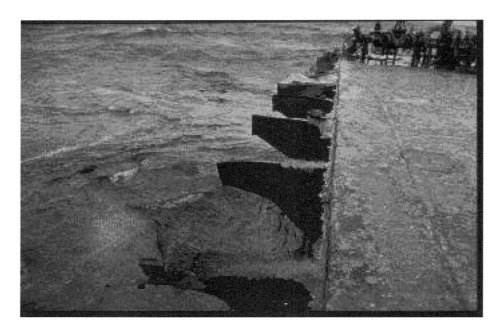

Figure 2.10: Kirki sans forepeak tank. Once again fairly sharp cut at aft end of forepeak tank. Deck had become wafer thin forward of this point. Source: Australian Maritime Safety Authority.

(Endurance Forepeak tank did not quite fall off). In all these cases, the pictures that emerged showed horrific corrosion in the Forepeak tank. The Tromedy attributed these casualties to "freak" waves. All these ships were fully classed to the highest rating.

The KIRKI is the best documented example of a vanishing forepeak tank. In 1991, this ship ran into bad weather off Western Australia, while loaded with a volatile crude. The forepeak ballast tank was horribly corroded. The hull structure failed on deck at the bulkhead between the forepeak tank and the forwardmost cargo tanks. The combination of hydrocarbon vapor escaping from the cargo tanks and the loose steel banging around started a fire, which was then put out by the sea. This process was repeated several times until the whole Forepeak tank just fell off, Figure 2.10

Thanks to heroic efforts on the part of the salvors, the ship survived. The KIRKI was fully approved by her Classification Society, Germanischer Lloyd. Her most recent Class survey was five months earlier. All her paperwork was in order. She was nicely painted. Yet when the Australians inspected this ship, they found massive corrosion not only in what was left of the forepeak, Figure 2.10, but in the aft segregated ballast tanks as well.[36] They found rust camouflaged with canvas. And they found the ship's safety gear, and some of machinery including the boiler safety valves in horrible condition. The Australians were at a loss to explain how the ship's Classification Society could have missed all this. Germanischer Lloyd for its part blamed "poor cooperation" on the part of the owner, Thenamaris.[37] In fact, owner and Class had developed the normal close working relationship.

In 1997, we had another massive structural failure in which a portion of the hull could be inspected after the fact. In January, 1997, the fully loaded, 20,000 ton Russian tanker, NAKHODKA, broke in two in the Sea of Japan in heavy weather. A large part of the cargo and the bow section came ashore on the Japanese coast. The Japanese government commissioned an investigation. The resulting report is an excellent piece of work: competent and objective.[79] From the bow, the Japanese found that the average corrosion in the deck steel was close to 40 percent. The rust was so bad that the underdeck supporting members had become detached from the deck. The Japanese had excellent wave data for this storm from a nearby weather buoy. They concluded that, if the ship had not been corroded, she would have easily weathered this storm. But although the Master hove to, the badly corroded structure could not handle even a moderately severe storm.[38] The wasted deck buckled, and shortly after the ship broke in two. The Japanese estimated that the corroded strength at the point where the hull failed was about half the original.[79][page 179] Like the KIRKI, this spill should have been a strong clue that something was terribly wrong. However, despite the fact that two clean-up volunteers suffered fatal heart attacks, the response by the Japanese public was muted. This casualty had nil regulatory impact.

In fact none of the 1990's structural problems had any real impact until very late in the decade. On December 11th, 1999, the smallish tanker,

---

[36] See `www.atsb.gov.au/marine/incident_detail.cfm?ID=33`, Photos 7, 8 and 9.

[37] The Australians were among the first to lose confidence in the IMO/FOC/Class triumverate. The parliamentary report, "Ships of Shame" issued in December, 1992 is a trenchant critique of the Tromedy.[62] This investigation was mainly motivated by the loss of six bulk carriers in rapid succession off Australia. But the KIRKI must have played some part in Australian thinking.

[38] The Japanese report also criticized the crew for not using a loading pattern that would have placed less stress on the ship. But the report admits that the pattern the ship used was perfectly legal, and, if it weren't for the corrosion, the ship would have been unscathed. The crew has the right to expect that, if it uses a legal loading pattern, the ship will be safe. The Tromedy is unable to overlook any opportunity to blame-the-crew.

ERIKA, was traveling south off Brittany loaded with 31,000 tons of heavy fuel oil. She ran into bad weather and developed a hull crack on her starboard side in way of tank number 2S, one of the segregated ballast tanks. This was the side the waves were coming from.

Over the next 24 hours the fracture extended upward to the main deck and then across the main deck. At this point the ship was lost. At 0610 on the 12th, the ERIKA, set out a distress signal saying she was flooding. Rescue services mobilized. At 0810, a rescue helicopter reported that the ship had broken in two. Probably about 10,000 tons were spilled at this time. The crew were rescued off the stern. The bow floated vertically bow up and had near zero drift. However, the stern was drifting toward the shore at 3 knots. Somehow the crew of the French tug, Abeille Flandre, was able to get the stern under tow. This feat was accomplished about 1440, with winds from the west at 45-55 knots, 7/8 m seas. The brave volunteers who were helicoptered to the stern remarked that the ship looked well-maintained on their return. Needless to say, they did not go into any tanks.

The Abeille Flandre was able to slow the drift toward the coast and the next morning, with the weather improving slightly, started towing the stern slowly westward. However, on the morning of the 13th, the tug noticed the stern was taking a list to port, and the spillage had stopped. Later in the morning the stern became more and more vertical and at 1450 in the afternoon, the stern sank 80 kilometers off the coast.

The ERIKA, was fully approved by her Classification Society, Registro Italiano Navale or RINA. In fact, she had undergone a *Special Survey* just 18 months earlier. Once every five years a ship is supposed to be thoroughly inspected. This is done in a dry dock, and it is called a Special Survey. For older tankers, the Class surveyor goes into every tank. Thousands of steel thickness measurements are taken. The process can take several weeks. If steel is found to be more than 25% wasted, then it must be replaced.[39] Most tanker owners let their steel deteriorate between Special Surveys and then negotiate with the surveyor as to how much steel has to be replaced.

25% thickness loss is horribly wasted steel. Steel corrodes very unevenly. Steel that is rusted down to a knife edge will be surrounded by steel that is barely discolored. You are in a dark, dirty, rusty tank. Much of the structure is essentially inaccessible or very dangerous to get to. How do

---

[39] The rule is actually slightly more complicated than this. Side shell plating is supposed to be replaced if it's wasted more than 20%. Secondary structure is allowed to be 30% corroded. Either way we are talking about an awful lot of rust.

In 1988, the survey rules were strengthened so that some tanks must be inspected at the Intermediate Survey, which takes place half way between each Special Survey.

you determine whether the steel is 20% wasted or 30% or 40% wasted? You take thickness measurements with an ultrasonic gauge. This works fine on unrusted steel because it easy to get a good coupling between the transducer and the steel. But the more wasted the steel, the harder it is to get a reading. So you take the reading on the least wasted spot. Thousands of thickness readings sound like a lot, but it's actually far less than one pencil sized reading per square meter. The readings are automatically biased toward the good side and by a lot.[40]

And that's before we start playing games. The owner chooses and pays for the thickness readings just as he chooses and pays for Class. Most owners have an on-going relationship with one or two thickness surveying companies. These people know how to maintain that relationship. In the early 90's I became interested in cargo tank bottom corrosion and had our ships' cargo tank bottoms carefully measured. To counteract the above biases, I laid down very strict rules as to where the measurement points were going to be taken, completely taking away the measurer's freedom to pick the point. This worked OK, except on the Hellespont Paramount where the numbers were obviously wrong. All the other ships showed substantial wastage in certain portions of the tank bottom with localized areas up to 20% loss. This ship had nil wastage almost everywhere with a just a few tiny areas up to 10%.

It turned out that the thickness firm I used was overbooked. For this ship, they had hired an experienced surveyor away from another firm. And

---

[40] Here's an extract from an Exxon report.

> In September 1980, a 250,000 dwt VLCC underwent Second Special Survey *without a class requirement for steel renewal.* [Emphasis mine.] Coincident with this survey, inspection of the structure by Exxon technical personnel alerted operating management to potential and unexpectedly high steel renewals of about 645 tonnes. These renewals were located primarily in segregated ballast tank stiffening and cargo/dirty ballast tank bottom plating. These findings were of concern not only due to earlier forecasts of much smaller steel renewals but to the fact that bands of ultrasonic thickness measurements taken during the Second Special Survey did not detect the problem.[72]

Exxon's management drew the obvious conclusion. Remember Exxon is not dealing with second tier Classification Societies. Exxon uses ABS and Lloyds.

> In Exxon, we found in the late 70's that typical Class Special Surveys were being done so badly that we could not rely on the results, and thus did our own.[30, page 6]

Decent owners never wait until Class tells then to renew steel. They know that, if they do, then at a minimum they will face very expensive problems down the road.

despite our crew telling him over and over that "this time" the owner wanted the real numbers, this surveyor assumed that this was pious fluff meant to be ignored. He even took to sitting behind the Radio Officer as the RO was transcribing the readings onto the computer, instructing him when to change the "bad" readings to "better" numbers. I had to fire this guy and redo all the readings. I believe this character was representative.

In short, between the outrageously generous wastage allowed, the difficulty in determining average wastage, the automatic biases in wastage determination and the commercial biases, ***it is routine that steel that is wasted 50% or more is passed in Special Surveys***. I have inspected tanks in which the rust underfoot was so thick that it crunched like snow on a very cold day, tanks in which you dare not touch a bulkhead because the rust would come down on your head in multi-kilogram sheets. In every case, the ship was fully classed to the Classification Society's highest rating. That is what happened with the ERIKA.[41]

Two years after the sinking RINA issued a report exonerating itself, saying the ship was basically sound, and blaming the crew for "mis-handling" a minor crack and turning it into a major failure. What the crew was supposed to do, RINA doesn't say. This attempt at blame-the-crew is insufferable nonsense.

The Maltese Flag State report is almost as useless, offering a potpourri of possible causes including corrosion, but failing to pin the blame on any one. After all RINA was Malta's duly appointed representative.

In fact the problem was massive corrosion abetted by an understanding purveyor of Classification services. The French agency Bureau d'Enquetes sur les Accidents en Mer (BEA) did its own investigation.[42] BEA discovered that tanks 2 Port (2P) and 2 Starboard (2S) were in bad condition at least as far back as April, 1993. In April 1997, a surveyor from Bureau Veritas called the condition of 2 port and 2 starboard unacceptable, a word rarely used by Class surveyors. His report comments on the absence of coating

---

[41] One area — just about the only area — where the new Joint Tanker Project Rules (see Appendix E) are significantly tighter than the old Rules, at least for big tankers, is in wastage allowance. The allowed wastage before renewal is required is now set in absolute terms and is between 2 mm and 3.5 mm depending on location. For a VLCC this translates to 10 to 20% loss of thickness. This is a substantial improvement but it is still a hell of a lot of rust. And the new Rules can do nothing to counter either the inherent biases or the commerical pressures facing the measurer and the surveyor.

[42] www.beamer-france.org/english/inquiries/pdf/Erika_Final_Report.pdf has an English translation of the BEA report.

and anodes. No problem; if Class is being obstreperous, change Class.[43] In February 1998, the owners (actually the third party managers, PanOcean) decided to change Class to RINA. But even RINA upon inspection rejected the ship mainly due to corrosion in 2P (2S was not inspected for reasons BEA does not explain) citing wastage of up 68%, holes between frames 80 and 82, and very severe corrosion of the plate welds. They also found oil residues in the segregated ballast tanks indicating past leakage from neighboring cargo tanks. The access ladders were so corroded that inspection was extremely dangerous. The report cited lack of coating in the 2 wings and the forepeak. Changing class was put off temporarily.

In summer of 1998 the ship underwent her fourth Special Survey in Bijela, Montenegro. About 100 tons of steel was renewed — a remarkably low number for a ship that had been rejected a few months earlier — and the ship switched Class from Bureau Veritas to RINA.

Between the fourth Special Survey and the sinking, the ship was inspected seven times by oil company inspectors. In none of these inspections did the vetters go into any tanks. BEA points out that the Flag State (the ship had had four) never inspected the structure other than through the Classification Societies. BEA found evidence that the Erika's captains had complained to the ship manager PanOcean on numerous occasions, especially about the condition of 2P and 2S.

The BEA report goes on to a detailed structural analysis backed up by crew reports and the results of underwater surveys of the wreckage. It concludes that the sequence was:

1. A leak of cargo from cargo tank 3C (3 center) to ballast tank 2S from a crack in the bulkhead due to corrosion. The crew deballasted 4S to reduce the list. At this point the crew noted cracking and buckling on deck at the forward end of 2S.

2. Buckling of the wasted transverse members in 2S. This generated a crack in the no longer supported side shell plating. This flooded 2S increasing the sagging moment. 3S started leaking.

3. The crack progressed vertically up and down the side shell. A large portion of the 2S side shell plating detached, flipped up on the deck, and then sank.

4. The crack now progressed along the bottom plating. The main deck

---

[43] Bob Somerville, President of ABS, tells this story. An ABS surveyor spied what looked like bad corrosion in a tank but he couldn't get close to it. He requested that the owner stage the area for a close-up inspection. The owner was so outraged that not only did he switch all his ships out of ABS, but he invoiced ABS for the cup of coffee the surveyor had been given.

buckled and "the vessel bent, as if her deck were hinged", a poetic way of saying the ship failed in sag.

In short, the cause was long standing corrosion in a segregated ballast tank about which the ship's owner, manager, and Class did almost nothing.

But what has gone virtually unnoticed is the role of environmental pressures in this spill. The ERIKA was a pre-Marpol tanker. As built her only pure ballast tanks were 3C and the Forepeak tank. But in 1990 she was converted to segregated ballast by changing 2P and 2S to ballast tanks *without coating these tanks*. Segregated ballast was required at age 25 under the 1992 Marpol amendments but many owners converted earlier due to charterer pressure.

Normally, all segregated ballast tanks are coated when built but cargo tanks including combined cargo/ballast tanks are not. Corrosion rates in segregated ballast tanks are far higher than those in combined cargo/ballast tanks where wastage is dramatically slowed by the film of oil on the tank steel and by the lack of oxygen from inerting. Besides it costs less than $6 per square meter to properly coat a tank in a newbuilding yard where you are dealing with brand new, shop-primed steel and the steel is still in conveniently sized blocks.

However, if you are converting an old cargo tank to segregated ballast then it will cost you more than 40 dollars per square meter to properly stage, clean, blast, clean, and coat the steel. For a big tank, this can easily be more than a half million dollars per tank.

Few, if any, owners spent this money, when they converted to segregated ballast. I know of none. They simply changed the piping around, maybe threw a few sacrificial anodes into the new ballast tanks, and hoped. The owners knew rapid wastage was inevitable. What they were hoping for was an understanding Classification Society.

The BEA report does not mince words. BEA on page 33 of the English translation concludes:

CBT is segregated ballast without separate piping systems.

> The problems which beset the Erika were apparently caused by her conversion to segregated ballast tanks which began in 1990 (CBT) and was only completed in 1998 (SBT 4 and 2). Neither the infrequent Flag State surveys, nor the port state and vetting inspections seem to have picked up this fact. The only people who were aware of this were the crew (but they had little opportunity for expert assessment) and of course the classification societies whose scope for action is undoubtedly limited by the

socio-economic context inherent in the operation of this type of
vessel. The various reports and opinions voiced make it abun-
dantly clear that after the August 1998 special survey, the corrosion of the 2 port and starboard ballast tanks had developed
apace, so weakening their structure that what followed became
inevitable

Delicately put.

In 1997, I inspected some tanks which had been converted to segregated ballast six years earlier without coating them. The wastage was so
severe that the horizontal *stringers*, which are the major structural members
running athwartship across the tanks, had become detached from the tank
bulkheads (walls). If you jumped up and down on these once massive plat-
forms, they reacted like a trampoline, except they made a lot more noise. I
scared the hell out of my fellow inspectors for a while by demonstrating how
much this improved my vertical. These ships were fully classed by Lloyds
Register.

Fortunately, these particular segregated ballast tanks were center tanks.
Unlike the ERIKA, they were not exposed to wave forces. But the job of the
stringers is to keep the side walls of the tank where they are supposed to be.
On this ship, the main deck had begun to ripple longitudinally as the tank
side walls had started to move together. This particular ship was owned
by a good guy. When he got our report, he quietly sold the ships he had
converted to segregated ballast. I was amazed he was able to find buyers.

Uncoated segregated ballast tanks are a prescription for disaster. Yet
this is what MARPOL/78 and the 1992 amendments resulted in. To be
fair to the regulators, they didn't tell the owners to used uncoated ballast
tanks. But on the other hand, they didn't tell them not to, when any fool
could have seen that was what was going to happen. If they couldn't figure
it out for themselves, they could have looked at the ships that had already
converted to segregated ballast.

The legal maximum for oily ballast for non-segregated tankers is 15 ppm,
which is low enough so that there is no sheen. With proper operation, this
is easily achievable. The ERIKA would have used about 10,000 tons of non-
segregated ballast per trip. As a non-segregated ballast ship, she would have
discharged less than 200 liters of oil per trip in her ballast or something like
2000 liters per year. As it was, the ERIKA put 30,000,000 liters of oil into
the sea.

Poorly thought through regulation with unintended consequences is what
happens when regulation is written by politicians in the emotional, media-
driven aftermath of a big spill. And media driven, emotional aftermath is

exactly what we got after the ERIKA. The French and the some of the other European countries went ballistic. They demanded that something must be done. The loss of the ERIKA was caused by the combination of uncoated segregated ballast tanks and criminally lax inspection by the ship's Classification Society. **Intelligent regulation would have outlawed uncoated ballast tanks and implemented a non-owner controlled hull inspection regime.** But the cry from the mob was "give us double hull" and the Classification Societies escaped again.

The double hull mantra was more than a little superfluous since double hulls were already mandated by the 1992 Marpol amendments. The only thing the politicians could come up with was a more rapid phase out of the Marpol single hulls. The EU quickly pushed through a rule that said no single hulls in European Union ports after 2015. IMO, scrambling to retain some semblance of control, came up with essentially the same new phase-in period in April, 2001.

The ERIKA generated a great deal of discussion about strengthening Port State Control. An organization called the European Maritime Safety Agency (EMSA) was set up to provide technical support to the Paris-MOU inspections. But nothing really happened. The ERIKA had undergone eight port state inspections in the three years before she sank. They all found superficial deficiencies, and in one case she was detained for a few hours. But the appalling condition of the tanks went undetected. There was almost no chance it would be discovered **since port state inspectors don't go in tanks.**

Class did not get off exactly scotfree. In December 2001, the EU issued a nebulously worded directive that gave it the right to *recognize* a Classification Society and to withdraw that recognition. The probable impact of this will be to strengthen rather than weaken the established Classes. The preamble calls for transparency with regard to Class data, but the law only requires the Classes to publish suspensions, withdrawals, a list of overdue surveys, and conditions of Class. The all-important inspection reports remain private. Neither IMO nor the EU did anything about the basic Class/owner conflict of interest.

But the Classification Societies were scared. They knew they were on shaky ground. Privately, they couldn't believe they had gotten off so lightly. Their response was *IACS*, the International Association of Classification Societies. IACS had been around since the late 60's, when it was formed by the seven largest Classes in a half-hearted attempt to regulate the competition that had broken out between the Societies with the emergence of Flags of Convenience. But as an attempt at a cartel, IACS was a bust. The individual Societies were too jealous of their own turf and prerogatives to cede any real power to IACS. IACS was a moribund operation. Few knew it existed; nobody paid any attention to it. IACS didn't even have an office.

But ERIKA was a close call. The big Classification Societies got together, set up a permanent office for IACS in London, and agreed to draft and abide by "harmonized" rules. In the case of tankers, as of April, 2006, the harmonized Rules will be those produced by the Joint Tanker Project.[65] This effort is important enough to merit its own section. See Appendix E. But overall these new Rules are fundamentally the same as the old. Harmonized is an apt participle.

IACS' job is to protect the status quo. The harmonized rules that emerge from the inter-Class wrangling tend to be least common denominators of the individual Class rules.[44] An individual Class can opt out of particular rule they don't like; this is called "reserving". IACS is a kind of mini-IMO.

Anyway the problem isn't so much the Rules, but how they are enforced. IACS made no basic change in the vendor/client relationship between individual Class and owner, nor the competition among the Classes for owners which is based not on the wording of the Rules, which with a few exceptions competition has guaranteed is already nearly the same across Classes, but which Class will most leniently enforce the rules.[45] On the front lines nothing changed.

I need to say something here. The problem is not an owner suborning an individual Class surveyor. In my 25 years as a tanker owner and operator, I have no first hand knowledge of a Class surveyor being bribed. I've heard third hand stories and it probably has happened; but individual bribery is a problem that any inspection system faces.

The reason why bribing of individual Class surveyors is so rare is that it is unnecessary. We never bribed a surveyor; but we worked very hard to develop a friendly relationship with *our* surveyors. Every shipowner does and it not difficult to do. The surveyors must walk a narrow line. On the one hand, they don't want to sign off on an unsafe ship which could come

---

[44] Consider the ill-fated NAKHODKA. She was Classed by the Russian Marine Registry of Shipping (RS), hardly a first tier Classification Society. Under RS Rules, the NAKHODKA was required to have a hull section modulus of 78.2 cm^{2}m. The section modulus is the single most important measure of a hull's strength. Under IACS Rules, the required section modulus for this ship is 74.4 cm^{2}m. If the NAKHODKA had been built to IACS requirements, she would have been 5% weaker.

[45] This is obliquely admitted in the IACS Code of Ethics which says in part "Competition between Societies shall be on the basis of services (technical and field) rendered to the marine industry but must not lead to compromises on safety of life and property at sea or to the lowering of technical standards." In other words, the customer is still king.

back to bite them if the ship gets in trouble. Also many of the frontline Class surveyors are professionals who simply don't like the idea of lousy ships. On the other hand, they have to keep the customer happy, lest he complain to his boss threatening to take his ships to another Class.[46]

The result, whenever there is a problem, however major, is a friendly negotiation. The owner's superintendent recognizes yes this must be fixed but the market is strong, the ship has a cargo, and we need some time. Together they come up with wording on the survey report which balances the conflicting requirements. In such an environment, the Rules can be pushed very hard indeed.

This is what happens when you are dealing with a first tier Class such as Lloyds or ABS. If you need to push the Rules even further, you switch to a second tier Class, such as RINA, where just about anything goes to keep the customer happy.

As a practical matter, the only real impact of the loss of the ERIKA was that some charterers became willing to pay a premium for double hulls. And many charterers instituted age requirements, refusing to charter ships over 20 years old. Since under the vetting programs, they had had inspectors on all these ships, they knew full well that in many cases this would force them to take a poorer quality, younger ship when a better, older ship was available. But it was a rational move on their part. They also knew they would get far less flack if the younger ship got into trouble than if the older ship did. One Exxon executive told me they were "no longer managing ships. They were managing perceptions".

---

[46] My experience is that the farther up the Class hierarchy you go, the easier it is to play games. To be successful in climbing the intra-Class ladder, you must know how to treat the customer.

2.12 Castor

Since the response to the ERIKA did not address the core problem, it was inevitable that the ERIKA would be repeated. And it was, again and again.

On New Years Eve, 2000, the CASTOR, a Cypriot flagged tanker carrying 29,500 tons of gasoline developed a twenty six meter crack across its main deck at the forward end of 4P, 4C, and 4S tanks. The ship was in the Western Med off Morocco. The weather was very bad. The ship requested refuge from nine different countries; and in each case was denied. For 40 days, she wandered the Mediterranean, a pariah, before her cargo was lightered in a risky operation in exposed waters off Malta.

The ship was classed by the American Bureau of Shipping. At first ABS was almost exultant. In February, ABS issued the following statement by President Robert Somerville.

> Since suffering the initial heavy weather damage, this vessel has been subjected to an extreme Force 12 gale with wave heights in excess of 8 meters without any further deterioration in its structural condition.
>
> Over the last 39 days it has been towed 1,000 miles across the Mediterranean, remaining intact without losing any cargo or causing any pollution. Only a remarkably robust, well-maintained vessel in stout structural condition could withstand such a beating and still deliver its cargo safely.
>
> At ABS we are as committed to eliminating the substandard operator and the substandard ship from this industry as the most vociferous legislator. But the difference between these rogues, who form such a small minority within our ranks, and the responsible members of the maritime community must be emphasized.
>
> Well-found ships can suffer heavy weather damage in extreme circumstances. That is not an indication of weakness within the industry's self-regulation mechanism. Rather the manner in which the parties concerned with the Castor responded should assure the public and and concerned governments that we are their allies in seeking to protect life, property, and the environment.[75]

The message was clear. Sub-standard owners and second tier Classification Societies (read RINA) might screw up from time to time, but you can trust a major Class like ABS.

But after the lightering, the CASTOR was taken to Piraeus and inspected. The tone changed. Here are excerpts from an April ABS Press release.

> Hyper-accelerated Corrosion Believed to have Contributed to Castor Damage. Preliminary findings highlight importance of tank coatings. April 10, 2001
>
> Following an exhaustive inspection and analysis of the damaged product tanker Castor, the Cyprus Department of Merchant Shipping and ABS have jointly announced preliminary findings that point to hyper-accelerated corrosion as the probable principal cause behind the structural failure. "The Castor has become a floating laboratory which is providing us with some surprising findings," said ABS Chairman and CEO Frank J Iarossi in announcing the preliminary results of the investigation.[47] "If these initial conclusions hold up, there will be significant implications for class and possibly wider implications for the manner in which the new generation of double hulled tankers should be constructed and maintained."
>
> "This indicates an annual corrosion rate of as much as 1.5mm compared to normal rates of about 0.1mm or less."
>
> "It must be remembered that the Castor had met all class requirements when the major steel replacement was completed, and had remained in class with no outstandings" he [Iarossi] added "We have always felt that the Rules are sufficiently conservative for any operational environment. Although it must be emphasized that the Castor was structurally sound, it did not sink, it did not lose any cargo or cause any pollution, and no one was injured or lost their life, if there are shortcomings in the requirements we need to rectify that, and do so quickly."

The maritime press immediately announced that ABS had discovered a new phenomenon which it dubbed "super-rust". There is no such thing. What there is is the same old combination of poor maintenance, and understanding/forgiving survey standards which eventually leads to a major hull failure.

To ABS's credit, in the end they did not attempt a laughably deceitful report as RINA did in the case of the ERIKA. (Of course, the fact that the ship inconveniently survived made a cover-up a bit more difficult.) ABS's

---

[47] Iarossi was ex-head of Exxon Shipping where he demonstrated his safety consciousness by reducing the crew of the EXXON VALDEZ to 20, with plans to go to 16.

Final Report[1] documents that the old steel in the area of the crack was in shocking condition.[48] Portions of the 16 mm deckplate were down to less than 6 mm. 15 mm webs down to 4.4 mm; 15 mm flanges down to 3.4 mm. Four contiguous deck stiffeners in the port tank were totally gone. See Figure 3.4 in the ABS report. Welds between the underdeck stiffeners and the plating were 95% gone.[49] The resulting structure had zip buckling strength.

> While the area of severe corrosion was limited, it did cover a large portion of the forward end of the No 4 tanks particularly the center tank. Survey and analysis of this structure leads to the conclusion that the wasted under deck longitudinals became detached during the heavy weather. This weakened the deck structure eventually leading to the buckling and then to cracking.[1, page III]

Gone are the claims of hyper-accelerated corrosion. The report does note that the wastage rate of the new uncoated steel was as much as 0.7 mm per year. This should not have surprised anybody for uncoated steel in a gasoline/ballast tank without any anodes.[50] The ABS report has some revealing pictures of the crack and the wretched condition of the original steel in the area of the crack.

The only reason why this ship survived was that she was (a) in a *sagging* condition at the time, (b) more or less evenly loaded in all tanks, and (c) in the Mediterranean. The deck failed in compression. The crack was being held together by the overall stress pattern in which the forward and aft ends of the ship are pushed up and the middle part sags down. For the ship to be lost, the bottom had to give way or the crack had to extend down the sides. The bottom, **which as built was 34% stronger than required by current rules**, had about 10% wastage but was still considerably stronger than a brand new ship, and was able to take the tensile stresses of the fairly short Mediterranean waves. ABS calculated that even in the very rough weather she encountered the worst bending moment was only 69% of her design bending moment. So the bottom was not overstressed in tension.

---

[48] There is a PDF version at `www.eagle.org/news/press/castorreport.pdf`. I am no fan of Class but ABS should be given full credit for publishing this report. In all my experience with Class, this is unique.

[49] Welds almost always corrode faster than the steel around them, often much faster.

[50] Wastage rates of this level and higher have been observed on many occasions. The figure 1.2 mm/year shows up as the top end of the normal range in the TSCF table of corrosion rates.[78, page 243]

An important difference between the CASTOR and the ERIKA/ PRESTIGE is that the CASTOR was in the gasoline trade. Gasoline has a density of about 0.75 as opposed to 0.95 and higher for heavy fuel oil. Because of the low density cargo, there was no need to keep some of the midships tanks empty to provide buoyancy in the middle of the ship. The CASTOR had no segregated ballast tanks. All her tanks were loaded including the 4P, 4C and 4S. This helped her survive in two ways.

- The wave loading on the side shell plating were much less than ERIKA/ PRESTIGE because the external pressure of the sea was partially balanced by the internal pressure of the cargo.
- More importantly, since the tanks were loaded more or less evenly both transversely and longitudinally there was very little shear stress. Shear stress is the stress that results from excess buoyancy on one side of the steel pushing it up and too little buoyancy on the other side pushing it down, in the same way that one side of scissors pushes the paper up while the other side pushes the paper down. Shear stress is the most important stress component in the side shell and the longitudinal bulkheads.

In short, the crack was being pushed together, the side shell and the longitudinal bulkheads were lightly loaded, and the crack did not propagate downward.

But it was near thing. ABS calculates that, as the ship was going thru the worst case waves, the stress in the deck in way of the crack did cycle into hog albeit at a low level (15% of design).[51] The Second Mate took some video during the storm. It confirms the ABS calculations, showing the deck pumping and spewing out geysers of gasoline. We were fortunate that the CASTOR was a considerably stronger ship than required by current rules. By the way, the video contradicts the ABS statement that there was no spill.

The ship's last Special Survey was in October 1997. In theory, at the end of the special survey there should be no areas with substantial corrosion. While quite a bit of steel was replaced, obviously this was not the case.

An Annual Survey in September 1999 found the deck set in way of 2C and 5C, and recommended thickness measurements and the tank be inspected. Annual surveys normally don't go into any tanks. It is quite unusual for an annual survey to pick up internal wastage or the deck to fail in a manner

---

[51] *Hog* is the opposite of sag. Hog occurs when there is more buoyancy than weight in the middle of the ship. In hog, the middle of the ship is pushed up by the wave, and the ends hang down.

that makes it obvious from the outside that something is wrong.

As a result of the September, 1999 report, repairs were made to the 2C and 5C deck in November 1999. The ship also completed her Intermediate Survey at the time and as part of that survey 4P and 4S were inspected. ***ABS surveyors were in the Castor's 4S and 4P 13 months before the casualty.*** One small piece of steel in 4S was replaced. The ABS report laconically observes:

> The gaugings taken during the most recent special and intermediate surveys did not reflect the areas of excessive corrosion in No. 4 tanks and therefore failed to adequately represent the condition of the vessel's structure.[1, page 29]

Business as usual.

An Annual Survey was carried out in August 2000 with no recommendations or repairs. At the time of the hull failure, the ship was fully classed with the highest rating by a first tier Classification Society with no outstanding recommendations.

Other than to temporarily intensify the port of refuge debate, CASTOR had no regulatory impact. The myth of no spill was accepted. In the end, everything had worked out just fine. ABS did not widely promulgate the final report. The only lasting impact of the CASTOR was super-rust which is still being used from time to time to explain the surprising amount of corrosion we keep finding in "remarkably robust, well-maintained" vessels. But within ABS, Bob Somerville must have finally realized there was something badly wrong with "the industry's self-regulation mechanism".

2.13   Prestige

Somerville's education was not finished. On the 13th November 2002, the ABS classed PRESTIGE was proceeding southbound at the southern end of the Bay of Biscay loaded with 77,000 tons of heavy fuel oil. In bad weather, the side plating in way of 3S, a segregated ballast tank, failed. The damaged extended into No 2A (aft) starboard, another segregated ballast tank. Both tanks flooded. The ship took on a 25 degree list. At this point none of the cargo tanks were breached, but the list was so bad that some of these tanks were leaking thru the tank hatches. The Captain counter-flooded 3 port, which drastically reduced the list and stopped this leakage, but increased the stress levels on the already damaged structure.

The Captain asked for refuge from Spain. It was not only denied but the Spaniards forced the ship farther off-shore. Six days later in deteriorating weather, the PRESTIGE failed in sag, broke in two, and sank.

This spill is a near carbon copy of the ERIKA. When the ship was built, the only segregated ballast tanks were 2A starboard and 2A port. When the PRESTIGE converted to segregated ballast as required by MARPOL, 3P and 3P became ballast tanks. But they were not coated. The 2A's, starboard and port, remained segregated ballast.

The ship's last special survey was in China in May 2001. Quite a bit of corrosion was found in 3P and 3S. 336 tons of steel was replaced. 18 months later the tank fails.

I don't know about you, but I find this tiresomely repetitive.

ABS made a half-hearted effort to claim the ship was in good shape. The fact that the ship had not only not survived but an underwater vehicle which cut some holes in the sunken hull had come back with steel in good condition (probably either cargo tank steel or some of the new 2001 steel) made this semi-feasible. But Somerville had learned his lesson. This time ABS settled for saying we don't know what happened, blaming the counter-flooding — yet another variant of blame-the-crew — despite the fact that the hull was already over-stressed in the listed condition,[52] and the Spanish for not providing refuge. The Spanish threw the Captain who together with the Chief Mate and Chief Engineer, remained on-board in perilous conditions, thereby allowing the ship to be towed offshore, into jail for 80 days.

More pavlovian screams about single hull from the European Union. In response in December, 2003, IMO moved the final Phase Out date of pre-

---

[52] Not to mention, that the Captain's only hope of getting the Spanish to allow the ship into shelter, was to stop the leakage from the tanklids.

Marpol tankers from 2007 to 2005, and the final phase out date for the Marpol single hull from 2015 to 2010, with a couple of loop holes. Needless to say, the fact that the PRESTIGE was single hull had nothing to do with her loss. The Classification Society system escaped unscathed,

In fact this time the Classification Societies did something very clever. They realized that at least European patience with the Classification Society system was running out. They knew the next time around pubic attention could no longer be focused on the bogus single hull issue. So they invented "goal based standards". This system envisions five *tiers* of regulation. At the top, goals (Tier 1) and functional requirements (Tier 2) along with verification procedures (Tier 3) would be set by IMO. At Tier 4, Classification Societies will provide prescriptive rules to "deliver the goals". At Tier 5, the shipowner "will provide further vital means to achieve the goals by way of effective maintenance, training, working practices, ..".

There's a great deal of isoistic babble in the "goal based standards" literature. The Tier 5 verbiage in particular is panglossian nonsense. But the intent is clear: insert Class so deeply into the IMO regulatory system that it can never be removed. Class already has tremendous influence within IMO, due to the fact that all the IMO committees are rife with Classification Society employees, especially in the key drafting positions. The goal based system would legalize and cement this influence. Class is petrified that a combination of IMO and the Port States would make the Classification Society redundant. The goal of "Goal Based Standards" is to ensure that this does not happen.

What "Goal Based Standards" does not do is alter in any way the vendor/client relationship between Class and shipowner. The real system remains "Fee Based Standards".

2.14   Regulatory Summary

So what have we learned from this pattern of "self-regulation" to use the Classification Societies' oxymoronic phrase, and media driven reaction to a select group of high profile spills.

- On balance, the oil companies have had a major beneficial effect. They introduced cargo tank inerting. It was a change in charterer attitudes that generated the big reduction in spillage immediately after the Amoco Cadiz, and again after the Exxon Valdez. In the past the oil companies set marginally decent tanker newbuilding standards. Unfortunately, in the last 20 years, the prime pillar of tanker design and operational standards, the major oil company's marine department, has crumbled and just about disappeared.

- The Flag States are useless. The Flags are competing for owners. The successful Flags are the ones that offer the shipowner the best deal. It's not regulation; it's an auction. Since the rise of the Flag of Convenience the only impact of the Flag State has been to strengthen the role of the Classification Society.

- IMO's record is dismal.[53]
    1. IMO forced pre-Marpol ships to segregated ballast without requiring that the new ballast tanks be properly protected, witness Erika and Prestige.
    2. IMO took 15 years to mandate inerting cargo tanks on all tankers resulting in something like 100 unnecessary deaths.
    3. IMO replaced pre-Marpol single hulls with Marpol single hulls increasing spillage in groundings such as the Exxon Valdez and trebling ballast tank coated area. See Section C.3.
    4. IMO replaced Marpol single hulls with double hulls, trebling ballast tank coated area again and insuring that all cargo tank leaks will be into the ballast tanks **without requiring that this space be inerted**.
    5. IMO has mandated all sorts of quality assurance red tape guaranteeing that more and more tankers will be operated by short-run obsessed hirelings rather than crews that care for the ship.
    6. IMO has failed to mandate twin screw. I'm foreshadowing here. See Section 6.5.

---

[53] Not all IMO regulation is bad. An example is Traffic Separation Schemes. But the coastal states involved would have done this with or without IMO.

7. IMO has failed to institute any system of builder liability. See Section 7.4.1.

We sometimes forget that IMO is a collective of Flag States and the big Flag States represent the shipowners. IMO's job is to impose as little new expense on shipowners as public outcry will allow. Ever wonder why IMO was so slow on inerting? Tanker owners didn't want the additional expense and there was no outside political pressure to impose something the public didn't understand. Ditto: twin screw.

- The Classification Society remains the key regulatory body. The shipyards control Class prior to delivery. See Chapter 5. The shipowners control Class after delivery.

- A few port states have instituted beneficial inspection programs but they don't go into the all-important tanks. Hull structure remains the preserve of the Classification Society.

In short, a Tromedy.

Chapter 3

The Nature of Tanker Spills

3.1 The Three Salient Features of Tanker Spills

Even the most cursory glance at tanker spill statistics reveals three striking features of the data which together pose a difficult problem for statistical analysis and a bit of a quandary for regulation.

1. **Spill size range is so large that it is nearly impossible to grasp.**
   Tanker spill volumes range from less than a liter to as much as 500 million liters. The UK has recorded tanker spills down to 0.3 liters. The largest tanker spill to date, the Aegean Captain/ATLANTIC EMPRESS collision, spilled 329,000,000 liters. **With respect to spill size, we are dealing with a number that can vary by a factor of a billion.** A billion is a figure with which very few of us have any day to day experience. This is important because normally when people use the word "large" they are talking about something that is maybe twice as big, or occasionally ten times as big as "small". But when we are discussing tanker spills, "large" has an entirely different meaning. Sometimes regulators forget this. In fact, "large" just does not say it. We need a larger word. I will call any spill at the upper end of the range, roughly 10 million liters or more, *brobdingnagian*.

2. **Almost all spills are lilliputian.**
   Table 3.1 summarizes a fairly typical sample of tanker spills. This particular sample contains all the tankship spills recorded in the USCG MINMOD database in the period 1992-2001 for which a positive volume spilled into the water was given. 84% of these 1,100 spills are listed at 100 gallons (380 liters) or less. This is true despite the fact

Table 3.1: Typical Tanker Spill Size Density

**All Tankship Spills in USCG MINMOD Database (1992-2001)
with a Non-Zero Volume in Water**

SIZE RANGE (gallons)	NUMBER	TOTAL VOLUME
1 or less	381	380
1 to 10	359	1,787
10 to 100	209	9,551
100 to 1,000	124	44,880
1,000 to 10,000	41	140,394
10,000 to 100,000	13	514,535
100,000 to 1,000,000	2	547,465
1,000,000 to 10,000,000	1	7,500,000
TOTAL	1,130	8,758,992

that the smaller the spill is the less likely it is to be recorded, or at least recorded accurately.[1] You will get the same kind of results with just about any reasonably comprehensive source of spill data. In 2003, the UK recorded 14 tanker spills. Nine of these spills was listed at less than 5 liters. Three of the remaining five were less that 100 liters. The other two were 750 liters and 2100 liters respectively. In 2001, the USCG instituted the MISLE system. Thru 2003, the system recorded 20 tanker spills. All but 5 were less than a 100 liters. **In terms of numbers, almost all tanker spills are less than a few hundred liters.**

3. **Almost all oil is spilled in a small handful of brobdingnagian spills.**

   Look at how unbalanced Table 3.1 is. In Table 3.1, one spill, the SURF CITY[2] represents 85% of all the volume in the MINMOD sample. In contrast all the spills of 100 gallons or less — 84% of the sample in numbers — represent less than 0.15% of the total volume. This too is typical of any sizable sample of tanker spills. In the MISLE database, the total spillage reported for 2001-2003 was 2.35 million

---

[1] The MINMOD database contains another 520 tankship spills but the volume is inconsistently coded as zero. We can be confident that almost all these spills were in the 1 to 100 gallon range.

[2] Cargo leaked into segregated ballast tank, exploded. See Section 3.3.

Table 3.2: Total annual spillage versus single biggest spill

(Based on CTX CDB as of 2005-03-18)

	TOTAL Liters	BIGGEST Liters	PERCENT	SHIP
1995	8,517,000	5,880,000	69%	Sea Prince
1996	86,781,000	84,400,000	97%	Sea Empress
1997	90,875,000	29,800,000	33%	Evoikos
1998	1,844,000	1,100,000	60%	Maritza Sayalero
1999	38,556,000	33,000,000	85%	Erika
2000	10,943,000	8,230,000	75%	Natuna Sea
2001	16,902,000	12,800,000	76%	Ife
2002	84,189,000	82,000,000	97%	Prestige
2003	35,224,000	35,200,000	99%	Tasman Spirit

liters. The three largest spills represented over 99% of this oil. The largest spill in this sample, the WESTCHESTER[3] main engine fire, alone accounted for 87% of this spillage. The spill size range is so immense that there is no way that even a very large number of small spills can approach the volume of a single brobdingnagian spill.

Worldwide, in a normal year, total tanker spillage is dominated by a single spill. Table 3.2 compares total spillage in the CTX Casualty Database with the single largest spill each year for the last ten years. In almost every year, two-thirds or more of the total spillage came from a single spill. 1997 was an exception but, even in that year, three similar sized spills (EVOIKOS, 29,800,000; NAKHODKA, 20,200,000; and DA QING 243, 18,900,000 liters) accounted for almost all the spillage.

It will be objected that the CTX database is missing lots of the little spills. This is certainly true; but it doesn't matter. It would take 1000 one liter spills, before the TOTAL column in Table 3.2 would change in the fifth digit. On average, we are spilling very roughly 50 million liters per year from tankers. It would take fifty thousand, 100 liter spills to change this figure by 10%. We could miss many more little spills than actually occur and the conclusion still holds.

Even back in the 70's when we were spilling a lot more oil, Figure

---

[3] Lost power due to crank case explosion, drifted ashore. See Section 3.5.

3.1 shows that the largest spill in any given year was roughly about half of all the oil that was spilled in year. ***In terms of volume, the handful of brobdingnagian spills are all-important.***

The twin facts that (a) almost all tankers spills are very small and (b) almost all oil spilled is spilled in a small handful of brobdingnagian spills poses a problem for regulation. Do you go after the rare but massive spill or the frequent, little spill? The pious response is "both". A brobdingnagian spill is in the common parlance "an environmental catastrophe". But even the smallest spill is an ugly nuisance. However in going after both, we must be careful to recognize they are very different animals, lest we concoct regulation that reduces the frequency of small spill at the cost of increasing the probability of a brobdingnagian spill.

And we must be wary of charlatans who misuse the lopsided spill statistics, as in "A 1992 IMO study estimated that an inner hull would have prevented spillage in 84% of all the groundings worldwide."[32][page 71] The reader is expected to conclude that double bottoms would have reduced spillage by about 80%. In fact, essentially all the grounding spillage is in the other 16%. ***We must distinguish between numbers and volume in dealing with tanker spills.***

Given such a situation, one would think that the main focus of regulation would be on preventing the brobdingnagian spill.

- It is the brobdingnagian spill that put almost all the oil on the water.

- It is the brobdingnagian spill that generates outrage and regulation.

In fact, the focus of regulation has not been on preventing tanker casualties at all. Rather regulatory focus has been directed at reducing the number of spills from smaller hull penetrations after the casualty occurs. So far regulation has done almost nothing to prevent the brobdingnagian spill.

Only the Tromedy could get so far off track.

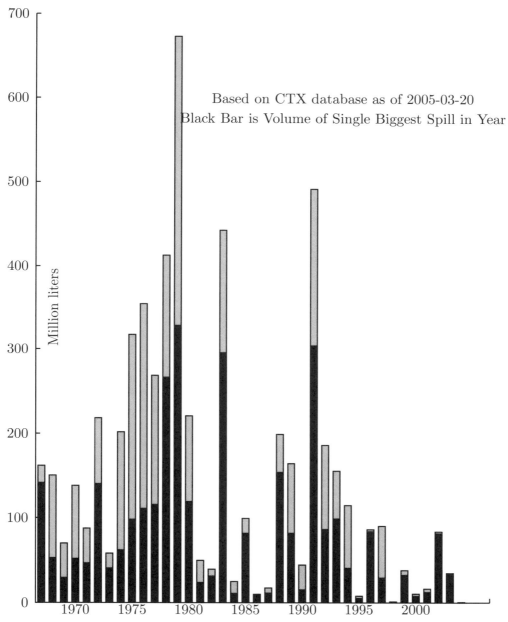

Figure 3.1: Annual versus Biggest Spill by Year

3.2   Spill Causality

Table 3.3 is a breakdown of the CTX Casualty Database (CDB) by initial cause. The first thing you will notice is that the initial cause is never a grounding, or an explosion, or a collision.

Let's get one thing straight. ***Groundings do not cause spills.*** I repeat a grounding is never the cause of a spill. It it a consequence of the cause of a spill. Groundings can be caused by navigational errors (TORREY CANYON, ARGO MERCHANT, EXXON VALDEZ), by conning errors (SEA EMPRESS, DIAMOND GRACE), by machinery failures (AMOCO CADIZ, BRAER, WAFRA), by insufficient maneuverability (AEGEAN SEA), by an anchor dragging (DONA MARIKA), by a poorly maintained channel (TASMAN SPIRIT [maybe]), by breaking loose from a berth, (JUAN LAVALLEJA), and a host of other reasons, even structural failure (NAKHODKA). To blame a spill on a grounding, is like blaming the runway for an airplane wreck on landing. Not only is "grounding" never the real cause of a spill, but by talking about grounding as if were the cause, we focus attention away from measures that could have prevented the grounding.

The same thing is true of fire/explosions and collisions. Ships don't ground themselves, nor all of sudden blow up, nor run into each other for no reason.

The CTX database tries to get at the real cause. For each casualty, the CDB has a sequence of event codes. Grounding, fire/explosion, collision and the like are never the initial event. In attempting to assign an initial event, the CTX does the following:

1. If there is actual documentation of the cause, we assign one of the causes in Table 3.3 which does not start with "Probable". Even here there are uncertainties. For one thing, we could be flat out wrong. More worryingly, there is a problem of defining initial. The CTX calls the BRAER a machinery failure. What happened was spare pipes on the aft deck were improperly secured. When they came loose in bad weather, the crew could not, or at least did not, re-secure them. The loose pipes clobbered the engine fuel oil tank vents, and sea water got into the fuel. Since there was no redundancy in the main engine system, the ship lost power, and drifted ashore. This spill could as easily be attributed to poor seamanship as a machinery failure. In such cases, CTX tilts toward bad design rather than "human errors" for the reasons laid out in Section 1.3.

2. In many cases, we have no actual documentation of the initial cause but strong circumstantial evidence. In this case, the CTX assigns one of the causes which start with the name "Probable" in Table 3.3. The CTX takes an aggressive approach in assigning probable cause, so we can be sure there are errors. We need more information on the cause in all these probable cases; but overall on a statistical basis, the numbers are almost certainly not misleading.

3. In some cases, we do not have enough evidence to be able to assign even a probable cause. In this case, the initial cause is left blank. At the time of writing, in 206 of 629 casualties, we could not assign a probable initial cause.[4]

Table 3.3 is central to the thesis of this book. Please study it carefully.

---

[4] Readers who have any information on these and other tanker casualties are implored to contact the CTX at cdb@c4tx.org.

Table 3.3: Breakdown of CTX Casualties by Initial Event

Based on CTX Casualty Data Base as of 2005-10-15T14:49:22

Initial Event	1960 ON			1995 ON		
	NO.	Volume (Liters)	Dead	NO.	Volume(liters)	Dead
HULL STRUCTURAL FAILURE						
Hull crack	48	18,425,199	0	35	91,371	0
Hull, cant link to corrosion	39	1,730,830,000	325	2	0	0
Pipe failure/leak	3	7,778	0	2	7,460	0
Hull, lots of corrosion	11	215,672,000	51	6	135,519,000	1
Probable hull failure	17	328,778,950	104	2	113,550	0
Hull, probably corrosion	1	0	2	0		0
TOTAL Hull Structural	119	2,293,713,927	482	47	135,731,381	1
RULES OF THE ROAD SCREW UPS						
Bad Giveway vsl response	5	25,623,500	41	1	83,500	0
Confirmed dance of death.	3	178,690,000	28	0		0
Failed to detect other vsl	2	335,890,000	35	0		0
Rogue vessel in wrong lane	2	6,638,000	64	0		0
Uncoordinated maneuver	2	29,800,000	0	2	29,800,000	0
Probable bad Rules of Road	25	146,675,000	13	12	6,276,000	1
Probable dance of death	9	304,262,000	176	1	9,450,000	0
TOTAL Rules of the Road	48	1,027,578,500	357	16	45,609,500	1
MACHINERY FAILURE						
Blackout	3	42,100,000	42	0		0
Crankcase explosion	1	2,030,000	0	1	2,030,000	0
Engine room flooding	2	50,000,000	0	0		0
Crankshaft failure	1	0	0	1	0	0
Steering gear/rudder failure	13	334,925,000	28	7	3,071,000	0
Shaft/sterntube failure	1	0	0	1	0	0
Stern tube leak	3	2	0	3	2	0
Seawater leak	2	103,000,000	0	0		0
Boiler Fire	2	0	9	0		0
Other/Unknown Machinery	40	209,982,800	0	11	1,652,800	0
Probable machinery failure	12	314,032,000	13	0		0
TOTAL Machinery	80	1,056,069,802	92	24	6,753,802	0
GUIDANCE/CONNING ERRORS						
Anchor dragged	5	11,360,000	0	0		0
Hit berth, mooring/unmooring	2	7,630,000	0	1	0	0
Conning error	8	209,711,000	26	3	86,707,000	0
Ship too deep for depth, swell	2	1,817,000	0	0		0
Tug contact/screw up	8	1,792,800	0	6	257,800	0
Probable guidance error	25	69,763,242	142	13	2,371,142	0
TOTAL Guidance/Conning	50	302,074,042	168	23	89,335,942	0
NAVIGATION ERRORS						
Navigation error	12	252,799,000	7	0		0
Bad charts on-board	1	0	0	0		0
Probable Navigation error	7	36,026,000	0	2	8,706,000	0
TOTAL Navigation Errors	20	288,825,000	7	2	8,706,000	0

Continued on next page

Initial Event	1960 ON			1995 0N		
	NO.	Volume (Liters)	Dead	NO.	Volume(liters)	Dead
BAD INERTING/HOTWORK						
Inert gas not working/bad	10	44,004,000	27	0		0
Stupid hotwork	3	3,490,000	16	0		0
Lightning strike	3	6,980,000	8	0		0
Bad purging/gas-freeing	3	0	16	2	0	13
Probable bad IG/hotwork	15	30,306,000	69	2	0	8
TOTAL Inerting/hotwork	34	84,780,000	136	4	0	21
BAD CHARTS, CHANNEL, BUOYS						
Bad channel depth	1	4,700,000	0	1	4,700,000	0
Incorrect charts	4	54,476,400	0	1	91,400	0
Hit submerged object	1	120,000	0	1	120,000	0
Probable navaid error	2	146,900,000	1	1	35,200,000	0
TOTAL Charts, channel	8	206,196,400	1	4	40,111,400	0
CARGO TRANSFER PROBLEMS						
Deballasting screw up	1	4,760	0	1	4,760	0
Hose failure, not unmoored	13	4,138,480	0	11	4,138,480	0
Other transfer screw up	37	7,595,678	0	28	708,201	0
Came unmoored	13	56,373,360	29	9	408,060	0
TOTAL Cargo Transfer	64	68,112,278	29	49	5,259,501	0
TOTAL KNOWN INITIAL EVENT						
TOTAL KNOWN	423	5,327,349,949	1272	169	331,507,526	23
NO INITIAL EVENT						
TOTAL No Initial Event	206	673,057,973	164	74	45,337,573	30
TOTAL KNOWN AND UNKNOWN						
TOTAL ALL	629	6,000,407,922	1436	243	376,845,099	53

3.3   Hull Structural Failures

In terms of spill volume, hull structural failure is by far the most important cause of tanker casualties. Table 3.3 is quite emphatic in this regard. It is almost as important as all the other causes combined. This is not only true of the entire post-1960 period but recently as well. The ERIKA and the PRESTIGE are only the latest in a long line of structural failures. If all we did was eliminate hull structural failures, we would cut volume spilled and tanker casualty deaths by a half. If you take nothing more away from this book than this simple fact, then I'm a happy man.

Given the importance of hull structural failure, the last thing we want to do is to produce tanker regulation that increases the liklihood of structural failure. But this in fact is what we have done. Twice! Once when we mandated segregated ballast without requiring coating. Secondly when we mandated double bottoms without requiring inerting. Moreover, the dysfunctional system for regulating newbuildings is ensuring that each generation of tankers is flimsier than the last. See Chapter 5.

Unless we do something drastic, hull structural failures will be a even bigger factor in the future than they were in the past. A large part of the second half of this book will be focused on building robust tanker hulls and maintaining them.

Table 3.5 lists all the Hull Structure spills greater than 1,000,000 liters in the CTX casualty database The fourth column, labeled E1, is the initial cause code. The hull structure cause codes are

HC	Hull crack, minor hull failure
HR	Major structural failure, lots of corrosion
HF	Major structural failure, corrosion unknown
HN	Major structural failure, corrosion not factor
HP	Pipe failure/leak
H_	Probable structural failure

HF does not necessarily mean that corrosion did not play a part, only that we could not establish that corrosion was important.

The fifth and sixth columns, E2 and E3, are subsequent events. The codes are

CN	Collision
EX	Engine Room Explosion
FD	Sank
FX	Fire/Explosion, cant say ER or PR or tank
PX	Pump Room Explosion File
RD	Rammed, hit while moored/anchored
RR	Rammer, allision, hit stationary object
TX	Cargo Tank Explosion/Fire.
TL	Ship scrapped or scuttled
WS	Grounding

The CDB tries to differentiate between cargo tank fires and engine room fires. They are fundamentally different animals. Most engine room fires are the result of a machinery failure. Most cargo tank fires are structural failures, at least since the imposition of cargo tank inerting.

The seventh column, labeled L, is what CTX calls Locale. The codes are

D	At repair yard
T	At fixed berth
S	At Single Buoy or other buoy based terminal
L	Lightering
H	Harbor (inside the Seabuoy)
R	Restricted Waters
O	Open Sea
?	Dont know

The eighth column, A, is Activity at time of casualty. The codes are

L	On loaded leg
B	On ballast leg
T	Tank cleaning (use instead of B)
l	Loading
d	Discharging
R	Repairing
?	Dont know

The ninth column is weather. This column shows the Beaufort Force if known, or HW (Heavy Weather) or (GL) gale or GD (good) or CM (calm).

The tenth column is the number of people killed.

Cargo leaking into segregated ballast tanks plays a crucial role in many tanker casualties. The CDB has a field, BT, that addresses this issue. The coding is:

Y	Confirmed leakage into segregated ballast tank
P	Leakage into segregated ballast tank extremely likely
M	Probable leakage into segregated ballast tank
N	Leakage into segregated ballast tank not a factor
?	Don't Know

The BT field is the 11th colum in Table 3.5. The ship names for which this field is either Y or P are shown in boldface.

Many of our Hull Failures are listed as "Probable" meaning we only have circumstantial evidence of a hull failure. Most of these spills are tank fires/explosions on a loaded ship. Structural failure is by far the most likely reason a loaded, inerted cargo tank would catch on fire. A loaded tanker is a quiet ship. Unlike the ballast leg, there is no tank cleaning, little deck maintenance of any kind due to the low freeboard, and only the most desperate tankerman would do hotwork anywhere near a cargo tank on a loaded tanker. Nothing much is happening forward of the accommodations on a loaded tanker, certainly not in any kind of weather. It's a safe bet that just about all tank explosions/fires on loaded tankers are structure related.[5]

Consider the KIRKI. In many spill databases, the KIRKI casualty is called a fire/explosion. In fact, this ship ran into heavy weather off West Australia while loaded with a volatile crude. The Forepeak ballast tank was very badly corroded. The hull structure failed on deck at the bulkhead between the Forepeak tank and the forwardmost cargo tanks. The combination of hydrocarbon vapor escaping from the cargo tanks and the loose steel banging around started a fire, which was then put out by the sea. This process was repeated several times until the whole Forepeak tank simply fell off. The fires had almost no impact on this spill, and most certainly were not the cause. The main difference between the KIRKI and most of the loaded tank explosions in Table 3.5 is that the ship survived.[6] As a bonus we

---

[5] If a ship is desperate enough to be doing hotwork forward on a loaded leg either on deck or in a ballast tank, then it's highly likely they are trying to repair dangerously corroded structure.

[6] One reason for this is that the Kirki's forepeak tank failed before the midships permanent ballast tanks. The pictures in Brodie[10] shows that the No. 7 ballast tanks were also horribly corroded, and not long for this world. Also cargo was leaking into the midships ballast tanks. But the Forepeak tank went first. When the midships tanks fail first, which is the case in many of the spills in Table 3.5, the ship often breaks in two and is lost. When the Forepeak ballast tank fails first (KIRKI, TOCHAL, GALP FUNCHAL), the ship has a pretty good chance of surviving.

have an excellent investigation report from the Australians including some pretty disgusting pictures of the corrosion.[7] As always, the KIRKI was fully approved by her Classification Society. See Section 2.11 for the gory details.

Not surprisingly, bad weather shows up in many hull failures. Most structural failures are in open waters in heavy weather. This does not mean that bad weather is a cause of structural failure. Rather the bad weather reveals that the structure is too weak. Tanker hulls are in theory designed to handle all the weather scenarios in Table 3.5. Either these hulls were not in fact so designed, or corrosion had weakened the structure to the point that it could not handle conditions it should have been able to.

But sometimes weather is not an immediate factor in which case it is a good bet the culprit is cargo leaking into a segregated ballast tank. Two of the most deadly of the sinkings in Table 3.5 were the BERGE ISTRA and the BERGE VANGA.[8] These ships were very large OBO's. *OBO* stands for Ore-Bulk-Oil meaning that the ships can carry both petroleum and dry bulk cargos such as iron ore. To do this they have a double bottom and a structure very like a double hull tanker. Both these ships sank almost immediately due to massive explosions in the double bottom.[9] The problem was that oil was leaking into the double bottom ballast tanks from cracks in the cargo tanks. In those days, the way a cargo surveyor checked for oil in a ballast tank was to use a mirror to send a shaft of sunlight down the ullage hatch. An experienced eye can tell if there is any oil, even a sheen, lying on top of the ballast water far below by the reflection. The crews of these OBO's were having so much difficulty keeping oil out of the double bottoms that they resorted to putting big buckets of water under the hatches. The cargo surveyor's mirror would see only the pail of clean water. This subterfuge cost them dearly. It was only a matter of time before the vapors in the double bottom were combined with a source of ignition.

Ballast tank leaks resulting in explosions are not confined to double bottom ships. Far from it. The SURF CITY explosion is an unusually well-documented single hull example. The loss of the ABT SUMMER, the second largest spill of all time, is another. In both cases, the Chief Mate discovered

---

[7] See www.atsb.gov.au/marine/incident_detail.cfm?ID=33.

[8] See also the ALGARROBO which killed 32, and the SINCLAIR PETROLORE which was the first of the really big post-war spills. All OBO's.

[9] In the case of the Vanga, this is well-founded conjecture. The ship sank so rapidly that not only did no one survive, they did not even have a chance to get off a distress message. The Istra sank almost as rapidly but miraculously there were three survivors, so we know what happened. The Vanga clearly was a repeat of the Istra. The owner, Bergesen, took the remaining vessels of this class out of the oil trade after the second sinking.

that cargo had leaked into a midships segregated ballast tank. In both cases, he went into the tank to find out how bad the problem was; and, while he and his helpers were in the tank it exploded. In both cases, the dead Chief Mate was blamed for the explosion. Blame-the-crew gone berserk.

A leak into a segregated ballast tank is the almost certain cause of the ANDROS PATRIA explosion, killer of 39, and the CASTILLO DE BELLVER sinking, third largest tanker spill ever. Cargo vapor in a ballast tank is by far the most likely cause of the KHARK 5 spill and the IRENES SERENADE sinking. It is probably the cause of the HAVEN explosion, the worst spill ever in the Mediterranean.[10] It was the cause of the BETELGEUSE explosion which killed 50 and destroyed the Bantry Bay terminal.[11] It is the most likely cause cause of the ODYSSEY and HAWAII PATRIOT losses.

Segregated ballast tank leakage is implicated in a dozen or more of the biggest pre-Marpol tanker casualties despite the fact that pre-Marpol tankers had only two or three segregated ballast tanks. Table 3.4 summarizes the importance of leakage into segregated ballast tanks in the CTX database. If you compare these spill volumes with those in Table 3.3, you will find that the sum of the Confirmed and Very Likely categories is larger than any non-hull structure related cause. **Hull structural failure is by far the most important cause of tanker casualties; and leaks into segregated ballast tanks are by far the most important cause of hull structure spills.**

The only difference between single bottom and double bottom ships in this regard is that in the latter the opportunities for such leaks are increased by at least a factor of two relative to a double sided ship and a factor of eight relative to a pre-Marpol tanker. See Table 2.2 on page 47. **The same owners who could not maintain 25,000 square meters of segregated ballast tank area are now being asked to maintain 225,000 square**

---

[10] So far I have not been able to determine the cause of this casualty with certainty, in part because of the owner's frantic legal efforts to avoid going to jail for manslaughter.

[11] The uncoated segregated ballast tanks on this Total ship were horribly corroded. It is unclear whether the cargo leaked into the tank and then exploded, or the wasted deck structure in the top of the ballast tanks failed in sag as they ballasted, allowing cargo into the ballast tanks which then exploded. We will never know. Everybody who could tell us, both on the ship and at the terminal, were killed. For our present purposes, it really doesn't matter.

The Irish Inquiry[60] was able to document not only that the segregated ballast tanks were in execrable condition and had been for several years, but also that Total executives knew this and, with the acquiescence of Bureau Veritas, the ship's Classification Society, **consciously decided not to do anything about it**, since Total intended to sell the ship. Fifty people were killed. Ten years after the MARPESSA this big tanker was not inerted. Yet no criminal charges were brought against anyone.

Table 3.4: Spills in which cargo leaking into Segregated Ballast Tank implicated

LEAK INTO SBT?	NUMBER	LITERS	DEATHS
DONT KNOW	60	573,797,841	158
NOT A FACTOR	9	2,443,448	44
LIKELY	19	341,549,000	86
VERY LIKELY	10	497,600,000	57
CONFIRMED	21	878,323,638	137
TOTAL	119	2,293,713,927	482

meters. With the entire tanker fleet going double hull, it is inevitable that we have had and will have oil leaking into the double bottom from cracks in the cargo tanks. And unless we do something, it is also inevitable that we will have double bottom explosions. That something is ballast tank inerting.[12] See Section 6.4.

---

[12]Ten of the top 13 hull structure spills in Table 3.5 involve an explosion, usually starting in a segregated ballast tank. None of these ballast tanks were inerted. If they had been, most of these brobdingnagian spills would have been averted.

Table 3.5: Hull Structural Failures, Spillage above 200,000 Liters

Based on CTX Casualty Database as of 2005-10-15T15:22:21

DATE	SHIP	Kiloliters	E1	E2	E3	L	A	WE	Dead	B	T	Brief Description
19910528	**Abt Summer**	305000	HF	TX	FD	O	L		5	Y		exp in perm ballast tank due to leak from cgo tank
19830805	**Castillo De Bellver**	296400	HF	TX	FD	O	L		3	Y		leak to perm ballast tank, NW Capetown, fire, sank
19910411	**Haven**	164700	HF	TX	FD	H	L		5	P		tank fire anch off Genoa, prob leak into SBT
19881110	Odyssey	155000	H_	FX	FD	O	L	HW	27	M		fire 700M E St Johns, probably structural failure
19800223	**Irenes Serenade**	120000	HF	TX	FD	H	L		2	P		fire lowering anchor Pylos, prob cgo in FP tank
19770223	Hawaiian Patriot	116400	HF	TX	FD	O	L	HW	0	?		hull crack off Hawaii, fire, broke in two, sank
19920416	**Katina P**	84700	HF		FD	O	L	HW	0	P		midships hull failure off Mozambique, sank,
19891219	**Khark 5**	82300	HF	TX		O	L	HW	0	P		ballast tank leak, exp off Morocco loaded,
20021113	**Prestige**	82000	HR		FD	O	L	10	0	Y		hull failure off NW Spain, bad corrosion in SBT
19601206	Sinclair Petrolore	60000	HF	FX	FD	O	L		0	M		self-unloading OBO exploded and sank, no details
19781231	**Andros Patria**	58800	HF	TX	TL	O	L	HW	39	Y		50 ft crack, then explosion in 3P, off NW Spain,
19680613	World Glory	53100	HF		FD	O	L	GL	24	?		broke in two in gale off Durban
19790108	**Betelgeuse**	47000	HR	TX	TL	T	d		50	Y		bad rust in uncoated bllst tank, explosion, 50 dead
19941021	Thanassis A	41200	HF		FD	O	L	TY	16	M		broke in two in Typhoon Teresa, prob corrosion
19880422	Athenian Venture	40000	H_	FX	FD	O	L		29	?		fire off Newfoundland, broke in 2, hull failure?
19770117	Irenes Challenge	39500	HF		FD	O	L	HW	3	?		hull failure off Midway, broke in 2, no details
19720611	Trader	34000	H_	WS	FD	?	?		0	?		Conflicting reports, need more info, cause is guess
19991212	**Erika**	33000	HR		FD	O	L	GL	0	Y		hull failure off Brittany due hvy corrosion in SBT
19720128	Golden Drake	32000	H_	FX	FD	O	L		0	?		"explosion on board" sank, Bulkpetrol Class, cause?
19640301	Amphialos	30000	HF		FD	O	L	HW	2	?		broke in two,storm off Cape Cod, Bulkpetrol Class
19691105	Keo	30000	HF		FD	O	L	HW	30	?		broke in two, storm off Nantucket, Bulkpetrol Class
19691125	Pacocean	30000	HF		FD	O	L	HW	3	?		broke in two, storm off Taiwan, Bulkpetrol Class
19701200	Chryssi	30000	HF		FD	O	L		0	?		hull failure, Atlantic, nil info
19710327	Texaco Oklahoma	30000	HF		FD	O	L	11	31	?		split in two, whole gale off Hatteras, overstressed?
19761230	Grand Zenith	28700	HF		FD	O	L		0	?		structural failure off Massachusetts, nil info
19760728	Cretan Star	28000	HF		FD	O	L	HW	36	?		hull failure, Indian Ocean, sunk with all hands

Continued on next page

DATE	SHIP	Kilo-liters	E1	E2	E3	L	A	WE	De-ad	B/T	B Brief Description
19900222	**Surf City**	28000	HF	TX		?	?		2	Y	leak into ballast tank, explosion off Dubai
19940124	Cosmas A	27000	H_	TX	FD	O	L	HW	10	M	broke in two, prob structural failure, need confirm
19800307	**Tanio**	24400	HF	FD		O	L	8	8	P	hull failure off Brittany, an early Erika/Prestige
19750404	Spartan Lady	21700	HF	FD		O	L	HW	0	?	broke in two in storm off New York, crew rescued
19910721	**Kirki**	20300	HR	TX		O	L	HW	0	Y	massive corrosion, Forepeak tank fell off, Australia
19970102	Nakhodka	20200	HR	WS	FD	O	L	HW	1	M	massive hull failure, Japan "20 to 50% corroded"
19741205	Cherry Vinstra	18800	H_			?	L		0	?	"hull defect, India" no other info
19901117	Berge Broker	15800	HC	HL		O	L		0	M	big hull rupture off Azores, very low lightweight
19790315	**Kurdistan**	14900	HF	TL		O	L	GL	0	P	hull failure Cabot Str, prob. rust in perm blst tank
19891004	Pacificos	11800	HR	HL		O	L	10	0	M	hull failure off East Africa, prob corrosion
19761015	Boehlen	11100	H_	FD		R	L	HW	0	?	sank. Brittany, bad weather, prob structural failure
19751229	**Berge Istra**	5000	H_	TX		O	B		38	Y	explosion in double bottom, 38 killed
19791029	**Berge Vanga**	5000	HF	TX	FD	O	B		40	P	Repeat of Berge Istra, dbl bott explosion, 40 dead
19880131	Amazzone	2470	HF			O	L	HW	0	M	hull failure in storm off Brittany, one tank holed
19800909	Derbyshire	2400	HF	FD		O	L	TY	44	N	DH OBO sank in typhoon, prob hatch cover collapse
19870106	Stuyvesant	2380	H_			O	L		0	M	big hull crack Gulf of Alaska, need confirmation
19871004	Stuyvesant	2220	HC			O	L		0	M	big hull crack Gulf of Alaska, need confirmation
19900919	Algarrobo	2000	HF	FD		O	B		32	M	O/O loaded ore, sank no message, prob dbl bot leak
19750908	**Pacific Colocotronis**	1760	H_	HL		R	L	10	0	Y	big hull crack in 3P off Holland, 70KT spill averted
19750513	**Princess Ann Marie**	1600	H_			O	L	HW	0	P	big hole strb side midships, made it to Dampier
19821226	Charalambos	1160	HF			O	L	HW	0	M	side plating fell off under tow, Yucatan, scrapped
19780526	**World Horizon**	830	HR			O	L	HW	0	Y	corroded forepeak tank fell off in hvy weather
20000916	Alambra	319	HR	TL		T	1		0	M	big crack at Tallinn, bad corrosion, scrapped
19890103	Thompson Pass	270	HC			T	1		0	?	"9 ft" bottom crack discovered at Valdez
19940602	**Tochal**	223	HR			O	L		0	Y	whole FP tank fell off, but only fwd fo breached

3.4   Rules of the Road Screw-Ups

Rules of the Road (ROTR) screw-ups is my grab-bag term for all the ways people manage to steer one ship into another. Every casualty caused by a Rules of the Road screw-up is a collision, but not every collision is a ROTR screw up. For example, the NASSIA[13] and BALTIC CARRIER collisions were caused by steering gear failures.

As Table 3.3 shows, Rules of the Road screw-ups have been the second most important cause of both deaths and spills.[14] The largest tanker spill of all time, the ATLANTIC EMPRESS/Aegean Captain collision, falls into this category.[15] Table 3.7 shows all the ROTR spills in the CTX Casualty Database with a spill volume greater than 200,000 liters. The relevant initial cause codes are

VB	Give-way vessel failed to maneuver
VD	Confirmed, one port2port, other stbd2stbd
Vd	Probable, one port2port, other stbd2stbd
VL	failed to detect other vessel in time
VR	rogue vessel in wrong lane
VU	Uncoordinated maneuver
V_	Probable Rules of the Road screw-up

The ATLANTIC EMPRESS collision appears to have been caused by horrible radar watch on both ships, abetted by illegal manning. The two ships were in and out of rain squalls at dusk. They did not adjust the anti-clutter controls on their radars correctly. Each ship apparently did not realize the other ship was there until immediately prior to impact. This is exceedingly unusual.

Since the introduction of radar in the 1950's, detection of the other vessel hasn't been the problem. Wheatley studied 174 collisions that occurred in

---

[13] Actually the bulk carrier Shipbroker had a black out. With no electrical power, she had no steering and ran into the NASSIA in the Bosporus killing 42.

[14] The Nova/Magnum collision which spilled 82 million liters does not show up in Table 3.3. These two ships were shuttling oil down the Persian Gulf for the Iranians during the Iraq/Iraq War. They were running at night without any navigation lights, and reportedly maneuvering to avoid a missile attack.[56, page 108] CTX concluded that this was a war casualty. War casualties are not included in the CTX database.

[15] The officer of the watch on the Greek Flag ATLANTIC EMPRESS was the radio officer. He had no deck officer's license. This was a regular practice on-board the Empress and, according to the crew, known to the owners. Despite this Flagrant violation of Greek maritime law, the Greek report says "We wish to say nothing that might be thought to be any criticism or complaint against those who were responsible for operating these two vessels."[12, pages 14-17] This is called Flag State control.

the Straits of Dover in the period 1968 to 1971.[80]. The average range at detection for the radar equipped ship was 9000 meters. The minimum required to avoid collision for even the largest tankers is less than 2000 meters **if both ships react correctly**.[20, pages 2.3-2.5] With modern radars, a sizable tanker is aware of every ship within 15 miles of her.

Paradoxically, almost all Rules of the Road screw-ups still occur in periods of low visibility or at least at night. The column labeled V in Table 3.7 is the visibility in miles or F for Foggy. One result of radar and the ease of detection was that the world fleet used it to maintain speed in periods of low visibility. In the Wheatley study which went back into the late 1950's, some of the ships did not have radar. Their average speed at time of detection was 4 knots. For the radar equipped vessels, the average initial speed was 10 knots. This increase in speed was almost certainly a smart decision economically. But it means that you better use the information the radar provides correctly.

To understand ROTR screw-ups, you must understand the Rules of the Road. The Rules are simple. There are basically only three.
1. Overtaking vessel must keep clear.
2. In crossing situations, the ship that has the other ship on her starboard side must keep clear. This ship is called the *give-way* vessel. The other ship is called the *stand-on* vessel.
3. In head-on situations, both ships should alter to starboard for a port to port passing.

The CTX CDB has a field called Encounter Type that applies only to collisions. The coding is

V	Overtaking
B	Crossing, own ship is give-way ship
C	Crossing, other ship give-way ship
H	Confirmed, head on or nearly head on
h	Probable, head on or nearly head on
c	Probable crossing
	Cant say

"Own ship" in this context means the tanker by which the casualty is known in the CTX database.[16] To analyze Rules screw-ups, the first thing you must know is the Encounter Type. Unfortunately, in many cases this essential fact is unreported and must be inferred.

---

[16] If a collision involves two tankers, the CTX database list the casualty under the ship that spilled the most, almost always the hittee. This has no implications for guilt.

Figure 3.2: Dance of Death

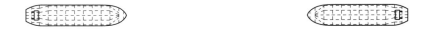

Sketch A. Perfect Head On Encounter

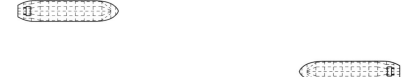

Sketch B. Displaced to Starboard

Overtaking tanker collisions are quite rare. As far as we know, the only one in the CTX database is the OLYMPIC GLORY which occurred in very confined waters.

As Table 3.7 shows almost all collisions occur in restricted waters or harbors. Most restricted waters now have Traffic Separation Schemes (TSS) in operation which set up one way lanes with a separation zone in between. The TSS rule is also simple: stay on the starboard side of the waterway. Most crossing situations are generated when a ship has to cross one of these traffic lanes. We were able to positively identify four crossing casualties in the CTX CDB. In this case, the fault usually lies with the give-way vessel, but in some of these cases the stand-on ship which is supposed to maintain course and speed contributes an unexpected maneuver. (See ENOIKOS/Orapin Global below.)

Most collisions result from a head on encounter. Herein lies the rub for, in this situation, the rules have a fatal ambiguity. If the ships are meeting perfectly end on as in Sketch A, barring lack of water depth or total stupidity, there is no problem. Both ships alter to starboard and that's the end of the story. However if the two ships are displaced to starboard as in Sketch B, then we have a problem.

In a classic 1977 study, Kemp asked a sample of ten randomly selected people what they would do if they were the captain of the two vessels in Sketch A.[40] As might be expected, their replies were random with roughly half the subjects going left and half going right. When Kemp repeated the question with a sample of ten experienced mariners, all ten turned to starboard to effect the port to port passing called for in the Rules.

Then Kemp repeated the process but this time with the ships displaced as in Sketch B. The ten subjects with no knowledge of the Rules of the Road all maintained course, undoubtedly perplexed as to why they were asked to consider such an obvious problem. The ten master mariners, however, were in a quandary.

A) Should they consider the situation to be a dangerous crossing, invoke Rule 3, and turn to starboard to effect a port to port crossing even though it means crossing the other ship's bow and decreasing the Closest Point of Approach (CPA)?

B) Or should they consider that a crossing situation does not exist and maintain course, or perhaps go to port to increase the CPA further?

In Kemp's experiment, when the two tracks were displaced by a mile, half chose (A) and half chose (B). This turning into the path of the other ship has been called the Dance of Death. The CTX Casualty Database uses the more prosaic cause codes: VD (confirmed Dance of Death) and Vd (probable Dance of Death).

Historically, the Dance of Death is by far the most common cause of collisions. The Andrea Doria-Stockholm may be the most famous case. The SEA STAR is less well known. On the night of December 19, 1972, the SEA STAR and the Horta Barbossa were proceeding on nearly complementary courses in the Gulf of Oman.[12, p 42-44] Clear weather, light wind. The ships were aware of each other at a range of 14 miles. Their courses were sufficiently displaced so that, if both had maintained course and speed, they would have passed starboard to starboard with a CPA of about one mile. The SEA STAR apparently regarded this separation as insufficient. At a range of about four miles, she went starboard to effect a port to port passing. The Horta Barbossa maintained course and rammed the SEA STAR amidships. In the ensuing fire, 12 tankermen died and 141 million liters of crude were lost into the sea, the eighth largest spill of all time.

The implication is obvious. The Rules of the Road do not resolve the ambiguity associated with end-on encounters. They only displace it to starboard slightly. In situations with good visibility, the residual uncertainty does not appear to be too dangerous. Several groups, principally in England and Japan, have attempted to apply random encounter theory (molecular analogies) to vessel collisions. When one asks, what is the probability that collisions would occur if ships made no attempt at avoiding each other, and then compares the results with actual collision incidence for regions as disparate as the Straits of Dover and the Inland Sea, there are very roughly one ten-thousandth as many actual collisions as predicted by random encounter theory. In good visibility, 9,999 out of 10,000 potential collisions are avoided. However, if one repeats the same analysis for collisions during low visibility, fragmentary evidence indicates that the ratio of actual to potential collisions is about one tenth — only about nine out of ten potential collisions are avoided. A one thousand fold difference in avoidance efficiency is a number well worth contemplating.

This striking difference is almost certain due to:

1. Acceptance of *lower* CPA's during good visibility; hence less need to maneuver.

2. ability to determine the other ship's intentions almost instantly by visual observations.

Baratt (1976) studied radar plots of collision avoidance maneuvers in the Straits of Dover, reaching some very interesting and, at first glance, surprising conclusions.[5] He found that the incidence of collision avoidance maneuvers was over twice as high during periods when visibility was less than a kilometer than when visibility was greater than a kilometer. In low visibility, mariners are unwilling to accept CPA's they regard with equanimity in high visibility. Hence many more maneuvers were initiated. Further Baratt found that not only were maneuvers twice as frequent during low visibility, they were initiated at greater range and they were more violent. Seamen, contrary to the impression one would obtain from some shoreside defenders of the Rules of the Road, are quite cognizant of the dangers of low visibility and feel the need to do something. Unfortunately, the Rules' prescription of early substantial maneuvers has not prevented the low visibility collision incidence from being a thousand times that of high visibility.

Most interestingly, Baratt found that non-standard maneuvers (altering to port) were over four times as frequent during periods of low visibility. Table 3.6 summarizes this finding. Mariners clearly feel that during periods of low visibility a starboard to starboard passing requires a higher CPA than in high visibility. Hence if they are displaced to starboard, the tendency to alter to port in low visibility when they would stand on in high visibility. When one is displaced well to starboard, the alternative of going starboard and crossing the other ship's bow is not regarded with great favor. And

Table 3.6: Maneuver Incidence

Visibility	Alter to Starboard	Alter to Port
>1 km	0.21/hr	0.08/hr
<1 km	0.28/hr	0.33/hr

with good reason as the SEA STAR found out. As the statistics reveal, many ships are making port alterations in bad visibility, in which case the starboard decision can easily lead to disaster.

Things have been getting better in this casualty category. By far, the most important reason for this improvement has been the adoption of Traffic Separation Schemes. Traffic Separation Schemes now exist in most congested waterways. Most waterways have a long axis and most traffic is along that axis. A TSS is little more than the rule that all traffic along the axis stay on the starboard side of the waterway. This simple rule does two things:

1. It cuts the number of head-on encounters by a large factor.

2. And if there are any head-on encounters in the waterway, they are unlikely to be displaced to starboard.

Many TSS's include radar surveillance to enforce the lanes and advise traffic of dangerous situations. This is called VTS (Vessel Traffic Service). The legal status of VTS is a morass into which I do not intend to venture, but currently VTS's have at best an advisory role. Worse, they often operate under self-imposed restrictions about what they can say, for fear of being blamed for a collision. The OREGON STANDARD/Arizona Standard collision is an egregious example. Their only useful role is to identify rogue ships (ships traveling in the wrong lane) and even then their enforcement powers are limited. But overall Traffic Separation Schemes have made a tremendous difference. We rarely have a Dance of Death collision in TSS waterways anymore.[17]

Technology has helped as well. In the mid-1980's ARPA was introduced. ARPA (Advanced Radar Plotting Aid) is a specialized computer inside the radar which projects the tracks of the ships on the screen, and displays the

---

[17] Traffic Separation Schemes have also been applied to areas in which there is no geographical funneling of the traffic, for example, in the approaches to a port. This is not a bad idea, but usually traffic approaches a harbor entrance from more than one direction which results in converging TSS's. I like IMO's French term for the area where the TSS's come together, *Zone de Prudence*. But a better name might be "time to talk".

CPA's, usually in the form of a "danger circle". It automates the plotting
that a watch officer was supposed to have done but often didn't simply because the calculations were so time consuming, that, if he did them with
any degree of frequency, he stood a good chance of losing control of the situation. ARPA eliminates plotting errors and omissions. This was important
because now both watch officers have a much better idea of the CPA if they
do nothing and, if the number is OK, they do nothing, avoiding a possible
Dance of Death. ARPA has undoubtedly prevented a number of collisions.[18]

However, ARPA does NOT resolve the basic ambiguity in the Rules.
ARPA assumes both ships maintain course and speed in its calculations. As
soon as this is not true, as soon as at least one watch officer feels a maneuver
is indicated, then the ARPA projections are incorrect and misleading.[19]

The ENOIKOS/Orapin Global is probably an ARPA-assisted collision.[20]
This wreck is also an interesting example of lack of communication, both
between the vessels and a VTS. On the evening of November 15, 1997, the
Orapin Global was westbound in ballast in the Malacca Strait off Singapore.
The ENOIKOS was eastbound loaded but her destination was Singapore,
which meant she had to cross the westbound lane to pick up the Singapore
mooring pilot. Both ships were under the surveillance of the Singapore VTS.
At this point, the westbound (north) lane is 600 m wide, then there is a 200
m wide buffer zone, and the eastbound deep water lane is 700 m wide. Since
both these ships are more than 200 m long, it is extremely tight quarters.

At 2041, Singapore VTS warned the Orapin Global that she was in the
buffer zone. The OG acknowledged saying she was overtaking a slower ship
and, as soon as she passed, she would come back to starboard to get back
in her lane. Meanwhile the ENOIKOS is looking for a break in the traffic
to turn to port and cross the westbound lane to get to the pilot boarding
station. It was night with visibility of 5 miles. With the OG's jog to port,
it looks to the Enoiks' ARPA that she can pass in front of the OG.

---

[18] The installation of an ARPA equipped radar became a requirement on all sizable
ships between 1984 and 1987. However, the regulations require only a single ARPA. This
makes no sense. The same rules rightly require two radars and the marginal cost of adding
ARPA to the second radar is less than $5,000. Yet many owners choose to save the $5,000,
which means the ship is one failure away from being ARPA-less.

[19] Modern radars display the other ship's course and speed on the screen. A sharp
watch officer could use this info to pick up the fact that the other ship is maneuvering
sooner than if he did not have this data. But to do this he has to remember the old course
and speed for all targets of interest. My experience is that few watch officers actually do
this. Rather they focus on the CPA's and the little "danger circle" ellipses.

[20] I am indebted to Captain Pierre Woinin for the following description of this casualty.
The conclusions about ARPA are my own.

At 2046, the VTS warned the Orapin Global of risk of collision with the Enoikos, but does not tell the OG the Enoikos's destination. At 2048, the VTS warns the Enoikos of risk of collision with the the OG. Both ships go hard to starboard to try to get back to a port to port passing. But at this point this is exactly the wrong thing to do. At 2054, the ships collide. At no point did the two ships talk to each other.[21]

The simple fact is that the only way of truly resolving the ambiguity in the Rules of the Road is for the two ships to coordinate their maneuvers. In plain English, they need to talk to each other. The deep sea merchant marine community had always resisted this simple solution, claiming lack of a common language and inability to positively identify which ship you were talking to. In 1986, the USCG correctly rejected these objections, pointing out that acquiring the limited vocabulary needed was not a big deal, and that with ARPA you could pretty easily identify the other ship by its relative location and course. In 1986 the USA passed the Bridge to Bridge Act which requires all sizable vessels in US Effective Economic Zone which extends up to 200 miles from the American coast to have common VHF equipment, maintain radio watch on a common frequency, have a rudimentary English capability, and to communicate in any situation where a collision is possible and agree on a coordinated maneuver. There have been no tanker Rules screw-up collisions in American waters since then.

In non-American waters matters have proceeded much more slowly. However, in 1988, IMO finally mandated common VHF equipment on all ships over 300 GRT which rules came into force between 1995 and 1999 depending on the size and type of vessel. The 1995 Amendments to the International Convention on Standards for Training, Certification, and Watchkeeping for Seafarers (STCW) requires that watch officers on all ships over 500 GRT on international voyages have a adequate knowledge of English "to communicate with other ships and coast stations". This came into force in February, 1997. IMO has published a simplified English vocabulary.

However, the language requirements have not been well enforced. Some countries continue to issue licenses to deck officers who have very little En-

---

[21] The Singapore courts found both captains guilty of speeding and recklessness and sentenced each to several months in prison. The Court found no fault with the VTS. It is in interesting that neither owner really contested the case; rather they left their Captains out to dry. Tanker owners are not famous for their loyalty to their crews, and their lawyers undoubtedly pointed out that attempting to put blame on Singapore in a Singapore court wasn't going to work. The public is left with the impression the spill was caused by two rogue cowboys. In hindsight, it is easy to say that the OG should not have passed slower traffic at this point, and that the Enoikos should not have tried to squeeze thru the apparent gap, but the real problem is a system in which people don't talk to each other.

glish. This is not that big a problem for tankers, big container ships, or passenger vessels where commercial realities require that at least the top deck officers have some English. But it can be a problem if the other ship is a bulk carrier or general cargo ship. Second tier owners and ship management firms are continually switching to the newest, cheapest nationality for crews. It takes a few years before these new crews acquire a little English. By that time, some other nationality is cheaper.

Unlike US waters, there is no requirement that ships in danger of a collision must communicate. In fact, the requirement to monitor Channel 16, the normal VHF bridge to bridge channel, lapsed in January, 2005. IMO adopted this much needed requirement mainly to make sure that distress calls were received. Channel 16 has now been replaced, at least in IMO's mind, by a fancier digital system that can only handle distress calls. A big step backward. For whatever reason, the ships still don't talk to each other.[22]

Technology to the rescue again. The last ten years have seen the adoption of three important technologies:

GPS With the introduction of GPS, for a few hundred dollars, every ship in the world can know where it is to an accuracy of a few tens of meters. It also knows its course and speed over the ground accurately. GPS

---

[22] The BRITISH VIGILANCE/Stena King is a particularly bizarre example. On the calm, clear night of March 25, 2002, the Stena King, a fully loaded 450,000 ton pre-Marpol ULCC was outbound from the crowded Fujairah anchorage, headed SE. The double hull VLCC British Vigilance in ballast was also outbound but headed NNE. The King was the give-way vessel but opted to go to port to pass in front of the Vigilance. She may have been confused by the fact that the Vigilance, which had just raised her anchor, was increasing speed at the time. The Stena King didn't make it. She hit the Vigilance in the aft most cargo tank on the port side. Despite the fact that the ships collided at fairly fine angle and at a relative speed of less than four knots, the bow of the King penetrated not just thru the double sides, but all the way thru the port cargo tank to the center tank. I saw the Vigilance in the Dubai repair yard a few weeks later. Massive damage to a nearly new tanker.

Miraculously, the Vigilance was headed for her first drydocking. Her cargo tanks had just been cleaned and gas freed. This was one of the few days every two and a half years that she would be free of petroleum vapor. There was no explosion. The King's forepeak was badly damaged but the damage stopped just forward of her No 1 starboard cargo tank, so there was no spill. What could have easily been the biggest spill in history was avoided.

There was no communication between the ships until after the contact. Here's the kicker. Not only did everybody on both bridges speak good English, the captains of both the Stena King and the British Vigilance were English. In fact they knew each other well. The captain of the Vigilance had served as mate under the captain of the King. But still they did not talk.

should just about eliminate navigation errors. See Section 3.6.1.

ECDIS But from a collision point of view, the important development is the combination of GPS, ECDIS, and ARPA. ECDIS stands for something like Electronic Chart Display system. It is similar to an in-car navigation system. Instead of paper charts, the ship is equipped with computerized charts that are displayed on a monitor. The neat thing about this is, when combined with GPS, the display can include the ship's own position, eliminating plotting errors. And when combined with ARPA, the display can include the other ships' position on the chart display, which means both watch officers accurately know their own and the other ships' position. When they refer to "ship at latitude such and such and longitude such and such", there is nil likelihood of talking to the wrong ship.

AIS To make matters even simpler, we now have AIS. *AIS* (Automatic Identification System) operates like a transponder sending out a signal to neighboring ships which identifies the ship name, IMO number, call sign, and size, location, course, speed, and rate of turn. The requirement to install AIS on all ships over 300 GRT came into force between 2003 and end of 2004. New radars and ECDIS systems have the capability of displaying the AIS info on the radar scope or on the ECDIS chart display.

There is simply no longer any excuse for not talking other than a common language. Even this could be handled by slightly extending AIS. Only a few bits of information need to be transmitted to agree on a maneuver. Select target. Press one button to indicate to the other ship you want to pass starboard to starboard, another to go port to port. He either agrees or requests the opposite with his two buttons. Repeat until agreement is reached.[23]

For all these reasons, it is reasonable to expect that Rules of the Road screw-ups will be less frequent in the future than the past. But if we are really worried about collisions, and we should be, then we must either

1. enforce a common language and the requirement to talk,

2. expand the AIS to perform the same function.

---

[23] Skippers in inland waterways have this simple conversation all the time. "One bell or two bells, Cap?" "Let's go two bells." "Two bells it is." As this little dialogue indicates, before radio this communication was carried out by whistle signals.

Rules of the Road screw-ups are not a tanker design problem. At this point, they are simply a communication problem. The regulatory solution is dead simple: enforce communication.[24]

---

[24] The Rules of the Road could use a number of other more secondary improvements. Over time the ROTR have become encrusted with pious and pernicious blather. We have already seen the "early and substantial maneuver" nonsense. The stand-on vessel is required to maintain course and speed BUT, if he thinks the give-way vessel is not responding properly, then suddenly it is his responsibility to maneuver. This puts the stand-on vessel in the impossible position of getting into the other man's head and introduces a whole new set of uncertainties into the equation. Lawyers love this one.

And the ROTR ignore simple physics. Consider the injunction to slow down if you find yourself in a dangerous situation. In fact, if you find yourself in a dangerous situation on a big ship, the last thing you want to do is throttle back or worse go astern. Reducing throttle on a large ship has nil immediate impact on speed. It takes over half an hour and five miles for a large tanker to stop by going astern. What does happen when a ship throttles back is that the rudder forces are drastically reduced and the ship's ability to turn is crippled. (A big ship going astern essentially has no rudder.) If you want to turn a big ship quickly, then you must go full ahead. The ship's speed won't change, but your rudder forces will be improved immensely. In fact, the quickest way to stop a big ship is full ahead and rudder hard over. Seamen know these things, but, thanks to the Rules of the Road, nobody wants to be caught going full ahead in a collision, so the ships' ability to maneuver is badly compromised just when they need it the most.

But there is only one really necessary change: enforce communication.

Table 3.7: Rules Screw-ups with Spill Volume over 100,000 Liters

Based on CTX Casualty Database as of 2005-10-15T16:35:27

L=Locale, A=Activity, TOD=Time.of.Day, V=Visibility, WE=Weather, EN=Encounter Type, TK=Talk?

DATE	SHIP	Kilo liters	E1	E2	E3	E4	E5	L	A	TOD	V	WE	Dead	EN	TK	Synopsis
19790719	Atlantic Empress	329000	VL	CN	FD			R	L	1915	R	5	26	h		coll w Aegean Captain off Tobago,appalling watchkeep
19721219	Sea Star	141100	VD	CN	TX	FD		O	L	NGT		GD	12	H	N	coll Gulf Oman, one Port to Port, one stbd to stbd
19791115	Independenta	111000	Vd	CN	TX	FD		R	L				43	h		Collision South end of Bosporus, cause?
19741109	Yuyo Maru 10	79500	Vd	CN	SC			H	L				34	h		coll w Pacific Ares in Tokyo Bay, cause?
19680229	Mandoil Ii	50500	V-	CN	TX	TL		O	L	DUSK	F	FG	11	c		collision off Oregon, probable B encounter
19791101	Burmah Agate	40500	Vd	CN	TX	WS	TL	H	L	NGHT		GD	32	h		coll w Mimosa inbound Galveston Bay, 30+ dead,cause?
19700428	Gino	39000	V-	CN	FD			R	L			FG	0	h		coll w Team Castor, no cause info, Gino was OBO
19771216	Venoil	34800	VD	CN				O	L		F		0	H	N	coll w Venpet off S.A. classic dance of death
19971015	Evoikos	29800	VU	CN	TL			R	L	2054	5	CM	0	B	N	coll spore crossing westbound lane hugh gash, 3 tnks
19930120	Maersk Navigator	29400	Vd	CN	FX			R	L				0	H		coll w Sanko Honour west end of Malacca, cause???
19760216	Nanyang	24000	V-	CN	WS	TL		O	L				0			coll in South China Sea, no cause info
19940330	Seki	18800	VB	CN				H	L	0200			0	C	N	hit while storing underway off Fujairah, 1P holed
19920919	Nagasaki Spirit	14100	Vd	CN	FX	TL		R	L	2320			30	h		coll w Ocean Blessing N end of Malacca, 30 dead
19720821	Oswego Guardian	11700	Vd	CN	FD			R	L		F		34	H	N	coll w Texanita near Cape, Texanita exp, sank,cause?
19970118	Bona Fulmar	9450	Vd	CN				R	L			FG	0	h		hittee off Dunkirk, OBO, 1 tank breached, 4mx3m hole
19900806	Sea Spirit	7770	Vd	CN				R	L				0	H		coll with LPG carrier Hesperus whose bow destroyed
19930603	British Trent	6890	VL	CN	FX	TL		R	L		F	CM	9			hittee off Ostende,port side, heavy fog, under vts
19701023	Pacific Glory	6000	VR	CN	TX	WS	TL	R	L				13	B		coll w ld tanker Allegro, Glory on wrong side?
19770813	Agip Venezia	5880	V-	CN				O	L				0	B		coll w Ramses II near Sicily, cause?
19780506	Eleni V	5320	V-	CN	TL			R	L		F	FG	0	B		cut in two by coll off Norfolk UK, heavy fog
19930817	Lyria	5290	V-	CN				O	L				0			collision with submarine off Toulon
19990115	Estrella Pampeana	4540	V-	CN				H	L				0	h		collision, Rio Plata, 1P tank breached
19900329	Jambur	3800	V-	CN	WS			R	L				0			coll in Bosporus, 1S,1C holed, no cause info, vol?
19941221	New World	3500	VB	CN	TX			O	L				8	C	Y	coll w burdened Ya Mawlaya which failed to give way
19710118	Oregon Standard	3240	VB	CN				R	L	0140	F	FG	0	H	N	coll SF Bay, wrong frequencies, advisory VTS useless
19810128	Olympic Glory	3170	V-	CN				H	?	0940	9	3	0	O		overtaking collision Houston Ship Channel, cause?
19740118	Key Trader	2790	VD	CN	WS			H	L	1401	F	3	16	H	N	dance of death w Baune in lower Mississippi River
19751112	Olympic Alliance	2220	V-	CN				R	L	NGT		FG	0			coll off Dover w frigate in traffic lane
19920418	World Hitachi Zosen	900	V-	CN	TX			O	L				1			coll w bulk carrier off Morocco, holed, fire in 1S
19850321	Patmos	842	Vd	CN	FX	WS	TL	R	L	0531	9	GD	3	H		collision S of Messina, fire, Patmos to port?
19711011	Texaco Caribbean	638	VR	CN	TX	FD		R	B		F	FG	51	H		fog, coll w rogue vessel, others hit wreck

105

Continued on next page

DATE	SHIP	Kilo liters	E1	E2	E3	E4	E5	L	A	TOD	V	WE	De- ad	N	E K	T	Synopsis
19990324	Min Ran Gong 7	543	V-	CN				R	?					0			collision off Zhouhai, nil info
20040322	Everton	494	V-	CN	FX			O	L	NGT				1			coll w trawler in Arabian Gulf
20021205	Agate	411	V-	CN				R	L	0535				0			coll E of Singapore with Tian Yu, hole P slop
19700320	Otello	319	V-	CN				H	?					0			coll n Vaxholm, some say 60-100KT, appears unlikely
19970803	Saraband	150	V-	CN				?	?					0			collision Malacca Strait, no real info
20010922	New Amity	138	V-	CN				H	?	1430				0			coll w tow in Houston Ship Channel, got bfo tank?

3.5 Machinery Failures

3.5.1 Statistical Summary

According to Table 3.3, Machinery Failures are the third most important spill cause. This may come as a surprise to some, for in many spill databases machinery failure is not a major factor, if it is mentioned at all. This is because most machinery failure induced casualties show up as something else in the spill databases.

One of the top twenty tanker spills of all time is the WAFRA. The WAFRA stranded off Cape Agulhas, South Africa in February, 1971. Upon grounding all six port cargo tanks were breached, and two of the six center tanks as well. She eventually was refloated, towed out to sea, and scuttled with the remaining cargo on-board. In all the WAFRA lost 40 million liters of oil into the sea. In most spill databases the cause is listed as "grounding". In one database, the cause of the spill is listed as "structural failure".[25]

In fact the WAFRA spill was caused by loss of engine power. The loss of engine power was caused by engine room flooding. The WAFRA was a steam turbine ship. The steam turbine cycle requires lots of sea water to condense the steam back to water. The engine room flooded because of a fracture in the piping that brings this sea water to the condenser. The real cause of the WAFRA spill was a machinery failure.

If the WAFRA had been a twin screw, two engine room ship, this failure would almost certainly not have resulted in a spill nor the loss of the ship. But this fact is obscured in all the tanker spill compendiums of which I am aware.

Other examples are legion. The AMOCO CADIZ[26] (steering gear failure) is often listed as a grounding. The BRAER[27] (loss of power) is usually listed as grounding. Ditto GENERAL COLOCOTRONIS[28] and OLYMPIC BRAVERY[29] The BRITISH AMBASSADOR[30] (essentially same failure as WAFRA) is called a sinking. The NASSIA[31] (loss of steering) and BALTIC CARRIER[32] (ditto)

---

[25] The structural failure listing will come as a surprise to the South African air force which had great difficulty sinking the ship.

[26] See Section 2.8.

[27] See Section 3.2.

[28] Lost power off Eleuthera. Worst spill ever in the Bahamas.

[29] This VLCC fortunately was in ballast when she lost power multiple times, drifted ashore in Brittany, and broke up.

[30] Condenser inlet line fractured, then poorly maintained sea valve failed.

[31] This is the second worst spill of all time in the Bosporus, killing 42.

[32] Steering gear failed. BALTIC CARRIER suddenly turned into path of oncoming ship. Incredibly, IMO blamed watch keeping on other ship.

are called collisions.

Table 3.8 shows all the spills in the CDB over 10,000 liters which CTX believes were caused by machinery failure.[33] The CTX Machinery cause codes are

MB	Blackout	MR	Loss of Steering
MC	Crankcase explosion	MS	Shaft/Sterntube Failure
MF	Engine room flooding	MT	Stern Tube Leak
MG	Bedplate/Bearing Girder	MW	Sea water line leak
MK	Crankshaft failure	MX	Boiler fire
ML	Cylinder Liner Failure	MY	Other/unknown machinery
MO	Fuel/lube oil line leak	M_	Probable machinery failure
MP	Propeller failure/damage		

The CTX database almost certainly under-estimates the importance of machinery failure. Many of our unknown initial causes involve engine room/fire explosions. This includes the JAKOB MAERSK[34] one of the biggest spills of all time. Something happened in these engine rooms to cause the fire. It is a good bet that in most engine room fires that something was a machinery failure. Check out the SEAL ISLAND[35] fire at St. Croix to see a rare case of a well-documented engine room fire. Rare here refers to well-documented. There is nothing rare about engine room fires. All it takes is a leaking fuel or lube oil pipe in the wrong place and we have a situation which can quickly escalate into a major casualty. See the TASMAN[36] for how easily this can happen.

---

[33] The AEGEAN SEA was not exactly a machinery failure. This massive fire and spill resulted from our imprudent machinery design philosophy which left the ship with insufficient low speed maneuverability to handle the weather conditions she encountered entering La Coruña. See Section 3.6.2. The ship was perfectly legal. Currently, there are no low speed maneuverability requirements.

[34] Ship touched bottom entering port, there was a jolt, and the engine room suddenly exploded. At this point I have no idea why. But something was wrong.

[35] Jury rigged lube-oil strainer dumped oil on hot turbo-generator when crew needed to change strainers. Crew could not take turbo-generator off line, because other generator not large enough to handle actual electric load rather than unrealistically optimistic Class Rule load. Three killed. Ship destroyed. She had just finished discharging, so nil spill, and no lessons learned.

[36] Two fuel oil pipe screws vibrated loose. Fuel oil sprayed onto generator exhaust manifold and ignited. Crew responded brilliantly, averted major casualty.

Table 3.8: Machinery Failure Spills

Based on CTX Casualty Database as of 2005-10-15T19:34:23

DATE	SHIP	Kilo-liters	E1	E2	E3	L	A	WE	De-ad	Brief Description
19780316	Amoco Cadiz	267000	MR	WS	FD	O	L	HW	0	steering gear failure, grounded Britanny, broke up
19930105	Braer	99600	MY	WS	FD	R	L	HW	0	lost power, seawater in BFO, pipes on deck hit vents
19921203	Aegean Sea	87000	M_	WS	TX	H	L	9	0	grnd Corunna, could not turn ship in bad weather,OBO
19830107	Assimi	60200	M_	EX	FD	O	L		0	ER fire, Gulf of Oman, cause uncertain
19750110	British Ambassador	56000	MW	MF	FD	O	L	HW	0	sw inlet leaked, vlv failed ER flooded,sank under tow
19831209	Pericles Gc	54100	M_	EX	FD	O	L		0	ER fire east of Doha, sank
19730602	Esso Brussels	50000	MR	RD	TL	H	L	CM	16	rammed by Sea Witch whose steering gear failed
19710227	Wafra	47000	MW	MF	WS	O	L		0	SW circ pump fracture, ER flooded, drifted aground
19760204	St Peter	44300	MY	EX	FD	O	L		0	"elec fire in ER" off W Coast, Columbia, sank
19770527	Caribbean Sea	35200	M_	FD		O	L	HW	0	ER flooded S of El Salvador, sank
19821126	Haralabos	31900	M_	EX	WS	H	L		0	ER fire, Ras Gharib, cgo transhipped
19891229	Aragon	29400	MY	HL		O	L	HW	0	lost power, big spill under tow near Azores
19671024	Giorgio Fassio	25000	MF	FD		O	L		0	Enigne room flooded, sank in Atlantic off S Africa
19720331	Giuseppe Giulietti	25000	MF	FD		O	L		0	er flooded off C St Vincent, no power, sank
19810329	Cavo Cambanos	24300	M_	EX	FD	R	L		6	fire in generator room Tarragona, fire, sank, cause?
19940313	Nassia	23500	MB	CN	FX	R	L		42	BC Shipbroker black out, no rudder, coll in Bosporus
19661024	Gulfstag	21000	M_	EX	FD	O	L		7	two engine room explosions, sank
19700131	Gezina Brovig	18800	MY	FD		?	L		0	cyl came thru crankdoor, broke SW main, sank
19740926	Transhuron	18600	MB	WS	TL	O	L	GD	0	A/C nipple failed, water on swbd, no power, grnd
19870623	Fuyoh Maru	11900	MR	CN	FX	H	L		6	coll w Vitoria in Seine "damage to helm"
19680307	General Colocotronis	6000	MY	WS	SC	R	L		0	grounded off Eleuthera after machinery failure
19761227	Olympic Games	5880	MY	WS		H	L		0	engine failure, Delaware R, 39 ft draft, grounded
20010329	Baltic Carrier	2900	MR	CN		R	L	GL	0	steering failure, collision, 6 m penetration
19770327	Anson	2330	MR	WS		H	?		0	steering gear failure Orinoco, grounded
20001128	Westchester	2030	MC	EX	WS	H	L		0	crankcase fire, grounded Mississippi River
19850928	Grand Eagle	1640	MY	WS		H	L	5	0	ship lost power, grmded near Marcus Hook

Continued on next page

Date	Name	Size								Description
20020814	Golden Gate	1520	MY	WS			H	L		0 entering Karachi, maybe mach, maybe comn, volume hi?
19760124	Olympic Bravery	842	MY	WS	FD		R	B		0 "series of engine failures", VLCC drifted aground
19840319	Mobiloil	624	MR	WS	FD		H	?		0 steering failure in Columbia River, grounded
19780321	Aegis Leader	586	MY	WS			?	?		0 grounded off Sumatra after machinery breakdown
19760119	Irenes Sincerity	582	MY	WS			?	?		0 "stranded after engine trouble", Baltic, nil info
19730624	Conoco Britannia	500	MY	WS			S	L		0 lost power mooring Humber SBM , ran over own anchor
19810725	Afran Zenith	302	M_	WS			H	?		0 grounding Elbe after machinery problems
19901015	Rio Orinoco	200	MY	GA	WS		R	L	0	0 mach problems, anchored, dragged, grounded G of St L
19990523	Parnaso	151	MR	CN			O	B		0 lost steering, collision South of Cuba
19981207	Tabriz	117	MY	RR			H	?		0 eng failure, hit jetty at Bandar Abbass
19840627	Vic Bilh	30	M_	UM	TX		T	d		0 unmoored by Afran Stream, too fast to keep steerage
19970118	Stolt Spray	20	MR	CN	WS		H	L		0 lost steering in Miss River, holed 1p, dh
19990227	Hyde Park	16	MY	CN			H	L		0 lost power loaded gasoline, drifted 13 M, many coll.

3.5.2 Machinery Failures versus Groundings

A major difference between hull structure and machinery failure is that a hull structural failure often results in a spill even if nothing else happens. (Put much more accurately, we ordinarily don't hear about a structural failure unless it results in a spill.) In the case of machinery failure, the machinery failure in and of itself usually doesn't result in a spill. Something else has to happen for a spill to actually occur.

Often that something else is the ship drifts ashore before power is restored. This is why so many machinery spills are listed as groundings. But I find it impossible to explain the inability of not only the public, but also regulatory bodies, to focus on the real cause and not on an effect. Some time this myopia reaches bizarre proportions. In November 2000, the fully loaded 88,000 ton tanker WESTCHESTER had a main engine crankcase explosion in the Mississippi River. Crankcase fires are a problem to which all big two-stroke diesels are prone. What happens is that lube oil vapor builds up in the space above the crankshaft and below the piston, usually due to a leak or a control problem in the lube oil system. Once that occurs all that is required is a source of ignition, and with all the rotating machinery in the crankcase, there are lots of possible sources. This is such a common problem, that the engines are fitted with blow-out panels to minimize the damage to the engine in the event of a crankcase explosion. It is probable that many diesel tanker casualties that merely list Fire/Explosion as their cause are crankcase explosions.

Without power, the WESTCHESTER drifted aground about 50 miles downriver from New Orleans, holed a tank, and spilled 2 million liters of her cargo. This was a very high profile spill, receiving extensive media coverage. Almost all these reports decried the fact that the ship was a single hull. Not one of them, at least not any that I have come across, even noted that the ship was single screw with nil propulsion redundancy. *This includes the official USCG investigation report.*

In 1996, there was an even more high profile casualty when the bulk carrier Bright Field lost power and rammed into the crowded Poydras Street wharf in New Orleans. Miraculously, no one was killed but at least 62 were injured. This generated a 99 page report by the National Transportation Safety Board.[37] The proximate cause was that the main engine tripped due to low lube oil pressure.[38] The NTSB report goes into great detail

---

[37] www.ntsb.gov/publictn/1998/mar9801.pdf.

[38] A trip is when the engine automatically shuts itself down when it senses something is wrong.

about the engine room deficiencies (see the disgusting list in the report's Appendix C), but never even mentions the fact that the casualty would have been prevented by twin screw.

Conversely, it seems that even the most spectacular machinery failure will receive little or no attention unless there's a big spill or a lot of non-crew deaths. In February, 1999, the HYDE PARK lost power at Mile 92 on the Mississippi River. She was fully loaded with 25,000 tons of highly flammable gasoline. The HYDE PARK then went on a 13 mile rampage, drifting downriver, causing multiple collisions including sinking a crew boat and a barge containing caustic soda, before power was restored. But the only damage to the tanker itself was a holed bunker tank and a 16,000 liter bunker spill. This miraculous escape received almost no publicity. The CTX has no evidence that USCG tried to figure out why the ship lost power.

3.5.3   The V-Plus Experience

Having said this, it is a blessed miracle that a machinery failure alone is generally not enough to cause a spill. There are about 3600 tankers over 10,000 deadweight tons afloat. ***All but about 16 of these ships are single screw. All but a handful of the world's tankers are a single failure away from being helplessly adrift.*** For some unfathomable reason, this cardinal fact has not penetrated the public consciousness.

Modern tankers are unreliable mechanically. My firm built four 442,000 ton tankers in Korea 2001 and 2002. These ships were built to far above Class standards. The supervision by my team was so rigorous that the Koreans made it clear we would not be welcomed back. They were manned by some of the best tankermen in the world. To my shame, they were single screw. We called these ships the V-Plus class.

Shortly after the first of our new superships was delivered in 2002, we began receiving disturbing reports from our Chief Engineers about the machinery. It began with main engine fuel oil piping leaks. On one ship, the Hellespont Tara, the fuel oil piping began leaking on her maiden laden voyage while headed down the east coast of Africa. This ship had so many of these leaks, that the Chief quickly went thru his entire stock of spares. He was forced to shut down one cylinder.[39] More pipes began leaking on him, and we were forced to go to the manufacturer, Sulzer, and ask if the engine could be operated with two cylinders down.[40] The reply "Maybe, if you, go

---

[39] The low speed diesels used on big tankers can operate with one cylinder shut down, at greatly reduced power.

[40] Sulzer like most big marine engine manufacturers has changed ownership and name

slow enough". The Chief managed to make a temporary repair of some of the pipes and the Tara, with 420,000 tons of cargo, limped down the coast to East London, South Africa where we were able to helicopter out some spares.

This experience turned out to a harbinger. By the time, we sold these four ships in early 2004, the V-Plus class had amassed a total of 3500 at-sea days. During that time, we had:

1) Ten involuntary total losses of power including one catastrophic liner failure.
2) Plus 13 forced reductions/shut downs mostly from leaking high pressure fuel oil piping. We had a total of 38 reported incidents of fuel oil piping leaks.
3) Plus 5 crankshaft and 1 camshaft bearing failures we know about.
4) At least five trips from the Piston Cooling Oil (PCO) system.[41]
5) Plus two badly cracked turbo-charger diffusers.

In only one of these incidents, a very minor one, could we find any evidence of crew error.

Most of the total loss-of-power incidents were quite short as Table 3.9 shows. (I will call this type of failure, a *minor* loss of power, even though applied to tankers the phrase is oxymoronic.) But one of the casualties was a catastrophic failure of a cylinder liner. (Continuing my pattern of understatement, I will call this sort of failure a *major* loss of power.)[42] In

---

several times in the last decade. Currently, I think its official name is WSND which stands for something like Wartsila Sulzer New Diesel. I'll just call it Sulzer.

Actually, it is incorrect to call Sulzer the main engine manufacturer. Sulzer and MAN-B&W, the two "manufacturers" of almost all big tanker main engines, actually build almost no such engines. Rather almost all the engines are built under license by massive machine shops in Korea, Japan, and now China. Sulzer and MAN merely furnish the design and the reputation. The same machine shop will build engines for a number of licensors.

This separation insures that, when something goes wrong, nobody's responsible. The licensee blames the design and says talk to the licensor. The licensor blames the material or erection procedure and says talk to the licensee. The only winners from this system are the lawyers.

[41] On these three story high engines, lube oil must be fed to the piston head to keep it from overheating. But the piston is moving up and down. To solve this problem, a Rube Goldberg-like set of lube oil pipe links and elbows follows the piston up and down inside the crankcase. How to tell if this contraption is leaking? The answer is a differential pressure sensor, but as the links open and fold they send out their own pressure pulses. If you set the pressure sensor so it can actually sense the leakage, you get false positives and unnecessary and dangerous main engine trips. If you set the pressure sensor to avoid this, then leaks go undetected and eventually you have a crankcase explosion.

[42] Very roughly a *minor* loss of power lasts an hour or less. A *major* loss of power lasts

Table 3.9: V-Plus Total Loss of Power Incidents, 2002-2004

Date	Ship	Length	Problem
20030419	Alhambra	abt 24 hrs	Liner in two pieces
20031119	Alhambra	<15 min	Trip due bad setting #9 PCO DP Switch
20030320	Metropolis	0:13	Trip due low Jacket cooling water press
20021119	Tara	<15 min	#9 CYL PCO IN DP (SHUT DOWN)
20030525	Tara	<15 min	#8 CYL PCO IN DP (SHUT DOWN)
20030511	Fairfax	0:06	#8 PCO DIF PRESS 06:45
20030710	Fairfax	0:10	#5 PCO DIF PRESS 04:42
20031008	Fairfax	0:17	M/E LO LOW PRESS 16:16
20040129	Fairfax	0:05	M/E OVERSPEED 01:01
20040521	Fairfax	0:02	#1 D/G TRIP HH TEMP COOL FW

these enormous engines, the cylinders are not bored as they are in your car. Rather each cylinder is made up of a separate very thick walled piece of pipe called a liner. This piece of pipe is about 1 meter in diameter and about four meters long. Each liner weighs about 5 tons. It is drilled with inlet ports, and all sorts of cooling and lubricating passages. On April the 19th, 2003, the main engine on the Hellespont Alhambra suddenly shut itself down. The crew discovered that one of the nine liners had split into two pieces. The top part was still in place but the bottom two thirds was totally detached and had fallen down about 10 mm. The only thing that was keeping the bottom portion from falling onto the crankshaft was that it had hung up on some lubricating fittings. If that had happened, the ship would have been helpless until a tug arrived. The main engine would have had to be totally rebuilt.[43]

---

a day or more. In between take your pick. Needless to say, there is nothing minor about any total loss of power on a big tanker.

[43] Despite our best efforts, we never learned why the liner failed. The Classification Society, Lloyds Register, was useless. Sulzer was less than cooperative. But in investigating the failure we learned a lot about how far the thermal stress levels in the liner had been pushed in the quest for more and more power out of the same engine. There simply were no margins. Most likely, the liner had a small manufacturing defect which combined with this imprudent design philosophy resulted in the failure.

This was the case in the fuel oil piping leaks. When we went to Sulzer on the fuel oil piping leaks, initially they feigned ignorance. But we later learned that they had already done a study on the problem which came to the same conclusion that our own study did. These pipes are subject to very high pressures pulses, up to 700 bar on every stroke of the fuel oil pumps. It turned out that the Korean pipe manufacturer had allowed microscopic

As it was, we were very lucky.[44] The Alhambra had just finished discharging in the Gulf of Mexico, so she had no cargo on-board. The Master let the ship coast past a nearby offshore oil platform until he was five miles away. Although they were sixty miles offshore, the water was still shallow enough so they could anchor. They anchored and gingerly removed the piston and failed piston liner.[45] They could then move to a safer anchorage under reduced power, and replace the liner with the ship's spare.

Worldwide there are currently about 3600 tankers with a deadweight of 10,000 tons or more afloat. All but a handful of these ships are single screw. If the V-Plus experience is typical, this means that on average there are ten "minor" total loss of power incidents every day, even if you are crazy enough to call any loss of power that risks a major oil spill "minor". **If my once every ten year number for major loss of power incidents is correct, then worldwide we are averaging one major tanker loss of power incident every calendar day.**

Of course, if you ask any tanker owner, he will tell you that his engine rooms have performed far better than ours did. I am convinced he is either lying or misinformed, possibly willingly misinformed. The V-Plus were better speced, better built, and better manned than just about any modern tankers out there. In a normal tanker operation, almost all minor loss of power incidents are not even reported to the owner. The crews know that however blameless they are the incident will be a black mark.[46] More importantly, they know the owner doesn't want to know. The owner probably knows about a major loss of power incident but, unless he decides to make an insurance claim, nobody else does. Even then it doesn't become public. No Classification Society will violate an "owner's privacy" for fear of losing

---

impurities into the steel. When the seamless pipes were drawn, these impurities generated minute scratches on the inner surface of the pipe. Since the pipes were designed with very little stress margin, the stress concentrations generated by these tiny scratches gradually grew into small cracks that eventually leaked. Sulzer blamed the pipe manufacture for poor quality material. The pipe manufacturer blamed the engine designer for not making the pipes thick enough. I think they were both right. But one thing is sure, our experience was not unique.

[44] The bulk carrier Selendang Ayu was not so fortunate. In 2004, she also suffered a broken cylinder liner, but drifted ashore on Unalaska Island, and broke in two. Six crew died, a USCG helicopter crashed, and a sizable bunker spill occurred.

[45] To do this, they had to invent and build a special lifting apparatus on the spot. Try blaming the crew on this one. (Actually that's what Sulzer did; but after pouring over the records and the engine data logger, neither we nor Sulzer could find any crew mistake.)

[46] On ships that are run by third party managers even if the crew reports a problem to the manager, there's a very good chance the manager will not transmit the report to the owner.

a customer. ***This silence is written into Class contracts. It is a legal requirement.***   The only time we hear about a loss of power incident is when it results in a spill.

There are a few exceptions. The Coast Guard grabbed the Bright Field logs before they could be sanitized. They found that the Bright Field had had at least two major loss of power incidents in the 11 months prior to the "minor" loss of power which caused her to clobber the Poydras Wharf. One lasted four days, the other a little over a day. That's twenty times the V-Plus major loss of power experience.

After the EXXON VALDEZ spill in 1989, ships loading at Valdez, Alaska were subject to unusual scrutiny. Based on Alyeska records, the Anchorage Daily News reported on 1992-11-22 (page A13) that, in the two plus years since the EXXON VALDEZ, there had been four total loss of power incidents on laden tankers in Prince William Sound alone. Here's a brief summary of the casualties in this article. Remember these are outbound (loaded) tankers only.

1989-07-31, Mobil Arctic Gyrocompass failed in fog. Ship returned to berth

1989-09-20, Atigun Pass Lost power between Bligh Reef and Glacier Island. Escort vessel held ship in shipping lane until power was restored one hour later.

1990-06-20, Southern Lion Lost power at about the same spot as Atigun Pass. Ship did not drift out of shipping lanes before regaining power. Sailed to Knowles Head for repair.

1990-08-04, Kenai Lost power near Rocky Point. Stayed in shipping lanes. Did not require help from escort vessels.

1990-11-14, Arco Prudhoe Bay Gyrocompass failed while still in Port Valdez. Went to container dock for repair.

1991-04-01, Arco Sag River Discovered a possible mechanical problem with its propulsion system while passing through Valdez Arm. Sailed under own power to an anchorage at Knowles Head.

1992-03-04, Exxon North Slope Bad propeller vibrations after leaving the Sound. Returned to Sound and escorted to anchorage at Knowles Head. Divers checked prop, found nothing. When engine restarted, vibrations were gone. Probably fouled fishing net.

1992-09-09, Brooks Range Lost power in Valdez Arm. Regained power before it required aid from escort vessels.

1992-10-20, Kenai Problem with steering system and headed toward Middle Rock. USCG estimates ship was about 100 yards from the rock, when escort vessel turned the ship back on course.

At the time Valdez was loading two to three tankers per day and these ships are in laden passage in Prince William Sound for less than 8 hours per trip. We are talking four total loss of power incidents – plus one loss of steering – in at most 2.5 ship-years of operation. This is roughly double the V-Plus numbers.[47]

Even if my time between loss of power incidents were low by a factor of ten, which is extremely unlikely, then worldwide we are still talking about one "minor" tanker total loss-of-power per calendar day, and a major tanker loss-of-power every ten days. Of course, only a small percentage of tanker loss-of-power incidents actually end up in a spill. But, given the consequences, any sane person has to regard these numbers as unacceptable.

The obvious solution is mandating twin screw. With twin screw, *properly implemented*, we could reduce the frequency of total loss of power incidents not by 20%, not by 50%, but by more than a factor of a 1000. This is the subject of Section 6.5.

---

[47] Gray reports that after the US Coast Guard encouraged American pilots to report loss of power/steering incidents, the frequency went from one per thousand port entries to one per hundred.[30][page 5] This is a truly scary number.

3.6   Conning/Navigation Errors

3.6.1   Navigation Errors

The CTX database distinguishes between navigation errors and conning or guidance errors. In a navigation error, the ship is not where she thinks she is. In a conning error, the ship knows where she is but gets into trouble anyway because someone misjudges the current or hits a berth or the like. The ARGO MERCHANT[48] which was 24 miles off course was clearly a navigation error. The SEA EMPRESS[49] in which the pilot misjudged the tidal set at the entrance to Milford Haven was clearly a conning error. Some spills are not so clear cut. You can argue the EXXON VALDEZ either way. The CTX rule is, if the spill almost certainly would have been avoided if the ship had had a properly functioning GPS and used it, then it is a navigation error. If it is not nearly certain that the spill would have been avoided if the ship had had GPS, then it is a conning error.[50] We called the EXXON VALDEZ a navigation error on that basis.

The CTX Guidance/Navigation cause codes are

GA	Anchor dragged
GB	Hit Berth, mooring/unmooring
GC	Conning error, misjudged current, turn, or the like
GD	Ship too deep for water depth, swell
GT	Tug contact or other tug screw up
GY	Other Guidance or Seamanship error
G_	Probably guidance error, need confirmation
NA	Navigation error, ship not where she thinks she is
NC	Bad charts on board
N_	Probably nav, error but need confirmation

Table 3.10 shows the spills in the CTX database which I have attributed to navigation errors. A fair number of the pre-Amoco Cadiz big spills were navigation errors including (TORREY CANYON, ARGO MERCHANT, ARROW). In many of those cases, the quality of the navigation was execrable. After the AMOCO CADIZ, the worst of the second tier tanker owners mostly disappeared or cleaned up their act a bit, and totally atrocious navigation errors have been reduced markedly. But even before this happened,

---

[48] The gentlemanly Cahill calls this "a matter of almost studied ineptitude".[13]

[49] A contributing factor was the failure to recognize the increased size of a Marpol tanker versus a pre-Marpol of the same deadweight.

[50] In the case of the SEA EMPRESS and many other conning error spills, GPS/ECDIS could have alerted the pilot to the tidal set a little earlier but one cannot say with near certainty that this would have avoided the grounding.

navigation errors represented less than 7% of the volume spilled and have killed just six tankermen. Since 1990, there are only two navigation errors in the CTX casualty database and we are not absolutely sure about those.[51]

There should not be any. With the advent of GPS and ECDIS, spills due to navigation errors should be a thing of the past. GPS of course is the Global Positioning System. For a few hundred dollars, every ship in the world can not only know exactly where it is, but also have accurate speed and course over the ground. ECDIS, computerized chart display, eliminates plotting errors.

There's always a way to screw up; but, despite TORREY CANYON and EXXON VALDEZ, navigation errors never were that important, and should be a non-factor in the future, even if we don't improve the current regulatory system. I worry a lot about tankers. But I don't worry much about tanker navigation errors.[52]

---

[51] Not all navigation errors are the crew's fault. In October, 1984, the fully loaded AGUILA AZTECA ran aground 8 miles northwest of Bermuda. It was broad daylight and calm weather. Visibility was good and Bermuda had been sighted. The ship's plotted position was correct. It turned out the only chart that she had of the area covered the entire Atlantic, North and South. On such a chart, Bermuda shows up as a dot and the reefs to the north of the islands not at all. The ship knew exactly where it was, but it did not know where the reefs that used to support the Bermudian economy were.

There have been a number of very similar groundings. Fairplay comments unfairly:

> In both instances, as in so many cases previously, subsequent enquiry found the groundings were entirely due to negligence and incompetence on the part of the vessels' crews.[73][page 23]

The assumption is that it is the crew's fault if the ship does not have the right charts on board. These people are living in the days when the Master supplied his own charts. In fact, the crew have no control over what charts are on board. But the Tromedy takes the standard out: blame-the-crew.

[52] Given the crews' almost slavish reliance on GPS, we need to

1. Mandate two completely separate GPS's, each with their own antenna. The systems should be interlocked so that if they disagree the crew is alerted in an unmistakable fashion. The marginal cost will be a few hundred dollars.
2. If the GPS loses its satellite fix and goes into "dead reckoning" mode for more than a few minutes, then it should stop displaying any position. Just blink zeros.

The big cruise ship Royal Majesty, equipped with a full panoply of modern navigational systems, went aground off Nantucket in 1995 when the GPS antenna wiring came loose. The crew was apparently unaware of the fact that the system had gone into dead reckoning mode despite a warning on the GPS display. They did no independent position checks from the time she left Bermuda, despite having a half-dozen alternatives. She ended up grounding 17 miles off course, in nearly the same place as the ARGO MERCHANT twenty years earlier.[13] I have no problem blaming abysmal crew performance on this one, but the ship should have had dual GPS.

Table 3.10: Lousy Navigation Spills

Based on CTX Casualty Database as of 2005-10-16T14:54:46

DATE	SHIP	Kilo liters	E1	E2	E3	E4	L	A	TOD	Vis	We	Dead	Synopsis
19670318	Torrey Canyon	142300	NA	WS	FD		R	L	0850	G	5	1	nav error, jumboized ship, poor Autopilot design
19890324	Exxon Valdez	41000	NA	WS			R	L	0009	3	3	0	nav error, master not on bridge leaving Valdez
19761215	Argo Merchant	29000	NA	WS	FD		O	L	0600		HW	0	grnd off Nantucket, putrid nav. bad operations
19750326	Tarik Ibn Ziyad	17400	N_	WS			H	?	2045			0	grounding Rio, cause uncertain
19790302	Messiniaki Frontis	14100	NA	WS			R	L	0459	G	CM	0	grounding, Crete, radar on wrong scale, no visuals
19700215	Arrow	12200	NA	WS	FD		R	L	0935	5	HW	0	grounded NS, broke up, horrible nav, operations
20001003	Natuna Sea	8230	N_	WS			R	L	0615	G	GD	0	grounded off Singapore, prob nav???
19730318	Zoe Colocotronis	5970	N_	WS			R	L	0255		GD	0	grnd PR, nav gear out of order, bad owner, cause?
19750106	Showa Maru	5290	NA	WS			R	L	0540			0	VLCC grnding, narrowest part of Spore Str. 2-3m DOP
19781012	Christos Bitas	4290	NA	WS	SC		R	L	1634			0	grnd off Milfordhaven, probably bad navigation
19800821	Texaco North Dakota	2860	N_	RR	FX	TL	O	?				0	hit new oil platform in GOM, charts not up-to-date
19031128	Petriana	1500	NA	WS	FD		R	L	0700	F		0	grounding hvy fog, cgo jettisoned, pilot susspended
19941002	Cercal	1470	NA	WS			H	L	1000			0	bad pilot nav , grnded entering Leixoes,1 tnk holed
19750815	Globtik Sun	1110	NA	RR	TX	TL	R	L	0130	G	3	6	hit platform off Galveston, bad charts, bad plotting
19890623	World Prodigy	1090	N_	WS			R	L	1640	7	3	0	grnd off Rhode Is. perfect conditions, nav or 2deep?
19980807	Ocean Gurnard	476	N_	WS			R	L				0	another Malacca Strait grounding, guessing nav
19700722	Tamano	378	NA	WS			R	L	0120		GD	0	hit ledge side of channel, Casco Bay, mishandled HBL
19861221	Thuntank 5	161	NA	WS			H	L	NGHT	B	8	0	grounding, very bad weather, "nav misinterpretation"
18930325	Gluckauf		N_	WS	FD		R	B		F	HW	0	grounding some say fog, no real cause info
19841001	Aguila Azteca	0	NC	WS	TL		R	L	DAY	G	CM	0	grnded, Bermuda, chrt covered N/S Atl,reef not shown

3.6.2 Guidance Errors

Guidance/conning errors are quite a different story. For one thing, guidance errors are much more important than navigation errors both in terms of deaths and spill volume. Table 3.11 shows the guidance error casualties in the CTX database. For another, guidance errors are not going away.[53] The largest post-1995 spill, the SEA EMPRESS, was a guidance error. Finally, there is no magical technological fix for guidance errors. However, there are a couple of things that could help.

As we have seen with the EXXON VALDEZ, some guidance error spills are in the gray area between guidance and navigation. In these cases the ship strays out of a channel or very restricted waterway due to a combination of imperfect navigation, current, and failure to issue/execute the right helm/power orders at the right time. GPS/ECDIS should help a lot in these situations. The combination of knowing exactly where you are and having that position immediately and correctly displayed on the ECDIS chart should alert pilots much more quickly when they are straying out of a channel. And in the case of lots of current, GPS gives the pilot better, quicker information on speed and course over the ground than he had prior to GPS.

Perhaps even more important is better vessel maneuverability. Current tankers are under-powered and under-ruddered. The IMO maneuverability requirements, for example a turning circle diameter of no more than five times the ship's length, are so lax that it is difficult to design a ship that violates them. Moreover, these are (nearly) full speed, deep water requirements. In shallow water, where maneuverability becomes paramount, the turning ability decreases by a factor of two or more. Slowing down doesn't help. As power decreases, the turning ability does not improve. The turning circles stay about the same — even though the ship is going slower. And then at still lower speeds, the ship loses steerage completely. There are no low speed maneuvering requirements.

This puts a huge burden on the pilot to get it right very early in the

---

[53] The field labeled POB (Pilot on Board) shows pilot status at time of casualty. The coding is

Y	Pilot was on board.
N	No pilot on board.
P	Ship was picking up pilot.
D	Ship was disembarking pilot.
?	Pilot status unknown.

In most moving guidance casualties, a pilot was on-board.

process. He has little ability to correct any errors. In some weather conditions, he is helpless. The AEGEAN SEA is the most famous example. This ship was at anchor off La Coruña when she was ordered into port. Weather was 20 to 30 knot squalls from the west. The ship needed to make a nearly 180 degree turn in order to enter the harbor. She was proceeding at very low speed both because she had just picked up her anchor, and immediately after making the turn she needed to pick up the pilot. After raising the anchor, the weather suddenly deteriorated as a freak squall with winds over 60 knots came through. The master was turning to port. On a single screw ship, this means the rudder must push the stern to starboard. But on a fully loaded tanker all the windage is aft. At the low forward speed, the rudder was not strong enough to push the stern to starboard, even though the master correctly went to full ahead. The ship went aground well before completing the turn. The ship was a double bottom OBO. Oil leaking into the double bottom caught fire, the ship was rocked by a series of explosions, and she ended up being destroyed and losing essentially all of her 77,000 ton cargo.

Both the master and pilot were blamed, despite the fact they had done nothing wrong other than fail to predict an abnormal weather occurrence. This was not a guidance error; it was a design fault. Nowhere in all the commentary on this spill that I have seen has anyone pointed out that the casualty would have been avoided if the ship were twin screw.

The simple fact is that big, single screw ships are nearly unmaneuverable at low speed. Consider the dilemma facing the pilot of the VLCC DIAMOND GRACE entering Tokyo Bay at 10 in the morning of 1997-07-02. Weather is calm, visibility is good. He is confronted with two fishing vessels dead ahead. No room on either side. The only way he can avoid them is to go to dead slow. (In doing this, he is following the Rules of the Road). Unfortunately, at dead slow, the ship has no rudder, no steerage way. A fully loaded, 250,000 ton ship drifts aground, spilling 1.5 million liters. This was called "pilot error" by the Japanese press. I suppose some environmentalists would have preferred he had run down the fishing boats, and avoided the spill.[54]

The best way of obtaining low speed maneuverability is twin screw. The main reason for mandating twin screw is engine room redundancy. But an

---

[54] Other examples abound. In the case of the MOBIL VIGILANT, the pilot went very slow and his ship turned into the Marine Duval as a result of bank suction overwhelming rudder forces. In the case of the VIC BILH, the Afran Stream proceeded fast enough to maintain steerageway and as a result sucked the VIC BILH off her discharging berth generating a fire and a spill. Either way you are screwed.

important by-product will be far better slow speed maneuverability. The slower the speed the more important and the more effective twin screw is. One of the worst of our Guidance casualties is the Edgar M Queen's hitting the Corinthos at Marcus Hook in January, 1975. The Queeny had part discharged at the Monsanto terminal and then had to proceed further up the Delaware River to complete her discharge. To do this, she had to make an 180 degree turn in the river. The ship was equipped with a bow thruster but it clearly wasn't enough. The pilot backed and filled for four minutes before proceeding upriver. But he still hadn't turned the ship far enough to miss the Corinthos which was discharging at a berth on the far side of the river. When this became clear, the Captain panicked and ordered full astern.[55] But the rudder was still hard to starboard. The rudder responded to the prop wash. The vessel's rate of turn slowed and, at a forward speed of less than two knots, the Queeny slid into the non-inerted Corinthos. 26 people were killed and 11 injured in the ensuing fire. Twin screw almost certainly would have prevented this killer casualty.[56]

Twin screw also allows the pilot the option of turning the vessel without stern swing. A rudder does not turn a ship in the direction the helmsman steers. Rather it swings the stern in the opposite direction, and only then does the ship start to go in the desired direction. In close quarters, stern swing can be critical. If you are right on the edge of a channel, you can't turn a single screw ship back into the middle. If you are too close to a ship passing port to port, you can't go to starboard without swinging your stern into the oncoming vessel. If you are a lightering ship and screw up your approach to the mother ship, you can't turn away.[57] Turning a twin screw by differential throttle swings the bow in the direction you want to go. Unlike a rudder, you can actually use your maneuverability when you need it most.

In many of the casualties in Table 3.11 and quite possibly in the case of the Tasman Spirit the largest spill since 2003, twin screw maneuverability could very well have made an important difference.

---

[55] This was exactly the wrong thing to do, and exactly what the Rules of the Road requires.

[56] Proper inerting and maybe double sides might have had considerable impact in mitigating the effects of this collision, but twin screw would have eliminated it.

[57] The reason lightering is always done on the starboard side of the mother ship is that the only way a single screw lighter can unmoor is for the mooring master to give a burst of throttle which for a clockwise turning propeller tends to push the stern to starboard, counteracting the rudder's swing to port. This is a poor substitute for real control.

Table 3.11: Conning Error Spills over 100,000 Liters

Based on CTX Casualty Database as of 2005-10-16T16:20:45

DATE	SHIP	Kilo liters	E1	E2	E3	POB	L	A	TOD	Vis	We	De-ad	Synopsis
19960215	Sea Empress	84400	GC	WS		Y	H	L	2007			0	pilot misjudged tide set, compounded by bad response
19740809	Metula	62300	GC	WS		Y	R	L	2218	G		0	grnd Str of Magellan, pilot error, no place for VLCC
19750131	Corinthos	42200	GC	RD	TL	Y	T	d	0029	9	CM	26	hit by E M Queeny, Marcus Hook, no IG, pilot error
19770207	Borag	33900	G_	WS	FD	Y	H	L				0	grounding Keelung , pilot on board, cause?
19700505	Polycommander	17600	GC	WS	TX	Y	H	L	0400			0	grounding near Vigo, pilot error? Cedre say 23 dead.
19680307	Ocean Eagle	13200	G_	WS	FD	?	H	L				0	"bumped 3 times" in San Juan channel, heavy swell
19780109	Brazilian Marina	11800	G_	WS		?	H	?				0	"struck submerged rock" S. Sebastiao channel, cause?
19830928	Sivand	7630	GB	RR		?	T	L				0	hit berth at Immingham, "negligent handling"
19711130	Juliana	7200	GA	WS	FD	?	H	L	1650		HW	0	anchored off Niigata waiting pilot, dragged, lost
19730805	Dona Marika	3000	GA	WS		?	H	?	2104		GL	0	anchor dragged in storm off Milfordhaven, why stay?
19910410	Agip Abruzzo	2800	G_	RD	TX	N	H	?	2300			142	hit by ferry Moby Prince while anchored, killer fire
19880713	Nord Pacific	2440	G_	RR		?	T	L	NGHT			0	hit berth while mooring Corpus Christi
19941003	Neptune Aries	2380	G_	RR		?	T	L				0	hit jetty at Cat lai, mooring
19970702	Diamond Grace	1550	GC	WS		Y	H	L	1005	G	CM	0	had to slow down in Tokyo Bay, lost steerage, grnded
19900207	American Trader	1500	GD	WS		Y	S	L	1620			0	grnd Huntington Beach CBM, too much draft for swell
19951117	Honam Sapphire	1400	G_	RR		?	T	L				0	Hit berth mooring at Yoshon, no cause info
19781230	Esso Bernicia	1220	GT	RD		Y	T	B				0	hit berth at Sullow Voe, tug caught fire, let go
19821108	Samir	1160	GA	WS	TL	N	?	?				0	"broke moorings" Casablanca, grounded, no other info
19851221	Arco Anchorage	904	GC	WS		Y	H	L	1626	3	CM	0	ran aground anchoring Pt Angeles, pilot error
19960927	Julie N	757	GC	RR		Y	H	?				0	struck bridge Portland ME, 30m opening for 26m beam
19690430	Hamilton Trader	635	G_	RD		?	H	L	DAWN			0	hit while anchored Liverpool, one tank holed
19810119	Concho	317	GD	WS		Y	H	L	DAY	9	CM	0	grounding New York Harbor, ship too deep for channel
19920830	Era	315	GT	RD		?	T	?				0	hit by tug berthing Pt Bonython, "rough conditions"
19960310	Mare Queen	238	G_	RD		?	T	d				0	hit by barge at Baytown
19931009	Iliad	235	G_	WS		?	H	?				0	grounding leaving Pylos, "human error"
19970807	Katja	196	G_	RR		?	T	L				0	hit quay at LeHavre ,ship dh, but port bfo tank not
20000608	Posa Vina	189	GT	RD		?	T	?	0830			0	tug punctured bunker? tank, unmooring East Boston
20021123	Tasman Sea	188	G_	RD		?	R	L			FG	0	hit while anchored off Tianjin
19950205	Berge Banker	143	G_	RD		Y	L	L	0940	G	3	0	hit by lighter Skaubay at GLA during mooring

3.7 Inerting/Purging/Hotwork

Almost all tanker cargos are highly flammable. Many are quite volatile. These are cargos that have to be handled very carefully. When they are not, bad things happen. Three conditions are required for a cargo tank to support combustion:

1. a suitable concentration of hydrocarbon vapors, not too lean, not too rich,
2. sufficient oxygen,
3. and a source of ignition.

Up to 1969, tankers relied largely on keeping a source of ignition away from the cargo. This was an inherently dangerous strategy and it didn't always work. The Esso fleet alone suffered three major explosions in the 1960's: ESSO PORTSMOUTH, ESSO DURHAM, and ESSO GLASGOW. The tank atmosphere was supposed to be too rich to combust but in fact this was often not the case due to tank breathing. During the day, the liquid and vapor in a cargo tank expands as it heats up. Some of the tank vapor is expelled to the atmosphere. At night, when the contents of the tank cools and contracts, outside air is sucked in. This is called *tank breathing*. At various points in this process, a highly combustible mixture exists in portions of the tank. The same thing was true during discharge and loading. The wonder is that there weren't more cargo tank explosions.

As we saw in Section 2.6, things came to a head in December, 1969 when we had three massive explosions in new VLCC's within three weeks. The cause was traced to the build up of static electricity in the tanks. The solution was to inert the tanks with a low O_2 gas from the boiler exhaust. It was a great step forward.

For the first time, it was possible to maintain a non-combustible mixture everywhere in the tank all the time. To aid in the process, the tanks are equipped with *Pressure/Vacuum* (P/V) valves. These are relief valves which open only if the internal tank pressure head gets higher than about 1.4 meters water or less than about 0.4 meters of vacuum.[58] This is done to protect the tank structure. These valves greatly reduce tank breathing (when they are not leaking which is often) and the resulting atmospheric pollution and cargo loss. A switched on crew can use the P/V valves to keep the pressure in their tanks always slightly positive. This totally eliminates the influx of oxygen into the tank and thereby prevents even temporary

---

[58] A positive pressure of 1.4 meters of water is about 14% higher than normal atmospheric pressure. A vacuum of 0.4 meters of water is a pressure about 4% less than atmospheric.

pockets of combustible mixtures. Few tanker crews do this consistently.

In any event, cargo tank inerting has had a tremendous impact on tanker casualties. Table 3.12 shows the IPH casualties in the CTX database. IPH is short for Inerting/Purging/Hotwork screw-ups. These are casualties caused by lousy inerting, bad purging, or by stupid welding. *Purging* is the process of replacing the inert gas/hydrocarbon mixture with normal air for tank inspection or repair. This had to be done carefully lest during this transition or afterwards we have a flammable mixture in the tank.[59]

Every IPH casualty results in a fire or explosion. But not all fire or explosions are caused by IPH. In fact, as we have seen, most tank explosions are caused by structural failures; most engine room fires are caused by machinery failures. The initial cause codes in Table 3.12 are:

FG	Inerting not working or bad
FH	Hotwork
FL	Lightning strike
FP	Bad purging, gas-freeing
F_	Probably bad inerting, purging, need confirmation

Despite the obvious value of inerting, it was not until 1984/1985 that inerting was actually required, and then only for tankers larger than 20,000 tons.[60] This criminally slow response almost certainly cost nine people their lives when the non-inerted SANSINENA exploded in Los Angeles in 1976. Ditto the AMERICAN EAGLE in 1984 which killed seven.[61] The 1979 CHEVRON HAWAII explosion which is blamed on lightning might have been avoided if the ship had been inerted. The 26 people killed in the CORINTHOS ramming might have lived. Most of the 50 people killed in the BETELGUESE explosion would have lived. The Tromedy's inexcusable failure to impose inerting reasonably quickly killed something like 100 people.

But eventually inerting was required. By 1990 almost all the ocean going tanker fleet was equipped with inert gas systems. Since 1990 just about all the casualties due to IPH screw-ups involved gas-freeing or a tank which supposedly has been gas-freed, usually in combination with hot work. A tank must be gas-freed for inspection, manual cleaning prior to dry dock or

---

[59] This can be done by pumping enough inert gas into the empty tank so that the hydrocarbon content is diluted to less than the lower limit which will support combustion, and only then introducing air into the tank. In my experience, few crews worry about this. Their focus in purging is to get the O_2 level as high as possible as soon as possible.

[60] The FIONA proved that you do not need a large tank to have an incendive build up of static electricity.

[61] The United States Coast Guard did not cover itself with glory on this issue. American Flag ships feature prominently in the IPH casualties. See also MONTICELLO VICTORY in 1981.

repair, and for repair itself. Any tank repair involves hotwork. There are any number of ways to mess up this dicey process. An incomplete purge can kill people by leaving deadly inert gas in the tank. The purge air can be introduced before the hydrocarbon concentration has been diluted below the lower flammable limit.[62] Pockets of gas can be skipped by a sloppy purge, or re-emerge later from any sludge and oil remaining in the tank. Now we have people working in the tank which means all sorts of possible sources of ignition.

These purging and manual tank cleaning casualties almost always take place when the ship is in ballast. While they kill people, they usually don't result in a spill. In the CTX tanker data base, Table 3.3, we have no spillage from tanker IPH casualties since 1995. In short, Inerting/Purging/Hotwork casualties are an important safety issue. We need to teach the crews to worry about hydrocarbon content as well as O_2 content when purging. But they do not represent an important cause of tanker spills.

This most certainly does NOT mean that tank explosions are not and will not be a problem. They most certainly are and will. But the critically important cause of tank explosions is not inerting/purging/hotwork mistakes. The critical important cause of tank explosions is structural failure, in particular leaks into non-inerted segregated ballast tanks.

In this regard, there is an important difference between inerting a pre-Marpol single hull, a Marpol single hull, and a double hull. In a pre-Marpol tankers, inerting the cargo tanks meant you inerted all the tanks forward of the accommodation except two or three segregated ballast tanks. Inerting the cargo tanks in a Marpol single hull meant that five to seven segregated ballast tanks are not inerted. But inerting the cargo tanks of a double hull means that the entire space surrounding the cargo tanks is not inerted.

---

[62] The ATLAS TITAN is a particularly ingenious example. In spring of 1979, this ship arrived at the Setubal, Portugal tank cleaning station properly inerted. But they could not totally pump out 5C because of some sort of piping or valve problem. So they lowered five air-driven pumps into the tank. About the time they had exhausted a full tank's worth of air into the tank, it blew up. Four people killed.

Table 3.12: Inerting/Purging/Hotwork Screw Ups

Based on CTX Casualty Database as of 2005-10-16T17:05:33

Date	Ship	Kiloliters	E1	E2	E3	L/O	A/C	De/ad	Synopsis
19790901	Chevron Hawaii	32200	FG	TX	FD	T	O	3	exp Deer Park, lightning combined with no inerting
19900609	Mega Borg	15800	F_	PX		L	L	4	Pump room exp while lightering, cause?
19731105	Golar Patricia	5880	FG	TX	FD	O	T	1	explosion off Canaries in tank being cleaned
19761217	Sansinena	4760	FG	FX		T	B	9	exp on non-inerted deck at LA, ballasting, 9 killed
19800311	Maria Alejandra	4660	F_	FX	FD	O	B	36	fire off Mauritania, tank cleaning?
19800403	Albahaa B	4660	F_	TX	FD	O	B	6	tank fire off Tanzania, prob tank cleaning screw up
19800403	Mycene	4660	F_	TX	FD	O	B	1	tank fire off Sierra Leone, prob tank cleaning?
19751028	Kriti Sun	3490	FL	TX	FD	S	?	0	fire Singapore SBM, lightning, prob in ballast
19810712	Hakuyoh Maru	3490	FL	TX		T	d	6	"struck by lightning" at Genoa, probably no IGS?
19820306	Golden Dolphin	3490	FH	TX	FD	O	?	9	stupid hot work, explosion E of Bermuda, sank,
19840226	American Eagle	582	FG	TX	FD	O	T	8	exp clning gasoline tank, GOM, static from sleeve
19850914	Sinoda	582	FG	TX	FD	O	T	1	exp while gas-freeing off Japan
19681020	Sitakund	526	F_	TX		R	B	3	tank exp. ballast, probably pre-IG tank cleaning
19610126	Esso Durham		F_	TX		O	T	0	tank cleaning explosion, hole in way of No 4
19691212	Marpessa		FG	TX	FD	O	T	2	non-inerted tnk clning explosion, sank
19691229	Mactra		FG	TX		O	T	2	non-inerted tnk clning explosion,
19691230	Kong Haakon Vii		FG	TX		O	T	0	non-inerted tnk clning explosion,
19731003	Texaco North Dakota		FP	PX		O	B	3	PR exp, draining gasoline to P/R bilge! no vent fan
19790419	Seatiger		FL	TX	FD	T	d	2	exp dsching Texas, sank, lightning,IG not being used
19790527	Atlas Titan		FG	TX	TL	T	B	0	put air driven pumps into cgo tank, explosion, CTL
19791213	Energy Determination		F_	TX	FD	R	B	1	exp in slop tank, bad inerting, sank
19791220	Choyo Maru		F_	TX	FD	O	T	0	explosion off Bali, tank clning, broke in two, sank
19810531	Monticello Victory		F_	EX		H	?	0	corroded bilge line to cgotnk left open,ER explosion
19861028	Omi Yukon		FH	FX		O	B	4	flush oil in bfo tank, no screen, bfo tank fire
19880831	Fiona		FG	TX		T	L	1	exp,static chg from stm leak, no IG, set off by tape
19920420	Seastar		F_	TX		O	T	2	tank clning exp in 3C 275M SE Hong Kong
19930925	Altair		F_	TX	FD	?	T	3	exp during manual tank cleaning tank not inerted
19931009	Omi Charger		FH	TX		H	B	3	hotwork in Galv. Bay, no proper inerting, explosion
19931031	Oslo Lady		F_	TX		D	R	5	tank exp while repairing, 1S ballast
19931101	Pink Star		F_	TX		H	?	0	slop tank exp anchored Falconara, hotwork?
19960730	Lido		FP	TX		H	T	6	tnk clning exp, blamed on "portable lamps"
19990111	Athenian Fidelity		F_	TX		O	B	5	explosion in 2C Caribbean, prob tank clning screwup

Continued on next page

DATE	SHIP	Kilo liters	E1	E2	E3	L O C	A C B	De- ad	Synopsis
20000130	Sletreal		F_	TX	FD	H	B	3	tank fire waiting to load at Cardenas
20010611	Heng San		FP	TX	FD	O	T	7	tank explosion while purging Arabian Sea

3.8 External Factors

Occasionally, the ship is not at fault. The ENNERDALE[63] and OCEANIC GRANDEUR[64] are spills in which the ship hit an uncharted rock. The URQUIOLA,[65] the 11th biggest spill of all time, may also have been the result of bad charts, compounded by an indefensible decision on the part of the harbor authorities. Since the size of tankers leveled off in the late 1970's, the "uncharted rock" problem has pretty much disappeared. Presumably the ships had already found all the rocks that were shallow enough to make a difference.

Bad channel maintenance is a continuing problem as Table 3.13 shows. The TASMAN SPIRIT,[66] the largest spill in the last five years, was probably the fault of a poorly maintained channel.

Outside tampering has caused a number of spills. Usually the motive is theft.[67]

---

[63] Now a famous dive site in the Maldives.

[64] Interesting example of hydrostatic balance. Ship with half her cargo tanks breached was exposed to currents up to 6 knots in the Torres Strait for three days, but spilled very little oil. See Section C.4.

[65] Considerable mystery surrounds the URQUIOLA. Ship with a draft of 19.6 m touched bottom on the way into La Coruña, in an area where the water depth was supposed to be 23 m. The harbor master ordered the leaking ship back to sea. On the way out, she hit bottom again in almost exactly the same spot, started to sink, then blew up, killing her master who had refused evacuation.

[66] A poorly maintained channel is only the most likely of a number of possible causes. Based on the CTX's current lack of knowledge, the spill could also have been caused by a simple pilot conning error. The TASMAN SPIRIT was a poorly operated, under-powered, single screw tanker. This may well have been the cause. Twin screw probably would have helped. Some sources claim — not too convincingly — the steering gear failed to respond.

[67] The weirdest case of tampering I know about occurred in the Suez Canal. The Suez Canal requires that the ships carry local "line handlers" when transitting the Canal. To prevent thievery on the part of the Canal line handlers, the ships carefully lock up everything including the engine room and the steering gear flat when going through the Canal. An 80,000 ton tanker was making an uneventful passage when suddenly the steering gear control alarmed and quit. The crew switched to the back-up control system and a grounding was averted. When the Chief Engineer went to the steering gear room to investigate, he found that the Canal line handlers had dropped a rope thru a small rope hatch, had somehow squeezed thru the hatch and down the rope, and had started dismantling one of the steering gear telemotors, presumably to sell it for scrap. When the alarm went off, they must have shinnied back up the rope.

The CTX cause codes for external factors are

CB	Navaid out of position or inoperative
CH	Charts incorrect
CD	Bad channel depth
CS	Hit submerged object, not bottom
C_	Probably external error, need confirmation
EP	Piracy
ET	External Tampering
EW	War damage

The cause codes CD and GD (ship too deep, Section 3.6.1) are fundamentally different. CD implies the charted depth was wrong. GD means the ship was over-loaded for the charted depth.

But sometimes the fault it is not so clear. In 1997, there were a spate of groundings in the channel leading out of Lake Maracaibo: NISSOS AMORGOS, OLYMPIC SPONSOR, and ICARO. The NISSOS AMORGOS, was a Marpol single hull and spilled 4 million liters. The other two ships were double hulls, and there was no spillage. The OLYMPIC SPONSOR, grounded in exactly the same place as the Amorgos, two weeks earlier. In these situations, the ship blames the locals for not maintaining the channel. The locals blame the ship for not staying in the channel. But the fundamental problem is the economic imperative to push channel depths right to the limit.

This is not an on-board problem. It is all very well to declare the master has final responsibility for safely loading his ship. But this is pious bunkum. Unless a master loads his ship to the maximum legal allowable, he will be replaced by a captain who will. The problem lies with the charterers and the ports. The charterers generally know when a channel is being pushed too hard. They could specify a less than legal max draft, but they never do. It would increase their transportation costs slightly. And besides if things go wrong, they won't get blamed.

After the OLYMPIC SPONSOR grounding, the ship's owner sued the charterer, Lagoven, claiming Lagoven's explicit order to load the ship to 38 feet caused the casualty. The arbitrators found that Lagoven had not violated a charter party clause which requires a charterer to order the ship only to "safe ports", upholding the long established principle that it the Captain's responsibility to load the ship safely. A triumph of legal tradition over common sense.

The only real solution is for the port state to set the controlling depth conservatively. You would think this would make sense. If there is a spill, it is the port state that will bear the pollution. But the responsibilities of the port state government are usually divided in a manner that pressures the authority in charge of the channel to set the controlling depth very aggressively. A day after the OLYMPIC SPONSOR grounding, the Maracaibo Port Authority reduced the maximum sailing draft from 38 feet to 36 feet. But the Captain of the NISSOS AMORGOS stayed in jail.

Table 3.13: Spills due to External Factors

Based on CTX Casualty Database as of 2005-10-17T12:06:11

DATE	SHIP	Kilo liters	E1	E2	E3	E4	E5	L	A	We	De-ad	Synopsis
19760512	Urquiola	111700	C_	WS	FX	FD		H	L		1	grnd in channel to Corunna, "uncharted rock" / 2 deep
19700601	Ennerdale	52200	CH	WS	FD			R	L		0	hit "unmarked rock" in Seychelles, now dive site
20030727	Tasman Spirit	35200	C_	WS	TL			H	L		0	chan?pilot?mach?, guess ship too deep for channel
19970228	Nissos Amorgos	4700	CD	WS				H	L	HW	0	ship too deep for Maracaibo channel
19700303	Oceanic Grandeur	1400	CH	WS				R	L		0	hit uncharted rock, 8 tanks holed, nil initial loss
19870702	Glacier Bay	785	CH	WS	HL			R	L		0	struck "uncharted rock" Cook Inlet, need to confirm
20041126	Athos I	120	CS					H	L		0	hit sunken pipe? at Paulsboro, big hull leak
19960311	Limar	91	CH	WS				H	L		0	grounded Boston in 35/36 ft with 33.75 ft draft

133

3.9   Transfer Spills

3.9.1   Introduction

Most tankermen will tell you that a tanker's toughest job is discharging
cargo; second toughest is loading. These activities not only stress the ship's
piping system and crew but also require good coordination between the
tanker and the terminal. If a terminal receiving oil were to close its valves
while a discharging tanker was still pumping, the pipes or hoses would burst,
and we'd have a very sizable spill on our hands.   If the pumper keeps
pumping when the pumpee has no room for more oil, same story.

Table 3.14 shows the Transfer spills in the CTX database. The relevant
cause codes are

TU	Came unmoored during cargo transfer
TD	Deballasting screw up
TH	Hose break/leak during transfer but no unmooring
TR	Other transfer screw up
T_	Probably transfer screw up, need confirmation

As Table 3.3 shows, transfer spills are among the most numerous in the
CTX database, but they tend to be small. In volume terms they are not a
big player, but there are a couple of areas where we could make important
improvements in the transfer system.[68]

---

[68] You can see that most of the CTX transfer spills are at the discharge port (activity
codes L and d). I would not make much of this. Most load ports are in countries which,
whether they are strict or lax, don't make spills public. The CTX database has no spills
at Ras Tanura/Juaymah by far the largest tanker load port in terms of volume. This port
loads half-a-dozen big tankers a day. Based on my experience, I'd be surprised if this port
averaged less than one spill a week, almost all of them quite small.

The CTX casualty database includes a site code, which can be used to identify the
port involved. But certain ports show up again and again. SV is Sullom Voe in the
Shetlands, VZ is Valdez in Alaska, MH is Milford Haven in Wales. This is much more an
indication of good reporting than poor port performance. However, it is clear that some
ports have more problems than others. Milford Haven in Wales combines large tides, high
tidal currents, a difficult entrance, and a lot of bad weather. It has been a famous hot
spot. The Oahu SBM is dangerously positioned, and as a result has much more than its
share of casualties. The "harbors" at Arzew and Skikda in Algeria are little more than
a series of poorly designed breakwaters. Not a good place to be in a mistral. They have
been the site of two of the worst transfer spills. This is not a book on port design, but
the CTX database clearly makes the case that some ports are a lot safer than others.

Table 3.14: Transfer Spills

Based on CTX Casualty Database as of 2005-10-17T12:24:09

Date	Ship	Kilo liters	E1	E2	E3	L O C	A C	TOD	We th	Po rt	De ad	Synopsis
19801228	Juan Lavalleja	52700	TU	WS		T	1		HW	AZ	0	Unmoored while loading at Arzew, need confirmation
19900916	Jupiter	3170	TU	HO	FX	T	d	0830		GL	1	Bay City pier failed from suction of passing ship
19741022	Universe Leader	3050	TR			T	d			BY	0	valve screw-up at Bantry Bay, cgo thru seachest
19981101	Giovanna	2000	TH	FX		H	d				0	underwater hose leak, Beirut, gasoline slick on fire
19851204	Amazon Venture	1890	TR			T	d			UE	0	"three malfunctioning valves", discharging Savannah
19771029	Al Rawdatain	1160	TR			T	d			GA	0	valve screw up discharging Genoa
19980608	Maritza Sayalero	1110	TH			T	d			CA	0	"broken hose", Carenero Bay, Ven.
19960308	Bunga Kesuma	906	TH			T	1			MA	0	"hose burst" while loading Bintulu, no cause?
19920717	Shoko Maru	374	TR			T	?			GB	0	2300 bbl at Texas City, no cause info
19990803	Laura Damato	294	TR			T	d			OZ	0	tampering, 2 seavlvs open, crew failed to check
19940501	Alva Sea	286	TR			T	?			PC	0	shore vlv failed, then temp hose failed, Balboa?
19950722	Jahre Spray	222	TU	HO		T	d		HW	DR	0	unmoored from Eagle Point in storm, two hoses parted
19961030	Once	158	TR			S	d			TH	0	dsching at Maptaphut SBM, no cause info
19960509	Anitra	151	TR			L	d			DR	0	valve screw up at start of discharge, Delaware Bay
19930519	Prime Trader	127	TR			T	d	0530			4	valve screw up at Jacksonville
20010314	Genmar Hector	115	TU	HO		T	d	1500	HW	GB	0	blown off Texas City berth, broke 2 chiksans
19890302	Exxon Houston	95	TU	HO	WS	S	B			BP	5	Oahu SBM chafe chain parted, vsl later went aground
19950806	Ariete	68	TH			H			HW	WS	0	hose break in rough seas at Conchan near Lima
19960809	Kriti Sea	59	TU	HO		T	d			AT	0	unmoored in thunderstorm, Greece, hose broke
19970918	Mystras	26	TR			L	d			DR	0	"possible valve misfunction", Big Stone Anchorage
19980702	Theotokos	24	TH			T	d			IN	0	"hose came away" at Columbo, cause unclear
20031022	Athina M	24	TH			T	d			AT	0	dsch arm disconnected at Agioi Theodoroi
19970103	Tove Knutsen	18	TR			S	d			HU	0	Tetney SBM, no cause info, er fire reported??
20001220	Randgrid	14	TR	HO		S	d			HU	0	crew released chainstopper remotely at SBM, bad GUI
20020425	Front Sabang	12	TR			T	d			SB	0	relief valve failed dsching Saldanha Bay
20020412	Petrotrym	10	TR			T	1			FL	0	"human error" at Flotta, nil cause info
19980821	Palmerston	9	TR			T	d			BR	0	lube oil spill discharging Brisbane, cause?
20010522	Tokachi	5	TH			S	d			TH	0	auto release coupling failure at Mahpathut SBM
19970526	Plate Princess	5	TD			H	B			LM	0	deballast screw-up in Lake Maracaibo
19991206	Almanama	5	TU	HO		S	1		BD	BU	0	blown off Butinge SBM, hose broke
20010705	Tasman	4	TR			T	1	0400		OZ	0	cgo in ballast, loading Melbourne
20041002	Flying Officer Nirmal	4	TR			T	d			IN	0	leak fr pipes discharging Vasco

Continued on next page

Date	Ship	Kilo liters	E1	E2	E3	L O C	A C	TOD	We th	Po rt	De ad	Synopsis
19990627	Arco Texas	4	TU	HO		T	d	1355		PS	0	unmoored while dsching at Ferndale
19960701	Provence	3	TU	WS		T	d	2245		UE	0	unmoored dsching Portsmouth NH, tide may be factor
19811129	Volgograd	2	TH			T	l			TN	0	tank overflow while loading Tallinn
20010128	Overseas Chicago	2	TH			T	d			BP	0	coupling malfunction at Barbers Point
20030913	Venture	2	TR			T	l			MH	0	cargo tank overflow at Milford Haven, IMO is right?
19990601	Histria Spirit	2	TR			T	l			BS	0	oily ballast?? at Odessa, nil info
19960205	Neptune	1	TR			T	B			PS	0	bfo tank overflw bunkering Anacortes, crew left post
19890311	St Lucia	0.477	TR			T	l			VZ	0	tank overflow at Valdez
20040219	Irving Eskimo	0.450	TU			T	d	1200	HW	UE	0	unmoored during disch by blizzard, Charlottetown
20010630	Sericata	0.300	TR			T	d			BR	0	leak in IG ovbd line? at Brisbane
20010523	Sericata	0.200	TR			T	d			OZ	0	screw up during manifold draining at Geelong
20030807	Sirius 1	0.130	TR			T	l			MH	0	gasoline overflow loading Milford Haven
20030221	Navion Anglia	0.100	TR			S	l			NS	0	100 l spill, disconnecting from Alba N SBM
20000820	Loch Rannoch	0.075	TR			T	?			SV	0	faulty cargo pump seal at Sullom Voe
20030505	Ragnhild Knutsen	0.003	TR			T	?			UK	0	Transfer spill at Finnart, but no cause data
20030727	Estere	0.002	TR			T	?			MH	0	transfer spill at Milford Haven, no cause info
20030501	Loch Rannoch	0.001	TR			T	?			SV	0	1 l spill at Sullom Voe, no cause info.
19600708	Esso Portsmouth		TH	TX		T	d			MH	0	unloading arm failed, spill, fire and explosion
19681212	Diane		TH	FX		T	d				0	fire from burst hose, while discharging
19890215	Maassluis		TU	WS	FD	H	B	0100	HW	SK	28	"broke moorings" Skikda, hit breakwater, hvy weather
19930827	Australia Ocean		TR			T	?			OZ	0	spill while "loading fuel" at Melbourne
19940411	Endeavor Ii		TR			T	d			SS	0	sea vlv problem discharging Sao Sebastiao
19950910	Halia		TR			T	d			BR	0	"hose coupling failed" discharging Brisbane
19951017	Kraka		TH			S	l			PG	0	Leak from hose at Mena Almadhi SBM, cause?
19951209	Handy Sonata		TH			S	?		HW	OZ	0	Wandoo SBM chain parted, cyclone Frank involved
19960228	San Giorgio		TR			T	l			CZ	0	"overflow of gasoline" loading Constanza, nil info
19960601	San Sebastian		TU			T	d		BD	SS	0	broke away during discharge at Sao Sebastiao
19990416	Bage		TU	HO		T	d			SA	0	unmoored while discharging Temadre, Brazil
20010802	S R Hinchinbrook		TH			T	l			VZ	0	lding arm disconnect, Valdez, ship flange too small?
20020513	Brotas		TR			T	d			ES	0	discharging Angra dos Reis, nil info
20030221	Nordic Blossom		TR			T	?			MH	0	transfer spill at Milford Haven, no cause info
20030603	Nordic Marita		TR			T	d			SS	0	hydraulic failure during discharge Sao Sebastian

3.9.2 Coming Unmoored

As Table 3.14 makes clear, the dominant cause in terms of volume and deaths in this spill category is unintentional unmooring almost always associated with unexpectedly high winds. Other transfer spills: hoses bursting, valve screw ups, up, etc can be limited by simply shutting down. A ship that becomes unmoored puts her entire cargo and crew at risk. This can result in disaster as in the case of the JUAN LAVELLEJA[69] and the MAASSLUIS[70] A basic problem here is that the mooring calculations on which the ship's mooring system is designed assume that the forces are more or less evenly distributed among the wires. On all ocean going tankers, the mooring wires are led to winches which are equipped with big drum brakes. Upon mooring the wires are tensioned with the winch and then the brake band is drawn tight against the drum with a big hand screw. When a mooring wire becomes highly loaded, we are counting on the brake to do three things.

1. Hold up to its rated capacity.
2. If the load on the wire exceeds the rated capacity, slip.
3. And then re-establish rated capacity after the wire has slipped enough to reduce the load to rated capacity.

If the brake does not hold up to its rated capacity, then more load is transferred to other wires than the mooring calculations assumed. If the wire does not slip at its rated capacity, then the wire can very quickly become overloaded and part, transferring all its load to the other wires. If the brake slips but does not re-establish its rated capacity, then we are back to transferring more load to the other wires than calculated.

The mooring brake is simply a large steel drum combined with a steel-backed, composite band. Sometimes the crew screwing down the band is a big strong guy; sometimes he's not.[71] The unpainted drum (it can't be painted) is sitting in the open on a tanker deck, a very corrosive atmosphere. Sometime the brake is wet; sometimes it's dry. Steel temperature on a dark colored (most are) tanker deck can vary by over 50C. To expect a friction brake like this to slip at the right time and not slip at any other time is totally unrealistic.

---

[69] Spilled at least 40 million liters of gasoline. Miraculously no fire.
[70] No miracle this time. 28 people fried.
[71] These winches must be continually tended to compensate for load and tidal changes. But with minimal crews fully employed loading/discharging the ship, sometimes this doesn't happen. A common trick on a tanker that is discharging is to set the brakes very lightly, so the winches pay out by themselves as the ship comes out of the water. This works only until you need the full holding power of the brake.

There are margins built into the calculations. Good owners attempt to fight the corrosion problem with stainless steel faced drums (should be a requirement but isn't). And hey the weather conditions in which a tanker mooring system is really stressed are not that common (thank God). But the drum brake is the wrong technology for this job.

The solution is constant tension winches. Constant tension winches use hydraulic motors to allow the crew to reliably set the release force and have that force maintained while an overloaded wire pays out.

Constant tension winches got a bad rep from ocean going tankermen when the first units tried proved to be unreliable, resulting in a couple of well-publicized casualties. Owners happily seized on this to go back to the cheaper drum brakes. But constant tension can be made to work. In 1907, Standard Oil built a twin screw tanker called the Iroquois. The Iroquois was coupled to a tanker barge called the Navahoe. The combined deadweight of the "Horse and Cart" was about 18,000 tons making this combination the largest tanker in the world at the time. The Iroquois successfully towed the Navahoe back and forth across the North Atlantic for 23 years.[52][pages 27-28] The Iroquois used a constant tension towing winch.[72]

In the Great Lakes where the trips are short, the ships spend a lot of their time moored, and the weather can be very bad, it was recognized that friction brakes simply couldn't do the job. Constant tension winches were mandated and have proven to be a God-send.

Constant tension winches should be mandated on all tankers.

---

[72] Tankermen claim that constant tension winches "walk". That is, if one winch is over-tensioned and releases slightly, the neighboring winches will then become over-tensioned and also release slightly. Opposing winches take up slightly, and the ship is now moored in a slightly different position. Repeat this process enough times, and the hoses/loading arms will part. This is true, but in the same scenario with friction brakes the brakes would either have released abruptly or wire(s) would have parted. The constant tension system gives any crew that has not fallen asleep time to react. The friction brake often does not.

3.9.3 Lightering

It doesn't show up in Table 3.14 but there is another transfer problem about which we should be very concerned: lightering. The standard long haul tanker is the prosaically named VLCC or Very Large Crude Carrier. A VLCC can carry about 320 million liters of oil. She will have a loaded draft in excess of 20 meters. This means that there are essentially no American ports that can accommodate these ships. Almost all American ports are limited to a vessel draft of 12 meters or less.

When VLCC's bring oil to the United States, they almost always have to off-load their cargo to smaller tankers at sea. The smaller tankers, called *lighters*, then actually deliver the oil to the refineries which in some cases are well in-shore. For example, the Exxon refinery at Baton Rouge is 200 miles up the Mississippi River.

This process is called *lightering*. Lightering normally takes place 20 to 50 miles offshore. A VLCC will offload to four or five lighters in a single discharge. The lighters have a deadweight of about 80,000 tons. Their loaded weight is about the same as a nuclear aircraft carrier. They are bigger than the largest ship afloat in 1960. The lighters may be small compared to a VLCC but they are still very big ships.

In order to lighter, the mooring master must bring this single screw, aircraft-carrier-sized tanker alongside the VLCC with the delicacy of a watch-maker, while both ships are moving thru open water at 4 to 6 knots. It is one of the more thrilling and spectacular sights in the industrial world. It is also an inherently dangerous process. I have never tired of watching this show and I have never failed to give a little sigh of relief when the two ships were moored together. As you read this, there are some half-dozen VLCC's being lightered off the Gulf Coast and another one or two off California. Lightering is also employed off China and in a number of other places around the world.

Once the ships are moored together, our problems are not over. Both ships are moving around in the sea. Wires can break. Double hulls with their tendency to roll exacerbate this issue. Someone has to make the correct judgment about when weather conditions are too lousy to keep lightering and the ships must break off. In a good market, the two ships are easily worth more than a $100,000 per day. There's an awful lot of economic pressure to keep pumping. (And an unmooring forces another dicey re-mooring.)

Most of all I worry about the crew on the lighters. These guys have it really rough. The toughest thing a tanker crew can do is load and discharge. A VLCC will take about two days to load. It will then have a 10 to 40 day relatively peaceful loaded leg in which to do maintenance and get ready for discharge. If she is discharging by lightering, she will take five to seven days to do so, depending on weather etc, a stressful period indeed, then there is a 10 to 30 day respite before loading.

A tanker in lightering service gets no respites. The time between when she finishes loading offshore to the time she begins discharging at the shore terminal is often no more than 12 hours. And as soon as she finishes discharging, it's another few hours and she has to begin the delicate offshore mooring process again.

Some operators of these tankers respond to this problem by putting extra crew on-board. Some don't. I have been at many lighterings where it was quite obvious that the officer on the other end of the VHF was dead-tired. Everybody tries to help. More than once while I was on-board, our guys caught a mistake in the making, and a bad situation was avoided. But it is not a good system.

Despite all these problems, lightering has an astonishingly good record **on the surface**. Table 3.15 shows all the casualties in the CTX database which were directly associated with lightering. But this table, like the 1998 National Research Council study on lightering,[18] does not account for the all important last leg of the trip. For every VLCC that is lightered, we will have four or five lighter port calls, that is, four of five 80,000 ton loaded tankers going up the Houston Ship Channel, the Sabine River, or the Mississippi River sometimes as far as Baton Rouge. Intelligent regulation would attempt to eliminate these dangerous excursions into confined and busy waterways.

There is one very important exception to lightering in the United States. And that is the Louisiana Offshore Oil Port or LOOP. LOOP consists of three large mooring buoys or *SBM*'s about 25 miles off the Louisiana coast. A VLCC or ULCC ties up to one of these buoys. The buoys are fitted with hoses. The hoses are connected to the tanker, which discharges the cargo to the buoy and then to an undersea pipeline that runs ashore, and connects directly to the refineries by other pipelines. The SBM eliminates the final tanker leg. Similar facilities exist throughout the world, but LOOP is the only SBM terminal in the United States.

The SBM-based system is far safer than lightering and then transporting 80 million liter cargos up rivers and bayous via tanker. It's also cheaper. In a non-tromedic world, there would be three or four LOOPS along the Gulf Coast, and inland tanker discharges would become a rarity.

Table 3.15: Lightering Spills (excludes last leg)

Based on CTX Casualty Database as of 2005-10-17T13:48:42

DATE	SHIP	Kilo liters	E1	E2	E3	L	A	TOD	V	WE	Po rt	De- ad	Synopsis
19900609	Mega Borg	15800	F_	PX		L	d	2330	G	CM	GM	4	Pump room exp while lightering, cause?
19960509	Anitra	151	TR			L	d				DR	0	valve screw up at start of discharge, Delaware Bay
19950205	Berge Banker	143	G_	RD		L	L	0940	G	3	GM	0	hit by lighter Skaubay at GLA during mooring
19980123	Red Seagull	72	HC			L	L				GM	0	hull crack discovered, lightering off Galveston
19950227	Florida Express	32		TX	TL	L	?				GM	0	exp in 3P in GLA bunker barge???
20000315	J Dennis Bonney	32	G_	RD		L	L				GM	0	hit by lighter while mooring, Southwest Pass
19970918	Mystras	26	TR			L	d				DR	0	"possible valve misfunction", Big Stone Anchorage
19930902	Red Seagull	25	H_			L	L				GM	0	spill while lightering GOM, probable hull crack
19951223	Hellespont Grand	2	HP			L	d			GD	GM	0	pit in unused ovbd disch line discoverd at GLA
19971008	Western Lion		HC			L	L				GM	0	crack at GLA, leak stopped after 1st lightering
20030619	Efxinos	0.000	TX			L	d				PG	4	exp at end of lightering off UAE, cause ?

141

3.10 A Digression: Groundings and Double Bottoms

I guess I've put off talking about groundings as long as I can. Groundings are never the real cause of a spill. But often one does not have a spill until the vessel goes aground, in much the same way that nobody is killed in an airplane crash until the plane hits the earth. This has induced some to come to the conclusion that the way to attack tanker spills is to reduce the spillage from groundings by mandating double bottoms.

Appendix C will consider the physics of this argument but, while we are talking spill statistics, we might ask ourselves how important are spills in which double bottoms might have made a difference in the overall spill picture?

The CTX database has a field called DB_DIFF, which is shorthand for: Would a double bottom have made a difference? This field applies only to groundings (plus a few oddballs), regardless of cause. The coding is

Y   Certainly, we have damage location and ideally supporting calculations

P   Probably, we have a rough idea of damage location, and it is favorable to double bottom, no calculations

M   Maybe, no real info on damage location, but low to medium impact grounding

N   Damage location known and not favorable to double bottom

?   Cant Say

W   Double bottom would have made things worse

Unless we have accurate damage location, this field is necessarily subjective.[73] But basically, all groundings in the CTX Database in which the ship was not lost or we have firm damage location and it is not favorable to double bottom, show up as either Y, P, or M.[74]

---

[73] The ALVENUS is an example of a grounding in which we can be confident a double bottom would not have helped. The ALVENUS hit the sea bottom in a manner that the bow was pushed up. The main deck split open forward with the rupture extending down to the waterline on either side. See Figures 3.3 and 3.4. The ship's single bottom was never penetrated. Paik has shown that modern double hulls are very weak when it come to deck buckling.[63]

[74] In general, if the ship breaks up or is entirely lost, it would not make any difference how many bottoms she has. There are a few cases where you can argue that the ship might not have been lost if she were double bottom. The TASMAN SPIRIT is a possibility, albeit a very weak one. In those cases, we have included the spill in Table 3.17. I've even included the URQUIOLA as a MAYBE even though I have no reason to believe that a double

Figure 3.3: Alvenus buckled after grounding. Source: R. Hann.

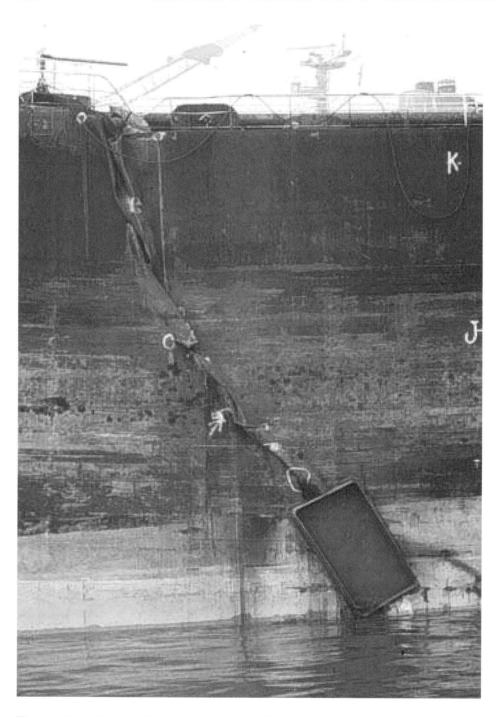

Figure 3.4: Alvenus fracture extended down to waterline. Source: R. Hann.

Table 3.17 lists these spills. The column labeled "?" is DB_DIFF. There's quite a few spills in this list and many infamous names. But Table 3.16 shows that all these spills were responsible for putting 542 million liters of oil in the water and killing two tankermen. ***These spills represent 9% of all***

Table 3.16: Summary of Spills in which Double Bottom Might Have Helped

ASSESSMENT	NUMBER	LITERS	DEATHS
MAYBE	35	301,722,800	2
PROBABLY	22	234,227,730	0
CERTAINLY	8	4,747,000	0
TOTAL	65	540,697,530	2

the oil spilled in the CTX spill database and less than 0.1% of the deaths. In other words, if double bottoms somehow worked perfectly — and had no negative side effects — they would reduce spillage by 9% and have a nearly negligible effect on deaths.[75]

Of course, double bottoms do not always prevent spillage in a grounding. The AEGEAN SEA is an obvious example. The 1997 grounding of the SAN JORGE off Uruguay is less well known. The general rule is that the larger the spill, the less effective a double bottom is in reducing spillage in percentage terms. In each of the four spills at the top of Table 3.17, it is difficult to make an argument that double bottoms would have reduced spillage by more than 50%. And, in each case, it is quite possible that there would have been little or no reduction. For example, in 1989, the US Coast Guard, by then a strong supporter of double bottoms, estimated that, if the EXXON VALDEZ had been double bottom, the oil outflow would have been reduced by at least 25% and by at most 60%.[16, page 156][76] Yet these top four spills represent more than half of all the volume spilled in Table 3.17.

---

bottom would have made any difference. In general, for every casualty in which you can make this argument, there is a casualty in which a single bottom ship was not lost but might have been if she were double bottom. Both the METULA and the EXXON VALDEZ are examples, albeit very weak ones. The AEGEAN SEA was a double bottom ship which conceivably might not have been lost had she been single bottom.

[75] This analysis is biased against the double bottom in that spillage prevented by double bottoms never gets into the database. For example, the double hull OLYMPIC SPONSOR had no spillage when she grounded in almost exactly the same place as the the single hull NISSOS AMORGOS which spilled 4.7 million liters. But the fact remains spillage from low to medium impact groundings is a small percentage of total tanker spill volume.

[76] The USCG never made this "internal memorandum" public so it is impossible to critique. I inspected the Valdez in the drydock in San Diego after the grounding. The damage was spectacular. Exxon ended up replacing 3,500 tons or 15% of all the hull

As you move further down the list in Table 3.17, you find more and more
spills in which a double bottom would almost certainly have made a big
difference in percentage spillage, often preventing the discharge entirely.[77]
In other words, the smaller the spill, the better double bottom works. But
overall we are talking about a maximum reduction of less than 5% in total
tanker spillage.

Some will say; so what? Even 5% is 2.5 million liters less oil in the sea
on the average each year. That alone would justify double bottoms. There
are two problems with this attitude:

1. It pulls the focus of regulation away from the real cause. See the
   WESTCHESTER spill for just one example. Addressing the real cause
   is the only way to have real impact on tanker spillage, not to mention
   loss of life.

2. Far more importantly, it turns out that double bottoms have three unintended side effects. They require a more complicated and inherently
   less robust structure. They increase ballast tank coating area by more
   than a factor of two relative to a double sided ship.[78] They represent
   a very real risk of losing the entire ship from double bottom explosions
   a la the BERGE VANGA and BERGE ISTRA.

Yet we have learned that structural failure is by far the most important
cause of both spillage and death, and segregated ballast tank corrosion is a
prime suspect in most large structural failures.

---

steel. My view is that a 3 m high double bottom would have not been penetrated in two
of the eight breached cargo tanks, 4C and 5C. These two tanks represented 17% of the
Valdez spillage. On the other hand, the two starboard ballast tanks, 2S and 4S, were both
damaged to a height of more than 3 m. On the Valdez, they contained no oil. On a double
hull ship, they would have had cargo. Overall, I can't see how a double bottom would
have made much difference. But a large portion of the oil would have been contained in
the double sides, which I'm guessing the USCG analysis ignored.

It is essential to distinguish between double bottom and double sides as soon as we start
talking spill reduction in groundings. Paradoxically, it turns out that double sides usually
have more impact on uncontained spill volume in major groundings than double bottoms.
See Section C.8.

[77] As always we must distinguish between volume and numbers. The HARDER project
examined a sample of 60 tanker groundings and found that an inner bottom would not have
been breached in 80% of these casualties.[47] Much earlier, Card, looking at a sample of 30
tanker groundings in US water through 1975, had come up with very similar results.[14]
Of course, almost all the oil was spilled in the other 20%.

[78] And a factor of eight increase in coated area relative to a pre-Marpol tanker. See
Table 2.2 on page 47.

In other words in going after at most a 5% reduction in spillage via double bottoms, we have not only overlooked far more effective means of preventing these casualties; we have compounded our biggest problem, big time.

I shouldn't be too harsh here. The misplaced focus on grounding is understandable in emotional, media terms. A big tanker on the shore is spectacularly obvious, a dramatic photo-op. What happened to put the ship aground is rarely photogenic, and often not even known at the time the oil comes onto the beaches. At that point, we move immediately to heart rending pictures of oiled and dying birds and anguished fishermen. The connection between grounding and damage is obvious. And completely superficial. We can't expect deep thinking from the public in the aftermath of a bad spill. But it is reasonable to expect some intelligence on the part of the regulatory process. Maybe not. It's the Tromedy.

Table 3.17: Spills in which double bottom might have helped

Based on CTX database as of 2005-10-17T13:57:04

Date	Ship	Kilo liters	E1	E2	E3	L O	A C	De ad	?	Synopsis
19760512	Urquiola	111700	C_	WS	FX	H	L	1	M	grnd in channel to Coruna, "uncharted rock" / 2 deep
19960215	Sea Empress	84400	GC	WS		H	L	0	P	pilot misjudged tide set, compounded by bad response
19740809	Metula	62300	GC	WS		R	L	0	P	grnd Str of Magellan, pilot error, no place for VLCC
19890324	Exxon Valdez	41000	NA	WS		R	L	0	P	nav error, master not on bridge leaving Valdez
19760425	Ellen Conway	36400		WS	TL	H	L	0	M	grnd Arzew, Nil info on this spill, volume suspect
20030727	Tasman Spirit	35200	C_	WS	TL	H	L	0	M	chan?pilot?mach?, guess ship too deep for channel
19821126	Haralabos	31900	M_	EX	WS	H	L	0	M	ER fire, Ras Gharib, cgo transhipped
19750326	Tarik Ibn Ziyad	17400	N_	WS		H	?	0	M	grounding Rio, cause uncertain
19790302	Messiniaki Frontis	14100	NA	WS		R	L	0	M	grounding, Crete, radar on wrong scale, no visuals
19780109	Brazilian Marina	11800	G_	WS		H	?	0	M	"struck submerged rock" S. Sebastiao channel, cause?
19931001	Frontier Express	8260		WS		R	?	0	P	grounding yellow Sea, no cause
20001003	Natuna Sea	8230	N_	WS		R	L	0	P	grounded off Singapore, prob nav???
19790227	Antonio Gramsci	7050		WS		R	L	0	M	grounding off Ventspils, no cause info
19730318	Zoe Colocotronis	5970	N_	WS		R	L	0	P	grnd PR, nav gear out of order, bad owner, cause?
19761227	Olympic Games	5880	MY	WS		H	L	0	P	engine failure, Delaware R, 39 ft draft, grounded
19950723	Sea Prince	5880		WS	FX	R	L	1	M	left Yosu terminal due to typhoon Faye, grounded
19970208	San Jorge	5880		WS		R	L	0	M	hit "uncharted rock" off Uruguay, dbl bottom
19750106	Showa Maru	5290	NA	WS		R	L	0	P	VLCC grnding, narrowest part of Spore Str. 2-3m DOP
19970228	Nissos Amorgos	4700	CD	WS		H	L	0	P	ship too deep for Maracaibo channel
19930616	Korea Venus	4280		WS		R	L	0	M	grounding west coat of Korea, no cause info
19800903	Esso Puerto Rico	3600		CS		H	L	0	M	hit submerged obj in Miss R, carbon black spill
19831125	Feoso Ambassador	3330		WS	TL	?	?	0	M	grounded off Qingdao, no info
19770327	Anson	2330	MR	WS		H	?	0	P	steering gear failure Orinoco, grounded
20001128	Westchester	2030	MC	EX	WS	H	L	0	P	crankcase fire, grounded Mississippi River
19850928	Grand Eagle	1640	MY	WS		H	L	0	M	ship lost power, grnded near Marcus Hook
19970702	Diamond Grace	1550	GC	WS		H	L	0	M	had to slow down in Tokyo Bay, lost steerage, grnded
19900207	American Trader	1500	GD	WS		S	L	0	Y	grnd Huntington Beach CBM, too much draft for swell
19941002	Cercal	1470	NA	WS		H	L	0	P	bad pilot nav, grnded entering Leixoes,1 tnk holed
19821108	Samir	1160	GA	WS	TL	?	?	0	M	"broke moorings" Casablanca, grounded, no other info
19890624	Presidente Rivera	1160		WS		H	L	0	Y	aground Del R., cause? same spot as Grand Eagle?
19890623	World Prodigy	1090	N_	WS		R	L	0	Y	grnd off Rhode Is. perfect conditions, nav or 2deep?
19810107	Jose Marti	1060		WS		R	?	0	M	grounding off/near Delaro, Sweden, cause?

Continued on next page

Date	Ship	Kilo liters	E1	E2	E3	L/O	A/C	De/ad	?	Synopsis
19860908	Viking Osprey	1040		WS	HL	H	L	0	P	touched bottom Del R., 1C holed, too much draft?
19851221	Arco Anchorage	904	GC	WS		H	L	0	M	ran aground anchoring Pt Angeles, pilot error
19900607	Bt. Nautilus	870		WS		H	?	0	Y	aground Kill van Kull, need cause
19870702	Glacier Bay	785	CH	WS	HL	R	L	0	M	struck "uncharted rock" Cook Inlet, need to confirm
19870206	Antonio Gramsci	670		WS		R	L	0	M	grounding near Porvoo LH, ice, no cause info
19840319	Mobiloil	624	MR	WS	FD	H	?	0	M	steering failure in Columbia River, grounded
19780321	Aegis Leader	586	MY	WS		?	?	0	M	grounded off Sumatra after machinery breakdown
19760119	Irenes Sincerity	582	MY	WS		?	?	0	M	"stranded after engine trouble", Baltic, nil info
19831222	San Nikitas	582		WS	FX	?	?	0	M	grounded Gulf of Bothnia, no other info
19830716	Manhattan Duke	580		WS		R	?	0	M	"stuck reef" off Port Moresby, no cause info
19730624	Conoco Britannia	500	MY	WS		S	L	0	P	lost power mooring Humber SBM , ran over own anchor
19831006	Theodegmon	476		WS		H	?	0	M	grounded in Orinoco, cause ?
19980807	Ocean Gurnard	476	N_	WS		R	L	0	M	another Malacca Strait grounding, guessing nav
20011018	Norma	392		WS		H	L	0	M	grounded departing Paranagua, Brazil
19700722	Tamano	378	NA	WS		R	L	0	P	hit ledge side of channel, Casco Bay, mishandled HBL
20010525	Jose Fuchs	363		WS		R	L	0	M	grnding, Moradela Channel, Chile, cause?
19810119	Concho	317	GD	WS		H	L	0	M	grounding New York Harbor, ship too deep for channel
19810725	Afran Zenith	302	M_	WS		H	?	0	M	grounding Elbe after machinery problems
19931009	Iliad	235	G_	WS		H	?	0	P	grounding leaving Pylos, "human error"
19950210	Mormacstar	127		WS		H	L	0	Y	grounded side of Sandy Hook Channel, nil cause info
20040910	Lucky Lady	120		WS		H	L	0	P	touched in approaches to Cilacap, volume suspect
20041126	Athos I	120	CS			H	L	0	M	hit sunken pipe? at Paulsboro, big hull leak
19960311	Limar	91	CH	WS		H	L	0	P	grounded Boston in 35/36 ft with 33.75 ft draft
20000401	Kingfisher	32		WS		R	L	0	M	grounded near Cilicap, no info on cause
19960701	Provence	3	TU	WS		T	d	0	P	unmoored dsching Portsmouth NH, tide may be factor
19920512	Aida	2	G_	WS		H	?	0	M	grounded entering Cienfuegos
19760911	Aegis Leader		MY	WS		?	?	0	M	grounded after drifting with engine trouble
19951211	Giulia Seconda			WS		H	?	0	P	"touched bottom" off Inchon, cause?
19970310	Olympic Sponsor	0.000		WS		R	L	0	Y	grnd lving Maraciabo, arbs say nav but not sure, dh
19970901	Icaro	0.000		WS		R	?	0	P	grnd Maraciabo,dh, no other info
19971109	Bunga Kertas		HC			H	L	0	Y	discovered 3 mm bilge keel crack at Port Stanvac
20030101	Vicky					R	L	0	P	Hit marked wreck of Tricolor, OBO
20030114	Four Island	0.000	H_			R	L	0	Y	cracks in No 6, leak into side ballast tank

3.11   Collisions and Double Sides

Since I've broken down and talked about groundings qua groundings and double bottoms, I suppose I have to do the same for collisions and double sides. Doubles sides have been sold as a means for reducing spillage from collisions. Table 3.19 shows all the collisions and *allisions* in the CTX casualty database in which the ship with the major spillage (almost always the struck ship) was not lost.[79] There's quite a few such casualties. Almost 15% of the CTX entries fit into this category. But overall the volume spilled is small. **The total spillage from such casualties is 164 million liters, about 3% of all the spill volume in the CTX database. Total known deaths are 26. If doubles sides were perfectly effective against such collisions, we'd have a nearly negligible reduction in overall spill volume, and a small reduction in deaths.**

But unlike double bottoms, I doubt if anyone who knows anything about tankers feels that double sides will have any real impact on a serious collision. Table 3.18 shows the depth of penetration (DOP) for all the collisions in the CDB where we have an estimate of that depth.

Table 3.18: Depth of Penetration in CTX Collisions

STRUCK SHIP	D.O.P. METERS	REL SPEED KTS	IMPACT ANGLE	DS ?
British Vigilance	13	4-5	35	DH
Esso Brussels	12	10-15	abt 90	SH
Keytrader	8	7-8	50	SH
Baltic Carrier	6	????	??	DH
Jambur	6	????	??	SH
Marine Duval	> 5	< 6	abt 90	SH
Alva Cape	> 2	2.5	90	SH

The ALVA CAPE/Texaco Massachusetts is particularly instructive. The Massachusetts which was the striker was traveling at no more than 2.5 knots. She was a 16,000 ton tanker in ballast. This is about the lowest impact energy one can reasonably expect in a serious tanker collision. Yet the penetration was more than 2 meters.[80]

---

[79] An *allision* is a casualty in which the ship hits a stationary object, usually a berth.

[80] In 2000, Brown et al did an extensive theoretical study of collision penetration.[11] They used four different computer models to estimate the depth of penetration of a 150,000

Double sides are required to be 2 meters thick. The only collisions in which you can expect the penetration to be less than this is when the striker is a tugboat or similar size craft at low relative speeds. In any major collision, this will not be the case.[81] It is highly doubtful that double sides would have had any impact on any of the collisions greater than 2000 KL in Table 3.19. Certainly, this was true in the case of the double hull BALTIC CARRIER, Figures 3.5 and 3.6. But these collisions represent 80% of all the volume in Table 3.19. *Collisions in which the inner side would not have been penetrated represent considerably less than 1% of all the spill volume in the CTX database.*

Double sides will have almost no impact on total volume spilled via collisions. A more effective means of reducing collision spillage is better subdivision, lots of small tanks, which would be a good idea for other reasons as well. See Section 5.7.

This does not necessarily means that double sides are a bad idea.

1. Double sides will prevent spillage in the fairly common minor spills resulting from tug contact or in some cases hitting a berth. Overall

---

ton bulk carrier into a 150,000 double hull tanker as a function of speed, angle, and longitudinal position. Even at a striking speed of 3 knots, the computed penetration was almost always more than 3 meters. At 7 knots, the computed penetration was generally 6 to 8 meters. These are only computer numbers, but they correspond reasonably well with real world data.

[81] Readers familiar with tanker regulation may be asking: why don't you use the IMO penetration data? The answer is: I can't.

A particularly bizarre result of Class confidentiality is *non-dimensionlization* of penetration data. The only entities that have a reasonably complete database on penetration are the Classification Societies collectively. But when IMO turned to the Classes for that information, they ran up against the confidentiality clauses in the contracts between Class and individual owner. To get around this, Class non-dimensionalized the data by ratioing it to the size of the ship. For example, in the case of side damage, they divided the depth of penetration by the beam of the damaged ship. This effectively hid the ship's identity, and along the way made it impossible to check the data for accuracy, completeness, etc. Even the IMO delegates who write the regulation do not see the real penetration data. Much worse, in using the non-dimensionlized data in evaluating new designs, IMO had no choice but to assume that the penetration is proportional to the size of the struck ship. For example, in the same collision, IMO assumes that a narrow ship suffers less penetration than a wide ship. This of course is total nonsense. The depth of penetration depends on the size of the striker, not the size of the struck. The whole system is not only totally opaque, but ridiculously biased against bigger ships. Non-dimensionalized penetration data is useless. Only in the Tromedy.

Figure 3.5: Helo view of double hull Baltic Carrier. Source: DR.

Figure 3.6: Close up view of Baltic Carrier penetration. Source: DR.

little oil is spilled from such casualties, but each such spill is a major nuisance or worse for the port involved.

2. Much more importantly, double sides have the ability to contain oil in the case of many groundings. Paradoxically double sides are far more effective at reducing spillage in groundings than double bottoms. This surprising feature of double sides is discussed in some detail in Section C.8.

On the down side, double sides result in a very large amount of coated ballast tank area which must be maintained, about twice as much as a Marpol tanker and roughly six times that of a pre-Marpol. Worse, they result in small cargo tank leaks being directed into the ballast space rather than showing up as a side shell leak. Some would regard this as a plus, but it most definitely is not. The most minor side shell leak is dramatically visible, caught right away, and reacted to. The spillage is rarely more than a few tens of liters, usually less than a couple of liters. There is nil danger of generating a far larger spill and fatalities from a an explosion. A leak into a ballast tank may go undetected for an extended period, which allows the leak to get bigger and at the same time generates a very real danger of an explosion in the ballast tank.[82]

Anyway the issue is politically moot. For better or worse, we are stuck with both double bottoms and double sides. ***And this means we must inert these spaces.***

---

[82] To counter this some owners, including me, fit gas detection systems in the double hull ballast tanks. This will probably be mandatory in the near future. But these systems are highly unreliable and difficult to maintain. Unreliable, difficult to maintain systems that are not essential to a tanker's everyday operation don't work.

Table 3.19: Collisions and Allisions in which ship survived

Based on CTX database as of 2005-10-17T16:11:50

Date	Ship	Kilo liters	E1	E2	E3	L O	A C	De ad	Synposis
19771216	Venoil	34800	VD	CN			O	L	0	coll w Venpet off S.A. classic dance of death
19930120	Maersk Navigator	29400	Vd	CN	FX		R	L	0	coll w Sanko Honour west end of Malacca, cause???
19940330	Seki	18800	VB	CN			H	L	0	hit while storing underway off Fujairah, 1P holed
19970118	Bona Fulmar	9450	Vd	CN			R	L	0	hittee off Dunkirk, OBO, 1 tank breached, 4mx3m hole
19900806	Sea Spirit	7770	Vd	CN			R	L	0	coll with LPG carrier Hesperus whose bow destroyed
19830928	Sivand	7630	GB	RR			T	L	0	hit berth at Immingham, "negligent handling"
19770813	Agip Venezia	5880	V-	CN			O	L	0	coll w Ramses II near Sicily, cause?
19930817	Lyria	5290	V-	CN			O	L	0	collision with submarine off Toulon
19990115	Estrella Pampeana	4540	V-	CN			H	L	0	collision, Rio Plata, 1P tank breached
19900329	Jambur	3800	V-	CN	WS		R	L	0	coll in Bosporus, 1S,1C holed, no cause info, vol?
19880903	Esso Puerto Rico	3600		CS			H	L	0	hit submerged obj in Miss R, carbon black spill
19941221	New World	3500	VB	CN	TX		O	L	8	coll w burdened Ya Mawlaya which failed to give way
19710118	Oregon Standard	3240	VB	CN			R	L	0	coll SF Bay, wrong frequencies, advisory VTS useless
19810128	Olympic Glory	3170	V-	CN			H	?	0	overtaking collision Houston Ship Channel, cause?
20010329	Baltic Carrier	2900	MR	CN			R	L	0	steering failure, collision, 6 m penetration
19740118	Key Trader	2790	VD	CN	WS		T	L	16	dance of death w Baune in lower Mississippi River
19880713	Nord Pacific	2440	G-	RR			T	L	0	hit berth while mooring Corpus Christi
19941003	Neptune Aries	2380	G-	RR			T	L	0	hit jetty at Cat lai, mooring
19751112	Olympic Alliance	2220	V-	CN			R	L	0	coll off Dover w frigate in traffic lane
19951117	Honam Sapphire	1400	G-	RR			T	L	0	Hit berth mooring at Yoshon, no cause info
19781230	Esso Bernicia	1220	GT	RD			T	B	0	hit berth at Sullow Voe, tug caught fire, let go
19890917	Phillips Oklahoma	941		RR	FX		H	L	0	hit anchored Fiona off Humber, cause?
19920418	World Hitachi Zosen	900	V-	CN	TX		O	L	1	coll w bulk carrier off Morocco, holed, fire in 1S
19960927	Julie N	757	GC	RR			H	?	0	struck bridge Portland ME, 30m opening for 26m beam
19690430	Hamilton Trader	635	G-	RD			H	L	0	hit while anchored Liverpool, one tank holed
19990324	Min Ran Gong 7	543	V-	CN			R	?	0	collision off Zhouhai, nil info
20040322	Everton	494	V-	CN	FX		O	L	1	coll w trawler in Arabian Gulf
20021205	Agate	411	V-	CN			R	L	0	coll E of Singapore with Tian Yu, hole P slop
19941001	La Guardia	397		RR			H	?	0	hit "fueling dock" at Aspropyrgos
19700320	Otello	319	V-	CN			H	?	0	coll n Vaxholm, some say 60-100KT, appears unlikely
19920830	Era	315	GT	RD			T	?	0	hit by tug berthing Pt Bonython, "rough conditions"
19960310	Mare Queen	238	G-	RD			T	d	0	hit by barge at Baytown

Continued on next page

Date	Ship	Kilo liters	E1	E2	E3	L O	A C	De ad	Synposis
19970807	Katja	196	G_	RR		T	L	0	hit quay at LeHavre ,ship dh, but port bfo tank not
20000608	Posa Vina	189	GT	RD		T	?	0	tug punctured bunker? tank, unmooring East Boston
20021123	Tasman Sea	188	G_	RD		R	L	0	hit while anchored off Tianjin
19990523	Parnaso	151	MR	CN		O	B	0	lost steering, collision South of Cuba
19970803	Saraband	150	V_	CN		?	?	0	collision Malacca Strait, no real info
19950205	Berge Banker	143	G_	RD		L	L	0	hit by lighter Skaubay at GLA during mooring
20010922	New Amity	138	V_	CN		H	?	0	coll w tow in Houston Ship Channel, got bfo tank?
19811207	Tabriz	117	MY	RR		H	?	0	eng failure, hit jetty at Bandar Abbass
20010423	Gudermes	84	VB	CN		R	L	0	coll w fishing vsl which had only deckhand on watch
20001104	Vergina Ii	83	G_	RR		T	L	0	hit pier, mooring Sao Sebastiao
20040220	Genmar Alexandra	83	G_	RD		T	d	0	hit by Bright Star discharging Mississippi River
20010523	Shinoussa	50	GT	RD		T	B	0	tug contact, unmooring Freeport, dh but hit bfo tank
20000315	J Dennis Bonney	32	G_	RD		L	L	0	hit by lighter while mooring, Southwest Pass
19970118	Stolt Spray	20	MR	CN	WS	H	L	0	lost steering in Miss River, holed 1p, dh
19980427	Barrington	17	GT	RD		H	B	0	bfo tank hit by trainee tugmaster in Brisbane River
19990227	Hyde Park	16	MY	CN		H	L	0	lost power loaded gasoline, drifted 13 M, many coll.
20040729	Eagle Memphis	8	G_	CN		H	?	0	coll w tug, both northbound??? in Miss. River
20000430	Princess Pia	2	GT	RD		H	L	0	tug contact, Rio Plata, why tug for loaded ship
20000328	Bahagia	1		RD		T	d	0	hit while unloading Belawan, pipe broke
20040802	Torm Mary	0.102	G_	RD		H	B	0	hit while bunkering Neches River
19711207	Texaco Denmark			CN		?	?	0	102000T volume, existence questionable, need info
19790225	Mobil Vigilant		M_	CN		H	L	0	coll w Marine Duval, bank effect, slo spd dop ¿ 5m
19840314	Yanxilas			CN		H	?	0	collision w Waheed, Kaohsiung, no other info
19920503	Geroi Chernomorya		V_	CN	FX	R	L	0	coll near Skyros, aft stbd cargo tank holed
19940708	Honam Pearl		V_	CN		R	?	0	coll with World Achilles in Malacca, nil info
19940801	Port Royal		G_	RR		T	?	0	hit dolphin, mooring at Corpus C.,poss mach failure
19940921	Patriot		G_	RR		T	?	0	hit pier leaving Hong Kong terminal
19941018	Amazon Venture		G_	RR		T	L	0	hit berth mooring at A. Theodoroi, holed 1 cgo tank
19960216	Stresa		V_	CN		R	L	0	coll w roro ferry in Malacca, port shell, nil info
19971127	Nordfarer	0	V_	CN		R	L	0	coll w Hoergh Mistral, no cause info
19980326	El Bravo			RD		H	?	0	hit by tanker Shauadar, Matanzas
19980427	Dubulti			CN		H	L	0	collison? entering Swansea, no real data,
19980520	Banglar Jyoti			CN		H	?	0	contact in severe storm, Chttagong, 1 tank holed,
19980529	Nunki			RD		R	?	0	holed by bunker barge off Kalunborg, horrible ship
19980924	Overseas Chicago		GT	RD		S	L	0	prob tug contact mooring Barbers Point SBM

Continued on next page

Date	Ship	Kilo liters	E1	E2	E3	L O	A C	De ad	Synposis
19990308	Navion Clipper		GT	CN		O	?	0	contact w tug during trials in North Sea, dh
19990701	New Venture		V-	CN		R	B	0	hitter in coll w Maritime Fidelity, prob ballast,
19990826	Senang Spirit		G-	RD		T	?	0	hit jetty at Port Fortin
19991026	Da Qing 50			CN		H	?	0	collision at Ningbo, nil info
20000115	Kapitan Rudnev		G-	RR		?	?	0	hit pier at Quebec
20000417	Antipolis			RR		?	?	0	contacted Panama Canal twice, why?
20000624	Gulf Star		GB	RD		H	L	0	hit berth with mooring, dh
20010504	Caspian Sea			CN		?	?	0	coll w fish vsl, India, nil info
20020325	British Vigilance	0	VU	CN		R	L	0	coll w B Vigilance, no comm despite know each other
20030429	B R Ambedkar		V-	CN		R	L	0	collision w fishing vessel off Kochi
20040331	Israa		G-	RR		D	R	0	hit dolphin while mooring at Jeddah shipyard
20040522	Kaminesan		V-	CN		R	L	0	coll w car carrier off Spore, comm w vts, other ship
20040526	Morning Express		V-	CN		R	L	0	coll w bulk carr, south coast of Korea, dh
20040708	Genmar Transporter			CN		R	B	0	coll lvng pilot pick up area Quangzhou
20040828	Astro Altair	0	MR	R		H	L	0	lost steering, hit ferry landing Mississippi River

3.12 Spill Summary

So what have we learned from our study of tanker spill statistics?

1. A "big" spill can be several hundred million times as large as a "little" spill. In terms of numbers almost all spills are at the very bottom end of this enormously large, hard-to-grasp spill range. In terms of volume, almost all tanker spillage results from the one or two largest spills each year. Regulators must be careful that in attempting to reduce the number of little spills, they do not produce regulation which increases the probability of a brobdingnagian spill.

2. By far the single most important cause of tanker spillage and tankerman deaths is hull structural failure, often abetted by advanced corrosion. No other cause comes close. Leaks into segregated ballast tanks have been particularly devastating. With the more complex structure, the drastically increased maintenance burden of double hulls, and the deterioration in structural standards (see Chapter 5), there is every reason to believe that hull structural failure will be even more dominant in the future that it has in the past. Building and maintaining robust tanker hulls should be the central focus of tanker regulation. It is the central focus of the second half of this book.

3. Historically, the second most important cause of spills is Rules of the Road screw-ups, tankers being driven into each other, primarily because the ships refuse to talk to each other. The solution is to enforce communication. This is not a tanker design problem, although improved maneuverability would be welcome. Thanks to ARPA, AIS, and the spread of English, there is reason to hope that this category of spills will be reduced dramatically in the future. In fact, there is considerable evidence in the statistics that this is already happening. But we need the same rules internationally that the US Bridge to Bridge Act enforces on all ships anywhere near the American waters.

4. The third most important cause is machinery failure. The prime culprit here is single screw. All but a handful of the 3600 sizable tanker afloat are single screw. This is preposterous. With deterioration in newbuilding standards, I expect this cause to become even more important in the future unless we do something. That something is fully redundant, twin screw with separate engine rooms.

5. The fourth most importance cause is guidance errors. There is no simple solution to guidance errors. But GPS/ECDIS should help in those casualties which are part navigation/part guidance. Twin screw and more power would help considerably by drastically improving low speed maneuverability and the pilot's ability to correct a mistake. Many guidance spills (and collisions and groundings) would be avoided by eliminating lightering and other trips into confined waterways in favor of building offshore SBM terminals.

6. Inerting/Purging/Hotwork casualties have become relatively unimportant with the implementation of inerting. Cargo tank inerting is one area where the tanker industry has done a good job, albeit belatedly. But we are still occasionally killing tankermen during manual tank cleaning due to lousy purging. And there is a pressing need to extend inerting to double hull ballast tanks.

7. Navigation errors, TORREY CANYON and EXXON VALDEZ notwithstanding, never were that important, and with GPS/ECDIS should become a complete non-factor. However, we should mandate separate, interlocked GPS's with unmistakable warnings when the satellite fix is lost.

8. Overall, transfer spills have not been a big player, but we need to improve mooring standards. Unintentional unmooring is the main cause of transfer spill volume. Mandating constant tension winches would be a big improvement. Reducing lightering in favor of SBM's would eliminate a very risky transfer operation, and more importantly the dangerous in-shore tanker leg.

9. Two ineffective means of reducing overall spillage are double bottoms in the case of groundings and double sides in the case of collisions. In both cases, even if they were perfectly effective at doing what they are claimed to do, overall spillage would be reduced by less than 10%, and they are far from perfectly effective. Neither of these measures address the real cause of spillage. Much worse, they increase the probability of ballast tank explosions, the single most important cause of tanker spills and tankerman deaths. If the Tromedy persists in mandating double bottoms and double sides — as it will — then we must address this issue.

Chapter 4

Category A Spills

4.1 Introduction

The CTX Casualty Data Base has a field which divides tanker spills into three categories as follows:

A) Spillage that results from small leaks, operational screw ups, and planned discharge of oily ballast water.

B) Spills that involve a major breach to one or more tanks, but not the loss of the ship.

C) Spills that result from the total loss of a tanker.

Very roughly speaking, Category A spills range in size from 1 to 1000 liters. Category B spills range from something like 1 kiloliter to say 10,000 kiloliters (occasionally 20,000 kiloliters or more), and Category C spills from 10,000 kiloliters to 300,000 kiloliters. The overall range is so large, that it doesn't make all that much difference if you move the boundaries between categories by a factor of two or more. At the boundaries it is more a matter of causality than size. A 2000 liter spill caused by somebody forgetting to close a valve would be Category A. A 500 liter spill caused by a bunker barge holing a tank would be Category B.

The CTX database attempts to be a reasonably complete compendium of post-1970 Category B and C tanker spills. But in terms of numbers almost all spills are Category A, and the great bulk of Category A spills go unreported. Because of this, is it impossible to do useful statistical analysis of Category A spills. But we can talk about these spills in qualitative terms, and hopefully gain some insights for tanker regulation. That is the purpose of this chapter.

Category A spills are pretty common. In my 120 ship-years of operating tankers, our ships have been involved in at least 20 Category A spills of which I am aware.[1] These are the discharges I know about. Unless a ship is in port or in US waters, most Category A spills go unreported. In my case, it wasn't so much that crews are hiding things but really a question at what point the discharge becomes so small that it is silly to call it a spill. A liter, a centiliter, a drop? It's a little like measuring shoreline. Do you count every little cove? If so, do you count every little wriggle in the coastline. If so, do you count every little jetty? If so, do you count every little shoreline rock?

I personally can't get too excited about the poor reporting of 1 or 2 liter sized spills. Even if every tanker over 10,000 tons had a 5 liter spill once a week — and they don't — we would be talking about 900,000 liters per year of unreported spillage spread fairly evenly in time and space around the world. This figure is dwarfed by all the other sources of oil pollution including bigger tanker spills. It would be less than 2% of the 50 million liters we know we spill annually from tankers on average.

Having said this, an unusual and perhaps unique feature of oil spills is that even a discharge at the very low end of the immense spill size range can be both quite noticeable and a bloody nuisance. Under the right conditions, an oil spill can spread to the point where its thickness is less than 10^{-7} meters, that is less than 10 molecules thick. This means that a half liter spill — the size of those containers of bottled water that the Yuppies carry everywhere – can cover an area of more than 1000 square meters. And despite the thinness of the spill, the interaction of light with these molecules generates a refraction pattern that in calm weather is easily visible from a distance of several miles. Finally, this ugly sheen or slick will normally persist for a matter of minutes, and in some case hours. In a sense there is no such thing as an insignificant oil spill. Even the smallest discharge can be a real irritant in a way that say a puff of smoke from a stack is not. Category A spills must be strongly discouraged.

At the same time, in controlling Category A spills, we must be careful to do so in a way that does not suppress little spills at the cost of increasing the liklihood of an astronomically more damaging brobdingnagian spill.

---

[1] Only one of these spills made it into the official databases. We will talk about that spill in the next section. I suspect this level of under-reporting is representative.

4.2 The Grand, Christmas Eve Spill

One of my Category A spills involved the HELLESPONT GRAND, a 420,000 ton tanker.[2] It was Christmas Eve, 1995. The Grand was lightering 40 miles off Galveston in rough weather, when the crew noticed a clearly visible sheen some 50 meters wide extending down current as far as they could see. Per law, discharge was halted, the US Coast Guard called, and a spill containment and clean up vessel was summoned from Houston. And I was summoned from my home in the Keys. Along the way, I called for a diver. When I arrived at the ship, I could see the sheen from the helicopter when we were still a mile or two away. The Coast Guard was already on-board.

The problem was that we could not figure out which of the ship's 28 cargo tanks was leaking. This is often the case in Category A spills. The means that we have for measuring the volume of oil in a 20,000 cubic meter or larger tank is accurate to at best a few kiloliters. With careful, repeated remeasurements, we should be able see a leakage of 2000 liters or more. Yet even after measuring and remeasuring none of the tanks showed any change in volume since the discharge was halted 12 hours earlier. Each person on-board had his own theory about which tank was leaking. I wanted to pull down each of the most likely tanks in turn to the point that they were *hydrostatically balanced*. (See Appendix C). Provided the leak was on the bottom, as we all thought, when we hit the right tank the leakage would stop. But the Coast Guard has a strict policy of no cargo or ballast operations during a spill until you are sure of the cause. This produced a Catch 22 for the poor Ensign JG on-board. No operations until we knew which tank was leaking; no way of determining which tank was leaking without operations. Neither he nor his boss on-shore was willing to break this bureaucratic logjam. So we sat and watched the oil leak out.

Fortunately, when the diver finally arrived, he discovered that the cause was a pencil sized hole in an unused ballast discharge pipe. He said it was little more than a steady dribble, like a badly leaking faucet. When he plugged the pipe, the leakage stopped. We transfered enough oil from the offending tank to pull the level of oil in that tank below the leak. After a period of testing, the Coast Guard allowed us to resume discharging. The Coast Guard and I went home in time for Christmas. The crew spent Christmas offloading oil.

---

[2] The Grand was the first ship ever registered under the Marshall Islands Flag. She was issued official number 00001. We all got a big kick out of this. I figured the Marshall Islands would never get 100 ships. But I badly under-estimated the power of Flag State competition. The Marshall Islands Flag now has over 35 million tons of ships.

I took a number of lessons away from this spill:

1. The glaring visibility of a spill that was at most a few hundred liters. If this spill had occurred in say the Houston Ship Channel, it probably would have been a major story on local TV that night.

2. The silliness and hypocrisy of offshore "oil spill containment and collection". The oil spill containment vessel, a sturdy offshore supply boat with several million dollars of special equipment and specially trained crews, manfully deployed its booms and bounced around in the nanometer thick slick for 12 hours, burning up resources and accomplishing absolutely nothing. The possibility of spill containment and collection in open water is one of the big lies that the oil industry has foisted on society. Even in the most favorable trial conditions it is possible to collect only a small proportion of oil spilled offshore. In all real world, open water spills, it is a wasteful public relations exercise.

3. The need to determine the cause of the spill before the Coast Guard arrives. Once I realized the Coast Guard was not about to alter its ostrich-like, do-nothing policy, it became apparent we had to determine the cause of the spill before the Coast Guard arrived on the scene.[3]

   We modified our loading program, the software the crew uses to determine that a particular cargo loading pattern is legal, so that it identified all the tanks that could be leaking from bottom damage — those that were *hydrostatically over-balanced* and ranked these in order of liklihood.[4] In a spill, the Captains were instructed to pull each tank down in turn to the point where they could no longer be leaking (*hydrostatic balance*) and, if the leak had not stopped, move to the next most likely tank.

Some months later, after we had the new software running in the office but before it had been deployed to the ships, the Master of one of my brother's ships, the Sea World, called me about 0600. He was discharging in the Gulf of Mexico. At first light, they had discovered a sheen. He couldn't tell which tank was leaking. The Coast Guard was on its way. What was he to do?

We quickly — if you can call an hour or more quickly — put his loading pattern into the new program, determined it had to be one of four tanks, and started transferring cargo from the most likely. No joy. By now it was after eight o'clock and the Coast Guard would be on-board in a half-hour.

---

[3] This reference to ostriches is a gross canard. Ostrich stick their heads in the sand to find water. Only humans as a species seem to be able to survive idiotic behavior. So far.

[4] See Section C.2 for an explanation of hydrostatic balance.

We turned to the second most likely tank. Almost immediately the leakage ceased. The Coast Guard arrived a few minutes later. They were pleased to find the leak had stopped and they could concentrate on the important task of filling out the reams of paperwork that any such call-out requires.

The ship resumed discharging a few hours later. If we had not determined which tank was leaking before their arrival, I suppose the ship would still be there. It turned out that the leak was so small, that identifying the source of leak by a diver would have been problematic at best.

The USCG do-nothing policy puts unnecessary oil in the water. But even if we were to get this nonsense changed, the crew is hamstrung by other parts of the Tromedy. When you need to transfer oil out of a leaking tank, usually the best, and often the only place to put it, is in a ballast tank. But under IMO rules, there can be no connection between the cargo piping and the ballast piping.[5] Some owners fit a spool piece in order to make an emergency connection, but per law the spool piece is not installed. Installing this big hunk of steel is a difficult, hour long job under ideal

---

[5] Presumably, the reason for this prohibition is to prevent owners from intentionally putting cargo in ballast tanks in order to carry more cargo. Whoever wrote this rule does not understand how a tanker operates. The one thing that is carefully monitored on all tankers, good tankers and bad tankers, is cargo volume. When the cargo is loaded, at least two and normally three parties – the terminal, the charterer, and the owner, carefully measure the volume in each tank. The terminal (seller) wants the numbers to come out high; the charterer (buyer) wants the numbers to come out low; the owner wants the numbers right (high means more freight but a bigger chance of cargo claims on discharge). The actual measurements, before and after each load, are taken by an independent cargo surveyor who unlike Class the owner does **not** hire. The cargo surveyor checks the ballast tanks. His measurements are witnessed by all the parties, and then compared with the terminal's numbers. Calculations are carried out to the tenth of a barrel, sometimes thousanths of a barrel. All parties keep and distribute records of these numbers. Afterall a VLCC cargo is worth more than 50 million dollars. This laborious process is repeated at every load port, and then again at every discharge port. An overloading would leave an extensive paper trail all over the world.

If any of these numbers don't match, the charterer withholds freight and goes after the owner for the missing cargo. Any attempt to put cargo in ballast tanks would be caught. Not only would it be caught by the cargo surveys; but it would make a godawful, expensive mess of the ballast tanks which would show up as a spill when the ship next deballasted. And it would both create an enormous safety hazard and render the owner's insurance worthless. Not even the most grasping owner would do anything so stupid.

In my 25 years in tankers, I've seen owners do all sorts of crazy things. But I have never seen nor heard of any owner intentionally putting cargo in a segregated ballast tank. And if it paid to do so, this rule would not stop him. Owners have stolen cargo by transferring a little of it into the ship's fuel tanks. In the past, this was not all that rare. This is one of the reasons why the cargo surveys are so meticulous. Legally, there can be no connection between the cargo tanks and the ship's fuel tanks.

conditions. The Tromedy has effectively outlawed one of the crew's more powerful spill reduction weapons. All tankers should be fitted with a double valved ballast/cargo connection protected with a seal. Crews should be encouraged to break the seal and transfer cargo into ballast tanks whenever it will reduce spillage.

4.3 Dribs and Drabs

4.3.1 Types of Category A Spills

Category A spills come in a number of varieties. Since Category A spills often go unreported, and, when they are reported, the accuracy of the data is highly suspect, it is impossible to draw any quantitative conclusions about these spills. But we can at least list the various kinds of Category A spills.

a) Deck dribs and drabs, Section 4.3.2.
b) Stern tube seal leaks, Section 4.4.
c) Bottom pitting, Section 4.5.
d) Fatigue cracking, Section 4.6.

We take a brief look at each of these Category A spills in the rest of this chapter.

4.3.2 Deck Dribs and Drabs

The most common Category A spills are dribs and drabs from the deck. A good tanker should be a clean ship. But spots of oil and grease can get on the deck, and transferred to the sea via the scuppers or occasionally by overflowing the *fishplate* in a rainstorm. All tankers have a big barrier or coaming, 200 to 400 mm high around the deck. This is called the fishplate. This coaming has a number of holes or drains in it called *scuppers*. The scuppers are normally plugged near shore. If a crew is careful and conscientious, the rainwater collected on deck can be decanted from below any film of oil, and the remaining oily liquid transferred to a slop tank.[6] If they are sloppy, some of the oil on deck gets into the sea.

The most effective way of controlling deck dribs and drabs is simple: white decks and topsides.[7] Most tanker owners paint their decks a dark color, usually a brownish red. This does an excellent job of hiding rust, dirt and oil. That is its purpose. If the decks are wet, even the rustiest, dirtiest red deck can look beautiful from a distance. A common trick when a tanker is going to have her picture taken is to wet down the decks. The topsides are usually black; that way you can not see the omni-present streaks of oil running from the scuppers to the water.

---

[6] To aid in this process, on our ships we fit a special decanting valve in the aft corners of the fishplate. This is an additional small valve placed as low as possible which allows the crew to drain from only the lowest portion of the puddle.

[7] The topsides are the portion of the hull from the deck down to the full load waterline, the part of the hull you see when the ship is fully loaded.

In the mid-80's we switched all our decks to a very light gray.   Our crews were not the least bit happy about this, but the quality of the deck maintenance improved markedly. Now the smallest bit of rust or oil was clearly and embarrassingly visible. They had to do something about it NOW. And the decks were noticeably cooler.

In our 1999 newbuilding programs, we went with all white ships including the topsides. Pure white from the loaded waterline to the top of the mast like the banana boats. Unheard of in tankers; much moaning and groaning from our crews; and lots of stupid white elephant jokes from the rest of the industry. But the decks on these ships were maintained to yacht standards. Dribs and drabs just about disappeared. The problem with a drib on these ships is that it makes a ugly black scar on the white topsides as it dribbles down to the water. The only way the crews could keep their topsides white was to stop the dribs and drabs. And they began taking extraordinary measures to do just that. We also obtained a massive reduction — more than 12^oC — in peak deck temperature from the pure white decks. This has extremely important implications for both tank corrosion and cargo evaporating into the environment. See Section A.2.2.

The first thing you should do when you visit a tanker is to check the color of the deck. If it's a dark color, or worse red, the ship's owner has already told you something very important. He'd rather hide his problems, than solve them.[8]

---

[8] Also check the color of the bottom of the engine room and pump room. This is confusingly called the tanktop. If it's dark — most are — you are not only looking at eventual pollution, but a safety hazard. A dirty tank top is an engine room fire in the making.

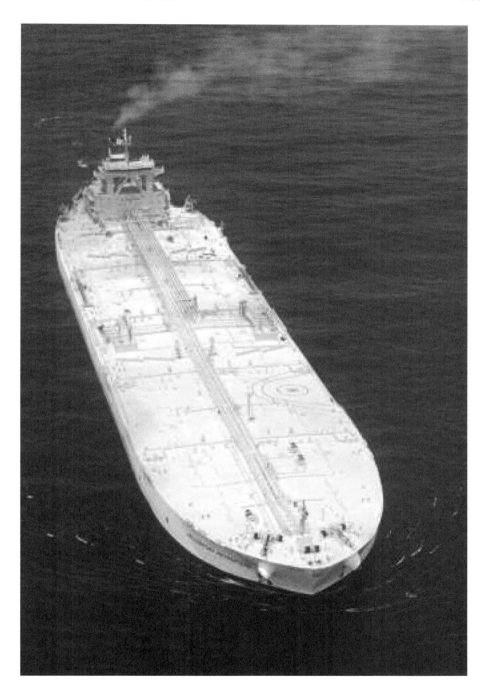

Figure 4.1: The All-White Tanker: Clean and Cool.

4.4   Stern Tube Seal Leaks

I suspect that stern tube seal leaks may be the second most frequent cause
of Category A spills. The propeller shaft on any ship, not just tankers,
rides in a big bearing at the aft end of the shaft. This bearing is lubricated
with hydraulic fluid. A series of spring loaded rings called seals keeps this
hydraulic fluid from escaping into the sea. Occasionally, these seals leak.
Based on our experience, I would guess this happens at least once every five
ship years on average. For tankers, these leaks tend to occur at the load or
discharge ports as the ship comes out of the water due to deballasting or
cargo discharge.

If a stern tube seal starts leaking, the crew has a certain amount of
control over the situation. By reducing the pressure in the shaft lubrication
system, they can reduce the leakage rate. If they reduce the pressure enough,
seawater will flow into the bearing rather than oil out. The leak will stop.

But this is a Faustian bargain. Reducing the hydraulic fluid pressure and/or allowing sea water into the bearing, greatly increases the risk
of a bearing failure which will totally immobilize the ship. Slightly reducing minimal stern tube leaks while at the same time greatly increasing the
probability of a massive spill or worse losing the whole ship, would seem to
be an unintelligent thing to do. But this is what is actually happening as
ports really crack down on Category A spills. Thank the Tromedy.

One intelligent response to stern tube leakage is the air seal. In this
system, the stern tube seal is fitted with an additional outer seal. The
sealing medium in the outer seal is air at a pressure which is slightly higher
than either the seawater or the hydraulic fluid on either side. If the seal
leaks, it will leak air, and the crew will be alerted to the problem by other
means than a spill. It doesn't always work; but it is a useful technology. It
is not required by current regulation.[9]

A still better idea is composite bearings. Almost all modern tanker stern
tube bearings are made of white metal, steel coated with a kind of tin. If salt
water gets into such a bearing, either by a crew screw up or a seal failure,
the bearing surface will corrode and the bearing will fail shortly thereafter,
immobilizing the ship. Composite bearings are a special fiber reinforced
plastic. These bearings will not corrode in contact with sea water and in
fact can be sea water lubricated. They can run for a long time, in some cases
indefinitely, in the case of a bad stern tube seal leak. Until the mid-90's,

---

[9] Very recently, a few tankers have gone back to seawater lubricated bearings.[43] Could
be a good idea, but I have no experience.

intelligent, first class owners specified the more expensive composite bearings to obtain this important insurance. Only lesser, cost obsessed owners used white metal.

But as we shall see in Chapter 5, the deterioration in shipbuilding standards have made it impossible to use composite bearings. Just about all big tankers built in the last ten years, including our own, have white metal bearings. These ships are a stern tube leak away from disaster.

4.5   Cargo Tank Bottom Pitting

4.5.1   Single Bottom Pitting

The bottom of all crude oil tanks is subject to a form of corrosion known as *pitting*. Almost all crude oils contain a certain amount of water. Most contain a significant amount of sulfur. On a long laden voyage, some of the acidic water in the crude settles out in a layer just above the bottom of the tank. This water combines with oxygen rich clumps of sludge to produce corrosion that starts out as a dimple but in some cases can develop into holes or *pits* that can drill thru the steel with remarkable rapidity.[21] Corrosion rates in tank bottom pits can be as high as 10 mm per year.[45, pages 3-4]

In single bottom ships, if the pit gets thru the bottom undetected, you will have a Category A spill. This is the kind of spill we thought we had on the Grand, but didn't. My ships have been involved in three of this variety of spill, all in the late 1980's. In a single bottom ship, it is child's play to stop a bottom pit leak if you know which tank is leaking. Simply transfer enough oil out of the leaking tank to establish *hydrostatic balance* at the bottom. As soon as the pressure of the sea water outside the tank is greater than oil pressure inside the tank, the ship will leak inward. Seawater will flow into the tank rather than oil out. In a pre-Marpol tanker, usually a transfer of at most a meter or two of oil out of a tank will establish hydrostatic balance. See Appendix C.

The problem, as we saw on the Grand and Sea World, is figuring out which tank is leaking. The location of the sheen tells you nothing. Not only is this determined by the local currents but the *bilge keels* direct the leakage all the way forward or aft depending on the current regardless of where the leak actually is.[10] There are only two ways of figuring out which tank is leaking: a diver, and intelligent trial and error.[11]

The counters against tank bottom pitting are:

1. Carefully blast and coat the tank bottoms preferably with a good solvent free epoxy. We found that Sigma's CSF worked well provided there was no salt on the blasted surface.[12] This requires a closely monitored combination of grit blasting and washing with desalinated water.

---

[10] Just about all tankers are fitted with a long very shallow fin at both outboard corners of the bottom. These fins, called bilge keels, are about 0.5 m wide and run 30% or more of the length of the ship. Their purpose is to reduce rolling.

[11] As we saw in Section 4.2, US Coast Guard policy prohibits the latter.

[12] The actual spec is less than 20 mg chloride per square meter.

2. Fit sacrificial anodes right on the bottom. This is crucial otherwise a single defect in the coating can produce the 5 mm/year plus pitting rate documented by Shell.[45, page 1] On our old ships we used the "one fat Greek/two skinny Filipino" approach. In this system, we welded a crank anode, which is just a long thin ingot of zinc, with a piece of rebar threaded through it. as low as we could on the bottom stiffener web. Then a hefty Greek officer or two Filipino crewmen would jump up and down on the anode until it was bent down onto the bottom.

3. Keep the tank bottoms free of pockets of sludge.

We started blasting and coating our cargo tank bottoms in the very late 80's. People thought we were crazy, spending something like a million dollars per ship. But we never had a bottom pit leak on any of our old ships after they had been so treated. Nor did we ever have to replace any bottom plate steel. Later in the 90's, owners of pre-Marpol tankers regularly ran up several million dollar yard bills replacing 100's of tons of badly corroded, flat bottom steel.

4.5.2 Double Bottom Pitting

With double bottoms, bottom pit leaks are a thing of the past? Yes and no. It is true that a bottom pit will not leak into the ocean. But the pitting is still going on. In fact, there is some reason to believe that bottom pitting may be more rapid in double bottom ships than single bottom. Here's a typical industry press report.

> When the first generation of double hull tankers were taken into service, their owners were startled to find that their state of the art ships were rotting away almost twice as quickly as single hulled tankers. Pitting corrosion in the inner bottom plating was taking place at an annual rate of between 1 mm and 2 mm. In some intance, pits were developed as deep as 7 mm to 9 mm within 5 years. That is 40% of the original plating thickness.[24]

In 1996, DNV predicted that, based on their owners' recent experience, double hull VLCC's would need "3000 to 5000 tons of steel replacement", double that of the worst pre-Marpol VLCC's.[9] The data upon which this intriguing statement is based is, of course, not available. In 1997, *OCIMF*, the Oil Company International Marine Forum, was concerned enough to issue a report entitled "Factors Influencing Accelerated Corrosion of Cargo Oil Tanks" which says

> Recent experiences of OCIMF members have indicated problems
> in new single and double hull tonnage from excessive pitting cor-
> rosion of up to 2.0 mm per year in the uncoated bottom plating
> in cargo tanks due, inter alia, to microbial induced corrosion
> processes. This type of wastage and the increased rate of corro-
> sion, which is much greater than that which would be normally
> expected, gives cause for serious concern.[59]

OCIMF is the major charterers' official tanker organization. Like the Classes,
OCIMF does not release data on individual ships. In October 1997, ABS
issued a Safety Advisory saying in part

> The Rule for cargo tank bottom is based on [a corrosion rate] 0.1 mm
> per year However, corrosion rates of between 0.16 mm and 0.24 mm
> per year are being reported on some double hull tankers less than three
> years old. After only two years of service one 150,000 dwt [double
> bottom] tanker experienced average corrosion-pit depths of between
> 2.0 and 3.0 mm in its cargo tank bottom plating.[71]

In 1999, Seatrade reported several instances of nearly new double hulls docking prematurely, allegedly for cargo tank bottom problems.[9] On the wa-
terfront, rumors abounded of double hull cargo tank corrosion including
whispers of the dreaded "super-rust". But as always with the Tromedy,
hard data is not available.

The favorite theory for the more rapid corrosion of double hull inner
bottoms is acid producing bacteria. The proponents of the bug scenario
argue that the inner bottom is insulated from the sea and therefore never
gets as cold as a single bottom. This is supposed to promote the proliferation
of the bacteria. I personally find this story uncompelling.[13] But thanks
to the Tromedy's inability to investigate its problems in an open, honest,
scientific manner, we simply don't know the cause of accelerated cargo tank
bottom pitting in double hulls if, in fact, it exists.

In any event, cargo tank bottom pitting is most definitely occurring on
double bottom ships. For our purposes, by far the most important difference

---

[13] There is nothing new about the pitting rates cited by OCIMF or ABS. My guess is
that the only differences between single bottom pitting and double bottom pitting are (a)
the absence of the stiffener web to bottom plate welding which served as a natural anode,
and (b) the use of Thermo-Mechanically Controlled Processed (TMCP) steel on the new
ships. TMCP steel has a much finer grain structure than the cold-worked steel used on
the older ships, which means many more active sites where corrosion can be initiated.

But this is just my guess. In the bad old days, an oil company marine department would
have instituted a real research program and got to the bottom of this problem. Now we
have nobody to turn to.

between single bottoms and double bottoms is that with the latter the leak is not into the sea, but into the double bottom space. At first glance, this would seem to be a benefit, another layer of protection for the environment. In fact, it's a guaranteed disaster. When a single bottom leak, the leak is immediately apparent, easily halted by a meter or two of cargo transfer, and eventually fixed.

With an inner bottom leak, even if you detect the leak, the only way you can stop it is to completely empty the tank. But this usually not possible. There is rarely enough room in the other cargo tanks; and, if there is, the transfer will probably violate over-stress the ship's structure.[14]

Much worse, there's a good chance the leak will go undetected for quite a while. In theory, the crew will discover the leak either by the double bottom gas detection system (if one is fitted) or in a routine tank inspection and take the appropriate measures. But the gas detection systems are notoriously unreliable and hard to maintain, and some crews don't inspect the double bottom for years on end. Most crude oil vapors are highly flammable. Sooner or later we will have an explosion in a double hull due to such leakage. We will have turned an easily handled Category A leak into a major spill or worse lose the whole ship. As we saw in Chapter 3, this will not be the first time this has happened to double bottom ships. The BERGE ISTRA and and BERGE VANGA explosions which together killed 80 crew are just two of a large number of examples. **Double bottoms must be permanently inerted.** Section 6.4 discusses this in detail.

And the top of the inner bottom must be both coated and anoded. Some owners are now coating double hull cargo tank bottoms but, according to the Korean yards, only Hellespont protects the coating with anodes. This is essential as we saw above. Otherwise the first defect in the coating will produce a leak in less than ten years, probably a lot less.[15]

---

[14] Readers familiar with hydrostatic balance (Section C.2) are asking themselves, why not ballast the the tank that is being leaked into to push the Live Bottom above the leak? No can do. *Almost all modern double hull tankers are too weak to allow a ballast tank to be safely flooded when the ship is loaded.*

[15] The skinny-Phil-fat-Greek system does not work on the structure-free inner bottoms. Hellespont had the yards weld short vertical pieces of 15 mm rod to the inner bottom. The anodes are laid on the bottom and attached to these rods with U-bolts.

We also need to keep these tanks sludge-free. With double bottoms, this should be piece of cake. But unfortunately the yards have exploited a loophole in the Rules to provide too few COW machines in double hull cargo tanks. See Section A.2.2. This problem has been recognized for at least ten years. With a decent regulatory system, this loophole would have been closed immediately. With the Tromedy, nothing has been done.

4.6   Fatigue Cracking

In the late 1970's, some tankers began experiencing a phenomenon that we had never seen in tankships before. Cracks were developing in the side shell, just above the loaded waterline, usually forward. Almost all the ships that had this problem were European built. If the tank was loaded at the time, it would start leaking at the crack. This was usually how the crack was discovered. Since the damage was generally high in the tank, hydrostatic balance was of no use. The crew's only recourse was to lower the level of oil in the tank to below the crack if they could, or to make some kind of temporary patch on the outside.

The cause was *fatigue cracking*. If steel is highly stressed first one way, and then the other, and this process is repeated long enough, the steel will eventually develop a crack. Anyone who has opened a can of coffee or a soup can with a dull can opener is familiar with fatigue cracking. The can opener leaves the lid still attached to the rim by a sort of tab or hinge. So you pull back the lid and then wiggle it back and forth. Eventually a crack appears in the tab, a few more wiggles and the crack advances all the way thru the tab, and the lid comes off. With luck, you haven't cut your fingers.

To generate fatigue cracking, two things are required:
1. High stress. The stresses must be large enough so that the structure is subject to significant deflection.
2. Cyclic loading. The stresses have to be back and forth, deflecting the structure first one way then the other. Over and over again.

Thanks to waves, ships at sea have always been subject to cyclic loading. But it wasn't until the late 70's that we started seeing fatigue cracking in tankers.

In the 1970's, European shipyards began having great difficulty competing with Japanese yards, in part because of Japanese wage rates, but much more importantly because the Japanese yards were more productive. The Class structural Rules had been drastically relaxed in the 1960's. The Manhatten is a graphic example. This 105,000 ton tanker was built in 1962 for Niarchos. She had a lightweight of 30,000 tons. By 1967, 190,000 ton tankers were being built with a lightweight of 30,000 tons.[16]

In the mid-70's some of the European yards started to push these weakened Rules very hard. They pushed down the overall scantlings, increasing stress levels. The ships became more limber as they got bigger. Worse, they

---

[16] By the way, the Manhatten had 45 tanks and two 16,000 KW main engines.[31] A modern tanker of this size will have as few as nine cargo tanks, and a single, 14,000 KW engine. This is called progress.

cut corners on structural detailing. Double curves became single curves. Single curves became flat triangles. The watchword was *design for producability*, that is, for minimum man-hours in welding and erection, with little concern for the internal stress flow. Many of the structures were plug ugly. Stress flows thru a structure in much the same way that water flows thru a stream. If the structure follows the stress flow, it is both efficient and beautiful. Nature often comes up with such structures. If a structure is ugly, unbalanced, it will create nasty stress concentrations, localized areas where the stress is many times what it would be in a smooth, flowing structure. It was in just such areas that the European tankers began having fatigue cracks. We have owned four big tankers built in Europe in the mid-70's. Three of them were crackers.

One of these ships was called the Hellespont Enterprise. It was a 320,000 ton tanker built in a Dutch yard called Verolme in 1976. Ships in this class started cracking very early in their trading life. (Crackers always do.) When I talked Basil Papachristidis into buying this ship in 1981, she was laid up in Brunei Bay. She had already suffered shell cracks at the deep loadline, midway between the bulkheads in just about every cargo tank. Her sisterships had suffered exactly the same sort of cracking. We knew about the cracking; but the price, $3,250,000 dollars which included about $500,000 worth of fuel on-board was impossible for headstrong idiots to pass up. The ship had cost the original owners $80,000,000 when she had been built 5 years earlier.

Besides we thought we knew how to fix it. There was a definite pattern to the cracking. There always is. All tankers are longitudinally framed. The skin is supported by a series of stiffeners which run fore and aft. These stiffeners are spaced about a meter apart. The skin and these stiffeners form the shell panels. These panels in turn are supported at intervals of every five or six meters by enormous ribs called *webs*. In the case of the Enterprise, design for producability had created a web which had a big triangular bracket on the forward side. But there was nothing on the other side. This simplified the erection sequence in the yard.

It also created a big hinge. Figure 4.2 looks down on this design. On the forward side of the web, the structure was very rigid. On the aft side, the shell plating was free to flex back and forth with the wave action. Think of the forward side of the web as the lip of the coffee can; the aft side as the lid. Not surprisingly it wasn't long before cracks started appearing on the inside edge of the shell stiffeners just behind the web, and only a matter of time after that that the crack would work its way thru the stiffener out to the shell.

The point I'm trying to make by getting into this boring technical detail

Figure 4.2: Design for Producability

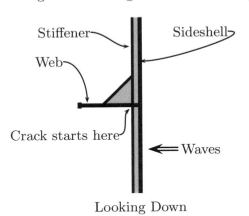

Looking Down

is that there is nothing subtle about this error. You don't have to be as structural engineer to know that Figure 4.2 is a terrible design. So why did the ship's Class, Lloyds, approve it? You will have to ask the Tromedy. All I know is that you will see the same kind of lousy design just about wherever you look in a modern tanker.

When we reactivated the Enterprise in 1985, we installed soft-nosed backing brackets on the aft side of the web to balance the brackets on the forward side. This eliminated the hinge, and we had no more cracks in this area. Unfortunately the Enterprise only traded for seven months before she was exoceted by the Iraqis in the Iran-Iraq War. The whole engine room was destroyed. No one was hurt. But the ship was a total loss. My guess is that, if we had been able to keep her, cracks would have shown up somewhere else. The structure was just too weak and too ugly.

Undeterred, in 1983 my brother and I talked Larry and Jim Tisch at Loews Corp into buying two 315,000 ton ships from Shell. They were called the Limnea and the Liparus. The Liparus had a short career as a film star. She was the mothership into which the mad tanker owner, Stromberg, abducted submarines in the Bond movie The Spy Who Loved Me.[17] These ships were built in Denmark in 1975. They were better ships than the Enterprise, but still the structure was marginal. These ships had a tendency to crack high in the shell just forward of the aft bulkheads of the forward most tanks. We never really solved this problem. We reinforced the area

---

[17] I can't say this was the worst Bond movie ever, but the tanker did have more personality than any of the characters. We renamed the Liparus, the Paradise, which is my candidate for the dumbest big tanker name ever.

and inspected it periodically. We knew where the cracks would be, so when we saw one getting started, we'd weld it up at the first opportunity. And wait for it to happen again. We traded these two vessels for 17 years each. During these 34 ship-years, we had two occasions where the crack reached the outer shell, the crew noted some cargo leakage. In each case, they were able to pull the level of the cargo in the tank down below the crack, and no one was the wiser.

Between 1985 and 1986, we bought four, 8 to 10 year old, Japanese built ULCC's, all around 400,000 tons. These were good tankers. The Japanese yards were slow to adopt the European design for producability philosophy. In the 1970's, they did not have the same economic pressures, and they were building ships for owners that at the time had real standards, including Daniel Ludwig, Exxon, and Chevron. We experienced nil fatigue cracking on these four ships. On these ships the structure was robust and full of curves. One ship, the Hellespont Embassy, built by Mitsubishi in 1976, had a particularly gorgeous structure. Walking thru the center tanks in the Embassy was like being in a cathedral. On the Embassy, the structure simply flowed. In 18 years of operation, we never experienced a structural problem of any kind on the Embassy. In particular, we never found a single crack on the Embassy. When we scrapped her at age 27 in 2003, she was a far better ship than the brand new ships we were taking delivery of.

The whole point here is **there is absolutely no need for, nor any excuse for, fatigue cracking in tankers**. To be as good as the Embassy, the Enterprise would have needed an extra 6,000 tons of steel. The marginal cost of extra steel is less than $500 per ton. For no more than three million dollars, or about 4% of the newbuilding price, the Enterprise lemon could have been an Embassy peach. One ship, properly maintained, serves trouble free for nearly thirty years and could easily gone another thirty in a more rational world. The other ship was a massive headache from the day she was launched, regardless of who operated her.

In the late 80's and early 90's, fatigue cracking reached epidemic levels. I was told by several people who would know that there were several ships in the Alaska to West Coast trade that had "thousands of cracks". Some of this, but only some of it, became public in a Berkeley study which documented 3629 cracks in ten ships.[6] Table 4.1 is taken from this report. Valdez suffered 36 spills between 1977 and 1989 most of them as a result of fatigue cracking. In addition, cracks in the Stuvyesant created two 2,000,000 liter spills: STUVYESANT(A) and STUVYESANT(B), in the Gulf of Alaska in 1987. After the 270,000 liter THOMPSON PASS spill at Valdez in 1989, the USCG sent Alyeska a letter saying it was changing its policy. Tankers with cracks

Table 4.1: Cracks in Alaskan Trade Tankers

TYPE	DWT	BUILT	No Cracks
Double Hull	39,000	1977	164
Double Hull	39,000	1975	24
Double Bottom	188,500	1979	327
Double Bottom	188,500	1980	177
Single Hull	70,000	1972	639
Single Hull	35,700	1973	321
Single Hull	153,200	1977	651
Single Hull	153,200	1977	457
Single Hull	153,200	1977	413
Single Hull	153,200	1976	467

would no longer be allowed to load. Up until then cracks were so common — the USCG, not the best looker, was finding six a year — that the policy was to load anyway rather than disrupt the flow of oil. By law, the Alaskan tankers had to be built in the USA. The uncompetitive American yards were among the most enthusiastic adopters of design for producability.

But alas, the Japanese were not far behind. In the late 1970's the tanker market went into a 15 year slump. This more or less coincided with the introduction of the Marpol single hull. But there were few tanker orders. Many of the world's big tanker yards went out of business. But the Japanese hung on desperately. To do this they pushed the Rules very hard, and forgot all about conservative design. This produced the so-called second generation VLCC.

A decent pre-Marpol 250,000 ton ship would have a hull steel weight of about 32,000 tons. As we have seen, with good detail design, these ships were just strong enough. The Marpol single hull of the same size had a steel weight of 26,000 to 28,000 tons. This was accomplished by extensive use of high tensile steel and aggressive use of computer models to convince easily-swayed Classification Societies that steel could be "optimized" away. See Chapter 5 for the details of how this works. The problem is that a 10 to 20% increase in stress over barely good enough generates a massive increase in cracking.

As a result, many of the Marpol single hulls were horrible tankers structurally, notoriously bad crackers. Some of them started cracking before they were delivered. The situation became so bad that in July 1990, MHI, the same yard that built the Embassy, had to recall six nearly new Marpol VLCC's for inspection and repair of cracking, and put another four brand new ships on "special monitoring".[42] Normally, this sort of thing is done privately. It is in everybody's interest: owner, yard and Classification Society to keep these problems within the family; and there is no governmental oversight that requires any disclosure. The only reason why this particular "recall" became public was that the withdrawal of tonnage was sufficient to produce an impact on spot tanker rates and wild rumors began circulating in the tanker market. MHI decided to go public to emphasize it really wasn't that bad. This recall is the tip of the iceberg. The second generation VLCC's were the worst fleet of ships since the Spanish Armada.

The situation appeared to improve with the introduction of the double hull. These ships automatically had more steel and were a little less limber than the Marpol single hulls. Far more importantly, some of the Marpol cracking was occurring in the first year of the ship's life. **This meant it was a warranty item.**[18] This woke the shipyards up. Some of the worst details were improved.

Class reacted by introducing *fatigue analysis*. This is an attempt to simulate the cyclic loading on each critical portion of the structure in order to estimate the structural detail's *fatigue number*, which is supposed to indicate how many years before it starts cracking.[19] To do this analysis, a slew of heroic and weakly supported, simplifying assumptions are required. In the end, the calculated fatigue number is little more than an index. A structural detail with a fatigue number of 40 is better than one with 20; but that's about all you can say.

All the yards cared about was that the cracking did not become apparent during the one-year guarantee period. So Class set the required fatigue number at 20. This proved to be enough to eliminate almost all the first year, warranty period cracking claims, and the yards were happy.

But cracking continues. Dubai Drydocks is easily the largest VLCC repair yard in the world. In 2002, this yard doubled its steel capacity from 1,100 to 2,200 tons per month, without increasing drydock or berth space. When I asked the yard why, I was told that the new double hull VLCC's were averaging 200 tons of new steel at their first special survey (age five), mostly repairing cracks. This was so much worse even than the Marpol single hulls that the yard had to make the new investment to keep up with

---

[18] Under the Tromedy, the yard's standard big tanker guarantee lasts for only a year. This idiocy is the subject of Section 7.4.1.

[19] Class calls this number the *fatigue life*; but the terminology is so misleading I can't bring myself to use it.

the demand.

An owner who wants Embassy-like freedom from fatigue will need to require that all the structural details have a fatigue number of at least 50.[20]

The crucially important point here is that fatigue cracking is a modern phenomenon. There is no record of any fatigue cracking on tankers prior to the 1970's.[21] It is never discussed in any of the technical literature. There is no evidence of any fatigue cracking in the pre-Wold War I Standard oil fleet whose average life was 36 years. See Section 2.3. The Hellespont Embassy proved that it is not difficult to build a tanker that does not crack, ever. Yet under the Tromedy, fatigue cracking in tankers is now assumed to be inevitable.[22]

---

[20] Surprisingly, this will add very little to the overall cost of the ship. See Chapter 6.

[21] Do not confuse fatigue cracking with *brittle fracture*, an entirely different phenomenon. During World War II, a number of tankers suddenly split in two on very cold days. The cause was a combination of bad welding technique and poor quality steel. Thanks to improvements in steel making, brittle fracture appears to be behind us.

[22] Here's a remarkably relaxed warning from an interesting source.

> Reduction in the expected fatigue life of the light scantlinged tanker will lead to a significantly shorter service life than shipowners have come to expect.[74][page 37]

The speaker is Frank Iarossi, Chairman of the American Bureau of Shipping, a leading approver of light scantlinged tankers.

4.7 Regulating Category A Spills

The system for regulating Category A spills must do two things:

1. discourage Category A spills by ensuring that the tanker owner bears the full cost of his ship's pollution,
2. do so in a way that does not increase the probability of an immensely larger, brobdingnagian spill.

The system has to recognize that Category A spills cannot be eliminated and, to pretend that they can, will be counter-productive. If the penalty for a Category A spill is set too high, then the owners and crews will be driven to measures that increase the probability of a multi-hundred million liter spill in order to avoid a ten liter spill. Crews' under-pressuring stern tubes to avoid a stern tube seal leak thereby accepting stern tube bearing corrosion which will eventually lead to a ship's being immobilized is a concrete example. Containing small leaks in a double bottom which will eventually lead to a brobdingnagian spill is another. In short, the penalty should fit the crime.

One good thing about oil spillage from an enforcement point of view is that it is so visible, so hard to hide. If a crime can be easily hidden and punishment evaded, and we know we are catching only a very small percentage of the criminals, then perhaps a punitive penalty is justified to compensate for that fact. This is not the case with oil spills, certainly not spills in and around ports. In fact, in many cases we can not only identify the culprit, but we can also make a reasonably good estimate of the size of the spill.

The proper regulatory approach to Category A spills is a schedule of fines. The fines should be set to an estimate of the cost of the damage caused by the spill. A fine system is fairly easy to administer, and keeps the lawyers out of the picture. Justice can be swift and sure; and the money can go to the victims, not the legal system.

It also avoids the prescriptive sort of regulation where an all knowing political system tells the industry how to avoid a spill, something it is very bad at doing (e.g. double bottoms). Fine the bastards, and let them figure how to keep the fines low.

I'd keep the fine system simple. The cost of clean-up is a very rough proxy for the cost of damage. Etkin and other have shown the unit cost of clean-up declines sharply with the size of the spill.[27] As long as we confine ourselves to Category A spills, spills less than say 10,000 liters, this is not unreasonable. There is a sizable fixed cost, at least psychologically, associated with the simple fact that a spill has occurred. This suggests a fine system of the form

$$fine = \alpha V^{\beta}$$

where V is the spill size and β is less than one.

For example, setting α to \$2000 and β to 0.5 generates the following schedule of fines.

SPILL VOLUME LITERS	FINE DOLLARS
1	\$2000
10	\$6400
100	\$20000
1000	\$64000
10000	\$200000

This is a ballpark approximation to the guesses at the cost of clean-up that we find in the literature.[27][Table 4] Of course, α and β can be adjusted as desired. The actual numbers are not important. The point is the system should be simple, quick, sure, and specific. And the political system should confine itself to picking α and β or the equivalent.[23]

For all the above reasons, I do not think Category A spills should be criminalized unless there is clear evidence of gross negligence. If there is, then the regulatory system must distinguish between negligence on the part of the crew, and negligence on the part of the owner and builder, recognizing that a crew can only operate the ship that it is given. The fiction that the Master bears all responsibility for what happens on "his" ship must be dispensed with. This is the favorite shield of lousy owners, compromised Classification Societies, and lazy regulators. In today's world, a ship master has no more control over the condition of his ship than a bus driver. If the

---

[23] We should not push this simplistic reasoning too far. That's what happened to the Transportation Research Board Committee for Evaluating Double Hull Tanker Design Alternatives.[49] This group simulated thousands of different sized spills in four locations in U.S. waters and concluded that spill "consequence" (read cost) varies very roughly as the 0.4 power of spill volume. If you believe this and the cost of a one liter spill is a generous \$2000 dollars, then the societal cost of the 40 million liter EXXON VALDEZ spill is two million dollars, far less than the value of the lost cargo. No one has ever mistaken me for a raving environmentalist, but this has to be low by a factor of 100 or more. Yet the TRB Committee recommends using this function in evaluating tanker designs.

If we want a fine system that covers the full range of spillage — not such a bad idea — then something like

$$fine = 500 + 1500V^{0.75}$$

generates roughly the same low end but a fine of about \$250,000,000 for an EXXON VALDEZ sized spill, a much more reasonable set of penalties.

bus is in bad shape, don't blame the bus driver. Blame the owner of the bus, the organization that was supposed to inspect the bus, and the shipyard that built the bus.

One of the biggest problems with Category A spills is that, since they are both common and visible, they become the focus of spill regulation, when in fact the focus of regulation should be on preventing the rare but brobdingnagian spill. A simple, sure system of fines is what we need for Category A spills. And then concentrate on the major casualties.

Chapter 5

The Deterioration in Tanker Building Standards

5.1 The Direct Analysis Downratchet

In 1999, my partners and I decided it was time to build new tankers. Our six old ships were still going strong. In fact, four of them were in better than as-built condition, and their as-built condition was considerably better than a brand new ship. But they were pre-Marpol, single hull tankers, so regardless of their quality and condition, they would have to be scrapped in the next six years.

Much more importantly, the timing looked right. The tanker market was flat on its back; the yards were dying for business, and the price of newbuilding was at an all time low in real terms. After protracted negotiations, we ordered four VLCC's at Samsung and four 440,000 ton ULCC's at Daewoo. The latter ships, the V-Plus class, were 50% larger than any tanker that had been built in the last 25 years. The reason why the negotiations were so difficult is that the yards, despite their desperation for business, were loathe to agree to our quality requirements.

We were aware that newbuilding standards had deteriorated drastically since the 1970's. We knew our barely satisfactory pre-Marpol tankers were ten to 15 percent "over-built" according to the 1999 Rules. The cracking of the MARPOL single hulls (Section 4.6) was so bad that it could not be kept entirely quiet, although we certainly didn't have the full story. We were acutely conscious of the structural problems associated with double hull. We knew that Class would regard the yard to be the customer and we tried to take steps to protect us from the first rule of retailing.

185

But we had no idea what we were getting into. Here's a list of just some of the problems that we will talk about in the rest of this chapter.

1. Structure that is so weak that it forces a set of loading restrictions on the ship which are so limited that as a practical commercial matter they are very difficult, and occasionally impossible to comply with.

2. A structure that by design can not handle even the most likely damage scenario.

3. Rampant misuse of the main structural analysis tool, the finite element method.

4. Rules that accept fatigue cracking as a matter of course.

5. Humongous tanks that are subject to sloshing resonance.

6. Ridiculously thin welding. Welds that had a 7 or 8 mm throat thickness on our mid-70's ULCC's would be 3 or 4 mm in thickness according to the new Rules. These tiny welds may well have exacerbated the EXXON VALDEZ spill.

7. Spaghetti-like propeller shafting resulting in a slew of stern tube bearing failures, rapid bearing wear down, and a very dangerous forced lubrication system.

8. Propeller shaft couplings that were 100 to 200% weaker than the couplings on our mid-70's built ULCC's.

9. Over-rated, under-designed main engines that broke down regularly.

It didn't take long to figure out the cause of this deterioration. I call it the "direct analysis downratchet". Here's how the *downratchet* works.

As we have seen, ship construction is primarily governed by the *Rules* of the Classification Society in which the ship will be Classed. The Rules are a multi-volume set of books or CD's which spell out in minute detail what can and cannot be done. But throughout the Rules, there is a general out clause which says something like "other arrangements may be approved [by the Classification Society] if it can be shown by direct analysis that they meet or exceed the above standard".

Sounds innocuous; but the result is that the yards are continually pressuring each Class to accept cost saving relaxations of the Rules by offering "a direct analysis" of some aspect of the design. Each yard has scores of bright young naval architects who do nothing more than work on beating the Rules. Once a contract is signed every kilogram of steel, every meter of welding, every gram of copper that they can save goes directly to the yard's bottom line.[1]

---

[1] Needless to say, the yards never offer a direct analysis that concludes that the Rule requirement is insufficient and needs to be strengthened.

Now you have to understand the web of relationships here. In the new-building process, the Classification Society's fees are paid by the shipyard. The yard is Class's customer. The first rule of retailing, the customer is always right, may not exactly apply; but Class must be very conscious of who is paying the bill.

The major Classification Societies are large bureaucratic organizations spread out all over the world. As far as that part of the Class that is domiciled in the shipbuilding countries and in the yards, owners come and go; but they have to live with the yards, their customers, permanently. In some cases, the yards and the local Class executives become very tight indeed.[2]

It is true that the shipowner picks the Classification Society and that, during the newbuilding process — but only during the newbuilding process — the owners want a stringent, tough Class. However, the yard can have a large if not determining influence on the owner's choice of Class. If an owner comes to a yard and asks for a Classification Society that the yard deems has been unreasonable, the yard will give the owner an inflated quote and point out that the owner can have the same ships Classed by a different society at a lower price. Usually this does the trick. In extreme cases, the yard will simply refuse to build to a particular Class's Rules.

In this environment, it is inevitable that some of the yard's "direct analysis" arguments are approved, even if it's not prudent to do so. As soon as that happens, the new lower requirement becomes the new standard, regardless of how imprudent the change is.

The Class involved can't admit it was wrong to approve the change. If it did, it would have legal problems on all the ships that had been approved with the change; not to mention some very angry owners asking why did you approve this mess on my ships and then not on his; and not to mention an extremely angry yard which bid the ship under the "new" rule and finds out it has to build the ship under the "old" rule. The other Classes have to fall

---

[2] This vendor/client relationship can go pretty deep. It is common practice for the yard and Class to have correspondence and discussions on an owner's ship without the owner's knowledge. If the owner asks Class for that correspondence, he will be told it is proprietary to the yard, even though it concerns his ship. The owner must explicitly get the right to this correspondence into the shipbuilding contract and in his pre-nuptial negotiations with Class.

It is not unusual for the yards to ask Class that an "unreasonable" surveyor be replaced. Even if Class does not transfer the surveyor, that surveyor will learn that he has made the customer unhappy. One of the reasons we always had one of our superintendents at every Class inspection was that it gave the Class surveyor cover against both the yard and the surveyor's own bosses. "What could I do? The owner's guy was standing right there."

in line. If they don't, their ships will be more expensive and they will lose owners. Having established a new lower standard, the yards then compete away the saving and must find new ways to save costs at that lower level. The process repeats itself. Each incremental click of the downratchet may not be large; but over time the ships get cheaper and lousier.

There are a couple of ways, an individual owner can try and protect himself from the first law of retailing.

Use an Owner-Oriented Office A common ploy among owners is to require that plan approval be done by a Class office where he has more influence than the yard. The Greek offices of the Classification Societies are correctly regarded to be "owner oriented". Their existence depends on being nice to the owners not the yards. A smart owner will negotiate that all plans must be approved in say Greece, rather than the office in the country of the yard. The yards will resist this strongly for they understand well the importance of the vendor/client relationship. But, when the yards are hungry for business, the owner can get this clause.

Pay Class himself We tried this.

Me to Yard Guy: "These survey fees Class is charging you are outrageous."

Yard Guy: "Yes, Dr. Jack, the Class fees are terrible."

Me: "Well, don't worry, we will pay the fees for you."

Yard Guy: "Oh no, Dr. Jack, we cannot do that. It would be against yard policy."

In 1999, three Korean yards, Daewoo, Hyundai, and Samsung, were hungry for our business; yet two out of three were prepared to walk rather than have us pay Class.[3] Samsung, temporarily agreed, but then pulled the agreement back, perhaps after consulting with the others.

I've heard that the offshore oil guys have gotten the right to pay Class but I don't know of any shipowner who has. In retrospect, I'm not sure it would have made as much difference as the yards feared. The Class guys in Korea know who the real customer is.

---

[3] The Class fees are substantial. In 1999, ABS quoted $378,000 for the first VLCC at Samsung, and about $320,000 per ship for each of the follow-on vessels.

Play one Class against another So we took another tack. Our specification required that the ships be built to both the American Bureau of Shipping (ABS) Rules and the Lloyds Register (LR) Rules.[4] This is not common, but other owners have done this. Then we asked for the option to pick the Class for each ship only at the very last minute, just before first steel cutting.[5] This was unheard of. And the yards didn't like it at all. In fact, at one time, all three yards almost simultaneously broke off the talks, mainly on this issue.

But this time we stuck to our guns and two of the yards accepted the clause. Now the Classes were competing for our business. We gave the first ship at Samsung to ABS; and the first ship at Daewoo to Lloyds; and we let both Classes know that the Class who did the best job would get the second ship, and so on down the line. This worked marginally well until we got down to the last ship, and the weapon evaporated. But by then a *relatively* high standard had been established, and a surprising number of the gray area decisions came down in our favor. The other owners' superintendents couldn't believe how well the Class surveyors stood up for the Hellespont ships.[6]

But obviously, this is no way to run a railroad. In fact, the only reason I'm going into this nonsense is to show how pervasive and how corrupting the vendor/client relationship is. Our minor victories over the downratchet were at best insignificant rear guard actions in the overall retreat from real standards.

---

[4] Inter-Class competition guarantees that the various Class Rules are almost the same. But there are some differences. In 1999, DSME claimed that dual approval added 750 tons to the 68,000 ton lightweight of the V-Plus. In general, ABS tends to be a bit tighter on structure and LR is definitely better on machinery. The new harmonized IACS Rules will remove these differences, often by going with the weakest.

The Joint Tanker Project estimates that the new IACS hull structure Rules will increase the steel weight of a VLCC by 3 to 4%. See Appendix E. But that's before the yards have had a chance to "optimize" against the new Rules. When the yards' structural whizzes get their hands on the new Rules, three percent will disappear quickly.

[5] First steel cutting is the formal beginning of the ship's construction.

[6] One final anecdote. We had negotiated an "instant arbitration" clause. In the event that there was a dispute between the owner's inspector and the yard about whether a particular piece of work met the Specification, either side could call in the Class Surveyor, who would then make an immediate determination who was right. The yards had originally accepted this clause with alacrity. But when Samsung realized they couldn't be sure which way the Surveyor would go, the yard wanted to renegotiate the clause. The meeting called to discuss this issue went nowhere and finally one of the yard guys in exasperation said "Why do you want this clause? You don't control Class, we control Class." Normally, he would have been right.

The rest of this chapter is a sad litany of the specific problems engendered by the vendor/client relationship between Class and yard combined with the downratchet. It is necessarily a bit more technical than the rest of the book. Unless you are a full time tanker person or regulator, I suggest you skim it. It's not the details; it's the pattern that is important.

5.2 Unreasonable Operating Restrictions: Lolling

It seems self-evident that a ship should be designed to handle all the operating conditions that it could reasonably be expected to face in normal commercial practice with a healthy margin for operator error. Current Class tanker rules use a different philosophy. The ship is designed to handle only a very limited set of loading conditions and then just barely.

This set of conditions is spelled out in the innocuously named *Trim and Stability Booklet*. The Trim and Stability Booklet will list some ten to fifteen tank loading patterns which the crew can legally use without exceeding the strength limits of the hull. Just about everything else is implicitly illegal. The yard's job is to make sure these conditions are as narrow as possible to save a bit of steel. Class doesn't seem to care as long as these restrictions show up somewhere in the paper work.

This philosophy was taken to particularly ridiculous heights in the case of the *one-across* tankers. In the late 80's, early 90's, the yards took advantage of the double hull's relative freedom from tank size restrictions to produce a series of 80,000 ton to 160,000 ton tankers that had only one column of cargo tanks. The cargo tanks in these ships extended from the starboard double side to the port double side.[7] More than half of the double hull tankers less than 160,000 tons that entered service between 1990 and 1998 were one across.[17] These ships had only six to eight cargo tanks, and each of these tanks extended the full width of the vessel save for the 2 meter wide double side on either side.

The one-across tankers have terrible spill resistance as even the proponents of double hull such as the US National Research Council have been forced to admit.[17, page 222][8]

A still worse problem with such wide tanks relative to the size of the ship is the *free surface effect*. When a tanker tilts or *lists* to one side or the other, the liquid in her tanks flows toward the low side increasing the list. This shift in weight is called the free surface effect. In extreme cases, it is

---

[7] To my knowledge, this had never been done before. The little Glückauf (3000 tons) and the Murex (5000 tons) had two columns of cargo tanks. Prior to double hulls, all pure tankers over 30,000 tons had at least three columns of cargo tanks.

[8] The methodology the National Research Council used is horribly biased against single hull ships (see Section D.2), but reasonably fair in comparing one double hull ship versus another. The NRC's mean side damage spill volume numbers for a 150,000 ton one-across double hull were nearly double that of the reference two across double hull, and the bottom damage numbers were one-third higher. Since these ships were double hull, they were exempt from the spill resistance requirements that the Tromedy imposes on non-double hulls.

possible for the free surface effect to capsize a ship. But in a normal two across or three across tanker, the tanks are narrow enough, so while the free surface effect must be allowed for, it almost never causes any real problem.

But in the one-across tanker, the free surface effect is so large that, unless all but one or two of the tanks are either completely full or completely empty, the ships becomes unstable. In this condition, the ship can be on even keel, then something, wave action or the wake of a passing ship, heels the ship ever so slightly; and, all of a sudden the ship will take on a 5 to 10 degree list. If the crew gets the ship back upright, she might all of sudden take a 5 to 10 degree list to the other side. This is called *lolling*.

The yards and Class knew these ships were unstable. No problem; they simply wrote into the Trim and Stability Booklet the requirement that at any one time there could be no more than 1 or 2 slack tanks. A *slack* tank is a tank that is neither completely full nor completely empty. Problem solved with a stroke of the pen.

Unfortunately, tanker crews have to load and unload tankers. And during the loading and unloading process, tanks have to be slack. The yards had developed contrived, complicated loading and discharging sequences that kept the number of slack tanks below the lolling limit; but in the real world, where a tanker crew is faced with time pressures, commercial requirements to avoid commingling different cargo parcels, these sequences were patently unrealistic.

The inevitable happened. These tankers experienced a series of lolling incidents. The most highly publicized casualty took place at Exxon's Baton Rouge refinery in 1993 badly damaging the terminal's loading arms.[36]

The whole concept of the one-across tankers was nuts. Very marginal savings in the cost of the ship while imposing all sorts of commercially costly restrictions in terms of both load and discharge time and the variety of cargos that could be handled, and nearly guaranteeing lolling casualties, some of which were bound to end up in terminal damage and spills.

Class never admitted that they had done anything wrong or stupid.[9] The Trim and Stability Booklet let the owner and crew know what they couldn't do. It was the owner's fault for accepting the design; and the crew's fault for not following instructions.

---

[9] In 1997 IMO passed Marpol Regulation I/25A which mandated positive initial stability "through design measures" for all tankers over 5,000 deadweight tons delivered after February 2002. This regulation is quite vague on the loading patterns to which this requirement applies. OBO's were exempted. Anyway owners had already stopped building one-across double hulls because the the oil companies didn't like them. Nothing has been done about the existing one-across-ers.

5.3 Hidden Restrictions: No Ballast in a Ballast Tank

This philosophy of restricting away our problems applies throughout modern tanker design. Steel is replaced with prohibitions. Don't want to put steel in the bow? No problem, just put a line in the Trim and Stability Booklet that says the ship can't operate with less than x meters draft forward, or can't operate with the forepeak tank empty. Want to reduce the hogging moment allowable? No problem, tell the crew they can't use all the ballast tanks even when the cargo tanks are empty. Combine that with a restriction on draft forward, and you end up with a ship which has absolutely no flexibility on the ballast leg. Need to inspect a ballast tank? Forget it. There's only one ballast configuration and it's the one that stresses the structure right up against the limit. Captain wants to get the ship a little deeper in the water in bad weather. Forget it, unless he wants to risk all sorts of problems for violating MARPOL.

When you talk to Class people about this problem, they invariably take the position that "It's not Class' fault. The owner accepted the conditions, so it's his fault." The most damning twist on this argument I know about is the ABS cargo tank density restriction. In 1997, ABS was falling behind in the race to see which Class could approve the flimsiest ship. The lightweight of a rule minimum ABS VLCC had become 500 to 800 tons more than that of a rule minimum DNV or LR VLCC. The owners were all going to LR and DNV in order to save a paltry $25,000 to $50,000 on an 80 million dollar ship. ABS felt it had to do something to "compete".

The solution was to change the design liquid density for the purposes of sloshing force calculations in the cargo tanks from 1.025 (sea water) to 0.90. This change was not widely promulgated. Not only did this mean that the owner could not legally load many crudes and heavy petroleum products in his cargo tanks, it meant he couldn't put sea water ballast in any of the cargo tanks including the *gale ballast tank*.[10] Many owners were not even aware of this new restriction.

But when we raised this with ABS personnel, we actually got the "if the owner wants to put anything heavier in the cargo tanks, he has to tell us" argument. The idea that the owner has to tell Class that he wants to be able to put ballast in the gale ballast tank was so patently ridiculous that

---

[10] Segregated ballast tankers have one or two *gale ballast* tanks. These are cargo tanks into which the Master is allowed to put seawater if he feels that the weather conditions are so bad that the ship's safety requires more ballast than he can carry in his segregated ballast tanks.

ABS backed off from this position in 2000. And did something even worse. The 0.90 is now buried in the Rules as a "calibration factor". The owner can now legally put sea water in his gale ballast tank, even though the tank is only designed for a 0.9 density liquid.

What Class's defense is really saying is Class have stopped being a regulatory body. Class originally was the creature of the underwriters who recognized from hard experience that, left to their own devices, owners would take bad risks and the underwriters were the ones who were going to pay. (The crews paid too but nobody cared.) The whole idea of Class or any tanker regulation for that matter is to prevent owners from being imprudent. In the modern world, where more than just insurers and crews pay for owner imprudence, the owners must be regulated. If Class won't impose reasonable design conditions, somebody else will have to step in.

5.4 Unfloodable Double Bottoms

Not only are ships built to the Class Rules designed to handle only an unrealistically restrictive range of operating conditions, they are not designed to handle even the most likely damage scenario. Double bottom tankers have an obvious characteristic: their exposure to flooding of the ballast tanks when loaded. The whole idea of the double hull is that it's a buffer between the sea and the cargo. If double hulls have any real purpose, you expect to use this buffer from time to time. Once the tanker fleet is fully converted to double hulls, it is nearly guaranteed that there will be multiple such floodings per year. If this were not the case, there would be no point in having double hulls. Yet the Class Rules ignore this obvious fact.[11]

There is a massive inconsistency in the IMO regulations in this regard. Marpol Regulations 25 and 13F(6) require that a tanker be able to withstand a whole range of flooding scenarios from a stability point of view. This ensures that the ship can withstand massive flooding without capsizing.[12] But structurally the ship is not designed to withstand **any** flooding of the ballast tanks when loaded.[13]

The standard Tromedy response on this issue is to say "Don't worry. In a flooding casualty like this, we can rely on the ship's ultimate strength." They are referring to the fact that a hull can be over-stressed in the sense that it will be deformed but still survive. But for a structurally optimized double hull in sag, there is little difference between ultimate strength and the stress required to permanently deform the hull. Normally when a tanker's longitudinal structure fails, it fails in buckling. This is a product of the Class Rules over-reliance on tensile stress. When it comes to buckling, double hulls tend to be strong in hog and weak in sag. Paik examined the ultimate longitudinal strength of nine existing double hull tankers.[63][page 138] He

---

[11] If a cargo tank starts leaking into the double bottom, there are only two ways the leak can be stopped:
  1. Empty the cargo tank entirely which is often impossible because of lack of room in the other cargo tanks.
  2. Ballast the tank being leaked into to establish hydrostatic balance at the leak, but the ships are not strong enough to allow this.

[12] The implementation of IMO Reg 25 leaves something to be desired. Class (IMO's enforcer) does not require the yards to check for flow through the inert gas lines on deck from high tanks to low. See Section C.9.4. If this happens, the standard stability analysis is worthless. But it doesn't matter; the ship's structure will fail first.
[13] Legalistically, this is not quite true. The new JTP Rules require that the tanks withstand the pressure associated with the flooded condition; but, since the immense sagging moment associated with loaded flooding is not applied, this is meaningless.

found that in sag most of these ships have almost no margin. For six of these ships, including all the VLCC's studied, the ratio of the moment required to induce progressive failure to the IACS design bending moment was less than 1.03. Flooding the midship ballast tanks on a loaded VLCC will impose a bending moment of about 1.6 times the IACS moment in the design wave.

5.5 Don't Allow. Don't Check

I could come up with any number of examples of the Classification Societies tacitly accepting bad newbuilding practice. I guess I picked the lightweight curve because it produced an intriguing quote.

An important determinate of the longitudinal forces on a ship is the *lightweight curve*, that is, how the steel weight of the ship is distributed along the ship. If a lot of this weight is near the middle of the ship, it increases the sagging moment, the tendency of the hull to sink in the middle, stressing the bottom plating. If a lot of this weight is near the ends of the ship, the hull will tend to hump up or hog in the middle stressing the deck. On double hulls, the yards can save a few tons of steel by pretending that the lightweight is more concentrated near the middle of the ship than it is. Class takes the Sergeant Schultz approach toward the lightweight curve: it knows nussink.

Not surprisingly, the yards have learned how to take advantage of this to build a weaker ship. On our V-Plus class with a lightweight of about 68,000 tons, Daewoo approximated all the steel weight with just five trapezoids — standard practice we were told. The inclining experiment revealed that the actual lightweight was 1,200 tons (about 2%) larger and a remarkable 0.7 m further forward than the design lightweight curve said it should be. The yard made an arbitrary adjustment to this clearly erroneous lightweight curve which added the weight and moved the center of this weight without adjusting the all-important hogging moment. This was accepted by both ABS and LR without any check.

At Samsung, the lightweight curve had this strange peak in the middle. When we asked what it was, we were told that it was the weight of the manifold piping. When we pointed out that the manifold couldn't possibly weight that much, the peak quietly disappeared. Nothing ventured, nothing gained.

In fact, the yards know exactly where all the lightweight is. They carefully calculate the weight and centroid of each of the 250 or so blocks that make up a big tanker. They must do this in order to lift and handle the blocks safely.[14] But these calculations have no impact on the lightweight curve that is used by Class.

When we used the block weights and centers instead of the Class approved pseudo-curve to generate the lightweight curve on the V-Plus, we

---

[14] Actually, the yards know the lightweight distribution well before they calculate the block weights. Modern CAD systems generate accurate estimates of the weight distribution fairly early in the design process.

found that it increased the critical hogging moment by 4%. The yards take advantage of the lack of Class oversight to fraudulently move the lightweight toward midships since they have figured out that on double hulls the decrease in hogging moment saves them more steel than the increase in sagging moment adds.

When I asked one ABS executive why Class allowed the yards to do this, he said "We don't allow it, but we don't check it." If this subtle distinction make sense to you, then you've gone a long way toward understanding the Classification Society approach to tanker newbuilding standards.

5.6 The Misuse of Finite Element Analysis

5.6.1 Pretending Computers Haven't Changed in 25 Years

Once we have a reasonably broad and conservative set of design conditions, we need to translate the resulting loads into actual structure. The main tool we have for this purpose is *finite element* (FE) analysis. For the purposes of this book, you don't need to know what finite element analysis is. All you need to know is that it a computer intensive method which, **properly employed**, allows us to estimate how the stresses flow thru a structure with far better accuracy than we could 25 years ago. The accuracy of the method depends on the *mesh size*, that is, how detailed your description or *model* of the ship is. A smaller mesh size means a better description of the structure but also a big jump in computer time.

When finite element first became feasible 25 or so years ago, computational resources placed a severe restriction on the effort. Because of the computer constraints, Class elected to go with a model that was limited to two or three midships tanks — usually one side only — and a mesh size that was one web frame longitudinally (about 5 m) and three or four stiffeners girth-wise. This was a reasonable decision 25 years ago but it resulted in an extremely limited tool:

1. A tool that could give only a very gross picture of the stresses in the mid body completely ignoring many critical "details" such as web and stringer corners.
2. A tool that required a great deal of judgment in applying boundary conditions, especially at the fore and aft ends.
3. A tool that could not model all sorts of interesting load conditions, including ballast exchange.
4. A tool that said nothing at all about the forebody and the aftbody nor the connections between the middle of the ship and the ends.

(1) was addressed by a second layer of FE models which used the results of the first layer (Phase I) to obtain boundary conditions for much more detailed models (Phase II) which analyzed a single web ring or stringer. Given the limits of the computer in the early 1980's, this was reasonable but the process of converting the Phase I model deflections into Phase II model boundary conditions was labor intensive, error-prone, and required a great deal of judgment. One problem with these judgment calls is that they are subject to commercial pressures and the downratchet. More basically, the process inevitably introduced errors and uncertainty into the analysis.

But a far more fundamental limitation of this approach is that many important problems simply cannot be analyzed at all. Ballast exchange which involves asymmetric loading of tanks extending the full length of the cargo area is an obvious example. On a VLCC at some points in the ballast exchange operation, we have loading conditions that involve more than 5 degrees of heel, and an overall level of torsional stress that the yards estimate is around 15% yield. But these stresses are not included in the design process since the finite element model required by Class can't estimate them.

Still more importantly, the forebody and aftbody are ignored completely. The forebody and aftbody are at least as critical as the midbody. These are areas where we see more problems than the midbody. The forebody is subject to the toughest external loads of any portion of the ship. Deflection in the aft body is critical to the all-important shaft reliability issue. The standard class FE model simply can't address these issues.

By 2000, it was no longer necessary to accept the constraints of this approach. Nor had it been for a long time. Computers are literally a million times more powerful than they were when FE was introduced into the Rules. If you outlined the tanker industry's standard FE model to an aircraft designer at any time from 1995 on, he would either look at you in disbelief or die laughing. The only proper model extent is the full ship. The proper mesh size girthwise is every stiffener (about 1 meter). The proper mesh size longitudinally is every frame, except where the frame spacing is more than three or four meters, it should be every half frame, but in way of the stringers it should be every quarter frame.[15] For the V-Plus, Hellespont belatedly developed a model that almost met this spec. It has about 300,000 nodes. In 2000, it took about two hours to solve a load case on a PC costing less than $4,000. Now it could be done in less than a hour on a computer costing less than $3,000. Such a model is not only now computationally feasible; it's dirt cheap.

Paradoxically, by eliminating all the Phase II work, adopting a full hull model will probably reduce rather than increase design cost. So why did Class stick with finite element models that were 25 years out of date?[16]

The answer is obvious. Better models would mean more steel. Both the yards and Class are using full hull FE models in their research work. If the yards felt they could save some steel by trotting out these models and

---

[15] One can reasonably argue it should be every quarter frame everywhere in the cargo tank length to keep the element aspect ratio nearly square.

[16] Under the new JTP Rules coming into force in 2006, the level of detail of the modelling is considerably improved.[65] But the model extent remains restricted to the midships three tanks. So almost all the above objections still apply. The Joint Tanker Project was a unique opportunity to switch the Rules to a full hull model base; but the downratchet prevailed.

showing the results to Class, you can be certain that the downratchet would assure that this would have happened a long time ago.

5.6.2   Orange instead of Green

A second problem with the industry's use of finite element is the way the results are interpreted. Sometimes our philosophy seems to be: if the stresses come out low, reduce scantlings. If the stress comes out high, it's an artifact of the model. Before finite element analysis came along, naval architects were acutely aware of the fact that they couldn't predict stress with any degree of accuracy. Therefore, for the most part they adopted conservative practice, used upper bound estimates of stress, and were careful not to move very far away from established practice.

But even so we made some mistakes, and came up with some very marginal ships. Under severe economic pressure from the Japanese, the European yards pushed the envelope and made a number of big tankers in the mid-70's that had systemic structural problems. As Section 4.6 chronicles, we've had some of these ships. Some of the failures were fatigue problems but others were more general including systemic cracking in the upper web corners, stringer buckling, etc.

When the first pictures of finite element analysis of tanker structure became available in the early 80's, I was blown away. This effort was spearheaded by Don Liu of ABS.[17] The FE models generate pictures which show stress level in colors: cool colors for low stress areas, and warm colors for the high stress areas. It was amazing; all the green and blue were in areas that had given us no problems; and all the problem areas were yellow and orange. In the usual color scheme, stresses above the legal level are red and stresses just below the legal level are orange. For the first time, we could see the stress flow and understand why we had failures in the corners of the upper webs and problems in the stringer toes. That's where almost all the yellow and orange were. It was obvious that this was a great tool. Now that we knew where all the yellow and orange areas are it would be an easy matter to make them green and blue. In fact, that was Liu's original idea: use finite element only to increase scantlings, and not allow any decreases.

That didn't last long. Instead of making all the orange, green and blue; the downratchet used finite element to make the whole structure orange. This is known as structural optimization. And the yards became very good

---

[17] Liu was involved in pioneering tanker FEA work by Chevron which dates back to the late 1960's.

at optimizing structure.[18] In 1999, when Hellespont went to the yards and told them that we wanted to reduce the maximum design stress by 10% below the stress that Class accepts (roughly make the ship yellow), they found that they had to increase the steel weight by about 7%. In other words, 70% of the structure was in the orange.

This is a prescription for disaster. The models simply aren't that good. Even the fine mesh recommended above leaves out all sorts of important details. And we don't know the loads or stresses that well. Anybody who thinks so should watch the yards during block fit-up. Often this requires a whole series of jacks and wedges and come-alongs. The induced deflection is far more than occurs in any design case. God knows what the residual stresses are.

In 2000, a Chevron VLCC being built at Samsung suffered extensive stringer buckling during the stagger test. In a stagger test, the tanks are filled in a checkerboard fashion to check for leaking welds. This was in calm water before the ship was even delivered. The failure was blamed on moving an access ladder hole from one location to another without redesigning the stringer. But if the structure had been anywhere near robust enough to go to sea, a minor change like this — locally compensated — should have had no effect. When you go to sea you need margins, and we don't have those margins.

Steel is cheap. The marginal cost to the yard of increasing a scantling is normally a good deal less than $500 per ton. If we increase the steel weight of a VLCC by 10% in an efficient manner, we will get a far more robust ship at a cost of about two million dollars, a little over 2%. That's intelligent regulation. We must adopt a more conservative design criteria. I would recommend an average reduction in design stress of at least 10%.

This will get us back to the good ships of the mid-70's, which by the way were not over-built.[19] We saw evidence of this on even the best of our

---

[18] Way too good. A structure can be meshed any number of different ways. The yards are experts at coming up with the model that minimizes calculated stress. And if they can't get the stress down to the number they want, then they go running to Class and ask that element stresses be averaged or in some cases be simply ignored as a model artifact. They never come running to Class pointing out the stresses look suspiciously low.

[19] The DERBYSHIRE was built in the mid-70's. As Faulkner found, she was certainly not over-built.[28, 64] Academicians Paik and Faulkner comment

> Over the period 1955 to 1992 (IACS UR S11), it appears that the allowable stress has slowly increased by about 10% to its present value of about 0.75 yield. No doubt this was mainly due to improved quality control leading to less fatigue, and so forth.[64][page 263]

The 10% deterioration in stress is a lower bound; and, sorry professors, it wasn't improved

mid-70's built ULCC's. Almost all these ships developed some cracks by age 15. In the "good" ships, these cracks were limited to a handful of localized areas. The owners eventually learn where these areas are and expect to have to repair a crack or two in these areas every docking. The mid-70's ships were much weaker than earlier generations. A 40,000 ton tanker built in the late 50's had a bottom plate thickness of about 35 mm. A very good mid-70's 400,000 ton ULCC — ten times larger — had a bottom plate thickness of 28 to 30 mm.

And if we are going to depend on finite element, then we should use the numbers that the FE models generate. There should be no averaging of stress across elements nor any rounding down of scantlings. In absolutely no case, should the design stress be more than yield.

5.6.3 Using Finite Element to Justify Ugly Design

There is an even more basic and pernicious problem with our current use of finite element analysis. Before FE came along, naval architects had to stick to structural concepts that were easy to analyze with the limited tools available. These structures tended to be simple and elegant. At their best, the structure flowed in a regular series of continuous rings — transverse, horizontal and longitudinal. Discontinuities, sharp corners, small radii were studiously avoided for everybody knew they generated high stress concentrations but nobody pretended to know how high.

With the advent of finite element, a new philosophy emerged. At some yards, it's called "design for producability". The idea is to stick together flat plates of steel in whatever way best suits the production process, and then use FE (aggressively interpreted, of course) to beef up the scantlings in the high stress areas that result. The result is complex and hard to follow stress patterns, small inserts of very thick plate, myriad discontinuities and sharp corners, plate thicknesses bouncing all over the place — plug ugly structure which violates the fundamental rules of good design. As the Class rules become more and more FE based, surveyors become more and more helpless to resist this development.

It's far from obvious that the yards gain much from this development. Elegant, simple structures tend to be the most efficient. But it's clear that owners, underwriters and eventually society as a whole lose big time. **We must find a way to align the yard's design objectives with society's.**

---

quality control. It was just the downratchet. Paik and Faulkner correctly argue for a 20% plus increase in ultimate hull strength.

5.7 The Case of the Disappearing Swash Bulkheads

Sloshing, like fatigue cracking and lolling, is another problem that should never have existed for tankers; and in fact never did exist in the pre-Marpol and earlier tankers.

A tank that is neither completely full nor completely empty is like a big basin. If you tilt the tank, the liquid will come flowing down to the low side. If you tilt it back, it will go flowing back to the other side. If you tilt it back and forth at the right interval, this motion quickly builds up to the point that the liquid in the tank is crashing back and forth in a massive wave. This is known as *sloshing resonance.*

Anyone who has carried a half-full basin any distance knows about sloshing resonance. Often the rhythm of your walk is fairly close to sloshing resonance period of the basin. The next thing you know the water is blasting back and forth, and, if you don't stop walking, all the water in the basin will hop out of the container with a big plop. Gold panners learned to control sloshing resonance so that all but the densest bit of material hopped out of the basin. It is not necessary that the back and forth motion be large to make all the liquid in the basin move as a body. What's important is that the back and forth motion be in synch with the time that it takes the liquid to flow back and forth, the so called *natural period* of the container.

For completely different reasons, ships also have natural periods. A ship moving thru waves will tend to pitch and roll at about the same interval almost regardless of what the wave pattern looks like. For a big tanker, this natural pitch period is generally around 13 seconds, depending on the ship's loading pattern. Coincidentally, the natural roll period is very roughly the same, or a few seconds longer.

Transverse sloshing in tanker tanks is rarely a problem. Even the widest tank has a transverse sloshing period of about 3 or 4 seconds, which is more than a factor of two below the ship's natural roll period, and the transverse motion inside the tank never really builds up.

But with the advent of the VLCC and the ULCC, we began to see 50 meter and even 60 m long center tanks. (The wing tanks on the single hull ships were subject to the MARPOL size restriction so they could be no longer than about 25 or 30 m.) These tanks when half-filled had a natural sloshing period, fore and aft, of 12 or 13 seconds, nicely in synch with the ship's natural pitch period.

The designers of these ships were aware of this problem. The solution was simple. They either divided the tank in two longitudinally, generating two half-length tanks. These half-length tanks had a sloshing period of 5 or 6 seconds, well away from the ship's natural pitch period. Or they inserted a *swash bulkhead* half way down the tank. A swash bulkhead is the same as a normal bulkhead but it has a number of small holes in it. The bulkhead is not liquid tight, so we still have a single long tank; but, from the point of view of a wave sloshing fore and aft in the tank, the swash bulkhead is effectively the same as a normal bulkhead. It's as if the tank has been turned into two half-length tanks, as far as sloshing is concerned. Either solution guarantees that the tanks never operate at sloshing resonance.

For double hulls VLCC's which are exempt from some of the MARPOL cargo tank size restrictions both the center and wing tanks are 50 meters or so long. In the original double hull VLCC's built in the early 1990's, these tanks were fitted with swash bulkheads. So far so good. Then the yards started playing downratchet games. The little holes in the swash bulkheads became bigger holes. The yards offered extensive direct analysis to show that it didn't really make that much difference. Then the bigger holes became a single massive hole in the top half of the bulkhead. The yards argued that sloshing was really only a problem when the tank was half-full or less, and in this case, the half-bulkhead would be nearly as effective as a full swash bulkhead. Then the half-bulkhead became little more than an oversized web frame. The yards argued that this was nearly as effective as a half-bulkhead because the tie-bars (beams stretching across the tank at about half-height) would break up the liquid motion, and beside they would beef up the structure at the ends of the tank to take the additional sloshing loads. By 2000, the swash bulkheads had just about disappeared.

In the mid-70's no one would even think about designing a tank to operate anywhere near sloshing resonance. But over the years, Class has allowed the swash bulkhead to atrophy and then disappear. The argument is that we can operate these tanks at resonance because we can predict the forces and beef up the structure to handle them.

This argument is a sad joke on a number of levels. Nobody has any way of accurately estimating sloshing forces at resonance, certainly not Class. The best of the current lot of Class tools is probably LRFLUIDS. When Daewoo applied LRFLUIDS to the case of the V-Plus' 64 meter long center tank, the program indicated that at resonance the tie beams would impose an important dampening on the sloshing. ABS's empirical gouge said the same thing. In 2001, the state of the art in sloshing analysis was the Hamburg Ship Research Institute's program which implemented a full two phase Navier-Stokes but only 2-D. Despite being 2-D, this is an extremely computationally intensive program. One run simulating a little over one minute in real time took a cluster of 8 Dual-Pentium PC's over two days to compute. The results showed that at resonance the tie beams will have almost no effect on sloshing. The basic wave form is a kind of U that sneaks under the tie-beams as it moves from one end of the tank to the other, not a sort of semi-harmonic wave as Class claims. (Any housewife who has had water slosh out of a basin could have told us the same thing.) The Hamburg results are far closer to reality but the people at Hamburg will be the first to tell you that they cannot accurately predict the loads imposed on the structure. But when this wave crashes into a bulkhead, it climbs over 15 m into the air.

The only reasonable thing to do is to stay away from sloshing resonance. And that means real swash bulkheads, not overgrown webs. And once you have real swash bulkheads, the move to oil-tight and far better sub-division is obvious. More, smaller tanks means better spill resistance, and far more flexibility in cargo parcels, ballast exchange, and tank inspection.

IMO has developed a series of methods to evaluate a tanker's propensity to spill cargo in the event of hull damage. The original method was aimed only at single hulls. It is badly biased against double sided and double bottom ships. In 1997, IMO corrected this by adopting a new method that was ridiculously biased in favor of double hulls. See Section D.2. All the IMO methods are biased against big ships in favor of smaller.

The original IMO method is reasonably fair in comparing single hulls against other single hulls of about the same size. It is based on a hypothetical collision and a hypothetical grounding. The collision involves a wedge penetrating into the hull about $B/5$ where B is the ship's beam. The grounding involves damage from the bottom up to about $B/15$. The collision/grounding is assumed to be equally likely to occur anywhere along the ship's side/bottom. The overall result of this analysis is the ship's Effective Oil Spill (EOS) number, which is the percentage of the ship's cargo which will be spilled on average given the IMO collision/grounding scenario. This IMO method is far from perfect but it is a reasonable starting point for evaluating a single hull's resistance to spillage.

Table 5.1 shows the IMO Effective Oil Spill numbers for four different pre-Marpol VLCC's and ULCC's all built in the mid 70's, and a typical single hull Marpol VLCC built in 1986. Under the regulations adopted after the Exxon Valdez spill, from age 25 on, the pre-Marpol ships must operate under either

IMO REG 13G4 30% of the side or bottom tanks non-cargo, usually but not quite correctly called called segregated ballast, or

IMO REG 13G7 usually known as Hydrostatically Balanced Loading (HBL).
See Appendix C for the simple, if sometimes surprising, world of hydrostatic balance. To over-simplify, an HBL tank is under-loaded to
the point where it will not spill oil from bottom damage.

For these ships, Table 5.1 shows the EOS numbers for each of these regulatory regimes. Table 5.1 makes a number of points including:

Table 5.1: IMO Effective Oil Spill Numbers
Arab Light, Summer Marks

| Design | Percent Cargo Spilled | | | Number of |
	As-built	13G7	13G4	Cargo Tanks
Hellespont Embassy, 1976	2.1	1.8	2.2	34 five across
Empress des Mer, 1976	2.6	2.2	2.4	35 three across
Shell L-Class, 1974	3.6	3.1	3.7	22 three across
Ludwig VLCC, 1974	3.4	2.9	3.3	22 three across
Typical Marpol Single Hull, 1986	4.3			13 three across

1. In terms of expected spillage, 13G7 is clearly superior to 13G4. 13G4
   involves keeping a number of tanks totally empty, which lifts the ship
   out of the water, while the remaining tanks are filled right up to the
   brim. From a spill minimization point of view, this is exactly the
   wrong way to go. See Sections C.2 and C.3. As Table 5.1 shows,
   often a ship will have a higher EOS number under 13G4 than if IMO
   Regulation 13G never existed. Talk about unintended consequences.
   13G4 also involves higher loss in carrying capacity than 13G7, less flexibility in multi-parcel loads, very high stresses, and most importantly
   ***putting ballast in tanks that were not designed to handle sea
   water***. As we saw in Chapter 2, sea water in unprotected tanks as
   a result of conversion to segregated ballast was the cause of both the
   ERIKA and PRESTIGE spills.
   However, very few pre-Marpol tankers used 13G7 when they turned
   25. Almost all used 13G4. The Tromedy in action.[20]

---

[20] The reason was that some charterers had a clear preference for 13G4 even though they
were aware of all of this. BP made "no HBL ships" an explicit rule. Chevron had a similar
policy, despite the fact they were using HBL on their own ships. The oil companies felt
they would get less flack if a "segregated ballast" ship had a spill than if a "hydrostatically
balanced" ship had a spill. It just sounded better. When I complained, one oil company

2. The Marpol single hulls have terrible EOS numbers. Like 13G4 ships, Marpol tankers operate with about a third of their tanks completely empty and the rest filled to the brim. The difference is that the designers reacted to the MARPOL requirements by making the ships very tall and the tanks very big, both of which exacerbate spillage further. One can argue that this was an acceptable price to pay to obtain segregated ballast. I find such an argument unconvincing. The nearly new EXXON VALDEZ would have spilled about ten million liters less oil if she had been an older ship.[21] In the Marpol single hull, the Tromedy came up with just about the worst spiller one can reasonably imagine.

But for present purposes, the interesting feature of Table 5.1 is the wide range in expected spillage under 13G7 for the pre-Marpol ships. Despite the method's bias against big ships, **the Hellespont Embassy spills 65% less than the L-class in the same casualty scenario.** The other two pre-Marpol ships are in between with the Empress des Mer much closer to the Embassy and the Ludwig V's much closer to the L-class.

This is a product of small tank size. The Embassy and the Empress des Mer have a lot more tanks than the other two designs. The Empress, which was built to the Marpol/73 restriction on tank size, has 13 pairs of wing tanks; the Shell L-class has 8. And in the case of the five across Embassy, the tanks are much more intelligently arranged.

The tragedy is that the big improvement associated with more smaller tanks costs very little. Shorter tanks mean:

1. sloshing forces are markedly reduced which saves steel,
2. much more importantly, a far more even distribution of transverse forces to the side shell and far better ability to withstand asymmetric loading and racking forces.

An egg carton is a very efficient structure. Cut out every other transverse corrugation and then see what you have to do to get the strength back. Because of the increased efficiency of the structure, limiting tank size doesn't require that much extra steel.

The Empress' lightweight, 60,656 tons, is nearly the same as other ULCC's of the same size with larger tanks built a year or two earlier. The Embassy's lightweight, 57,628 tons, is actually a bit smaller than other good pre-Marpol tankers of her size but it is easily the best tanker structure I have ever seen.

---

executive told me "he was managing perceptions, not ships".

Our old ships all went HBL.

[21] See Section C.3.

When we reluctantly scrapped the Embassy at age 27, we had not found a single crack anywhere in her hull structure. She is an instructive exception to the even-good-ships-have-a-few-cracks philosophy accepted by Class. In other words, small tank size is not expensive. My kind of regulation: substantial effect on spillage at nil economic cost.

In the case of current massive double hull tanks, we have just the opposite effect: immense forces in the critical lower hopper area near the transverse bulkheads, in way of the centerline buttress, and at the stringer corners and web toes, despite the Class Rules' staying away from any really difficult loading condition. The bottom bracket of the centerline buttress on the V-Plus has a 57 mm web and a 60 mm faceplate, both High Tensile Steel. The center tank lower web toes have 50 mm faceplates. That's way too much stress in one place.

Everyone at ABS and LR I have talked to off the record about the swash bulkhead issue thinks it's absolutely nuts to build 50 meter long tanks without a swash bulkhead. So how did we end up in such an imprudent situation? We already know the answer "the direct analysis downratchet". The disappearance of the swash bulkheads is one of the most dramatic examples of the downratchet in action that I have come across.[22]

---

[22] When we speced the 440,000 ton V-Plus, we had no idea the yard, Daewoo, would attempt to build a 64 m long tank without a swash bulkhead. Such a crazy notion never crossed our minds. When we belatedly realized the yard's intentions, I was aghast. But the contract was already signed. Our protests to the yard were politely refused. The first V-Plus was a Lloyds ship. I went to Lloyds and told them this was unacceptable. They agreed it was "bad practice", but the precedent had been set on earlier ships and there was nothing they could do. I made the specious argument that the precedent had been set on VLCC's not ULCC's. But they were not prepared to upset their long-standing relationship with Daewoo.

Under the contract both LR and ABS had to approve the drawings. So I went to Bob Somerville, the President of ABS. I told him that this was ridiculously imprudent and by the way, if ABS required swash bulkheads on the V-Plus as part of their plan review, I would award them the second ship at Daewoo. Somerville went to his top structures guy, Don Liu, and asked him if the ship should have swash bulkheads. Liu said of course. The word went down that the plan reviewers should require the swash bulkheads.

The yard was livid. On several occasions thereafter Somerville complained to me about "how much it had cost ABS to 'give' us the swash bulkheads" indicating that Daewoo had successfully pressured one owner to switch a six ship order away from ABS. He was attempting to talk me into giving ABS the last two V-Plus hulls, as a reward for ABS's selfless sacrifice. But I'm sure he was telling the truth.

This is how the Tromedy works.

5.8   Calibration Factors

Buried in the Class Rules are a bunch of numbers that don't make any physical sense. We've already seen one case in the 0.9 factor that ABS inserted in the sloshing force calculations. The idea is that our design method is too conservative so we need to "calibrate" it to actual experience. In practice, this means that some other Class has used a less conservative method, and so far nothing terrible seems to have happened. This is a horrible design philosophy, and an open invitation to commercial pressures, precisely what happened in the ABS design cargo density situation. The change wasn't based on anything other than the other Class Rules required less steel.

Here's a more egregious case. Class claims that it designs the ship on a 20 year basis, that is to the situation which has a probability of 0.5 of being encountered in twenty years.[23] This in itself is a revealingly strange philosophy. It implies that a ship should be built to last only twenty years. But even if you accept this open invitation to shoddy construction, do you want to design so that there is 50% chance that the ship won't make it to age 20? Suppose you knew that every airplane was going to be scrapped at age 20. Would you accept a 50% chance that it would break in two in flight before then? A 1% chance maybe, 5% if you really want to be imprudent, but not 50%.

In fact, the ships are not designed to even this dubious criterion. For example, when you go into the Rules, both ABS and LR, they say "compute the design sloshing forces on the basis of a pitch that is 60% of the 20 year pitch". I've asked a number of ABS and LR people where this 60% came from and got either blank stares or a semi-circular argument to the effect that this is the way the Rules have been and we haven't seen any real problems yet. Forget the fact that we only recently got rid of the swash bulkheads on big tankers and most cargo tanks are not slack most of the time, so we have no real experience. The point is that the ship is not being designed on the basis of the 20 year encounter, but something much less.

There are many other calibration factors hidden throughout the Rules. I'm sure there are many I don't know about. Class is so good at hiding stuff, that it's not just outsiders that are in the dark. A rational regulatory process would get rid of all calibration factors unless they are strongly supported by experimental evidence from carefully designed and publicly documented tests. And then make sure that these remaining calibration factors are very publicly documented, so owners who would prefer not to use them are alerted to their existence.

---

[23] The new JTP Rules talk about a 25 year design life. But they use the same probability of encounter, 10^{-8}, as the old Rules. There has not been any real change in this regard.

5.9 Forebody and Aftbody

Calibration factors are rampant in the forebody rules. In part this is because the finite element models haven't as a matter of course extended to this part of the hull. In part, it is because the forces, especially in the forebody are particularly difficult to predict. This means we should be particularly conservative.

Unfortunately, this is not the case. Class goes to some trouble to estimate peak slamming pressures and then immediately applies a bunch of calibration factors of unknown or dubious origin.[24] In many cases, the resulting scantlings are lower than the less highly loaded structure in the midbody. The result is that forebody damage is still the most common form of structural failure.

Another big problem is structural continuity. Hellespont was amazed to find out that the yards felt no compulsion to extend the main horizontal members, the inner bottom and the double side stringers, into the forebody or aft body in any reasonably continuous manner. Most were abruptly ended with minimal scarfing brackets and new flats and decks placed at whatever level suited the yard in the ends of the ships.

At the aft end, longitudinal bulkheads deteriorate abruptly into a series of widely spaced pillars with no shear strength whatsoever. The yards argue that this is required by machinery arrangement issues but both the Hellespont V and U have real longitudinal bulkheads extending to the aft peak tank and the engine room works just fine. Even the upper deck is abruptly ended, usually just aft of the accommodations with a big increase in vertical deflection.

Transversely, the engine room is inherently weak due both to the narrow sterns now being used and the large hole in the structure forced by the main engine. There is essentially no transverse structure between the forward and aft engine room bulkheads in the centerline third of the ship. Once again the yards claim that this is required by machinery arrangement. In fact, the web just aft of the main engine and just forward of the boilers and generators could be effectively filled in without affecting the engine room operation.

Class seems to have no rules that prevent this. They even allowed upper deck stiffeners to be cut at the pump room bulkhead in direct violation of the rules for primary longitudinal members. The argument seems to be

---

[24] Slamming occurs when the ship's bow comes out of the water and then smashes into the sea.

these are not high stress areas so we don't have to worry about it.[25] But the fact is that the stresses are not even analyzed. And the best way to turn an area that should not be a problem into a problem is with structure that violates basic principles of good design.

Another big problem in the aft body is hull deflection and its impact on shaft and engine bearing loads. Amazingly, Class doesn't even require this deflection to be calculated, despite the fact that there have been a rash of stern tube bearing failures and the repair yards are reporting very rapid weardown of VLCC shaft bearings. Needless to say shaft bearing reliability is absolutely crucial to these single screw ships.

One way to reduce hull deflection in way of the shaft would be to extend the main deck aft. The yards have fallen into the bad habit of stopping the main deck at the aft side of the accommodations. This not only makes the hull aft of this point more limber; but also puts a bad kink in the deflection curve in way of the main engine. I suspect but can't prove that some of the V-Plus' main engine problems may have been abetted by this kink. Our liner failure and most of the crankshaft bearing failures were in this area. Anyway it is very bad design.

Class' basic posture toward the aftbody is less-than-benign neglect.

---

[25] Class has conveniently forgotten about the Bridge class. These OBO's: Tyne Bridge, Kowloon Bridge, et al had interrupted longitudinal members at the pump room bulkhead. All but one had serious to debilitating cracking in this area. The exception was the DERBYSHIRE. She didn't have time to display this cracking. She sank with the loss of 44 lives after trading only three years.

Great Britain was the Flag State. It issued a standard Flag State report: bad weather, just one of those things. The ship's Classification Society, Lloyds Register, agreed. But the father of one of the crew was a ship surveyor. Being a Tromedy insider, he knew about the Bridge class cracking. He naturally figured the cause was cracking in way of the pump room. He and other relatives mobilized public support and eventually two underwater surveys were undertaken. It turned out the problem was not pump room cracking. It was either woefully under-designed (but Class legal) hatch covers[28] or buckling of the bottom plating.[64] Neither aspects of the ship structure could be expected to survive even a moderately bad Pacific storm. Sometimes the ships are so bad, you don't know which part of the Rules to blame.

5.10 Welding

Welding is one of the more dramatic examples of the deterioration in new-building standards since the 1970's. It seems that most of this deterioration took place in the 1980's. In 1990, Exxon rather courageously allowed me to inspect the EXXON VALDEZ in the drydock in San Diego about nine months after the grounding. The real eye opener was not the damage, as extensive as it was, but the welding. Just about everywhere in the damaged areas the stiffener webs had pulled cleanly out of the welds leaving the welds on the shell plating. The welds were tiny. They looked like continuous tack welds.

This structure never had a chance at resisting the ship's riding up on Bligh Reef. As soon as the stiffeners popped out of the tiny welds, all the strength in the structure disappeared. In many cases the stiffeners themselves were hardly deformed at all. They never came into play. When I asked the Exxon superintendent if these little welds were legal, he angrily nodded yes.

In the bad old days, the standard filet welds in a large tanker cargo tank had a throat thickness of 6.4 mm (9 mm leg length). Under current rules, much of the filet welding in the tank area has a required throat thickness of 3.2 to 4.0 mm. And Class allows the yards a 10% negative margin. (This is explicitly written into the IACS "Quality" Standards.) So often the actual weld is less than 3 mm throat. To expect any penetration at all with such welds is crazy talk. Those are the welds I saw in San Diego. Miniscule.[26]

And senseless. The yards can easily lay down 5 mm plus throat welds with a single pass. When Hellespont asked the yard to increase all welds in the V-Plus cargo tank area to 5.3 mm throat — after the contract had been signed — the price was $44,000; and it cost the yard far less. Bigger welds would cost almost nothing. Whatever argument — probably nothing more than the downratchet — led to the current weld sizes, it should be abandoned. Welds corrode much more rapidly than the other steel. And as the Valdez showed, these tiny welds fall apart on impact.[27]

---

[26] The new JTP Rules will have a minimum throat of 4.2 mm, 3.8 mm after we apply IACS quality. A much too small step in the right direction.

[27] Among other things, this kind of welding makes a mockery of so-called grounding resistant structure. A great deal of effort has gone into analyzing energy absorption in a grounding and designing structure to absorb this energy with less damage. In my view this effort is misplaced on at least three levels:

    1. The analysis is hopelessly artificial. For example, in many cases the bottom is modeled as a cone. There is not a great deal of reason to expect structure that is designed to work against a cone will do much good when the ships hits a real bottom such as Bligh Reef.

Double hulls generate welding problems we never had to face in the single hulls. A particularly critical weld is at the lower hopper corner. First problem is that this weld is difficult to do because of the restricted space. The only reasonably sure way of laying down the root pass is manually (semi-automatic in yard parlance). This should be a requirement. Otherwise it is nearly certain that the root pass will not fill in the bottom of the notch.

BP built a series of four VLCC's as Samsung in 1998 and 1999. Toward the end of the program, ultrasonic testing revealed some flaws in the hopper weld. When they gouged out the area, they found a series of voids in the bottom of the notch. At great expense, the yard had to redo all the hopper welds. I don't think these ships were unique. I think the BP guys did a better than average job of inspecting this weld.

However, the biggest problem is that a great deal of stress is trying to turn a corner at this weld. I have no idea why we don't roll this corner as if it were the bilge radius. But if we are going to have a sharp corner and a natural stress concentrator, we must radius the weld very carefully.

Given a series of failures in hopper welds in double hull tankers operating in the North Sea, LR is finally starting to address this issue. LR performed a super detailed FEM of the hopper corner with a mesh size of T/12 where T is the thickness of the inner bottom. Unsurprisingly, the minimum radius of the weld is critical to the maximum stress in the corner. With a "Class standard" weld, the max stress was 660 N/mm2, ***almost three times yield***. In laymen's terms, the computed stresses in the area were three times those required to permanently deform the steel. No wonder the hopper welds were failing.

Another area where the Rules have fallen apart is post-weld heat treatment. The most egregious case I know of is Daewoo's refusing our Lloyd's surveyor's request to stress relieve the critical welds between the upper rudder casting and pintle casting to the 82 mm thick plate that connects them on the V-Plus.[28] The yard was just following standard practice these days. In

---

2. Far more importantly, the energy that results in the loss of a ship in a grounding and a brobdingnagian spill (e.g. TORREY CANYON, AMOCO CADIZ, BRAER, URQUIOLA, AEGEAN SEA, etc) is not the ship's kinetic energy. It comes from the subsequent pounding by the sea or the cargo exploding. In many of these spills, the ship drifted ashore, not at the speeds TRB analyzed.

3. Regulation should be focused on preventing the grounding in the first place, not going after at best modest reductions in spillage in low to medium impact groundings.

But one thing is sure. With welds like these, there will be nil energy absorption regardless of how the steel is arranged.

[28] This request was refused despite a haphazard welding sequence which thermally

defiance of good engineering practice ***even for non-critical areas***, stress relief is no longer required under either ABS or LR Rules. In this case, the LR surveyor, Richard Beckett, strenuously and courageously objected. But Lloyds failed to support its own surveyor when the yard pointed out that stress relief was not explicitly required by the Rules. Not only are the days when the surveyor's word was law long since gone; the yard put Lloyds on notice that the surveyor's behavior was unacceptable and asked for his dismissal. In the yards' view, the surveyor has no right to require anything that is not explicitly in the Rules. Sadly that's essentially the Societies' position as well.

Hellespont had to pay extra for the heat treatment. The cost was trivial, $2,000. The yard was just making the point that a surveyor had no right to exercise his judgment. Obviously, if a yard doesn't have to heat treat this critical weld, there are almost no welds that it does. In the 1970's, Class required stress relief on all welds in excess of 40 mm thickness. The downratchet has been working big time in this area.

---

cycled the thick steel several times.

5.11   The Stern Tube Bearing Saga

Propeller shafting is a graphic example of the Tromedy's dangerous short-sightedness.[29] On tankers, the aft end of the propeller shaft rides in a large bearing called the stern tube bearing. There were at least eight stern tube bearing failures *on brand new VLCC's* while we were in Korea. A stern tube bearing failure generally leaves a single screw ship adrift and helpless. The only good thing about these particular failures is that they occurred so rapidly — in two cases before the ship was delivered — that the ships had not yet loaded oil. These failures are shown in Table 5.2. When I was

Table 5.2: Known Sterntube bearing failures on Brand-new VLCC's

YARD	HULL NO	DATE
DHI	5109	1998-08-17
HHI	1089	1998-05-08
HHI	1090	1998-07-03
DHI	5120	1999-01-05
DHI	5121	1999-01-28
HHI	1164	1999-10-26
SHI	1241	1999-12-02
SHI	1241	1999-12-02

still active in tankers, it was a rare month in which I did not hear reports or rumors of yet another shafting problem on young VLCC's. On several occasions, I was told by the repair yards that new VLCC's were showing up at their first docking with very rapid bearing weardown. In July, 2001, HHI 1090 was again out of service with major stern tube bearing problems. Thanks to the Tromedy's ability to hide its problems, we can be sure there were many shafting problems I didn't hear anything about.

A stern tube bearing can either be made of a fiber-reinforced composite or steel faced with a tin alloy called white-metal. In the old days, most first class owners favored the more expensive composite, in part because if the bearing became flooded with salt water it would continue to operate for a considerable length of time, while the metal bearing would quickly corrode and fail. Since all the Table 5.2 failures involved composite rather than white metal bearings, the immediate reaction was that there was something wrong

---

[29] See Devanney and Kennedy[23] for a much more complete description of this problem and the closely related issue of shaft alignment.

with the composite material. Several owners replaced a newer composite material with a composite material that had proven itself for over 25 years in hundreds of large tankers, and which in the opinion of most of the tanker industry including myself was superior to white metal. Two of these proven bearings failed almost immediately.

Attention then turned to alignment. This was a natural assumption. The Class approved alignment procedure used by the yards is very crude. Over the years, the yards had somehow received Class permission to bore the stern tube at the block stage, then weld the stern tube block in place, align by piano wire with the ship still on blocks, and hope. In fact, until the new LR limit on misalignment came into force in 2001, there are no concrete requirements with respect to alignment at all. It was suspected correctly that the yards were taking advantage of the Rules and the self-aligning characteristics of the composite bearings to be very sloppy in alignment. However in late 1999, LR itself carefully aligned two shafts using modern strain gauging techniques with the ship afloat at maximum alongside draft. Both these bearings failed before the ship completed trials. Alignment may be lousy but it was clearly not the root cause.

The Tromedy's "solution" to the problem is to use white metal bearings and high volume, forced lubrication in place of the traditional oil bath system. This is a dangerous work-around, not a solution. The repair yards are reporting rapid weardown in the white metal bearings. It's only a matter of time before they begin failing. High pressure lubrication is an invitation to blown stern-tube seals, and more importantly forces the the crews to make an impossible choice. If a stern tube seal starts leaking on a ship — and this happens fairly frequently (see Section 4.4) — the crew's normal response is to reduce the pressure in the stern tube lube oil system to nearly the same as the external sea water pressure. In an old style oil bath lubricating system, this generally halts the leak with nil increase in the chance of a bearing failure. If the crews attempt this with the current forced lubrication system, they face a high risk of a disabling bearing failure. But if they don't reduce the lube oil pressure, they face the certainty of a large fine (if not detention) at the next port, and a very displeased employer.[30]

So what is the real cause of the bearing failures? As Table 5.3 shows, over the last twenty five years, shaft diameters have decreased by at least fifteen

---

[30] Here's a confident prediction. When we have the first massive stern tube bearing spill, the investigation will reveal that the crew reduced the stern tube lube oil pressure. All will agree that this terrible lapse of judgement was the cause of the spill. The Captain and Chief Engineer will spend some time in jail. The Tromedy will impose more detailed paperwork procedures to prevent this sort of human error in the future.

percent for the same torque. This is a product of both higher strength material and the downratchet.   Since shaft bending goes as diameter to the fourth power, the net effect is that bending within the bearing itself has increased by more than 75% for the same propeller weight. At the same time, propellers have become bigger and heavier due to the decrease in main engine RPM.

Table 5.3: Reduction in Shaft Diameter, 1975-1999

SHIP	SHP	RPM	DIAM (mm)	Comment
Embassy, 1976	45,000	85	1,010	Smooth turbine torque
VLCC, 1999	44,640	76	820	Large torque pulses

There are no Class restrictions on shaft bending within the bearing. However, there is one Class that has the capability to study at least a part of this problem. Bureau Veritas (BV) has a program which has the ability to model bending within the bearing and determine the resulting pressure distribution and oil film thicknesses within the bearing. Figure 5.1 shows a typical result. Figure 5.1 is based on an alignment that was acceptable to class on the grounds that the misalignment at the aft end of the bearing was small (1.0e-4 radians) and the nominal pressure (bearing load versus overall bearing area) was a reasonably conservative 6.3 bar, well below the Class limit of 9.0 bar. But what counts is the distribution of the pressure within the bearing and the standard Class approved method simply cannot address that issue. In this case, the BV results show the pressure on the aft 10% of the bearing averages 140 bar, well over BV's recommended (and none too conservative) maximum of 100 bar. At this pressure, the lubricating film thickness is a miniscule 31 microns.

Figure 5.1 is the reason why the composite bearings failed immediately while the white metal bearings have taken longer. There is only one area where white metal bearings are better than composite; but in that area they are far better.   That area is heat conductivity. The conductivity of white metal is over 30 times higher than that of the composite material. The composite bearing relies on the lubricating fluid to conduct away the 7.5 KW of heat generated in a VLCC stern tube bearing. But most of that heat is generated in the high pressure portion of the bearing where the film thickness is much too thin to do the job. The composite bearing burns out almost immediately. White metal has a great deal more ability to conduct

Figure 5.1: Sterntube bearing pressure and oil film thickness

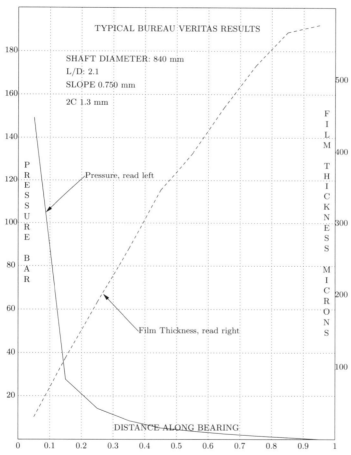

FIGURE 13.1 AFT STERN TUBE BEARING PRESSURE AND FILM THICKNESS

the heat away itself, so there is no immediate burn out despite the thin film thickness. But that doesn't change the fact that the pressures are very high, in fact far above the yield point of the white metal. Rapid weardown will occur, and premature failure is inevitable. We will see a lot of VLCC's dead in the water due to bearing failures. The only real question is: how many will drift ashore?[31]

There's a twin lesson for regulation in the bearing failure saga.

1. When the problem surfaced, the yards responded with alacrity **because the failures occurred during the warranty period or earlier**. The yards were on the hook, so they quickly came up with a solution.

2. However, **the solution was designed only to get the ships through the warranty period** (generally one year) or at least make the crews the culprit for failing to maintain lube oil pressure.

The solution was only a solution as far as the yards were concerned. But that was good enough for the Tromedy.

---

[31] Hellespont decided to go with a 15% thicker shaft than Class requires. This brings the shaft diameter almost back to the standards of the 1970's and reduces bending in the bearing by over 70%. With this system we were able to get the maximum local pressure according to BV down to 50 bar from 165 bar. It also allowed us to go to a two bearing system, to obtain the flexibility we needed with respect to bending moment and shear force at the main engine coupling. Since this was not required by the Rules and, due to lack of foresight on our part, had to be implemented with a change order, the yard charged us an extra $106,000. The actual marginal cost to the yard was far less than $50,000.

However, when you make this necessary change, you must be careful to beef up the hull structure in way of the shaft. It is essential that the hull be stiffer than the shaft, lest the changes in hull deflection between sagging and hogging impose large local loads on the bearings. On a VLCC, this will require 100 to 200 tons of extra steel in the aft end of the ship, at a marginal cost of about $75,000.

5.12   Crankshaft Bearings and Bearing Girders

There are any number of other machinery problems I could cite. The down-ratchet works everywhere. In Section 3.5.3, we talked about the V-Plus loss of power incidents including a catastrophic cylinder liner failure. But to me the most disturbing V-Plus problem was the five main crankshaft bearing failures in ten ship-years. If a brand new ship can have bearing problems like these, what does that say about an older ship. The Sulzer technicians we called in were not surprised. One commented "you have to expect bearing failures in these new engines". We had the material of our failed bearings analyzed. There was nothing wrong with it. The bearings were simply under-designed.

As the Sulzer tech remark hints, on our mid-70's built diesel driven ships, we rarely if ever saw a crankshaft bearing failure unless the crew screwed up. Why do we have this problem now?

The cause is a variant on the downratchet called cost-down/re-rate. The latest generation of tanker main engines, designed in the mid 1980's, adopted a very aggressive design philosophy. This included using cylinder pressures and temperatures never used in tanker service before. All these engines had lots of teething problems; but, after a series of modifications, a marginal level of reliability was achieved.[32]

As soon as that happens, it is time to *cost-down* and *re-rate*. Cost-down is the process of going through the design and finding items that are "over-designed". For example, Sulzer determined that the original bearing girder design on its VLCC main engine was needlessly conservative. The *bearing girder* is the slab on which each main crankshaft bearing rests. It looks something like the part of a guillotine you put your neck into. These cast slabs are welded into the engine bedplate. A 7 cylinder engine will have 9 bearing girders. Sulzer came up with a thinner bearing girder with sharper corners, saving maybe a few hundred dollars per bearing girder. Class approved.

At about the same time the engine was re-rated. The maximum power was increased by about 6% from 3,837 KW per cylinder at 74 RPM to 4,161 KW at 76 RPM. This was done with a stroke of the pen. Change a few control settings to allow a higher cylinder pressure and slightly higher RPM,

---

[32] The long tanker market slump in the 1980's meant that the engines were rarely used at full power during that period. When tanker rates are very low, it pays an owner to *slow-steam* since the loss in revenues is less than the savings in fuel. But as soon as the market tightens up, he wants to go as fast as he can. The performance of the engines during the slump was misleading.

and presto a more powerful engine, with no increase in cost, thereby keeping
the engine "competitive". Class had no problem with this.

Of course, stresses, pressures, inertial forces, temperatures are all increased; but hey the engine sort of held together at the last rating. Time
to push the envelope a bit. And if the crankshaft bearings start failing,
it's only two thousand dollars per bearing. There probably will only be a
couple of failures per ship in the warranty period. Cost of doing business.[33]

Alas, Sulzer's pushing the envelope on the bearing girders turned out to
be a disaster. In early 1999, rumors began circulating of big problems in
tankers with recently built Sulzer engines. Despite the fact that is in everybody's interest — where everybody is defined to be the yard, the engine
licensor, the actual engine builder, the ship's Class and the owner — to keep
problems quiet, it became semi-public that 10 VLCC's had had cracks in a
total of 21 bearing girders.[34] All these ships were fitted with the Sulzer engine with the re-designed bearing girder. Sulzer blamed the Korean builders
for casting defective bearing girders and in fact the Korean casting quality
was lousy. The Koreans responded that they had cast the girders to Sulzer
specs and with Sulzer quality control.[35]

What a mess. The only way to fix the problem was to replace the 250 ton
bedplate for which there was no provision in the engine room design. The
whole engine room had to be taken apart. Ships had to go into the yard for a
multi-month, multi-million dollar repair, all to save a few thousand dollars
per ship.[36] This problem resulted in no spills, so it never received any

---

[33] At least two loaded VLCC crankshaft failures have become public: the
Front Tobago in May, 2002 and the Orpheus Asia in July, 2002. In the case of the
Orpheus Asia, she drifted for thirty hours, before a tug could take her under tow. By
then she was within twenty miles of going aground in Taiwan. I don't know the details,
but I would not be surprised if these were bearing related.

[34] The bearing girder problem was first discovered on a Shell tanker named the Murex,
the fourth to bear that illustrious name. The original Murex was still going strong at age
24 when she was sunk by a U-boat. The most recent Murex lasted less than five years
before she had to have her main engine essentially replaced.

[35] Fortunately, we heard about this problem in time to insist on the original bearing
girder design, cast in Japan with better quality control. Sulzer never admitted they had
made a mistake, but they eventually went back to the original design as well.

[36] I don't mean to point a finger at Sulzer here. The problem is the Tromedy. Competition without regulation guarantees that the other major engine "manufacturer", MAN-
B&W, is no better. Thanks to the Tromedy's code of omerta, it is impossible to obtain
real casualty data. But I do know of at least one MAN bedplate replacement — the Texaco
Suezmax Ohio Star in Singapore in April-June 2000 — with rumors of five more. Talking
to the Korean yards, it is clear that the MAN engines are very sensitive to bedplate deflection and attendant bearing problems. Maersk is a very large tanker/containershipowner.
They probably operate more big two-stroke diesel engines than anybody in the world.

attention outside tanker circles. But it is a accurate indicator of the Class approved design philosophy which permeates both tanker hull and tanker machinery.[37]

In private communications, they talk about MAN engines with connecting rod problems, thrust bearing problems, and more crank case explosions due to bearing failures on MAN engines than Sulzer. And yet the brand new, Sulzer engined, V-Plus had five main bearing failures in ten ship-years!

[37] We were so chastened by our experience with modern main engines, we decided to do a little re-rating ourselves. Our V-Plus crews were instructed to never operate our engines at more than 85% the misnamed Maximum Continuous Rating. We never had to do something like this with our old turbine ships.

5.13   The 15% Rule

I could go on and on. The downratchet works everywhere. Rudder stock dimensions, steering gear torque,[38] propeller blades, ridiculously optimistic electric power loads resulting in the requirement to keep two generators on-line when the reliability analysis assumes that only one will be needed,[39] awkward and dangerous outfitting including **pump room ventilation ducts that don't go to the pump room bottom**,[40] etc, etc. But I'm sure you are getting as bored with this litany as I am.

Table 5.4 shows one last example: main engine shaft couplings. We are

Table 5.4: Deterioration in Main Shaft Couplings, 1975 to 2001

	1975	2000
Power	45,000 SHP	44,640 BHP
RPM	85	76
Engine Torque Pulse	nil	80%
Flange Thickness	220 mm	140 mm
Coupling Bolts	14 x 150 mm conical	12 x 95 mm reamer

not talking about losing 15 to 20% here. We are talking about losing 150 to 200% despite the much harsher design conditions associated with the diesel

---

[38] The rudder/steering gear design method Class uses is inherently optimistic on top of which it is based on the ship's service speed. A tanker's top calm water speed is more than a knot faster than the service speed at which point the forces on the rudder are at least 15% higher than those it was designed for. For the V-Plus the standard naval architectural rudder design method yields a design torque of 970 ton-meters.[44][page 383] The LR design torque was 780 ton-meters. True to the tradition of the AMOCO CADIZ, the ABS design torque was a puny 590 ton-meters.

[39] On the Samsung VLCC, Class approved a 980 kilowatt generator. We found we needed 1260 KW to ensure that in nearly all normal operations only one generator would have to be on-line. For the V-Plus Class approved 1200 KW; we found we needed 1450. Even under the unrealistically optimistic Class assumptions, you could not start the Emergency Fire Pump without first bringing another generator on line. The Class approved emergency generator was 250 KW, a toy. We found the minimum needed on the V-Plus was 440 KW. Insufficient installed power was a critical factor in the killer SEAL ISLAND fire.

[40] The rule is that the ventilation duct had to extend down to within 1 meter of the bottom of the cargo pumps, which made sense for a single bottom ship where the pumps are fitted on the actual bottom of the ship. But in a double bottom ship the pumps must be raised 2 to 3 meters above the bottom and put on their own little deck. This leaves an extremely dangerous space below the pumps unventilated. But the downratchet never works backwards, so the rule stayed as it was.

and its massive torque fluctuations. I know of three shaft coupling failures in new VLCC's, which means we can be sure there have been many more. The repair yards tell us there is no chance of unscrewing the shaft coupling bolts when the new V's come in for their first docking. They expect to have to drill them out since they all been over-torqued and badly fretted. And what does the owner gain for taking these massive risks? He saves a few thousand dollars per ship which he will give back to the repair yard on the first docking. This is the downratchet gone berserk.

Table 5.4 is an extreme case, but it's very difficult to find any scantling or parameter that is not at least 15% weaker on the new ships than the old. As a result, large tankers built to current Class Rules are far less safe and less reliable vessels than those built 25 years ago. And the mid-70's ships as a group were not over-built. They were at best just good enough. Yet in the same period the potential liabilities associated with large tanker casualties have increased one hundred fold. It makes no sense.

Chapter 6

The CTX Standard Tanker

6.1   The Basic Requirements of a Good Tanker

So what should a good tanker look like? The basic requirements are simple.

1. Lots of small tanks, regularly arranged.

2. Sufficient structural strength to avoid the problems outlined in Chapter 5.

3. All ballast tanks properly protected and permanently inerted.

4. Fully redundant, twin screw.

I'll call a ship meeting these requirements a *CTX standard* tanker as opposed to a *Class standard* ship, a ship built to the minimum required by Class Rules.[1] The rest of this chapter gets into the specifics of implementing these four principles, of building a CTX standard ship.[2]

---

[1] Actually, a true CTX Standard ship would also be capable of handling a full vacuum in the top of the tanks, and be fitted with a passive vacuum system to reduce spillage per Section C.9.2. But for present purposes this is icing on the cake.

[2] A tanker newbuilding is governed by two documents: the Contract, and the Specification. The Contract is about 40 pages of basic legalese. The Contract references the Specification which is a detailed technical description of the ship to be built. A tanker Specification can easily run to 300 pages. This chapter most definitely does not constitute a newbuilding Specification. In a Specification, the devil is in the details. You must have the language just right. You must not leave out anything. This chapter discusses some of the principles upon which a Specification should be written. The CTX has a project underway to produce a model tanker newbuilding Specification which will be made freely available, when it is finished.

But the point I want to make here is that the CTX standards are not expensive. The required increase in structural steel over a Class standard ship will be about 15%. The lightweight of a Class standard VLCC is about 40,000 tons. The lightweight of a CTX VLCC will be about 46,000 tons. This increase in steel weight, most of which is simply thicker scantlings, will cost about three million dollars. Extending the inert gas system to the ballast tanks will cost less than $500,000. Twin screw is the most expensive part of the package. On a VLCC, it will cost about six million dollars, The overall increase in initial cost will be about ten million dollars, or about 15%.[3] Here's what the owner gains in return for the increase in cost:

1. More operational and commercial flexibility.
2. A reduction in draft for the same amount of cargo.
3. Less off-hire time.
4. Fewer, shorter drydockings, and lower drydocking cost.
5. More speed. A Class minimum VLCC has a single main engine of about 26,000 KW and a loaded speed of 15.5 knots. A twin screw VLCC to CTX specs will have two 18,000 KW engines and a loaded speed of 17.5 knots. More revenue in a boom.[4]
6. A far longer investment life.
7. Far better slow speed maneuverability.
8. Good spillage characteristics in single tank breaches.
9. Ability to withstand engine room flooding.
10. A 1000 fold increase in time between total loss of power incidents.
11. A big reduction in ballast tank explosions. Just how big will depend on how well the ballast tank protection is maintained. If it is maintained properly, then we are talking multi-order of magnitude reductions.

---

[3] At the time of writing, the fully built up cost of a Class minimum VLCC in a world competitive yard is somewhere around 70-75 million dollars. But few owners pay this price. In a tanker market slump, few ships are ordered. The shipyards, desperate for business, compete the newbuilding price down to their marginal cost. For a Class standard VLCC, this is about 55 million dollars. When the tanker market goes into boom, the orders flood in, and the newbuilding price quickly rises, usually peaking out at close to double the marginal cost, or about 120 million dollars. A counter-cyclic owner can have a CTX standard VLCC for far less than it will cost a lemming owner for a Class standard VLCC.

[4] The basic tanker market cycle is a five to ten year slump in which the average rates barely cover operating costs interspersed with short booms in which the rates are five to ten times or more the non-boom rates. It is simply smart business that a tanker be designed to take advantage of the booms. A Class standard ship is not.

One of the few owners who really understood this was Daniel Ludwig. Ludwig's parsimony was legendary. But his VLCC's were fitted with 33,000 KW power plants when other less miserly VLCC owners were using 22,000 to 26,000 KW.

I've done the present values, and I'm personally convinced that the additional investment associated with a CTX standard versus Class standard ship — with the possible exception of twin screw – can be justified from a purely selfish, owner's point of view. In other words, the net economic cost of vastly improved standards is almost non-existent

So why are owners building such crappy ships? I think there are four reasons:

1. ***Many owners are dumb and/or uncaring.*** Some are distant investors, such as German doctors and dentists, who are in the hands of promoters and hirelings.[5] They know nothing about the ships they are investing in. Some are short-term speculators figuring they will unload the ship in the next market up-tick on the first fool that comes along.[6] Some are internal oil company politicians who want to bring in a newbuilding program as cheaply as possible and get promoted out of the marine department as a reward. Some are simply deluded. They actually believe that the Tromedy is giving them a pretty good ship.

2. ***Owners are in a hurry.*** It's strange. A shipowner will agonize for months or more before deciding to order some new ships. But once the decision is made, he wants the ships now. Usually, the shipowning organization is split in such a way, that the guy negotiating with the yards does not have the option of not buying. His only choice is which yard, and the yards know it. If the yards stand firm on standards — and they are not above talking to each other — then it comes down to price. In order to get real concessions from the yards, the owner must be prepared to walk; and most are not.

3. ***Many owners feel helpless.*** They don't know how to to get a CTX standard ship. In their view, the downratchet is so entrenched that there is no way that an individual owner can make more than superficial changes in the prevailing standard. God knows, I have a lot of sympathy with this position.

4. ***The owners are concerned about mandatory age restrictions.*** If a great ship such as the Embassy is going to be legislated out of existence as rapidly as the lousiest of ships, it changes the owner's investment calculus dramatically.

---

[5] Much current newbuilding is being financed by German KS partnerships. These are totally tax shelter driven schemes in which the quality of the ship is a non-factor.

[6] Anybody foolish enough to buy a tanker during a boom isn't going to care about ship quality.

We will address all four of these issues in Chapter 7. But for now the point is that ***the extra cost of a CTX standard ship versus a Class standard ship, after adjusting for the additional revenue earning capability, is nearly negligible, provided there are no age restrictions.***

6.2 Egg Carton

A good tanker should have lots of little tanks regularly arranged. With the deck removed, the ship should look like an egg carton. Table 6.1 shows the CTX tank arrangement standards. The table assumes we are dealing with a double sided ship. This level of sub-division automatically eliminates

Table 6.1: CTX Cargo Tank Sub-division Standards

Type	DWT	Minimum Subdivision
Aframax	100,000	3x6
Suezmax	160,000	3x7
VLCC	300,000	3x9
V-plus	440,000	4x9
VV	560,000	4x11

just about all stability problems. It also ensures that the tanks will never operate at sloshing resonance, regardless of filling level.[7] We don't have to try and design the structure against sloshing forces which we cannot predict. It spreads the stresses around evenly.[8] For all these reasons, the extra steel required versus a Class standard tank arrangement will be negligible, as we saw in the case of the Embassy, Section 5.7. Structurally, the extra sub-division comes for free.[9]

Commercially, the additional sub-division results in a far more flexible ship. And it ensures a ship with good spillage characteristics in low to medium impact groundings and collisions. Roughly speaking, **a CTX standard tanker will have a largest tank which is about one-third the volume of the largest tank on a Class standard tanker.**

The main cost of the extra tanks will be piping and valving. But the owner, at some loss in parcel flexibility, may eliminate a good deal of the additional piping, if he so chooses, by making some of the tanks *free-flow*: that is, connecting adjacent tanks with sluice valves so that operationally they are a single tank.

---

[7] Just to make sure, the Specification should explicitly require no restrictions on slack tanks. And it should specify that the liquid density in any sloshing calculations should be that of sea water.

[8] This is particularly important given the more stringent loading requirements we shall impose on the hull structure in the next section.

[9] The structurally efficient Embassy had an average tank size of about 12,000 m^3. It is not exactly a coincidence that the maximum CTX tank size is about the same.

But cargo piping only costs about 800 dollars per ton of pipe. Even if the owner does not use free-flow, we are talking at most a couple of hundred thousand extra dollars on a VLCC.

Small tank size is a no-brainer.

6.3 Robust Structure

6.3.1 Design Loading Conditions

As we saw in Chapter 5, it is essential that a tanker's structure be robust enough to handle all the operating conditions that it could reasonably be expected to face in normal commercial practice with a healthy margin for operator error. Further, a double bottom tanker must be able to withstand at least localized damage to the double bottom. To translate these two simple, reasonable principles into structural requirements, I have to get a little technical. For the non-specialists, the important point is that these two principles are easily achievable, not even particularly expensive.

The main CTX structural loading requirements are:[10]

1. **The ship must be able to flood any contiguous pair, trio or quartet of ballast tanks when loaded to scantling draft.**

   This is the strength counterpart of IMO Regulation 25.[11] It will set the design sagging moment. For a 300,000 ton VLCC, the resulting design sagging moment will be just over 1,000,000 ton-meters as opposed to the IACS requirement of about 600,000 ton-m. This requirement will add about 1000 tons of steel to a VLCC at a marginal cost of about $500,000.

2. **The ship must be able to empty any transverse combination of cargo tanks across with all other tanks at full load departure condition.**

   This is a shear force requirement. It will push the allowable shear force envelope for a VLCC up 50% from around 20,000 ton to about 30,000 tons. Sounds like a lot, but it is easily accomplished by making the inner sides and longitudinal bulkheads out of high tensile steel, without reducing the thickness. On the Samsung VLCC, this requirement cost us about $66,000 for which we received a tremendous increase in flexibility.

3. **In the no cargo condition and for a full range (0 to 100%) of bunkers the ship must have the ability**

   (a) **to completely fill all ballast tanks,**

---

[10] These conditions of course are in addition to the standard Class requirements. Once again this is not a Specification. CTX's model tanker Specification runs some 30 pages for the hull steel alone. Here we are talking only the basics.

[11] And it will push the yards toward smaller tanks.

(b) to allow any single ballast tank, including the forepeak tank, to be empty when all other ballast tanks are full.

This requirement will set the design hogging moment. For a VLCC, it will result in a hogging moment allowable of just over 1 million ton-meters as opposed to the IACS requirement of about 670,000 ton-meters. The extra hogging moment will cost about 600 tons of steel ($300,000) Without 3(b), there is no way to inspect a ballast tank in ballast nor to perform proper ballast exchange.[12]

4. **The range of hull deflection in way of the shaft(s) must be less than 2 millimeters.**

   This is a lot more prescriptive than I would like. The design process here should be:

   (a) Make sure the propeller shaft diameter is big enough so that bending within the shaft bearing is small enough so that we can safely use composite bearings. To do this you will need a shaft diameter about 15% larger than IACS requires.

   (b) Make sure the hull in way of the shaft(s) is stiff enough so that the engine room can go from full hog to full sag without imposing unacceptable local bearing pressures.

   For Class standard VLCC's, the full range of hull deflection in way of the shaft is 5 mm or more. Based on what I've seen, we need to get this down to 2 mm in order to use composite bearings, and not be dependent on forced bearing lubrication.

   On a VLCC, this requirement will add about 200 tons of steel in the aftbody.

5. **The fatigue number (aka fatigue life) must be 50 or greater.**
   Fatigue number is an unsatisfactory proxy for good structural detailing. But, given the current environment within which the yards operate, there is no other way to enforce decent design details.[13] A fatigue number of 50 or more will get rid of the ugliest consequences of "design for producability". If the overall structural concept is sound, if

---

[12] These CTX design loads are very roughly equivalent to those suggested by Paik and Faulkner, after studying the Derbyshire failure.[64] Their recommendations were based on the finding that the forces associated with the IACS design wave were likely to be exceeded much more frequently than the Class Rules anticipate.

[13] Actually, a meaningful yard guarantee (Section 7.4.1) will automatically create a new, far more robust design philosophy.

the structure flows with the stresses, this requirement will cost nearly nothing.

6.3.2 Scantlings

We need to convert these design requirements into scantlings in a conservative, repeatable fashion. This will require a full hull, fine mesh finite element model as outlined in Section 5.6. The regulatory process should both develop the guidelines for such models and also develop an in-house finite element capability meeting those guidelines with which it can check, at least on a random basis, yard designs.

The finite element results must be interpreted conservatively. This means:

1. **Conservative design stress.** If the yards are going to push everything right up to the limit — make the whole structure orange – then we need to re-define the limit. For starters, I'd put a 10% margin on the current Class allowable stress and buckling criteria. This is the most expensive of the CTX structural standards. It will add about 3,000 tons of steel to a VLCC at a marginal cost of about $1,500,000. But it will get the structure back in the yellow, about where we were in the mid-70's.

2. **Abjure calibration factors.** Get rid of all the calibration factors unless they are unambiguously supported by well designed, completely documented, repeatable experiments.

3. **Eschew silly games.** No playing with liquid densities. No messing around with the lightweight distribution. No averaging of element stresses. No rounding down of scantlings. Limits on insert size and plate thickness changes. The same rules for structural continuity and alignment in the forebody and the aftbody as in the midbody.

4. **Welding.** Current filet welding practice make a mockery of any attempt at structural redundancy. Go back to the weld thicknesses and penetration requirements of the 1970's. The cost will be negligible.

For a much more complete list of the CTX structural requirements, see the CTX Model Tanker Specification.[19]

6.4   Inert All Double Hull Ballast Tanks

In Chapter 3, we learned that the single most important cause of single hull spillage and tankerman deaths is leakage of cargo into segregated ballast tanks followed by a fire or explosion. With the advent of the double hull, the interface area between cargo tanks and segregated ballast tanks is more than five times what it was for pre-Marpol tankers. The implication is obvious. The double hull ballast tank space must be inerted. This simple requirement accomplishes two crucial goals:

1. When we have a cargo leak into a ballast tank, there will be a far lower chance of a fire or explosion.

2. A double hull VLCC has 225,000 square meters or more of coated ballast tank area. That's about 35 football pitches (50 football fields for the Yanks). No matter how good the coating spec and the owner's supervision in the yard, it is inevitable that somewhere in this vast area the coating will break down locally. If and only if the ballast tank is both properly inerted and properly anoded, this local breakdown will not spread nor lead to deep localized corrosion which in turn will eventually generate leaks between the cargo and ballast tanks.[14] Not to mention a horrific recoating cost or worse steel renewal. Owners of non-inerted, double hull VLCC's are looking at a fifteen million dollar ballast tank recoating bill between ages ten and 15, earlier if the original job was not done right. (But as in the case of the pre-Marpol segregated ballast tanks, few will actually do the job. ERIKA and PRESTIGE; here we come.)

Inerting double hull ballast tanks is neither difficult nor expensive. The first step is double scrubbing.

6.4.1   Double Scrubbing

I first began thinking about inerting ballast tanks in the late 1980's. The 15 year old epoxy coating in the top of the segregated ballast tanks in our mid-70's built tankers was breaking down badly. We were getting deep localized corrosion in the under-deck area, especially in the weld seams and around vent holes. The tanks had been well-anoded and were normally pressed up during ballast legs. It was clear that the bulk of this wastage was taking

---

[14] See Appendix A for the details of what I mean by properly inerted and properly anoded.

place on the loaded leg when the ballast tanks were empty. An empty ballast tank offers ideal conditions for atmospheric corrosion: wet, salty and often hot. The literature seemed to promise a ten-fold reduction in steel wastage rates if we could hold the O_2 content in the tank atmosphere to less than 5%.

By this time, the tankers that Loews had bought had been merged into Basil Papachristidis' Hellespont fleet. I approached my partners at Hellespont about doing a full scale test. They wanted no part of it. So I went to my kid brother, Dave; and in 1990 he agreed to try it on one of his tankers, the Empress des Mer. Dave's first name is Crazy.

The reason why Hellespont rejected the idea was sulfur. Tanker fuel, which is the dregs of the refining process, generally contains 3 to 4 percent sulfur. This means the stack gas coming out of the boilers contains 1500 ppm sulfur dioxide. It is highly acidic and highly corrosive. To reduce the SO_2 content, tankers use a *scrubber*. A scrubber is little more than a big shower that sprays seawater into the stack gas. The seawater cools the stack gas, condensing much of the water vapor in the boiler exhaust. Much of the SO_2 dissolves into the condensed water which is drained out of the bottom of the scrubber and discharged overboard. A good scrubber, properly maintained and operated will cool the stack gas from about 200C to about 17C above the seawater temperature, removing 95 to 97% of the sulfur.

The resulting gas still contains 50 to 100 ppm SO_2. It is smoky, smells of sulfur, and it still generates sulfur related corrosion, which can be seen in the IGS piping and in the cargo tanks near the inert gas inlets. Hellespont did not want this sulfur in the ballast tanks. Neither did Dave.

My plan was to back up the first scrubber with a second. The problem was that nobody knew how effective the second scrubber would be including the scrubber manufacturers. Dave blew $75,000 and installed the second scrubber in series with the first and we waited for the results. I was hoping for a factor of five reduction and had ordered a set of Draeger tubes, a sampling device, which registered in the range 10 to 50 ppm SO_2. When the system was turned on, we got no reading. After checking the obvious possibilities, we obtained more sensitive Draeger tubes.

To my astonishment, we found the second scrubber was nearly as effective as the first, removing more than 95% of the remaining sulfur and reducing the SO_2 content to less than 2 ppm at full load on the inert gas fans. At deballast volumes which are typically one-fifth cargo discharge rates, the sulphur content drops down to 0.2 to 0.3 ppm. You can get more than this on a winter day in New York city with an inversion. In fact, the

Draeger tubes we ended up using were developed to measure atmospheric pollution.   The double scrubbed stack gas is clear as a bell and has no smell.[15]

The reason why the second scrubber is so effective is that it reduces the stack gas temperature from about 17C above seawater to only 2 or 3C above seawater as shown in Figure 6.1.[16] This condenses a very large portion of the water vapor in the gas which in turn pulls out most of the remaining sulfur.

Figure 6.1: Double Scrubbing Schematic

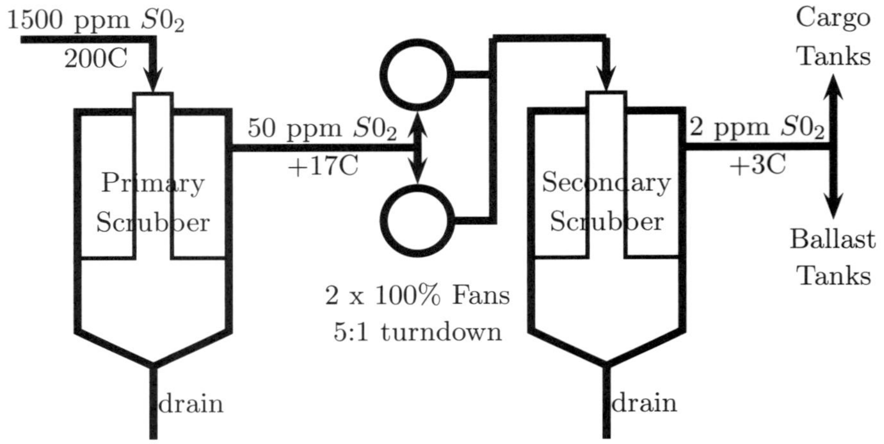

Hellespont became an instant convert, and we installed the second system on the Hellespont Grand. When we did this, I had the crew purposely scrape holes in the coating in about 240 spots in one of the ballast tanks, and carefully measure the steel thickness at each of these spots. Fourteen months later we went back into this tank and remeasured these spots.

There was no wastage.[17] You did not need the thickness gauge to tell

---

[15] This creates a real safety hazard. Single scrubbed inert gas is smokey and smelly, so the crew had some warning if inert gas is not where it is supposed to be. Double scrubbed gas looks beautiful, but it is deadly. Section A.4 outlines the additional safety measures that need to be implemented.

[16] Figure 6.1 is based on full cargo discharge rate which for a VLCC will be about 15,000 cubic meters per hour. When the ballast tanks are being inerted, the deballast rate is normally 4,000 cubic meters per hour or less. At these rates, the SO_2 content of the double scrubbed gas will be less than 0.3 ppm.

[17] The actual measured mean wastage was 0.009 millimeters, but this was clearly mea-

you that. The 1 to 2 cm diameter bare spots were like new except that they were covered with a very thin black film. There was no scale and no evidence of the 15 year old coating being lifted at the edges of the bare spots. The tank was well-anoded so there was plenty of white calcareous deposits in the tank from the ballast legs. But what was really interesting was there was no red or brown anywhere in the tank. At the top of the tank, where the coating had broken down earlier we had had some leafing corrosion, layers of red-brown rust that typically forms in corners. But now the leaves had turned black. I broke off one of the leaves and sent it to a lab. It was almost all magnetite, Fe_3O_4.

Corrosion proceeds from iron to magnetite, Fe_3O_4, to ferric oxide Fe_2O_3, better known as rust. The inerting had reversed this process. **We had created reducing conditions in the tank.** There will be no rust in such a tank.

Hellespont immediately converted all our pre-Marpol segregated ballast tanks and, as long as we maintained the anodes and the inerting per Appendix A, corrosion in the segregated ballast tanks was history. As an important by-product, we were putting much cleaner, dryer gas into our cargo tanks. Sulfur related corrosion in the cargo tanks essentially disappeared as well.

6.4.2 Purging Double Hull Ballast Tanks

It was clear from the start that our double hull new buildings would have inerted ballast tanks with double scrubbing. But we were now faced with two new problems:

1. In order to inspect an inerted tank, you must remove all the deadly inert gas and replace it with high quality fresh air everywhere in the tank. This is called *purging*. How to reliably purge (and re-inert) the warren of steel in a double hull ballast tank?
2. Class Rules.

The solution to the first problem turned out to be surprisingly easy. A double hull ballast tank is a series of cells formed by the transverse web frames and the longitudinal stringers/girders in double side/bottom. My idea was to turn the tank into a series of longitudinal ducts by maximizing the openings in the transverse webs and minimizing the openings in the longitudinal members. At one end of the tank, we ran an injection pipe from the deck down to nearly the centerline. This injection pipe had an

---

surement noise. The standard deviation of the measurements was 0.113 millimeters, ten times that of the mean.

orifice in it in each of the ducts. Air for purging (or gas for inerting) would be pumped through the injection pipe into one end of each of the ducts, flow to the other end of the tank, and exhaust out the tank lid at the far end.

Mike Kennedy, Hellespont's technical guru, wrote a program, which he called VENT2D (Mike's not a good namer), to model the gas or air flow through the cells.[18] VENT2D indicated that not only would the idea work, but it also gave us an idea of how to best size the orifices. We did a careful set of trials on both the first Samsung VLCC and the first V-Plus. In each case, Mike installed a series of O_2 sensors in several tanks, fully inerted these tanks, then blew fresh air into the tanks through the injection pipe, and measured the rise in oxygen. The actual numbers were considerably better than the purposely conservative computer results. We found we were able to safely blow out a double hull ballast tank in less than two hours. When you inspect one of these tanks, you can feel the wind from the air being injected on your cheeks anywhere in the tank. It is very comforting.

Class was a bit more difficult. It wasn't exactly that Class was against inerting double hull ballast tanks, but the Rules had not been written with this possibility in mind. And while we were drastically reducing one enormous risk (ship blows up due to cargo leaking into ballast tank), we were slightly increasing another far more minor risk (structural damage due to over/under pressurizing a ballast tank). Bureaucracies have a lot of trouble with this kind of change.

Initially, we followed a don't-tell/don't-ask policy. We didn't say anything special; just went ahead and installed the system. On the Samsung VLCC the extra cost of double scrubbing and ballast tank inerting was less than $400,000. The Class plan approval guys could see what we were doing; but we fobbed them off with semi-dishonest, Clintonesque statements about how we were going to use the system. They didn't push the matter.

But after the V-Plus class had been in successful operation for some time, we needed to get the system approved. What we were doing was technically illegal in that we were not venting the ballast tanks as required by Rule; not to mention inconsistent with all our lavishly documented ISM procedures and checklists. Sooner or later a port inspector or ISM auditor or somebody was going to catch this, and there would be hell to pay. The first V-Plus, the Hellespont Alhambra, was an LR ship. So we approached Lloyds for approval. They turned us down flat.

---

[18] Hellespont has made VENT2D available without cost. You can download it from `www.hellespont.com` if you accept the copyleft terms.

Time to play the same old game. The second V-Plus, the Hellespont Metropolis, was an ABS ship as a result of the swash bulkhead deal (Section 5.7). I went to ABS, explained the situation, pointed out the tremendous increase in safety, went thru all the measures we had put in place to prevent over/under pressurization — we were using the same system that Class had already approved for every large tanker cargo tank in existence – and, oh, by the way, if you approve this system for the Hellespont Metropolis, we will switch one (maybe all) of the other V-Plus' to ABS.[19]

The technical merits of our argument must have been persuasive. ABS not only approved the system, but developed a whole set of official recommendations for inerting double hull ballast tanks, which is remarkably similar to the Hellespont system.[61] Lloyds and the other classes have now done something similar. There is no longer any impediment to inerting double hull ballast tanks.

There is absolutely no excuse for not mandating that all double hull ballast tanks be inerted forthwith. Failure to do so will kill a lot of tankermen, and put a lot of oil in the water.

---

[19] ABS took so long to approve the system that we sold the single screw, V-Plus ships before I had a chance to live up to my end of the bargain. Somehow I don't feel guilty.

6.5 Twin Screw

6.5.1 The Importance of Redundancy

Total Loss of Power

Worldwide there are currently about 3600 tankers with a deadweight of 10,000 tons or more afloat. ***All but 16 of these ships are single screw.*** 99.6% of all tankers have one main engine, one propeller, and one rudder. If our experience with the V-Plus (Section 3.5.3) is typical, this means that on average there are ten "minor" total loss-of-power incidents every day, even if you are crazy enough to call any loss-of-power that risks a major oil spill "minor".[20] ***If my once every ten year number for "major" loss-of-power incidents is correct, then worldwide we are averaging one major tanker loss-of-power incident every calendar day.*** In fact, we have good reason to believe, that the V-Plus reliability was better than an average newbuilding.

Even if the time between tanker loss-of-power incidents is lower than the V-Plus by a factor of ten, which is extremely unlikely, then we are still talking about one "minor" loss-of-power per calendar day, and a major loss-of-power every ten days. Of course, only a small percentage of tanker loss-of-power incidents actually end up in a spill; but as we found out in Chapter 3, those spills account for at least 20% of overall tanker spillage. Given the consequences, any sane person has to regard these numbers as unacceptable.

They become totally unacceptable as soon as one realizes that total loss-of-power incidents can be reduced by several orders of magnitude or more by mandating twin screw, that is, two main engines, two propellers, and two rudders arranged in two engine rooms in such a manner that any failure in one engine room does not affect the other. To get a feel for the power of this redundancy, we must make some assumptions about the length of the loss-of-power.[21] For the sake of argument, let's assume that a "minor" loss-of-power lasts one hour, and a "major" loss-of-power lasts a day. If we have a twin screw ship, then to have a total loss-of-power, the second loss of power must occur while the first incident is still happening.

---

[20] It was a "minor" loss of power that resulted in the Bright Field ramming the Poydras Street wharf in New Orleans injuring at least 66 people.

[21] Under the Tromedy, ships don't report most failures, and the owners and Class won't tell us about the failures they know about. We have no real data on either Mean Time Between Failures nor the Mean Time To Repair. I have no choice but to make up numbers that seem reasonable.

If twin screw is properly implemented, so that loss-of-power incidents on-board a single ship are independent, then using my numbers the probability per at-sea day of the second engine room going down in a second "minor" incident while the first is down in a "minor" incident is 1/2,160,000 or on average once every 6000 ship-years. The probability of the second engine room going down in a "minor" incident while the first is down in a "major" incident is 1/900,000 or once every 2500 ship-years on average. The probability of the second engine room going down in a "major" incident while the first is down in a "minor" incident is 1/21,600,00 or once every 59,000 ship-years The probability of the second engine room going down in a "major" incident while the first is down in a "major" incident is 1/9,000,000 or once every 25,000 ship-years. Table 6.2 summarizes these numbers.

Table 6.2: Frequency of Total Loss of Power
Individual Ship

	MINOR	MAJOR
Single screw	1 per year	1 every 10 years
Twin screw	1 every 1,703 years	1 every 25,000 years

3600 Ship Fleet

	MINOR	MAJOR
Single screw	10 per day	1 per day
Twin screw	2 per year	1 every 7 years

There are a number of academic caveats required here: Poisson distribution, independence, etc. But the point is crystal clear. Propulsion redundancy — properly implemented — can reduce tanker total loss-of-power incidents not by 20%, not by 50%, but by a factor of 1000 or more.[22]

This is just simple common sense. Airplane engines are orders of magnitude more reliable than tanker engine rooms. Yet no one in his right mind would use a single engine airplane across the Atlantic on a routine, commercial basis. In fact, one would probably be regarded as a bit of a dare devil to cross the Atlantic once on a single engine plane. You'll probably make it; but, if 3600 people try it, it is nearly certain that someone will not. Right now there are 3600 sizable tankers out there routinely playing daredevil.

---

[22] Properly implemented is a key phrase. See Appendix B for technical details.

Loss of Steering

We also learned in Chapter 3 about the importance of steering systems. Loss of steering has put at least 335 million liters of oil in the water — about ten EXXON VALDEZ'S — and killed 28 people.[23] The Class Rules and SOLAS talk about requiring redundant steering gears; but this is not true in any meaningful sense. What is redundant is the control system (partially) and to a certain extent the steering gear motors. There are a multitude of possible failures and interdependencies – including loss of electric power, damage to the rudder, rudder stock, or rams, loss of hydraulic fluid, etc. which will render the ship rudder-less.[24] The double hull BALTIC CARRIER had such a "redundant" system. But it lost steering and turned into the path of the Tern causing the biggest spill ever in Danish water. So did the SORO, a nearly new fully loaded VLCC which in 1997 drifted to within 40 miles of the Hebrides after losing her under-designed steering gear to the proverbial "freak" wave. It's simple. A redundant rudder system means two rudders.

Low Speed Maneuverability

Finally, we learned in Chapter 3 about the importance of improved maneuverability, especially at low speed. The AEGEAN SEA (80 million liters) and the CORINTHOS (22 dead) are the most famous examples of casualties caused by abysmal low-speed maneuverability. But there are plenty of other examples where better maneuverability could have made a big difference including SEA EMPRESS, DIAMOND GRACE, TASMAN SPIRIT, and possibly even the TORREY CANYON. Twin screw would improve the low speed maneuverability of a tanker by an order of magnitude, as well as freeing the pilot from the stern swing problem.

Neither Class nor IMO has any requirements with respect to low speed maneuverability.

---

[23] Even if we don't count the 42 people killed in the NASSIA collision, where the loss of steering was on a non-tanker.

[24] The situation is similar to a twin engine, single rotor helicopter. The helicopter can fly with one engine down provided the engine doesn't fail in a way that screws up the downstream power train. But nobody would call this a fully redundant system.

CTX Twin Screw Casualties

Table 6.4 is the twin screw equivalent of Table 3.17 for double bottoms. Every casualty in the CTX database has been rated as follows:

Y   Twin Screw almost certainly would have made a difference
P   Twin Screw probably would have made a difference
M   Twin screw might have made a difference
N   Twin screw would not have helped
?   Cant Say
W   Twin screw would have made things worse

As in Section 3.10, this rating is necessarily subjective, but unlike Section 3.10 where I was purposely generous, here I have tried to be very conservative. Table 6.3 summarizes the results in the same way as Table 3.16 did for double bottoms. For twin screw, where I was strict, I put 850 million liters and 54 deaths in the Certainly and Probably categories. For double bottom where I was lenient, I had 113 million liters and 0 deaths in these categories. Given all this, it is nuts that any tanker is single screw. The single screw

Table 6.3: Summary of Spills in which Twin Screw Might Have Helped

ASSESSMENT	NUMBER	LITERS	DEATHS
MAYBE	29	358,891,700	74
PROBABLY	34	329,428,000	48
CERTAINLY	31	524,614,800	6
TOTAL	94	1,212,934,500	128

tanker developed at a time when the only losers from a loss of a tanker due to machinery failure were the shipowner, the cargo owner, and the crew. The shipowner and the cargo owner could — the owner still can — buy their way out of the risk in an imperfect insurance market, a market which gives only the most modest credit for ship quality and reliability. Nobody gives a damn about the crews.

Now we have a situation in which we understand that the cost to society of an oil spill can easily be orders of magnitude larger than the loss of a ship or a cargo. This is reflected in multi-billion dollar risks somehow spread among the charterers, insurers, governments, and that portion of mankind that lives or plays beside the sea. But, the way the Tromedy works, the owner of the ship (unless it's an oil company)[25] and the yard that built the ship bears almost none of this risk. Now you know why 99.6% of all the tankers in the world are single screw.

---

[25] It is not a coincidence that most of the existing twin screw tankers, including nine ships for the Alaska-West Coast trade, were built for oil companies, which can't insure themselves out of a risk of oil spill.

Table 6.4: Spills in which twin screw might have helped

Based on CTX database as of 2005-10-17T16:11:50

Date	Ship	Kilo liters	E1	E2	E3	L O	A C	De ad	?	Synopsis
19780316	Amoco Cadiz	267000	MR	WS	FD	O	L	0	Y	steering gear failure, grounded Britanny, broke up
19930105	Braer	99600	MY	WS	FD	R	L	0	Y	lost power, seawater in BFO, pipes on deck hit vents
19921203	Aegean Sea	87000	M_	WS	TX	H	L	0	P	grnd Corunna, could not turn ship in bad weather,OBO
19960215	Sea Empress	84400	GC	WS		H	L	0	M	pilot misjudged tide set, compounded by bad response
19830107	Assimi	60200	M_	EX	FD	O	L	0	M	ER fire, Gulf of Oman, cause uncertain
19750110	British Ambassador	56000	MW	MF	FD	O	L	0	Y	sw inlet leaked, vlv failed ER flooded,sankunder tow
19831209	Pericles Gc	54100	M_	EX	FD	O	L	0	M	ER fire east of Doha, sank
19730602	Esso Brussels	50000	MR	RD	TL	H	L	16	P	rammed by Sea Witch whose steering gear failed
19710227	Wafra	47000	MW	MF	WS	O	L	0	Y	SW circ pump fracture, ER flooded, drifted aground
19760204	St Peter	44300	MY	EX	FD	O	L	0	P	"elec fire in ER" off W Coast, Columbia, sank
19750131	Corinthos	42200	GC	RD	TL	T	d	26	P	hit by E M Queeny, Marcus Hook, no IG, pilot error
19770527	Caribbean Sea	35200	M_	FD		O	L	0	P	ER flooded S of El Salvador, sank
20030727	Tasman Spirit	35200	C_	WS	TL	H	L	0	M	chan?pilot?mach?, guess ship too deep for channel
19821126	Haralabos	31900	M_	EX	WS	H	L	0	M	ER fire, Ras Gharib, cgo transhipped
19891229	Aragon	29400	MY	HL		O	L	0	M	lost power, big spill under tow near Azores
19671024	Giorgio Fassio	25000	MF	FD		O	L	0	P	Enighe room flooded, sank in Atlantic off S Africa
19720331	Giuseppe Giulietti	25000	MF	FD		O	L	0	P	er flooded off C St Vincent, no power, sank
19810329	Cavo Cambanos	24300	M_	EX	FD	R	L	6	M	fire in generator room Tarragona, fire, sank, cause?
19661024	Gulfstag	21000	M_	EX	FD	O	L	7	M	two engine room explosions, sank
19700131	Gezina Brovig	18800	MY	FD		?	L	0	Y	cyl came thru crankdoor, broke SW main, sank
19740926	Transhuron	18600	MB	WS	TL	O	L	0	Y	A/C nipple failed, water on swbd, no power, grnd
19790302	Messiniaki Frontis	14100	NA	WS		R	L	0	M	grounding, Crete, radar on wrong scale, no visuals
19870623	Fuyoh Maru	11900	MR	CN	FX	H	L	6	P	coll w Vitoria in Seine "damage to helm"
19680307	General Colocotronis	6000	MY	WS	SC	R	L	0	Y	grounded off Eleuthera after machinery failure
19761227	Olympic Games	5880	MY	WS		H	L	0	P	engine failure, Delaware R, 39 ft draft, grounded
20010329	Baltic Carrier	2900	MR	CN		R	L	0	Y	steering failure, collision, 6 m penetration
19740118	Key Trader	2790	VD	CN	WS	H	L	16	M	dance of death w Baune in lower Mississippi River
19770327	Anson	2330	MR	WS		H	?	0	Y	steering gear failure Orinoco, grounded
20001128	Westchester	2030	MC	EX	WS	H	L	0	Y	crankcase fire, grounded Mississippi River
19850928	Grand Eagle	1640	MY	WS		H	L	0	Y	ship lost power, grnded near Marcus Hook
19970702	Diamond Grace	1550	GC	WS		H	L	0	P	had to slow down in Tokyo Bay, lost steerage, grnded
19820820	Corinthian	1470		EX	FD	?	?	0	M	engine room fire, flooded, sunk,no other info

Continued on next page

Date	Ship	Kilo liters	E1	E2	E3	L O C	A C	De ad	?	Synposis
19760124	Olympic Bravery	842	MY	WS	FD	R	B	0	Y	"series of engine failures", VLCC drifted aground
19840319	Mobiloil	624	MR	WS	FD	H	?	0	Y	steering failure in Columbia River, grounded
19780321	Aegis Leader	586	MY	WS		?	?	0	P	grounded off Sumatra after machinery breakdown
19760119	Irenes Sincerity	582	MY	WS		?	?	0	Y	"stranded after engine trouble", Baltic, nil info
19730624	Conoco Britannia	500	MY	WS		S	L	0	Y	lost power mooring Humber SBM , ran over own anchor
19810725	Afran Zenith	302	M_	WS		H	?	0	P	grounding Elbe after machinery problems
19901015	Rio Orinoco	200	MY	GA	WS	R	L	0	P	mach problems, anchored, dragged, grounded G of St L
19990523	Parnaso	151	MR	CN		O	B	0	Y	lost steering, collision South of Cuba
19950205	Berge Banker	143	G_	RD		L	L	0	P	hit by lighter Skaubay at GLA during mooring
19981207	Tabriz	117	MY	RR		H	?	0	P	eng failure, hit jetty at Bandar Abbass
20000315	J Dennis Bonney	32	G_	RD		L	L	0	M	hit by lighter while mooring, Southwest Pass
19840627	Vic Bilh	30	M_	UM	TX	T	d	0	P	unmoored by Afran Stream, too fast to keep steerage
19970118	Stolt Spray	20	MR	CN	WS	H	L	0	P	lost steering in Miss River, holed 1p, dh
19990227	Hyde Park	16	VB	TX		H	L	0	Y	lost power loaded gasoline, drifted 13 M, many coll.
19660616	Alva Cape		VB	TX	WS	H	L	33	M	coll w Tex Mass, very low speed, 12 ft penetration
19700701	Agip Ancona		MR	WS		R	?	6	Y	Lost steering, Bosporous. Killed 6 people on shore.
19700800	Ampunia		MB	WS		?	?	0	Y	Burn out of main generator. 16000T spill?
19711018	Anita Monti	0	MY	EX		O	L	0	P	ER fire, lube oil leak on steam valve towed to Med
19760911	Aegis Leader		MY	WS		?	?	0	Y	grounded after drifting with engine trouble
19770415	Universe Defiance		MX	SC		O	B	9	M	Boiler room fire off West Africa, sunk
19770600	Norse Queen	0	M_			O	L	0	Y	VLCC power failure, towed to Algoa Bay, lightered,
19790225	Mobil Vigilant		M_	CN		H	L	0	M	coll w Marine Duval, bank effect, slo spd dop ¿ 5m
19800206	Scorpio			EX		?	?	0	M	ER fire, Straits of Florida, towed in, no other info
19800824	Chaparal Ii			EX		O	?	0	M	ER fire, Freeport, Bahamas, ER flooded
19810201	Aikaterini			EX		R	?	0	M	Engine Room fire off Maryland, towed in, cause?
19810505	Humilitas			EX	WS	H	?	0	M	engine room fire off Naples, no cause info
19810520	Anna Xyla			EX		?	?	0	M	engine room fire, Jebel Dhanna, no cause info
19810629	Polluce			EX		?	?	0	M	fire in ER off Genoa, towed in, no other info
19810827	Yannis K			EX	TL	O	?	0	M	ER fire off Nova Scotia, towed in, scrapped
19810905	Globe Maritima		MY		TL	O	?	0	Y	mach failure E of Bahamas, towed in, scrapped
19820112	Point Milton		MY			O	?	0	Y	engine failure off New Jersey, towed in
19820518	Mar Corrusco		MY			?	?	0	Y	engine failure off Trapani, towed in
19820608	Manamaria			EX		?	?	0	M	ER fire Med, towed in, no other info
19820616	Ogden Willamette		MY			O	L	0	Y	ER flood, expansion joint, lost power, abandoned
19820815	Patris			EX		H	?	0	M	ER fire Bombay, no other info

Continued on next page

Date	Ship	Kilo liters	E1	E2	E3	L O	A C	De ad	?	Synposis
19820919	Citlali		MY			?	?	0	P	"machinery damage" off New York, towed in
19840704	Atia C		MY	TL		?	?	0	P	"engine damage" off Djibouti, scrapped
19881019	Kition		MY			?	?	0	P	ER flooding off Capetown, no power, towed in
19881226	Boni		M_	EX		?	?	0	M	ER fire, towed in, no other info
19900819	Livi		MY	WS		?	?	0	P	adrift during typhoon off Taiwan, went aground
19901106	Star Connecticut		GC	WS		S	B	0	M	conning error lving Oahu SBM, er flooded
19910716	Tonje Cob		MY			?	?	0	P	engine failure, towed to Balboa
19911110	Svangen		MY	FD		O	B	0	P	leak in engine room of Algeria, sank
19920703	Yellow Fin			EX		O	L	0	P	ER fire off Sri Lanka, had to be towed in
19920920	Briolette			EX		O	?	1	M	fire in engine room, towed to Subic
19930219	Carlova		MY			O	?	0	P	engine breakdown off Sidi Kerir, towed to Greece
19930428	Amazonas			EX		R	?	2	M	ER fire leaving Sao Sebastiao, no other info
19931025	Avon	0	MY			O	?	0	P	main engine breakdown off West Africa, towed in
19940528	Esso Demetia			EX	TL	O	?	0	M	ER fire off Libya, cause?, scrapped
19970117	Chestnut Hill	0	MS			O	B	0	Y	tailshaft seized, North Pacific, towed in
19970302	Soro	0	MR			O	L	0	Y	lost steering gear to "freak wave" drifted nr Scotld
19971012	Yusup K	0	MY			R	L	0	P	lost power and drifted toward Scotland, towed in
19980929	Moruy	0	MR	WS		H	L	0	P	lost steering, grounded Champlain, FP tank holed
19990428	Olympic Symphony	0	MR			H	L	0	P	lost steering Brisbane R., near (6-10m) ramming
19990629	Alandia Stream	0	MY			R	L	0	P	drifted 11 hrs off Orkneys after loss of power
20000727	Iris Star	0	MY			R	L	0	Y	lost power, escort tugs saved Bosporus grounding
20001010	Michael		MY	TL		O	?	0	P	main engine damage NW Columbo, scrapped
20020502	Front Tobago	0	MY			O	L	0	Y	mn engine failure, towed all around China Sea
20020722	Patriot			EX		O	?	0	M	ER fire off Abacos, towed in, cause?
20020726	Orpheus Asia	0	MK			O	L	0	P	crankshaft failure, 30+ hr adrift off Taiwan
20030325	Pactol River	0	MY			O	?	0	P	adrift due engine problems off Tunisia, towed in
20040828	Astro Altair	0	MR	R		H	L	0	Y	lost steering, hit ferry landing Mississippi River

6.5.2 The Cost of Twin Screw

The argument against twin screw is straightforward: it costs too much. In fact, twin screw would cost less than double hull, especially on big tankers. The first twin screw tanker I ever saw was a ULCC improbably called the Nanny. It was 1979 or 1980. My brother and I had a port agency in Cayman Brac which at the time was an important lightering area. (The Caymanians pioneered offshore lightering of big tankers.) When I went out to the ship, I couldn't help notice the twin funnels and the extreme beam. Then I saw the twin rudders, slightly canted. I knew I was looking at something special.

Once aboard all the crew could talk about was the marvelous maneuverability of the ship which they repeatedly demonstrated during the subsequent lighterings, once turning the ship in little more than twice her own length. The Cayman mooring masters couldn't believe it. It was a whole different ball game. But what turned me on was the fuel consumption.

The Nanny was the brainchild of Stig Bystedt of the Swedish yard Uddevallavarvet. The knock on twin screw for tankers was that, due to the blocky nature of the hull, you could not get a decent flow pattern around the propellers. The result was very poor fuel consumption.

Bystedt solved this by utilizing a *twin skeg* design. An example is shown in Figure 6.2. In effect, each propeller has its own hull. Properly implemented, the flow into the propellers is as good as that for a well-designed single screw stern. But the ship can be much beamier. For the same deadweight, this means a shorter ship which generates important savings in hull steel. It also partly compensates for the additional wetted surface of the twin screw. And it results in a shallower draft ship, allowing larger cargoes into draft limited ports.[26] Finally, the propellers are more lightly loaded which increases the propeller efficiency.[27]

The Nanny was a 500,000 ton ULCC. Her fuel consumption was almost exactly the same as that of a good single screw tanker of the same size and vintage. Since then considerable work has been done on twin screw tanker hulls. Much of this work has been done at SSPA, the Swedish state towing tank in Goteborg. SSPA now claims they can produce a twin screw tanker

---

[26] This was the economic rationale behind the Nanny. She could carry more cargo into Rotterdam than the largest tanker in the world.

[27] Twin skeg ships are wider and **less tall** than a standard double hull of the same capacity. This means less outflow in casualties in which the inner bottom is breached. The depth and draft of the Stena V-Max (see below) is 25.6 and 19.0 m, The depth and draft of a single screw VLCC is about 31.25 and 22.25. The single screw VLCC with a 2.4 m higher oil column will spill something like 15 million liters more oil in an Exxon Valdez type casualty. See Section C.3.

Figure 6.2: Twin Skeg Hull Form

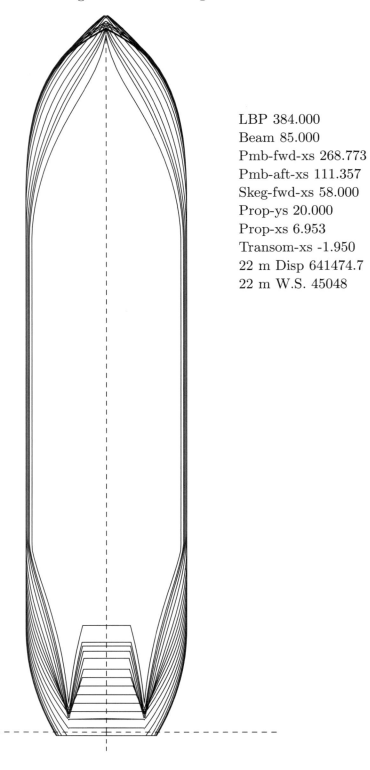

LBP 384.000
Beam 85.000
Pmb-fwd-xs 268.773
Pmb-aft-xs 111.357
Skeg-fwd-xs 58.000
Prop-ys 20.000
Prop-xs 6.953
Transom-xs -1.950
22 m Disp 641474.7
22 m W.S. 45048

hull with 6% lower fuel consumption than a single screw ship of the same capacity.[2, p 3][28]

In 1993, we asked the Korean yards to quote a 3 million barrel twin screw ULCC. The price numbers they came up with, before any bargaining, were about 10% more than an equivalent single screw ships. Our own internally generated cost estimates were in the range of 5 to 8%. Best guess at what a double hull adds to the cost of a tanker is about 7%.

The relative affordability of twin screw has been clouded by the fact that, with one exception, all the recent twin screw tankers have been specialty ships. Twin screw has been used in North Sea shuttle ships. But these ships have all kinds of requirements that conventional tankers do not. Recently, nine twin screw tankers have been built for the US West Coast–Alaskan trade at more than double the cost of a same sized, single screw ship built in the Far East. But these American Flag ships must be built in the USA. Just about any ship built in San Diego will cost more than twice what it will cost in Ulsan.

The one "normal" twin screw tanker built in the last 25 years is the Stena V-Max class. Stena, a Swedish company, is one of the maybe four tanker owners I admire. In 2000 Stena built two twin screw VLCC's at Hyundai. These ships cost approximately 10 million dollars more than a Class minimum ship.[69][page 255] But Stena builds to a considerably better Specification than Class requires. Probably 3 or 4 million of the extra dollars were due to to Stena's refusal to accept Class standards. Part of the remainder was due to the uniqueness of the project and the limited beam of the Hyundai building docks.

If twin screw became the norm as double hull has, then the additional cost would become even less noticeable than the additional cost of the double hull has.

But it won't happen without regulation. Even a 10% increase in initial cost will be more than all but the most committed owner, such as Stena, will accept. And with some superficial justification. In 2002, Hellespont developed a twin screw ULCC. We then went to both Exxon-Mobil and Chevron-Texaco, who we figured would be the most environmentally oriented charterers. We asked them if they would pay a small premium for

---

[28] This may be slightly optimistic. The Stena V-Max with an installed power of 42,990 BHP has a service speed of 16.9 knots loaded, 17.7 knots ballast. Our SHI VLCC with virtually the same carrying capacity had an installed power of 44,600 BHP (about 30% more than normal) had service speed of 16.8/18.2 knots loaded/ballast. Adjusting for the extra power, the SHI would have had service speed of 16.6/18.0 and virtually the same average speed. Certainly, there is no power penalty going with twin screw.

a twin screw tanker, pointing out the thousand-fold increase in reliability. They said no. Stena has had the same experience. The V-Max receive no premium in the spot market.

Twin screw, like double hulls, will require regulation.

6.5.3   Twin Screw and IMO

So what has IMO been doing with respect to twin screw? I bet you think I am going to say "Nothing". Would that this were the case. IMO is busy drafting and passing regulation that is strongly biased against twin screw. Sometimes the Tromedy really pisses me off.[29]

Here's what happened. Somebody decided that there should be a double bottom under all pump rooms.[30] The rationale behind this is to allow the pump room to keep pumping in any damage in which the vertical penetration is less than 2 meters from the baseline. (The *baseline* is the lowest level of the outer bottom.) Unfortunately, the wording doesn't say this. The wording requires a 2 meter high double bottom under the pump room. For a single screw ship, where the bottom of the ship under the pumproom and the baseline are the same, the wording and the intent are the same.[31]

But for a twin skeg ship, the wording does not match the intent. Figure 6.3 shows the problem. In a twin skeg design, there is a sort of ramp between the skegs. This ramp extends from the transom down and forward. The angle and curvature of this ramp is critical to the hydrodynamic performance of the twin screw. When the ramp reaches the forward end of the engine room (the aft end of the pump room), the situation looks like Figure 6.3. The ramp is still well over 2 meters above the baseline. (In Figure 6.3, the baseline is the bottom of the drawing.) No problem. The cargo pumps in the pump room are above the inner bottom. The ramp continues forward and downward until it finally merges with the outer bottom.

But under the IMO rules we must have at least a 2 meter high double bottom, ***even if the outer bottom is already 2 meters above the baseline***. This is senseless since the whole concept of the double bottom was to guard against a two meter penetration from the baseline. The drafters

---

[29] As usual, Class is no help. The new Joint Tanker Project hull Rules assume a single screw ship. For one thing, they are limited to a length/beam ratio greater than 5, while the ideal length/beam ratio for a twin screw tanker is a good deal less than 5.

[30] The pump room is a space just forward of the engine room where the cargo pumps are located.

[31] More basically, if the goal is to keep the pump room pumping, that's what the regulation should have said, rather than outlawing superior alternatives such as floodable pumps. But the Tromedy is fixated on double skin.

Figure 6.3: Section at Aft End of Pump Room

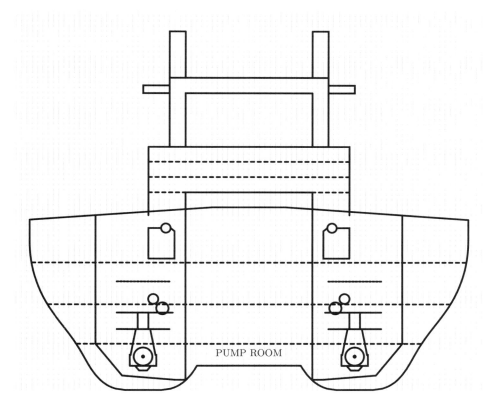

PUMP ROOM

of the double hull legislation had not anticipated the re-entrant hull form
of the twin screw. The twin screw can live with the original double hull
legislation drafted in the very early 1990's. It only means lifting the inner
bottom somewhat in the aftmost cargo tanks at a slight loss in capacity and
structural robustness. Stupid, useless, but not a show-stopper.

However, putting a 2 meter double bottom under the pump room causes
a serious problem, because the cargo pumps must be just above the level of
the inner bottom in the cargo tanks to properly empty the tanks. (Figure
6.3 like all good twin skeg designs pushes the pump room bottom as high
as it can and still have the cargo pumps at the correct height.) The double
skeg designer has only two choices in complying with the new pump room
inner-bottom rule:

1. A steeper ramp and a substantial jump in fuel consumption; not a
   good way to conserve resources.
2. Push the whole pump room forward at a major cost in steel, wetted
   surface, and capacity.

In 2004, I went to IMO in London to extoll twin screw and complain
about the anti-twin screw regulation.[32] The staff listened patiently, offered no counter-arguments, but pointed out they could do nothing. IMO
is merely a facilitator. Legislation is written by the Flag States. In fact,
the IMO staff is forbidden from taking sides in any debate. Their job is to
be an honest broker, a mediator, to help find a workable compromise when
necessary. Don't talk to us; talk to your Flag State.

Yeah, right. Let's see; who is my Flag State? I guess it's the Marshall
Islands. Hell, I started the Flag, so it should be my Flag State. Not any
more. The Marshall Islands now have 24 million tons of tankers registered
under its attractive purple flag. I'm sure the owners of all these ships would
just love to have their expensive single screw toys made illegal.

And herein lies the core problem with IMO. **IMO is a Flag State
organization.** The big Flag States (Panama, Liberia, Marshall Islands)

---

[32] A similar problem exists with bunker tanks. A neat feature of a twin skeg hull is
that the bunker tanks can be between the skegs where they are not only way above the
baseline but also totally protected from side damage. In 2002, IMO wrote the same kind
of single screw centric regulation for bunker tanks that it has for pump rooms, although
at least here there is some justification for properly drafted regulation. There have been
quite a few minor spills resulting from bunker tank sides being breached by tug contact,
hitting a berth, and the like. However, putting a 2 m thick layer between the ramp and
a bunker tank above it is totally useless from both a grounding and a collision point of
view. But it does eat up a lot of volume, forcing the designer to go back to the much
more exposed location outboard of the engine rooms. (Not to mention generating a big
area for hydrocarbon vapor build up.)

are charades, beholden to shipowners. IMO represents the status quo. The shipowners are never going to willingly step on their own toes.

This does not mean that IMO never passes legislation. IMO passes regulation for two reasons.

1. It is forced to by public outcry from a particularly photogenic spill. The Tromedy (owners, Class, the FOC's) is very worried about losing control. So whenever it feels its control is threatened unless it does something, it will do something. As we have seen, usually that something is very poorly thought out and always involves a great deal of careful grandfathering of the existing ships. But the Tromedy will do what it must to maintain control.

2. To seem busy. The Tromedy has developed an impressive bureaucracy in Class, the FOC's and at IMO. In periods when this apparat is not under pressure from public outcry, there are a lot of idle hands. That's when we pass the isoism sort of regulation, masses of increasingly detailed paperwork and procedures. This accomplishes three goals.

   (a) The Tromedy can argue that it is hard at work on the pressing issues facing vessel regulation, which everybody agrees are human factors which are best addressed by forcing the crew to fill out more forms.

   (b) It creates jobs for the Tromedy bureaucrats. Bigger staffs mean larger salaries for the managers of this process.

   (c) For shipowners and ship managers, it creates substantial barriers to new entrants.

I decided not to waste my time going to **my** Flag State, and presenting the case for legislating the existing Marshall Islands, single screw tanker fleet out of existence.

Chapter 7

How Should We Regulate Tankers?

7.1 The Importance of Transparency

It is time to talk about how we should regulate tankers. But before I do I need to call you attention to one of the most corrosive, self-defeating aspects of the current regulatory system: its ability to hide its problems.

This book is an obvious, if minor, example. I've been in the tanker business for nearly 30 years. Yet in making my arguments, I've had to rely on carefully sanitized reports, anecdotes, inferences, hints, and slips of the tongue during bar conversations. I can really only talk knowledgeably about what has happened on our own ships. What I, an insider, know is the tip of the iceberg. Non-tankermen (which includes most IMO delegates) have not a clue.

The Tromedy does an excellent job of enforcing omerta, a code of silence. This starts at the ship level, where crews don't report problems unless they absolutely have to. They know that their bosses regard a problem-free ship as a good ship.[1] Any casualty is a black mark on their record.

If the ship does report a problem to a superintendent, the superintendent decides whether to report this to the next level up and so on. Each level makes this decision in full knowledge that any reported problem is a black mark, and that in many cases the next level up doesn't want to hear about problems. Unless the problem is a major one, the owner almost certainly

---

[1] A small step in the right direction is the Nautical Institute's Marine Accident Report Scheme in which crews are encouraged to report problems anonymously. But at best this will give us a small sample of unauditable reports from only the best of crews.

never hears about it, in part because everybody knows he doesn't want to hear.

If the problem is so major that the owner and/or Class become involved, that's as far as it goes. The owner knows that if his customers, the oil companies, hear about a problem they will be less likely to charter his ships. Even if the charterer knows the ship and the operation are excellent, he will prefer a poorer ship that had not reported any problems. That way, if there is a big spill, the charterer can't be blamed for hiring a ship knowing that it had had problems.

And if the Tromedy has given him a lousy ship, the last thing an owner will do is to complain. Quite the contrary, he extols the ship and its builder to one and all, hoping to find some fool to whom he can sell the ship.[2] And the unfortunate buyer's lips are sealed for the same reason. It must be a great comfort to the yards to know that however bad their ships are, they will never hear anything but praise from their customers, at least in public.

The ship's Classification Society also has a big stake in secrecy. For one thing, Class's customer, the shipowner, wants any problem to remain quiet for obvious commercial reasons. It is well understood that Class will respect the "owner's confidence". Any Class that broke that rule would quickly lose all its customers to its competitors. This is written into Class contracts. Here's Lloyds Register's wording.

---

[2] I've been that fool. In 1986, I inspected a British built VLCC called the Windsor Lion. The tanks were gorgeous, strongly built, unusually well protected with coatings and anodes. The engine room was a bit strange. But at the time I didn't know much about engine rooms, and there was nothing suspicious in the Class (LR) records. On my recommendation, we bought the ship and renamed her the State.

What an idiot. The engine room was an operational disaster. Breakdown after breakdown. The generator control system was so erratic, prone to blackouts, that we ended up gagging the governors, an extremely dangerous practice. The State's worst habit was breaking main maneuvering valve stems, rendering the ship powerless for 10 to 12 hours. This happened four times in the less than two years we owned her. The State was eating up all our best talent. The other ships were being neglected. But we were able to keep the State's problems to ourselves.

In mid 1988, we sold her to the Iranians who renamed her the Avaj II. Two days after we delivered her, the Avaj II had a major boiler explosion. The German Chief Engineer died of a heart attack. The Avaj II traded sporadically after that. The Iranians never complained.

I later learned from a friend who grew up in Tyneside that this class of tankers were the first turbine ships Swan Hunter (of Glückauf fame) had built in forty years. They had simply forgotten how to build a steam turbine ship. The fact that the engine rooms were a disaster was well known among the Geordie mafia, but they kept it within the clan.

The Tromedy is almost always able to keep even the most egregious problems under wraps.

> LR will keep confidential and not use or disclose to any third party any technical information or operating data derived from the Client in connection with the Services except as may be required by law or as may be requested by the Client. This obligation will survive termination of the Contract.

Throughout Class paperwork, the regulatee is accurately called "the Client".

But Class has its own stake in secrecy. Major casualties often reflect on the Class itself. In any major casualty, it's a good bet that the design (approved by Class) or the Class's survey procedures could be called into question.

Given this system, the chances of even an insider finding out the real truth about other owners' problems are nil. It almost never happens unless a problem has reached pandemic proportions or there's a high profile spill.

Sadly, IMO itself is involved in the problem hiding. The Flag State casualty reports are not made public.[3] These reports are not even kept in the normal IMO library. Even IMO's "public" summaries of the Flag State reports are kept on a password locked web page. The data on which IMO regulations are based is not open to public scrutiny. In fact, in some cases, the IMO delegates themselves are not allowed to review the raw data, in part because of Class confidentiality clauses.[4] It is wishful thinking to expect intelligent regulation to come out of a star chamber.

This must change. If we don't know what the problems are, we can't correct them. Any decent regulatory system must be transparent. All casualty reports and all survey data, whatever its source, should be made public as a matter of course. The raw data on which any regulatory analysis or regulation is based must be publicly available.

The question is: how can we obtain this transparency?

---

[3] Individual Flag State may if they choose make a report public, but IMO has agreed that it will not.

[4] IMO scrupulously respects the Classification Societies' confidentiality. A particularly bizarre example is the case of the collision/grounding penetration data (Section 3.11). If you are beginning to think that IMO, the Flags of Convenience, and Class are tightly bound together, you are right. It's not just that they all in the final analysis depend on the shipowner and shipyards for their daily keep. It is also a network of symbiotic personal relationships. IMO, Class and Flag State managers all have a big stake in the status quo. For them, one goal of IMO/FOC/Class regulation is continued employment. And they understand that they all must work together to that end.

7.2   What Won't Work

We begin by eliminating the usual suspects.

7.2.1   Cremate Class

The Classification Society system must go. This book has been one long, sad litany of Class failures to properly regulate tankers. And indeed why would we ever think that a system based on the regulatee — sorry the Client — choosing and paying for the Regulator would work? If a building contractor chose and paid the Building Code inspection company, would we not expect sub-standard buildings? And if each such inspection company wrote the building code to which it inspected, would we not expect sub-standard building codes?[5]

As bad as Class has been for tankers, it has been far worse for bulk carriers. If you want to see how well the Classification Society system really works, unfettered by public outcry from oil spills and oil company concern resulting from that public outcry, check out dry bulk carriers. Since 1995 inclusive, the CTX tanker database has 54 tankermen killed in tanker casualties. In the same period, with about the same sized fleet and far safer cargos, there have 68 bulk carriers lost and 463 bulk carrier crewmen killed.[46, 35] The overwhelmingly important cause again is structural failure, usually abetted by corrosion.[62] This is not the place to get into the bulk carrier tragedy; but, if anyone has any lingering doubts about depend-

---

[5] Self-regulatee influence extends to the very top. The Clients are well represented on Class board of directors and other governing/advisory bodies. In 2004, the 12 man ABS Board was made up of 3 employees, 4 shipowners, 2 offshore rig contractors (Class approves offshore drilling rigs), and 3 cronies. My experience is that these bodies pretty much rubber stamp whatever Class management decides. But if the unthinkable were to happen, and Class management went against the Clients' interests, we can be sure the various Boards/Councils/Members would be heard from.

ing on Class, take a look at the bulk carrier record.[6]

The reason the Classification Society system has been a failure is obvious: the regulatee chooses and pays the regulator. There is no amount of tweaking that can overcome this fundamental flaw.[7] In any replacement to the Tromedy, neither the shipowner nor the shipyard must choose the regulator.

7.2.2 Forget the Flag State

Since the rise of the Flags of Convenience, Flag State regulation has been an oxymoron. The only role of the Flag States has been to strengthen the Classification Society system. Once again the reason is obvious. The Flags are competing for owners. The successful Flags are the ones which offer the shipowner the best deal. It's not regulation; it's an auction. Forget about Flag State control. It is not worth discussing.[8]

But this is as good a time as any to address the but-things-are-going-so-well argument. You don't have to be paranormal to figure out what the Tromedy's first line of defense will be: if Devanney's right, why have we had

---

[6] Class's legal posture is interesting. Class wants the priviledge of approving ships but not the responsibility. The Classification Societies have consistently argued that they have no legal liability for any of the consequences of their survey activities. IACS is quite out front about this:

> Such a certificate [the Class certificate] does not imply, and should not be construed as an express warranty of safety, fitness for purpose or seaworthiness of the ship. It is an attestation only that the vessel is in compliance with the standards that have been developed and published by the society issuing the classification certificate.[34]

So our tanker regulatory system is based on private entities, chosen and paid for by the owners, which entities cannot be held accountable for their mistakes.

[7] It has been suggested that we go back to the days in which a single Classification Society had an effective monopoly within each Flag State. This is a non-starter for a bunch of reasons; most obviously, owners would still be able to shop for a Classification Society by changing Flag.

[8] Some have suggested that the Flag State hire and pay Class, rolling the Class fees into the tonnage tax. Do these people think the owners will be any slower to change Flags, than they are to change Class? Anyway compared to the Flags of Convenience, the Classification Societies are pillars of professionalism. Whenever we wanted something important from Class, I usually led the effort myself. When we needed a concession from the Flag State, I could delegate the job to just about anybody in the organization and know that approval would be forthcoming.

The FOC's are well aware of how competitive their business is. It is not that easy to start up a real Classification Society. To set up a new Flag of Convenience, all you need to do is find a nation that wants to make a few easy dollars.

so little spillage recently? As this book went to press, there had been no brobdingnagian spills since the TASMAN SPIRIT in mid-2003. Before that you had to go back to the PRESTIGE (2002) and the ERIKA (1999). Look what a good job we are doing.

Actually the performance of the last five years is fairly typical of the post-Exxon Valdez era and not much better than the middle 1980's. See Figure 3.1. Stretches of several years between high-profile spills are common.

And the fact is that there have been some important improvements.

1. The combination of charterer vetting and embryonic port state control has forced the absolute worst operators to get out of the business or clean up their act at least superficially. This has had some real benefits, especially in Rules of the Road screw ups and navigational errors.

2. Likewise Traffic Separation Schemes and new technology such as GPS and ECDIS have made a major dent in collisions and navigation errors.

3. All (almost) cargo tanks are now inerted. This was not the case until the mid-late 1980's. Killer cargo tank explosions have been avoided, or at least turned into a situation that the crew could handle.

4. The pre-Marpol ships that the Tromedy pushed to non-coated segregated ballast tanks are now being retired. All segregated ballast tanks on tankers are now coated. A big change.

Question: in which of these four improvements did the Classification Society/Flag State play an important role? Answer: none of the above.

It is also true that with the forced retirement of all pre-Marpol tankers — good and bad — and the paucity of orders during the 1980's, the tanker fleet is now quite young. Thus, problems associated with coating breakdown and resulting severe corrosion have not yet reached puberty. But this is not an improvement, it's merely a deferral. And the order of magnitude increase in ballast tank coated area guarantees that when these problems reach maturity, we will face a massive mess.

It is also true that starting in the very early-1980's there was a major shift in tanker trades away from the the structurally stressful route around the Cape of Good Hope to much milder weather routes such as Persian Gulf to China. Now with the impending drop in Atantic Basin oil supply and the increased dependence on the Persian Gulf, the pendulum is beginning to swing back.

In short, the current lull in spillage is due to number of factors which have almost nothing to do with Class or the Flag State, combined with a very large dose of good luck. It most certainly is not due to the fact that we are building robust, reliable, maintainable, maneuverable tankers, as the next brobdingnagian spill will demonstrate.

7.2.3 Immolate IMO

IMO as currently constituted is a collection of Flag States. But in tankers (and bulk carriers), the major Flag States are owner dominated charades. At its core, IMO is a shipowner organization. IMO's job is to impose as little new expense on shipowners as public outcry will allow.

Technically, IMO has been a disaster. To recap,

1. IMO forced pre-Marpol ships to segregated ballast **without requiring that the new ballast tanks be properly protected**.
2. IMO took 15 years to mandate inerting cargo tanks on all tankers resulting in something like 100 unnecessary deaths.
3. IMO outlawed any practical connection from the cargo tanks to the ballast tanks, depriving the crew of their single most valuable after-the-fact spill reduction tool.
4. IMO replaced pre-Marpol single hulls with Marpol single hulls markedly increasing spillage in groundings and trebling ballast tank coated area.
5. IMO replaced Marpol single hulls with double hulls, trebling ballast tank coated area again and insuring that all cargo tank leaks will be into the ballast tanks **without requiring that this space be inerted**.
6. At the same time, IMO implicitly relaxed its own tank-size limits, one of the few truly intelligent IMO requirements, producing among other things the nonsensical one-across tanker.
7. IMO has mandated all sorts of quality assurance red tape guaranteeing that more and more tankers will be operated by short-run obsessed hirelings rather than crews that care for the ship.
8. IMO not only has not brought transparency to tanker regulation; it has institutionalized secrecy and the withholding of casualty data.
9. IMO has done practically nothing about the downratchet and the deterioration in tanker newbuilding standards. In particular, IMO has done nothing about fatigue cracking.
10. IMO has failed to mandate twin screw. In fact, it has passed and is passing regulation which is severely biased against twin screw. IMO has never shown any interest in machinery reliability.
11. IMO has failed to institute any system of builder liability.
12. IMO has become hopelessly intertwined with the Classification Society system, which infestation is currently being institutionalized in the form of "goal based standards".

Despite this abysmal record, some people have argued that IMO could be turned into a super-national body which would enforce a a single international system under a super-IMO.[9] This would well and truly establish a regulatory monopoly. But there would be no checks and balances. Given IMO's record to date, this is a truly scary thought. But there is no need to debate these issues. If a system based on a super-IMO had real teeth, it would be regarded as an unacceptable infringement of national sovereignty. Even if this were a good idea, which it isn't, it couldn't happen

At this point, we probably can't get rid of IMO. But we certainly cannot base our tanker regulatory system on this ponderous collective of Flag States.

---

[9] In some variants, this super-IMO would hire and pay Class for the inspection services.

7.2.4   Use the Underwriters?

A tanker regulatory system could conceivably be based on the underwriters. This system would retain Class, but have the insurers choose the Class and pay for the inspections. This system is theoretically attractive in its use of incorruptible, unemotional market forces.[10] But it would require that the underwriters do a good job of reflecting the relative risk between a poor ship and a good ship in setting the premia. This might happen in a competitive insurance market.

Unfortunately, the key insurance market for our purposes, the Protection and Indemnity or P&I market, which pays crew death/injury and pollution claims is about as uncompetitive as you can get. I don't want to go into any detail here, but the P&I market consists of strange cartel of mutual *Clubs*. This cartel (known as the Club of Clubs) bargains as a single entity in laying off its pollution risk on the market at Lloyds and elsewhere. From my experience, the Clubs have little internal tanker technical competence. Much, much worse, they are shipowner controlled. In fact, each Club is simply an agreement among shipowners. That's why they call it a Club. To expect this mess to set individual ship premia more or less correctly is hopelessly unrealistic.

Much more basically, our regulatory system should be focused on the rare, brobdingnagian spill. Very rare events are hard for even the most efficient insurance market to handle well. In order for insurance to have a positive influence on design and operation, you need a large enough sample of casualties so that the poor risks are clearly revealed despite the fact that a good ship can get unlucky and a bad ship can get lucky. Thankfully, brobdingnagian spills are too rare for this to happen.

Too many practical problems. We must reluctantly reject an underwriter based system. In fact, one can argue as Plimsoll did, that we would be better off if the owners could not insure themselves out of the spill risk.

---

[10] I'm been told that something like this happens in passenger ships where liability per passenger is substantial, and the individual Club retains almost all the risk. If a Club inspector (interestingly the insurers do **not** use Class) finds something wrong, you fix it immediately or lose your insurance. But I have no personal knowledge. It doesn't happen in tankers.

7.2.5 Cling to the Charterer?

A charterer based regulatory system has some real pluses. The oil companies, together with a few port states, have been the only really beneficial factors in tanker regulation. The oil companies gave us cargo tank inerting, cowing, and most of the other useful developments in tanker safety. The oil companies know more about tankers than anybody. We have a charterer vetting system already in operation, on which we could build.

A charterer based system, **in which the vetters went into the tanks**, could conceivably work in tankers. But nowhere else. And it probably won't even work in tankers as the big oil companies distance themselves from transportation, turning things over to oil traders and oil producers, who are far less sensitive to public outcry from spills.[11] The oil company tanker knowledge base has diminished radically in the last twenty five years, as the marine departments have been downsized or broken up to be replaced by managers who are far more worried about public perception and bean counting than technical reality.[12]

And we still have the problem of who pays for the inspections. Already the vetting system is being strained as some oil companies are being accused of not pulling their weight, unfairly taking advantage of their competitors' expensive inspections to avoid paying for their own.

Finally and most basically, there is something contradictory about asking buyers to police sellers. The oil companies' legitimate responsibility to their shareholders is to obtain transportation services as cheaply as possible. At best, a regulatory role puts them in a very conflicted position. One practical result is that every time the tanker market tightens up and it becomes expensive to be choosy, the oil companies' tanker quality standards loosen drastically.[13]

A charterer based system cannot be counted on in tankers, and the system we come up with should work for other types of ships as well.

---

[11] You think tankers owners are bad. Tanker owners are a choir of angels compared with oil traders.

[12] From what I saw in Korea, the top independent owners now have better technical standards than the oil companies. The shipyards agree. The Korean yards divide their customers into three quality categories: *Asian*, *European*, and *Greek*. In Korlish, an *Asian* owner wants the cheapest ship Class will accept, a Class minimum ship. A *European* owner will require modest improvements over Class minimums. The Korean yards lump all the major oil companies in the *European* category. An owner who wants something significantly better than Class minimums is put in the *Greek* category. I suspect that this surprising terminology is due to the fact that in the Greek system there is often a direct link between the owner and the guys who have to operate the ships.

[13] Or they buy the oil delivered from oil traders who have no standards.

7.3 Port State Control

So by process of elimination, we are left with the Port States. It could be worse. The Port States are the main environmental victims of poor regulation. They have a real stake in robust, reliable, well-operated tankers. The Port States can have very effective power as OPA 90 proved. Most importantly, few Port States are shipowner or shipyard controlled. ***The new system must be built around the Port State.***

7.3.1 Current Status of Port State Control

Port state control (PSC) of tankers is not a new idea. The Australians pioneered Port State inspections.[62] The USCG has been doing Tank Vessel Evaluations since the EXXON VALDEZ. However, it is the Europeans who have the most influential PSC system, the Paris MOU, www.paris-mou.org. The Paris MOU now comprises 20 countries including Canada (East coast only). The system involves not only inspecting 25% of the tankers calling at the members ports, but also
1. a centralized database,
2. a scheme for targeting high risk ships for inspection,
3. guidelines for inspections and detentions,
4. rules for black-listing ships and an agreement to bar black-listed ships from entering any signatory port.

Periodically, the MOU does no-holds-barred statistical summaries of deficiencies and detentions by Flag and Class. Particularly egregious ships make the "rustbucket" list complete with disgusting pictures. In 2002, the European Union set up an organization, the European Maritime Safety Agency, to provide technical support to the Paris MOU effort.

The Paris MOU has spawned a number of regional copycats including the Acuerdo de Vina del Mar, a 1992 agreement among South American Port States, and the Tokyo MOU, a 1993 agreement amount Pacific Rim nations including Canada (West Coast), www.tokyo-mou.org. A common database at www.equasis.org has been establised where detention data is exchanged.

In short, Port State Control (PSC) has become an established fact of life for tankers.[14] And it has done considerable good in forcing the truly awful operators to either upgrade their paperwork and cosmetics or leave most of the major trades.

---

[14] In fact, there are too many countries involved in Port State Control. When FOC's like Cyprus and Malta become MOU signatories, it is time to start restricting membership.

But there are two basic problems with Port State control of tankers to date:

- The inspectors don't go in the tanks. Both the ERIKA and PRESTIGE had undergone multiple Port State inspections shortly before they suffered massive structural failure. The PSC effort has left hull structure in the hands of the Classification Societies.

- The Port State efforts are having no impact on tanker design and construction. In two very intense years in Korea, the issue of Port State regulation came up never.

In order for Port State Control to have real impact on tanker spillage both these fundamental faults must be rectified.

7.3.2   Tank Inspection

In order to make Port State Control truly effective for tanker, the first requirement is that the PSC inspectors must go in the tanks. I'll use MOU as a shorthand for any PSC organization, whether it be a regional MOU, the USCG, or other.[15]

Frequency   Whenever a ship makes an MOU port call, the MOU headquarters should assign the tank(s) to be inspected. These assignments should be based on a combination of past inspection reports, and time since last inspection with a substantial bit of randomness thrown in.[16] The shipowner must not be able to accurately predict which tanks will be inspected. Nor should he be able to get all his tanks inspected at once. This would allow him some flexibility in picking the inspection state, and by picking the same inspection state over and over again, the checks and balances of multiple, different inspection bodies could be avoided.

A neat feature of a PSC system is that it is not dependent on a single inspection organization. A USCG inspector might be followed by a UK or

---

[15] The PSC organizational structure is still evolving. Presumably, the US will come to its senses and join at least the Paris-MOU; but, as long as there is good exchange of information, including the inspection reports, it doesn't really matter.

[16] Ships with marginal or questionable inspection records would be assigned more tanks, more frequently than normal. But the difference should be created probabilisticly. The Paris MOU is switching to a risk based schedule in which ships with good records will go to a two year schedule. This is too non-random. No owner or crew should be completely certain that the ship won't be inspected at the next port call. I was always impressed by the extra effort our crews took when they knew a TVE was imminent.

French inspector. There will be no pressure to cover up for the last inspector's mistakes or omissions — a dramatic change from the Class system. And even if a Port State with strong shipowner influence is part of the system or a chauvinistic inspector decided to favor ships of his own Flag, it would not make all that much difference. Any forgiving inspections would be caught sooner or later, mostly sooner.

Transparency All tank inspection data/reports must go to the central MOU clearing house. All such reports without exception should be made available to public scrutiny. For the first time, we will be able to do systematic analysis of our problems to decent scientific standards. A revolutionary change from Class enforced omerta. And the bad guys will be exposed. This is not that different from the current Paris MOU system except that the full inspection reports including pictures would be made available.

Standards This is not the place to try and develop detailed tank inspection standards but the basic concept would be quite different from Class. Class's ridiculous and impossible to enforce acceptance of 20% or more wastage would be chucked. ***In a well-protected, well-maintained tank, there should be nil wastage, regardless of the age of the ship.*** Appendix A outlines how this can be accomplished. Among other things, it will require that the segregated ballast tanks be inerted, something we must have for safety reasons as well. Unlike Class, which gives old ships a break, the standards will not be age dependent. Exactly the same standards will apply to a 40 year old ship as a brand new ship. Once again our model should be airline regulation.

PSC inspectors would flag minor coating breakdown combined with either poor inerting or cathodic protection and require that it be fixed before the next inspection. Anything more would require immediate steel renewal and re-inspection. In other words, good owner standards. This is a complete change from Class standards; but is is not a pipe dream. This is the way the old Hellespont ULCC's operated in the last five years of their existence. Robust ships, continuously maintained to these standards will never require any steel renewal.[17] If you don't know a good tanker owner, think Navy standards.

Detention and Blacklist The current Paris MOU rules are fine. The inspector has the power to detain the ship. The ship can appeal with the

---

[17] Crews will have to get bigger, but that's a good idea for a lot of reasons.

burden of proof on the ship. No more friendly negotiations with the surveyor, and then threatening to switch Class if the surveyor is inflexible.

Objections The Tromedy will fight this expansion of the PSC function tooth and nail. The Tromedy will produce all kinds of objections including:

Ship Delays We need to realize that tank inspection under the current system is far more difficult than it need be or should be. People make a big deal about the difficulties of tank inspection. But it is not rocket science. Any competent inspector knows within minutes of entering the tank whether or not the tank is in good condition or not. The difficulties arise when one is trying to determine whether a lousy tank is still marginally acceptable to Class or so lousy that even Class can't accept it. One can spend days in a tank fruitlessly debating this conundrum; and weeks arguing about just how much new steel is required to move the tank from unacceptably horrible to acceptably horrible. If Port State control imposes real standards on tank condition, tank inspections will go much more smoothly and quickly.

However, tank inspection will still be a very substantial effort. Tanks can be and should be inspected underway. This does three thing:

1. There is no ship delay.
2. The time pressure is taken off the inspector.
3. And he gets to see the ship in operation.

Inspectors must be prepared to ride the ships. This is not a major problem. There are few major tanker routes where it not possible to put an inspector on-board via helicopter one or two days prior to arrival or taken an inspector off one or two days after departure.[18]

Too Expensive Since the inspections are not under owner control, they need not be as comprehensive as the pseudo-inspections undertaken by Class. In the past, the Tromedy's response to lousy surveys was more lousy surveys. Corroded ships are not wasted in just one isolated location. The right combination of targeting and randomness will reveal the ships with problems without having to inspect an inordinate number of tanks. We can handle the problem with fewer, but far less forgiving, tank inspections than Class currently undertakes.

---

[18] Since most of the MOU ports are tanker discharge ports, the ballast tanks would be inspected prior to discharge. The cargo tanks after.

Anyway the world is already paying for three entirely different systems: Class, charterer vetting, and the Port States. Class may be ineffective but it is not cheap. An owner of a VLCC can expect to average $60,000 per year in Class fees. The Class system will atrophy and disappear — or turn into inspection services hired by the Port States — as underwriters and charterers recognize it is not doing anything.

How are you going to do Special Surveys? Special Surveys will have far less importance in the new system than they do under the Tromedy. Special Surveys should be non-events as they are now for the few really good tanker owners. However, there a couple of items that can only be inspected in a drydock. The tailshaft and anchor chains are examples.

Tanker owners who wished to stay in the MOU's good graces would have to inform the MOU of any impending docking. MOU headquarters could assign/hire an inspector to a docking to produce a report for the MOU for these items. In general, dockings should not be used to inspect tanks. The owner could be billed by MOU for the expense but have no role in the choice of the inspectors or what they do. Hired in inspectors would be audited by random re-inspections from MOU staff.

Blackmail PSC inspectors have enormous power in single handledly being able to detain a ship. It is inevitable that some will abuse this power, in some cases in an attempt to blackmail the owner. But there are a lot of checks and balances built in. It is highly likely that subsequent inspection will be in another country. An unfair inspection will be revealed at that time and the MOU headquarters should investigate.[19] A ship should have the right to appeal any detention and call for an immediate reinspection. Worst come to worst, the ship can go to court to obtain compensation for an unfair detention. This occured in Canada in 2004 with the ship, a bulk carrier called the Lantau Peak, winning a four million dollar judgement. The decision was overturned on appeal, but the point is that the whole procedure is out in the open and the normal justice system can be brought in when required. Contrast this with the Class system where everything is hidden and the inspection service is bribed as a matter of course.

---

[19] The head inspector's identity needs to be part of the public record.

How can PSC affect design and construction? The Tromedy will not
   raise this issue; but it is an excellent question, and the subject of the
   next section.

The only real reason why the PSC inspectors have not gone in the tanks
is the assumption that the Flag State and Class can handle this function.
The record clearly shows that this is not the case. ***Port state control
needs to view itself not as an adjunct to the IMO/FOC/Class
triumverate, but a complete replacement.***[20]

---

[20] The MOU's generally say they will enforce only recognized (read IMO) international
conventions. But the IMO regulations are a spotty hodge-podge of kneejerk reactions
to big spills combined with largely unnecessary redtape. There really aren't any IMO
regulations dealing with robustness of hull structure, not to mention machinery reliability,
or shipyard liability.
   As a fairly minor example, Australian inspectors were stymied when they wanted to
detain a ship for unsafe mooring wires. But since there are no IMO regs on moorings
wires — and there probably shouldn't be — this would have violated the Tokyo-MOU.
The Port States should simply go with the inspector's judgement. If the ship doesn't like
it, it can appeal.

7.4 Regulation of Design and Construction

There are four separate aspects to the pre-delivery regulatory issue:
1. Builder Guarantee and Liability
2. Construction Rules
3. Design Approval
4. Construction Supervision.

7.4.1 Builder Guarantee and Liability

Yard Guarantee

The single most important improvement we could make to the pre-delivery process is a meaningful Builder Guarantee. Here's a typical (abbreviated) shipbuilding guarantee.

> The Builder for the period of Twelve (12) months after delivery guarantees the Vessel and all her parts against all defects discovered within the this Guarantee period which are due to defective material, construction miscalculation or negligent or other improper acts of the Builder.
>
> ....
>
> The Builder shall have no responsibility or liability for any other defect whatsoever in the Vessel than the Defects specified in Paragraph 1.[clause immediately above]
>
> ....
>
> Nor shall the Builder in any circumstance be responsible for any consequential losses or expense directly or indirectly occasioned by the reason of the defects specified in paragraph 1.
>
> ...
>
> The guarantee contained above replaces and excludes any other liability, guarantee, warranty and/or condition imposed or implied by the law, customary, statutory or otherwise by reason of the construction and Sale of the Vessel to the Buyer.

Basically, the yard will fix anything that falls apart in the first 12 months, rewarranty of maybe six months, and that's it.[21] You will get a much better

---

[21] Owners can do a certain amount of haggling, get a few additional months here, a word change there, but nothing really significant. And the all important exclusion of consequential liability is sacrosanct.

guarantee when you buy a toaster. ***Much worse, it explicitly absolves the yard from any consequential liability.***

With such a guarantee and with the builder absolved from all real responsibility, the yard's design objective becomes: build the cheapest possible ship that won't completely fall apart in the first 12 months — something that the yards have become very good at. They really have no choice; it has become a commercial imperative.

Contrast this with the situation in the aircraft industry. Here are the typical guarantee terms for a commercial aircraft purchase.

1. Full warranty for five years.
2. Rewarranty of two years.
3. Service Life Policy. Primary structure including landing gear and movable surfaces are guaranteed for 12 years in the sense that cost of replacement is shared between builder and buyer with the builder proportion decreasing linearly from the end of the full warranty period to zero at 12 years.
4. Similar terms are provided by the engine manufacturers.

If shipbuilders faced airplane warranty terms, their design objective function would change markedly. An aircraft style guarantee would take us thru the first Special Survey by which time the majority of design/manufacturing defects will have shown up.

And the service life policy would dictate that major failures anywhere in the first two special surveys would expose the yards to big financial penalties.

Such guarantees generate another benefit. Since the aircraft and engine builders are on the hook, they take a real interest in how the vehicles are maintained. For example, the airplane engine builder is involved in every major inspection and overhaul of his engines. He has a strong pecuniary interest in calling out poor maintenance and operating policies in a way that a regulator does not. If he can prove that the maintenance/operation is not per manual, he is off the hook. This in turn puts real pressure on the owner to do his maintenance correctly, pressure he can't affect by threatening to take his Classification fees elsewhere.

Yard Liability

Along with a real guarantee, the yard must be prepared to accept the same kind of liability that an airline manufacturer accepts for the consequences of improper design or manufacturer. My guess is that this alone will be enough to dissuade a yard from building a single screw tanker.

Impact

I can't overstate the impact that a real guarantee and real liability would have on the yard design and construction process. The whole design philosophy would change completely. The question would no longer be: can we sneak this saving of half a ton of steel passed a compliant Class? This is the wrong question. The question would become: is the saving of $250 worth the increased chance of a big problem down the road? This is the right question. It would be the end of the downratchet.

The shipyards are full of Quality Control people. When we were in Daewoo, the total yard workforce including contractors was about 18,000. Over 500 of these people were Quality Control. Their job was to enforce the yard quality standards. Which they did, but in the negative sense, as in "no more than yard standards". Their real job was to be a buffer between the owner's inspectors and the actual workers. Most of the QC guys spoke some English; few of the real workers did. When a owner's superintendent wanted to talk to a worker about how something should be done, the job of the QC guy was to step in and explain to the owner's man that the work was being done to yard standards, had passed all the yard QC checks, (he has extensive paperwork to prove this) and there was nothing to worry about. There was usually some rapid fire Korean as well which we interpreted to mean "don't worry about this foreigner, I'll take care of it".

I hired a local to teach our people some Korean. It did me no good, but our Greeks and especially our Philippinos picked it up quickly. Our guys would wait until there was no QC person around and then talk to the worker or foreman about the job. It was amazing how often this would work. Most people would rather do a good job, than a poor job.

If the yard was subject to a real guarantee and real liability, the role of the yard QC people would change completely. If there were a problem down the road, the first heads to roll would be Quality Control. Now this immense QC effort would be directed at actually improving quality rather than keeping the owner's people from slowing down production.

A real guarantee plus liability will be quite expensive. My guess is that at least initially it will be as costly as all the specific improvements laid out in Chapter 6. And it should be. The ships are too cheap. But the difference will be all-important.

Implementation

Because it is such a wrenching change, the yards will go ballistic before they will accept a real guarantee and real liability. It will have to rammed down their throats. To expect that defender of the status quo, IMO, to do any ramming is preposterous.

The only way it will happen is for port states to refuse to allow any tanker into their ports unless it is built by a yard that is willing to offer such a guarantee and accept such liability. Unfortunately, the current ships will have to be grandfathered.[22] The yards will undoubtedly refuse to even talk about such a change; but, if say the Paris-MOU plus the USA holds its ground, the yards will crack.

The Japanese and Korean yards are petrified of the immense new ship-building capacity in China. They know they can't compete with Chinese wages; but they are in much better position to accept a real guarantee than the Chinese. The Koreans and Japanese can build good ships if they want to. The Chinese may not be able to for at least a while. Once the Koreans and Japanese realize that this is the only way that they can pull tanker orders away from China, they will cave. All the MOU has to do is to is to make sure to promulgate this requirement during a slump in the shipbuilding market.

The port states must require a real builder guarantee and impose real liability on the ship yards. Right now the owner (and for some convoluted reason the charterer) bear all the responsibility and the yard none. Contrast this with the automobile case. Does anybody ever sue a car owner for buying an unsafe car? Or in the case of a charterer, for riding in an unsafe cab? Of course, not. They correctly go after the car maker. We must do the same with tankers.

---

[22] This will put the tanker owners on the port states side. Owners are always in favor of a change that makes tankers more expensive *as long as their current ships are grandfathered.* It increases the value of the existing ships. This is the reason few tanker owners resisted double bottoms.

7.4.2 Construction Rules

One can argue that, if we had proper builder guarantees and liability, we wouldn't need Class-style construction rules. But we have to guard against throwing the baby out with the bath. Even if we are able to enforce real guarantees and liability, there will be a difficult transition period.

The Class Rules embody a great deal of experience. If it weren't for the downratchet, they wouldn't be that bad. All we really need to do is reverse the downratchet – put that 15% plus back in – use finite element correctly, require twin screw, ballast tank inerting, and lots of tanks; and we'd have a pretty decent tanker.[23]

I am going to surprise you. I think IMO could do this. I can imagine IMO setting non-prescriptive rules such as the loading and flooding requirements of Section 6.3.1 and setting structural analysis standards such as Section 6.3.2. IMO has already imposed similar requirements with respect to stability (See Marpol Reg 25).

I could see IMO, properly prodded, imposing twin screw in the same way it imposed double hull. I could see IMO, properly prodded, imposing ballast tank inerting and smaller tanks. IMO through the FOC's is an owner controlled organization. Owners will not resist an improvement in newbuilding standards as long as their current ships are grandfathered. The key phrase here is "properly prodded". In the past the only way to prod IMO is with a big spill or unilateral port state action.

The port states can be the cattle prod. If the Paris-MOU+USA informs IMO that they will not accept new tankers complying with IMO regs unless the regulations include the above measures, IMO will respond. If not, then the MOU develops those measures on its own.

Either way we end up with non-prescriptive, non-Class Rules consistent with Chapter 6.[24]

---

[23] Of course, we'd have to change some of the stupider aspects of the IMO Rules, including the anti-twin screw bias (Section 6.5.3). If the (dubious) goal is the ability to withstand a 2 meter vertical penetration from the baseline without involving a cargo or fuel oil tank, then say so. If the goal is to keep the pump room operational in the face of such a penetration, then say so. And the inane prohibition against a connection between the cargo and ballast tanks (Section 4.2) should not only be dropped, it should be reversed. Such a connection, properly valved, should be mandated.

[24] Since these rules will be non-Class, they will be far better insulated from the downratchet, if over my dead body the corrupt Class system is allowed to survive.

7.4.3   Design versus Spec

Currently, the owner doesn't buy a design from the yard. He buys a *Specification* or Spec. The Spec describes the ship in functional terms making copious references to the Class Rules and "Builder Standards". As drafted by the yard, it is a very carefully worded document. The yard is then free to implement the Spec as it sees fit. This gives the downratchet a great deal of wriggle room. With good owners, the Spec is the subject of endless haggling, with the owner's people trying to make the Spec as tight as possible, and the yard trying to keep it loose and general. It's a terrible way to design a ship.

One of the crazier aspects of the Tromedy is that it forces each owner to try and write his own rules. Good owners have so little faith in the current Class rules that few will accept a totally Class minimum ship. Each tries to protect himself by adding a phrase here to the Spec or tacking on this or increasing this or changing the wording there and so on. This generates all kinds of inefficiencies in the design and production process. More basically, it turns design into a contract drafting debate. Speaking for myself, I would have been far happier buying a proven, robust design, then semi-blindly attempting to come up with a Specification that might protect me against some of the worst aspects of the downratchet.

I believe large commercial ships, especially large tankers and passenger ships, should be treated like commercial aircraft. That is, the design (not a Spec) must be approved by an independent public body. This body could be IMO, enforcing construction rules acceptable to the port state MOU's; or it could be a body set up by the port states directly, such as the European Maritime Safety Agency.

In this context, design should be defined to include the fifty or so drawings and supporting analyses that truly define a ship. The yards divide design into (a) *basic design*, and (b) production design or working drawings. This division can also serve as the natural definition of design for approval purposes. The public body would approve the *basic design*. In many situations, especially with unusual or special purpose ships, the basic design is produced by a non-yard design house. This happens all the time in offshore rigs. It's an excellent division of labor. A naval archtectural firm which sees a niche or in collaboration with an owner with special requirements develops a design, gets it approved, and then sells it or puts it out to bid to the yards.

If the system only approved robust, reliable designs, all owners wishing to order a standard tanker would be comfortable with simply purchasing one of the approved designs and picking a color.[25] This standardization would reap economies in both design and production which would go a significant way toward paying for all the improvements that we must have.

7.4.4 Construction Supervision

Once again a real guarantee and proper builder liability will take a great deal pressure off the construction supervision problem. A real guarantee will put yard the QC team on the side of good ships.

However, owners will still want to have their own people in the yards, at least until the new regulatory system earns their confidence. The question then becomes how do we resolve disputes between the owner's inspector and the yard. Suppose the owner's man thinks a particular edge on a bracket is not ground as smoothly as the approved design calls for, and the yard QC guy thinks the edge meets the design tolerance.

There are two ways to go here:
1. Rely on standard contract law.
2. Set up an instant arbitrator.

All shipbuilding contracts have methods for resolving disputes between the Buyer and Seller. Usually, this involves a standard arbitration process. The problem with this is that by the time the arbitrators reach a decision months after the process is started as to whether a particular edge is ground smoothly enough to meet the requirements, the ship is probably already afloat. The overly sharp edge (which will result in very early coating failure) is a fait accompli. The best that the owner can hope for is some sort of compensation. Quite clearly, the normal arbitration process doesn't work for the multitude of minor disagreements that can arise on the production line. The standard arbitration process should be reserved for the really major disputes for which it was designed.

What is needed in an instant arbitrator who can be called in and make an immediate ruling. This person cannot be paid by either the owner or the yard. Nor need he be domiciled anywhere near the yard — probably better if he isn't. No yard is more than 24 hours away from anywhere.[26] What would work is to have IMO (or the MOU equivalent) set up an arbitration office. In the event of a dispute, an IMO guy would be called in and make his ruling. The IMO office and its salaries would be paid out of general

---

[25] To paraphase, Henry Ford, they can have any color they want as long as it is white. See Section A.2.2.

[26] In some cases, e.g. working drawings not consistent with design, the instant arbitrator can resolve the dispute from a distance.

IMO funds. The loser pays the travel expenses associated with a particular dispute.

We had a version of this in Korea. The instant arbitrator was of all people, our Class surveyor. I was gambling that our ability to change Class up to steel cutting on the next ship would keep the surveyor honest.[27] Both yards accepted the clause without demur, I assume because they were used to having their way with Class. My Greeks were very worried about the clause for the same reason.

It worked far better than I expected. In fact every time my guys said, OK let's go to instant arbitration, the yard fixed the problem without our ever having to call in the surveyor.

I'm not sure why. Maybe the local foreman/QC guy simply didn't want to take the chance the decision would go against him and the resultant loss of face. It was just easier and less hassle for him to do the job right. When yard management saw what was happening, both yards came to us and tried to get the clause eliminated as both "unnecessary" and "detrimental to our close relationship". They were not successful.

Instant arbitration works. All that is required is the threat of a fair decision.

---

[27] Also unbeknownst to the yards, I had negotiated the right to fire the head surveyor with Class prior to signing the contracts.

7.5 Final Points

There you have it, my suggestion for a regulatory process to replace the Tromedy. I'd like to make two final points about the system I'm advocating:

1. The role of Class.
2. No age restriction.

The Role of Class

For all the depressing reasons we've spent 280 pages wading through, the Classification Society plays no regulatory role in my proposed system. We cannot have the regulatee (aka Client) choosing and feeding the regulator. Does this mean the Classification Societies would disappear? I don't think so. Class is an inspection gun for hire. The problem is that this gun has been hired by the wrong people: the yards prior to delivery, the owners after delivery.

We will still need tanker inspection services and the Classification Societies have some terrific inspectors: smart, tough, and experienced. I expect to see port states hiring Class people for port state inspections. I expect to see owners hiring Class people for yard supervision. I know I would. I expect to see IMO hiring Class people to help write the new Rules and as instant arbitrators.

I have no problem with this at all. I have a lot of respect for many Class guys, especially the surveyors in the trenches. Very few of them can be bribed. It is the the Class system, where bribery (called fees) is so routine that it goes unnoticed, that I have a problem with. Reinhold Niebuhr once said

> The problem of the age is not imposing morality on the individual, but imposing morality on the organization.[58]

Niebuhr wasn't talking about the Class system. But he could have been.

No age restriction

Nowhere in my regulatory system is there any restriction on vessel age. This is intentional. A mandatory age limit would be a death blow to the kind of robust tanker I envision. As soon as you tell an owner that a ship will be worthless after age X, where X is any number less than 50, he will rightly try and build a ship that is designed only to survive to age X. And if you design a ship that can only survive to age X, you automatically have a ship that will be a problem at age 0. An age restriction is an open invitation to shoddy design. In order for a ship to be a good ship, it must be designed to last forever.

Under the Tromedy, the calls for an age limitation are understandable. Unless a ship is properly maintained, she will deteriorate, and sooner or later that deterioration will cause a casualty. We have talked at length about scores of such casualties including ERIKA, CASTOR, and PRESTIGE. The Tromedy failed miserably to force badly deteriorated ships out of service. The people who call for an age limitation have correctly lost faith in the Tromedy's ability to identify and remove deteriorated ships. They are using age in an attempt to counter the Tromedy's failure.

But there are two requirements for a safe ship.

1. The ship as originally designed must be robust and reliable.
2. And she must be maintained in an as-new condition.

An age restriction guarantees that the new ship will be flimsy and unreliable, while at the same time doing nothing about the Tromedy's failure to control deterioration. In fact, an age restriction promotes deterioration as the ship approaches the age limit.

Under the new system, many tankers will be forced out of service at a very young age; but well-built, well-maintained ships will trade until a change in technology renders them economically obsolete. The port states must make it clear that, *unlike Class*, there will be no age-related standards. Exactly the same standards will apply to a 40 year old ship as a brand new ship. Conversely, any ship meeting those standards will be welcome in MOU ports regardless of age.

Allow me one final story. The offshore drilling rig market is similar to the tanker market, highly cyclic with prolonged slumps. In 1988, I was involved in convincing Jim Tisch at Loews to invest in offshore rigs. We bought four rigs at less than 5% their replacement cost. My group was responsible for these rigs for a short while. But in 1989, we bought Diamond Offshore and 30 rigs. Diamond had an experienced rig management team, so control of all the rigs was placed in a separate subsidiary. The venture was successful and in 1995 Diamond expanded by purchasing Odeco, another large drilling contractor.

Odeco had an old drillship called the Clipper which was scuffling about Asia. The vessel was reportedly in bad condition. Diamond's management was not fond of drillships, and had decided to scrap her. Jim Tisch asked me to inspect the vessel in Singapore.

As I approached the rig in the Singapore anchorage, I decided the Diamond guys were right. Externally, she looked terrible. Nothing but the rig itself had been maintained. But when I went into the tanks, I found them in remarkably good shape; and the structure looked awfully strong for a relatively small ship.

Going through the ship's papers, I discovered that the Clipper had been built as a 25,000 ton tanker in 1953 at Newport News Shipbuilding. At the time, Newport News built good ships.[28] In 1976, she had been converted to a drillship at Mitsubishi. At that time all her tanks has been reblasted and recoated to a high standard. In 1995, almost all that coating was still in near-perfect condition. Buried in an old file cabinet, I found a midship section drawing. To my astonishment, the bottom plate was 38 mm thick. This was a 25,000 tonner. At the time I had good Japanese built 400,000 tonners whose bottom plate was 28 mm thick. The other scantlings were nearly as impressive.

That night I called Jim and told him that there was no way I could reproduce a hull as good as this 42 year old ship. The decision to scrap the Clipper was reversed. The Clipper was cleaned up, fitted with dynamic positioning, and a modern drilling rig. In 1997 at the age of 44, the Diamond Clipper set several deep water drilling records. Given proper maintenance, there is no reason why she won't still be drilling 20 years from now.

The key to good ships is not age. It's setting up a system that
a) produces robust, reliable tankers, and
b) identifies ships that have been allowed to deteriorate, and removes them from service, regardless of age.

The Tromedy does neither. We must change it.

---

[28] In 1962, Newport News was my first employer. I used to take my lunch breaks at the statue of the founder, Collis Huntington. The inscription was a quote. "We will build good ships here. At a profit if we can; at a loss if we must; but always good ships." Sounds corny but at the time, the yard had not had a labor stoppage in its 70 year history. Just after I left, the yard was bought by Tenneco, a conglomerate. Tenneco's first move was to get rid of the Huntington statue. Within six months, the yard suffered a prolonged strike.

Glossary

Advanced Radar Plotting Aid (ARPA) System which projects other ships' course on a radar screen based on current course and speed.

allision Casualty in which ship hits a stationary object, usually a berth.

Automatic Identification System (AIS) A transponder-like capability which provides vessel name and principle particulars to other ships in neighborhood. In a recent development this data can be displayed on the radar screen next to vessel's position.

ballast Seawater carried on tanker when she has little or no oil cargo, in order to sink the ship deep enough to provide proper propeller and rudder immersion and to avoid structural damage from bow slamming.

ballast leg The portion of a voyage during which a tanker is returning to an oil producing region carrying no oil.

brobdingnagian Spill larger than 10 million liters. Almost all oil spilled by tankers is spilled in a handful of brobdingnagian spills.

charter Contract between tanker owner and charterer (q.v.) by which tanker owner agrees to provide oil transportation services. Charters can be for a specified number of voyages (voyage charter) or for a period of time (term charter). A voyage charter for a single voyage commencing within a few weeks of the charter agreement is called a spot charter.

charterer A buyer of tanker transportation services. The tanker owner's customer.

Class Shorthand for Classification Society q.v..

Class Rules A Classification Society's vessel construction requirements.

Classification Society Entity which inspects ships for a fee and certifies that the ship meets its requirements.

Condition of Class Inspection or repair required by Class which if not complied with could result in the ship's being de-listed, q.v.

continuous survey Inspection of vessel machinery by a ship's Chief Engineer in lieu of inspection by Classification Society surveyor.

cow-ing Crude oil washing, the process of cleaning a tank by high pressure jets of crude oil.

cracking Steel fractures due to repeated cyclic loading of under-designed or corroded structure.

Dance of Death Collision in which one ship alters to port and the other to starboard due to the ambiguity in the Rules of the Road in an encounter in which the ships are displaced to starboard.

de-listing The removal of a ship from a Classification Society for failure to meet the Society's requirements.

deadweight Carrying capacity of the ship in tons. Includes the ship's own fuel.

deballasting The process of pumping ballast water out of the ship, almost always into the sea.

design for producability The philosophy of designing hull structure to minimize erection man-hours with little or no regard to its effect on structual performance.

Electronic Chart Display System (ECDIS) Electronic display similar to in-car navigation systems but shows not only own ship's position on chart, but also other ships' positions as well.

finite element method (FE) Computationally intensive method for estimating the stresses throughout a structure by dividing the structure up into little pieces.

Flag of Convenience A country who registers ships without regard to the nationality of the beneficial owner for the purpose of collecting registration and tonnage fees.

Flag State The country where the ship is registered.

free surface effect The transfer of liquid in a tank to the low side of a ship reducing stability and increasing list.

gale ballast tank A cargo tank into which the master is allowed to put ballast if the ship's safety requires it.

give-way The vessel that is required to alter its course to avoid a collision by the Rules of the Road.

hirelings Entities which manage ships they do not own.

hog Condition when there is more buoyancy that weight in the middle of the ship. The middle of the ship humps up and ends droop down. Most double hull tankers in ballast are in a strongly hogged condition. Or hog can be caused when the peak of a big wave is near midships. Hog is the opposite of sag (q.v.).

hotwork Welding or cutting steel.

hydrostatic balance Situation in which the external seawater pressure at the top of tank damage is equal to the internal tank pressure at this point. See Appendix C for what this means.

IACS International Association of Classification Societies. An organization of the largest Classification Societies which attempts to remove differences in Class rules.

IMO number Unique seven digit number assigned to each ship. Remains with a ship for its entire life and is not reused.

independent A tanker owner who has no oil of his own to move. Relies on renting out his ship to an oil company or trader.

inert gas Gas containing less than 5% oxygen, usually obtained from the boiler exhaust.

inerting The process of pumping low oxygen gas into the empty portion of a tank.

International Maritime Organization (IMO) Offshoot of UN which attempts to facilitate agreements between Flag States (q.v) on matters relating to ocean transportation. Voting is on the basis of the size of each country's fleet.

isoism The requirement for extensive documentation of all operating procedures, combined with external audits to ensure that these paperwork requirements are complied with.

lighter The tanker to which oil is transferred by lightering (q.v.). These tankers are typically one-fourth or one-fifth the size of the tanker being lightered. But they are still enormous ships, roughly the size of a large air-craft carrier.

lightering The process of transferring cargo off-shore from extremely large tankers to smaller tanker whose draft is small enough to allow them to enter the destination port.

lightweight The weight of the ship when empty of fuel and cargo in tons.

lightweight curve Longitudinal distribution of the ship's own weight.

loaded leg The portion of a voyage during which a tanker is carrying oil. The revenue earning portion of the trip.

lolling Ship suddenly listing to one side or the other due to insufficient stability.

manning agent Company which provides crew to owners and ship managers. Almost always domiciled in the country of the crew. In many countries, derives substantial income from kick-backs.

Marpol tanker A single hull tanker meeting the MARPOL/78 segregated ballast requirements.

member state A government which has agreed to comply with the IMO (q.v.) conventions.

OBO Ore-Bulk-Oil. Tankers that can also carry dry bulk cargos such as coal or ore. These tankers have double bottoms and usually double sides.

OCIMF Oil Company International Marine Forum. The major oil companies official tanker organization through which some of the oil company tanker experience was transmitted to the rest of the industry. Now largely defunct.

one-across tanker Double hull tanker in which a single cargo tank extends from one double side to the other.

pitting Rapid localized corrosion of cargo tank bottoms.

port state The country where the ship loads or discharges.

pre-Marpol tanker A single hull tanker built before MARPOL/78 required segregated ballast.

Pressure/Vacuum (P/V) Valves Tank relief valves which will open if the over-pressure in the tank is more than 1.4 m water (14% higher than normal atmospheric pressure) or the under-pressure is more than 0.4 m vacuum (4% lower than atmospheric pressure).

purging The process of replacing the inert gas/hydrocarbon mixture in a tank with normal air for tank inspection or repair.

sag Condition in which the forward and aft ends of the ship are pushed up and the center portion drops down. When a tanker is fully loaded, there is usually more weight than buoyancy near the middle of the ship creating sag. Or sag can be created when the trough of a big wave is near midships.

scantlings Size and thickness of steel structural members

scrubber Apparatus for removing sulfur from stack gas by spraying the gas with sea water.

segregated ballast System in which sea-water ballast is (almost) never carried in cargo oil tanks.

shipper A buyer of transportation services. The shipowner's customer. In the tanker market, charterer is a synonym.

Single Buoy Mooring (SBM) Large buoy in deep water connected to shore by pipelines into which very large tankers can discharge avoiding lightering (q.v.) and the subsequent in-shore trip by the lighter.

slack tank A tank that is neither completely full nor completely empty.

slop tanks Small cargo tanks fitted with heating coils. Tank cleaning residues and other oil-contaminated water is directed to these tanks where the oil and water is allowed to separate, and then a portion of the underlying seawater is decanted and pumped overboard. The remaining mixture of oil and water is called slops. Cargo is loaded on top of the slops, and the slops are pumped ashore at the next discharge port.

sloshing resonance Situation which develops when the motion of a tank due to the ship's motion is in sync with the motion of the liquid in the tank resulting in a massive wave crashing back and forth within the tank.

slow-steaming Operating at reduced speeds during market slumps when the savings in fuel is larger than the loss in revenue.

Special Survey Extensive set of Classification Society inspections which take place every five years at a drydocking.

stand-on The vessel that is (sort of) required to maintain its course by the Rules of the Road.

steering gear Massive hydraulic rams or vanes used to turn the rudder.

stern tube seal Spring loaded rings which keep the propeller shaft lubricating oil from leaking into the sea.

stringer Large horizontal tank structural members, mini-decks, whose job is to keep the tank walls in position.

surveyor Classification Society inspector.

surveys Classification Society inspections.

swash bulkhead Non-watertight partition within a tank designed to avoid sloshing resonance, q.v.

tank breathing Diurnal expansion of gas and liquid in a cargo tank resulting in tank vapor being expelled into the atmosphere during the heat of the day. Often followed by outside air being sucked into the tank during the coolest part of the night.

Tank Vessel Evaluation (TVE) Annual inspection of tankers calling at USA ports by the United States Coast Guard.

Traffic Separation Schemes (TSS) The imposition of one-way lanes in restricted waterways.

Trim and Stability Booklet Document which describes the cargo and ballast loading patterns which a tanker crew may legally use.

trip Main engine or generator shutting itself down upon sensing a dangerous condition.

Tromedy Current System for Regulating Tanker Industry.

twin skeg Catamaran-like stern used in twin-screw tankers to improve propeller flow and reduce fuel consumption.

Ultra Large Crude Carrier (ULCC) Tanker whose deadweight (q.v.) is larger than 320,000 tons.

underwriters Ship's insurers.

Very Large Crude Carrier (VLCC) Tanker whose deadweight (q.v.) is between 200,000 and 320,000 tons.

vetting Tanker inspections by oil company personnel.

Appendix A

Tank Steel Protection

A.1 Introduction

In Section 7.3, I made the bold claim that tankship tank steel can be maintained in as-new condition with nil wastage indefinitely, where indefinitely means 20 years, 30 years, forever. This appendix explains how this can be done, with a particular focus on double hull ballast tanks. In so doing, I will assume some knowledge of tanker jargon, although anyone should be able to follow the main argument.

When it comes to tank steel protection, a tankerman has three weapons.
1. Surface Preparation and Coating
2. Cathodic Protection
3. Inerting

These weapons depend on each other. He must use them all, and use each one correctly. If and only if he does, the tank steel will not deteriorate. We will take each of these in turn in the next three sections.

However, I have to make one pre-condition here. The initial ship structure must be strong enough, so it is not subject to fatigue. If the steel starts cracking, there's nothing any steel protection system can do. Cracking will destroy the coating, mess up the inerting, and produce micro-anodes in the steel which will corrode.

Eliminating fatigue cracking is not difficult. As the Hellespont Embassy proved (Section 4.6), we simply need to go back to the structural standards of the good Japanese yards in the mid-70's.[1] This appendix assumes a robust structure in which the deflections are small enough, so there is no fatigue cracking.

---

[1] Plus a little, just to be sure.

A.2 Coating

A.2.1 Surface Preparation

This sine qua non of any good coating is surface preparation. Unless we get the surface prep right, we are totally screwed. The problem is that the shipyards regard coating as a nuisance, which is fobbed off on sub-contractors, who compete with each other strictly on price.[2] The yard's all encompassing goal is don't disrupt the production schedule. If coating becomes a production bottle neck, as it easily can, the yard will try to do all kinds of terrible things to get back on schedule. At least until the new regulatory system has taken hold, the owner must be prepared to provide plenty of supervision to counter this pressure. Hellespont used a yard team of between 14 and 20 people at each of Samsung and Daewoo. Half this effort went to coating and surface prep. It helps to choose a yard with multiple, parallel coating lines. That way the yard has some flexibility as to which owner get screwed the most when they get behind.

Primary Surface Preparation

All structural steel without exception must be blasted to ISO 8501-1 (SA3) and immediately shop primed with inorganic zinc primer with a minimum dry file thickness of 20 microns.[3]

Some Japanese yards have taken to not shop-priming steel that will not be coated as in the cargo tanks. This is a no-no. Once the ship is in operation, the normal cargo tanks will spend almost all their life inerted and should never experience sea-water. However, we must remove all the corrosive mill scale. And, during construction, the tanks are not only exposed to the salty air in the yard, but more importantly are filled with sea water for the stagger test, inclining experiment, and sea trials. Shop primer is needed to protect the uncoated cargo tank steel during this period.[4]

---

[2] But quality is not expensive. The Hellespont yard teams noted tremendous differences in sub-contractor quality, all of whom were presumably being paid about the same. Some sub-contractors regularly got it right the first time. Others had to do the job over and over again. After a while, the Hellespont ships stopped getting the poorer contractors.

[3] In the yards never ending quest to save money and more importantly push up welding speeds, the ratio of zinc in the zinc primers has started to drop. There must be at least 2 kg of zinc per liter of shop primer. The yards try to get by with 15 microns but they can go to 20 microns without affecting weld quality or speed.[54][page 156]

[4] There were several reports of "super-rust" in the cargo tanks on brand new VLCC's just about the time the Japanese adopted this pernicious practice.

Edge Treatment

The yards cut steel with plasma arc torches. This results in an extremely sharp edge. There is no way that paint can stick to these edges. Surface tension forces suck the coating away from the corner. This is known as *pull-back*. Pull-back is inversely proportional to the radius of the corner. To control pull-back, we must convert the edge into a reasonably smooth arc with a minimum radius of at least 2 mm.

The yard attempts to do this with manual grinding: a slow, expensive, unhealthy, hard to monitor process. Hellespont found the only way to control grinding quality was a physical standard. At both SHI and DSME, we prepared little samples of steel in which the edges were ground and smoothed to our Specification. These samples were signed by both owner and yard. When there was dispute, a sample would be brought out, and, if necessary, the instant arbitrator would be brought in to compare the sample with the edge in question, and make a ruling. This process worked marginally well, but it was a terrible trial for all involved. But it must be done. Otherwise the coating will start breaking down on the edges in five years or less.

It would be far better if the yards worked edge treatment into the normal production process. One way to do this would be to have an edge treatment station at or just after the cutting stage in the panel line. A computer controlled edge milling tool would follow the torches around and, where instructed, round the edges perfectly. Everybody wins.[5]

This will happen when and only when the regulatory process demands proper tanker quality.

Secondary Treatment at Block Stage

In the CTX system, the segregated ballast tanks, the gale ballast tank(s), the slop tanks, and the bottom half-meter of the remaining cargo tanks will be coated. All these areas must be re-blasted to ISO 8501, Sa 3 (white metal) to a surface profile of between 75 and 125 microns per NACE RP 0287.[6] Full re-blast (rather than re-blasting only areas where the primer is

---

[5] Both the US Navy and the yards have experimented with milling tools for rounding edges, in at least the case of the Navy with some success. (Private communications with Rich Parks and Steve Cody of Navsea.) But the key is to integrate the edge treatment into the normal steel processing.

[6] The yards claim Sa 3 is "impossible" even though it used to be the standard spec for old steel. This is nothing more than the downratchet. In fact, the difference between Sa 3 and Sa 2.5 is just a little extra time, a little more care. The Diamond Clipper (Section 7.5) was reblasted to SA 3 at age 23.

"damaged") accomplishes four ends:

1. Smooths off and further rounds the edges.
2. Blasts off any weld spatter.
3. When the yard blasts plate for shop priming, they do so with an overly fine grit that results is a profile height of 30 to 50 microns. This is much too smooth for good coating adhesion. Adhesion falls off very sharply below 75 microns. It is essential the yards use a coarser grit for the reblast.
4. It eliminates all kinds of counter-productive arguments between the yard guy and the owner guy about whether or not the primer in a particular area is "damaged".

The chloride content of the re-blasted surface must be no more than 25 mg/M2 per ISO 8502-9. The yards have no problem meeting this spec at the block stage in the paint sheds but it must be checked.[7]

Secondary Treatment at Erection Stage

The yards can easily do an excellent job of surface prep and coating at the block stage if they decide to (read "are forced to"). The environment in the ballasting and coating sheds is controlled (or at least can be) and the surface is easily accessible.

Erection seams are a bit more difficult, but not nearly as bad as the yards pretend. The yards claim that the best they can do is hand grinding or wire brushing which is both very labor intensive, and in terms of surface preparation accomplishes nearly nothing. Adhesion to hand tooled surfaces is typically one-fourth or less than that for a properly blasted surface.

The first priority with respect to erection seams is to minimize the damage to the existing block coating from the welding. Normally a yard will simply go in and weld, allowing sparks and debris to spew all over the place, burning the coating wherever they fall. As long as all the yard has to do is daub a little paint on the burn spots, this is the cheap approach. The owner must require protection of the existing coating by blankets, welding boxes

---

[7] Soltz argues strongly for a salt spec of 2.5 mg/M2.[70] To obtain this level, a pre-wash with demineralized water (conductivity less than 50 microSiemens/cm) is required. It's not a lot of extra work for an important bit of insurance.

When we installed UHP water blasters on-board the V-Plus, we were treated to a graphic demonstration of the importance of salt. The only freshwater on-board was distilled water which contains nearly no salt. When we UHP blasted the deck with this water, we found that the steel would not turn (start to rust) for close to two days. This is on a tanker deck at sea. In repair yards, grit blasted steel will often start turning in two or three hours, which is a sure sign that the surface has far too much salt on it.

and the like, localizing the damage to the seam itself. The best way to do this is to require spot blasting and full recoat of the burn spots.

For the cargo tank seams (including the slop tanks and gale ballast tanks) which are uninterrupted by stiffeners and other structure, ultrahigh pressure water blasting using robotic crawlers is acceptable. These little machines vacuum up the water as they go, and, if and only if the yard uses low conductivity water (50 microSiemens/cm or less), will result in an easily obtainable, low labor cost, acceptable substrate.

For the other seams, including all the erection seams in the double hull ballast tanks, hand UHP water or dry vacuum blasting to SA 2.5 must be used.[8] The same spec applied to any ballast tank coating damage by the welding.

In either case, the max salt spec of 25 mg/m2 must apply. This is especially true if a tank has been immersed in salt water during a dock cycling. This is easily achievable; all the yard has to do is high pressure wash with low salinity water.

---

[8] The yards claim they cannot use UHP water blast in an enclosed space because of all the misting. But in fact entire failed VLCC double bottom coatings have been redone underway with water blast, using a number of techniques. The simplest is a can on the blaster which the operator pushes on to the surface.

A.2.2 Coating

Material

When it comes to coatings, I will limit myself to talking about epoxy, which is the standard tank coating technology used by the yards. There are some intriguing alternatives to epoxy that should be explored, but under the Tromedy haven't. As a result we – or at least I – don't have enough experience to talk about them confidently.[9] Anyway epoxy can do the job **if we do it right**.

The choice of an epoxy coating for tanks should be based on the following main criteria:

1. **Adhesive strength.** Adhesion, perhaps the single most important number, is a measure of the coating's ability to resist being lifted off the surface by corrosion or bubbling.[10] Big is better. We want a coating with an adhesion of at least 140 bar per ASTM D 4541.

2. **Permeability.** Permeability is a measure of ease with which water can work its way thru the coating. Small is beautiful. The less moisture that gets thru to the steel surface, the less corrosion and the less chance for bubbling. We are looking for a moisture permeability of 0.05 g/m2/day/mm Mercury or less per ASTM E-96.

3. **Glass Transition Temperature.** If an epoxy coating is heated, it will eventually reach a temperature at which at which the coating will become semi-plastic with some of the polymers rearranging themselves. This is called the Glass Transition Temperature or GTT. If the coating is repeatedly cycled through this temperature, the coating loses strength, becomes brittle, and eventually cracks. For most epoxy coatings, the GTT is somewhere between 50C and 60C. Unfortunately, the temperature in the top of tanker ballast tank with a dark deck on

---

[9] This is not true. I have extensive, successful experience with water-born inorganic zinc. As far as I am concerned, water-born zinc — pioneered by Daniel Ludwig for tankers — is immeasurably superior to epoxy for all above water, exterior surfaces. Orders of magnitude better in adhesion and abrasion resistance, never bubbles, never lifts, and, if scratched all the way through, sacrifices itself to protect the steel. But while many yards could do inorganic zinc in the 1970's, thanks to the downratchet, I have been unable to get any newbuilding yard to lay down zinc. So I won't discuss inorganic zinc coatings in this book. Anyway the key coating problem is the ballast tanks and inorganic zinc is not the right choice for inerted tanks, where a failure in the scrubbing system might generate a very acidic environment, which would clobber the zinc coating.

[10] The fancy name for bubbling is osmotic pressure. The most common way bubbling happens is there a speck of salt on the steel surface. If moisture worms its way thru the coating to this salt, we have a bit of highly concentrated salt water. This will attract more water in an attempt to reduce this concentration generating a bubble in the coating.

a sunny day in the tropics will be 55C to 65C or higher. This is the reason why ballast tank coatings invariably start breaking down from the top.[11] As we shall see below, the best way to fight this to keep the top of the tank cool, but still we want a coating with a high Glass Transition Temperature, at least 55C.

4. **No solvent** With current catalyst activated coating technology, there is absolutely no need to use any solvent. Solvent-less or 100% solids coatings are not subject to solvent entrapment and overall weakening of the coating matrix as the solvent interferes with the curing process. 100% solids coatings are a little trickier to apply, but anybody can learn to do it, especially if they are provided with a heated, plural component spraying system.[12]

5. **The Right Filler** Many so-called premium coatings use a hydroscopic filler such as clay or calcium carbonate.[13] Cheap but exactly the wrong thing to do. This attracts water and swells and weakens the coating. There are all sorts of alternatives. Hellespont's experience indicates that aluminum or aluminum oxide make a good filler.

Current coating technology is capable of giving us epoxy coatings with quite remarkable strength and permeability. ***The core problem is that the yards care about none of the above.*** What they want is ease of application over a wide range of weather conditions using poorly trained sprayers, usually provided by sub-contractors. Most importantly, they want a product that will cure quickly. The production schedule is the only thing that counts.

The paint vendors, especially the part of the organization that is in the yard's country, regard the yard as the real customer. Owners come and go, but the yards are always there and they buy a huge amount of paint. The paint makers go to great lengths to make their coating acceptable to the yards. And if that means compromising coating quality with thinners,

---

[11] A Shell superintendent once told me a story that illustrates the importance of temperature. On Shell's first generation of LNG carriers, the epoxy coating in the top of the ballast tank started breaking down seriously after about 7 years, about normal. But in the bottom of the tanks, cooled by both the sea and the cargo, the coating was in perfect condition after 27 years.

[12] Plural component systems mix the resin and the catalyst right at the spray nozzle. This assures accurate, thorough mixing, far less wastage, and no use of thinners. It is the only way to go.

[13] This was a big step backward from the 1970's where coal tar was the filler of choice. The clay fillers have moisture permeabilities 30 times higher than coal tar.[53, p 167] But coal tar coatings are black, and the Tromedy, more interested in decor than performance, decreed that ballast tank coatings should be light colored. Nuts.

dilutants, accelerators, and anti-sag additives, well, everything's a balance.[14]

The owner has two jobs.

1. Figure out what the best coating is.
2. Making sure that the coating he bought is the coating that actually goes on the ship.

In 1997 in anticipation of our newbulding program, we tested five "premium" ballast tank coating products:

1. Devoe Amercoat 238.
2. Hempels Multistrength 4575.
3. International Paints ENA.
4. Jotun Penguard.
5. Sigma Tankshield.

The test consisted of coating the top portion of one web frame in one of Hellespont Embassy's segregated ballast tanks with each of these products. The blasting and coating was done by our own people to a high standard. The test was considerably shorter than I would have preferred, a little under two years. As expected, all five coatings looked fine after two years; but the International ENA and Hempels 4575 tested much better than the other three on both the scratch test (a measure of the coating's ability to fight being lifted at the edge of corrosion) and the pull off test (a more direct measure of adhesion). These two products also had much better permeability numbers than the other three.

Interestingly, these two products were not designed for ballast tanks. They were both *anti-abrasive* epoxies, developed to withstand the rubbing and pounding that the topsides take from fenders, mooring lines, and cargo hoses. To this end, the normal, cheap clay filler was replaced by an aluminum powder. The result was a clearly stronger, less permeable coating. The paint makers had not offered it as a ballast tank coating, because they assumed that owners would not pay the additional cost.

We ended up going with the Hempels 4575. It tested a bit better than the ENA and had a higher Glass Transition Temperature.

Now began the struggle to actually get that product on the ship. In January, 2001, shortly before actual steel erection began, Hempels came to

---

[14] Strangely over-thickness is as bad a problem in the newbuilding yards as under-thickness. Most owners do a reasonable job of checking if the coating's too thin. The yards hate to put another coat on because it might disrupt the production schedule. So they lay it on thick. In repair yards it is normal to allow for 30% more paint than necessary to meet the thickness. The newbuilding yards normally allow 100%. But overly thick coats are not good, especially if solvent is involved. They generate solvent entrapment and result in the paint vendors putting all kinds of crap in the coating to prevent it from sagging.

us with earth shattering news. They had suddenly discovered that the eight year old 4575 product had terrible immersed adhesion and would have to be replaced with their standard ballast tank coating. We were incredulous. We quietly bought some 4575 on the open market and did the same immersed adhesion test. The results were excellent. The more we investigated, the more the Hempels story kept changing.

Eventually we found out what had happened. In testing, Samsung had discovered that they could not reliably put one coat of 4575 on one day, and then re-coat the next. In certain cases the inter-coat adhesion was non-existent. The second coat simply fell off. They would have to wait two days before re-coating. Samsung only has one paint coating line, so doubling the re-coat interval would play havoc with the yard's entire production schedule. Samsung a major, major Hempels customer demanded that Hempels do something.

The dispute went on for a couple of months, escalating to threats of full-on law suits. When our top paint guy, Kostas Liopiris, finally figured out what was going down, he pointed out to Samsung that all they had to do was properly ventilate the coated blocks while they were curing, and they would be able to recoat the next day. Samsung brought in fans and proved Liopiris right. The 4575 adhesion problems suddenly disappeared.

The struggle was not over. We had written into the contract that the paint must be made in the Hempels' plant in Singapore, rather than Korea. The relationship between the yards and the Hempels subsidiary in Korea – actually it was Korean company part owned by one of the yards – was much too close for comfort. And we bought a $60,000 infrared reflectance tester which produces a signature of a paint sample and commissioned software that would catch any significant variations in that signature. Liopiris, who is a bit of a showman, arranged a gala demonstration of the machine for the yard and the local Hempels personnel. Much murmuring and some sucking of teeth. Paint was sampled daily. On several occasions, paint was rejected on the basis of these tests.

Our unreasonable requirements were driving up cost. Something had to be done. In June 2002, Hempels informed us that regrettably they could no longer produce the paint in Singapore because the Singaporean supplier of the aluminum powder could no longer deliver powder to Hempels spec. They would have to make the paint in Korea. Once again there were strange inconsistencies in the story. We said forget it, whoever was producing the powder could ship it to Singapore. The other side claimed that was impossible because of time constraints. This time discussion became so heated that at one time Hempels threatened to sue me for libel.[15] The yard playing innocent by-stander warned of immense liabilities if production were delayed. We lobbed legal counter-threats back, and held our ground. Miraculously on the day before they were supposed to run out of paint, a whole container full of Singaporean paint was discovered. After that things went pretty quiet on the paint front. Our main job became keeping the contractors from tossing thinner into the paint. For repeat offenders, the technique is to kick the pot over and walk away.[16]

The only reason for recounting all this nonsense is to make the point that, thanks to the Tromedy, coating technology is far ahead of our actual use of it. The yards could give us much better coatings, but that's not the goal. The goal is to slop on something that will last for a year, with minimal impact on the production schedule.

Application in Ballast Tanks

The CTX system in the segregated ballast tanks is three coats with a stripe coat on the edges and seams before each coat. And a final fourth coat in the underdeck area. Each coat should have a dry file thickness of at least 200 microns and no more than 300 microns.

The main problem at the block stage for the owner is obtaining reasonably even coverage including enough coating on the edges while avoiding overly thick coats elsewhere. This implies that edge stripe coats must be applied by spray whenever possible. Brush or roller removes the paint from the high points. And keeping the yard away from the thinner. The yards are addicted to thinner to make the coating easier to spray, but all they need to do is use the right nozzle tips, replace them when they are supposed to, and, if necessary, control viscosity with temperature. Better yet, use plural component spraying.[17]

At the erection stage, the big problem is to minimize the amount of damage from weld splatter. The owner's people have to prevent the welding from starting until the entire area is protected. The welders only care about getting the welding done.

After the yard thinks its finished, all weld splatter and other debris must

---

[15] For my part, I wouldn't do business with Hempels again even if they offered to gold plate the ships for free.

[16] A much better solution is plural component spray, page 297.

[17] And the whole process could be vastly improved, from both the owner's and the yard's standpoint, by using robots for much of the work. The yacht yards are far ahead of the ship yards in this regard.[77]

be removed from the tank. The tank must be perfectly clean. Otherwise, the tanks are virtually uninspectable both prior to delivery and afterwards. After delivery the weld splatter will rust, requiring detailed individual attention to determine whether this stain is merely a bit of metal stuck to the coating, or a real pinhole. An impossible task when you are talking about 250,000 square meters of steel. The crew must know that every stain is a pinhole and needs fixing.

After the tanks have been ballasted during trials they should be reinspected and any holidays touched up. All this is simple common sense; but not normal yard practice. The Owner must get these procedures into his Specification.

Application in Cargo Tanks

The coating schedule for the slop tanks should be the same as for the segregated ballast tanks. In the gale ballast tank(s), the CTX spec is two stripe and two full coats plus a third coat in the underdeck area.[18] In all the tanks, the underdeck stiffeners must be flat bar. Otherwise the underdeck area is impossible to clean and impossible to inspect.

As we saw in Section 4.5, the big corrosion problem in inerted cargo tanks is bottom pitting. The problem here is that all crudes contain some water, and almost all crudes contain sulfur. On the loaded legs, the acidic water in the crude settles out and forms a thin layer below the oil. This can generate rapid pitting and leaks from the cargo tanks into the inner bottom, whereupon we have a dangerous mess. All the cargo tank bottoms should be full coated up to about 0.5 m above the bottom.

This coating must be backed up by anodes. These can be pitguard style anodes attached to the webs in the center tanks. But in the wing cargo tanks, there is no structure at all to attach the anodes to. Hellespont solved this by having the yards weld short vertical pieces of 15 mm rod to the inner bottom. The anodes are laid on the bottom and attached to these rods with U-bolts.

It is very important that the cargo tanks be kept clean. A key component in cargo tank bottom pitting is sludge.[45] Clumps of sludge set up oxygen differential cells between the steel under the sludge and the surrounding steel in which the surrounding steel plays the anode. Keeping a double hull

---

[18] Gale ballast tanks must be used fairly frequently in a double hull. The high freeboard often requires them to be used toward the end of discharge during lightering. The bad roll characteristics in ballast (due to the high roll radius of gyration) require them to be used in any kind of beam sea when in ballast.

cargo tank clean should not be difficult.

Unfortunately, the downratchet has resulted in too few crude oil washing machines in big double hull cargo tanks. The number and arrangement of COW machines is determined by *shadow diagrams*. The requirement is that 85% of the tank steel not be shadowed from at least one machine.   But double hull cargo tanks are so free of structure, this requirement can be met with one or two machines in an immense tank, whereas it would take 3 to 5 machines in the same sized pre-Marpol tank. Problem is that the machines are too far away from the surface they are supposed to be cleaning. The effective jet length of a COW machine is no more than 20 m. But in modern double hull VLCC's, you will often see machines which are supposed to be cleaning surfaces 30 m or more away. As a rule of thumb, you will need to add at least one machine per tank more than Class requires.

Many owners coat the underdeck areas in their cargo tanks. I have nothing against this, but, provided the inerting system of Sections 6.4 and A.4 is implemented, I don't think they get much for the $500,000 to $700,000 this will cost on a VLCC. The coating in the cargo tank underdeck is hard to inspect and nearly impossible to touch up. If the tank is properly inerted per Section A.4, then underdeck coating is unnecessary. We had no measurable wastage on the uncoated underdeck of the V-Plus class after 2.5 years.[19] If a cargo tank is not properly inerted, you can't count on an underdeck coating for more than 5 to 10 years.

But there is one important improvement to this inerting system we should consider and test. For less than $200,000, we could undercool the inert gas using a variant of the system used on LNG carriers. If we under-cooled the gas by only 5C, we would be putting dry (RH 60%) rather than super-saturated gas into the tanks. I don't think this would do anything for the ballast tanks because of the water lying on the bottom, but it would be the end of any chance of corrosion in the top of the cargo tanks.

---

[19] I have to make one caveat here. Hellespont disallowed TMCP (Thermo Mechanically Controlled Processed) steel in the 1999 newbuilding programs. TMCP steel has a finer grain structure than cold worked steel and improved notch toughness. But it also has a lot more active sites on the grain boundaries where corrosion can start. We decided to go with the steel we knew. Most of the world's steel mill are converting to TMCP which after investment is cheaper to make than cold worked steel. A prohibition against TMCP may not be realistic in the future. I really don't think it makes any difference. The technical literature claims it does not.[81, 38] But since this research was sponsored by the steel mills, I can't be absolutely sure.

A.2.3   Inspections

At Hellespont, we had a strict rule against ever putting sea water in a tank that was not full coated. For a normal cargo tank — as opposed to a slop or gale ballast tank — the only situation where one might be tempted to violate this rule is inspections. In the past, a common inspection technique was rafting. The tank was ballasted and the inspectors floated about on an inflatable dinghy. This was dangerous, resulted in poor quality inspections, and clobbered the uncoated steel. Hellespont replaced rafting with a hanging staging system based on bridge painting equipment. This gave good access to the entire top of the tank. We blasted and painted entire ballast tank underdeck areas underway with this system. But the surveyors were unfamiliar with it, and unwilling to use it. In a rare bit of intelligent regulation, IMO has mandated walkways which give decent access to a large part of the tank, for all ships built after 2004. With these walkways, there is no longer any need for rafting.

Some owners insist on a seawater washing via the COW machines prior to tank inspection, as a safety measure. Hellespont found that on old-style single bottom tanks, the extra seawater wash accomplished nothing. The key to cleaning the tank is enough COW machines and a thorough crude oil wash. The key to safety is careful measurement of the tank atmosphere prior to entry and during the inspection. This is even more true on the easily cleaned double hull cargo tanks, once again provided they are fitted with enough COW machines. (If not, all the washing in the world, won't clean the tank.) In double hull cargo tanks, seawater wash accomplishes almost nothing, other than provide a false sense of security and tear up the steel.

It's simple; do not put saltwater in an uncoated tank.

White Decks

Keeping the tank steel below the coating's Glass Transition Temperature is critical to coating life in the top of the ballast tanks. The single most important means of doing this is hull color. Table A.1 shows the reflectance of a range of colors. Reflectance is the percentage of the incoming solar energy that is not absorbed by the surface. A black surface will absorb almost all the sun's radiation. A favorite tanker deck color is dark red. Such a deck will absorb at least 60% of the solar energy.[20] Even a very light

---

[20] Green, another favorite deck color, is worse. Green is a cool color to our eyes precisely because it is so good at absorbing the sun's radiation. That's why plants use it.

Table A.1: Solar Reflectance

COLOUR	REFLECTANCE
Black RAL 9005	3%
Machine Grey RAL 7031	10%
Silver Grey RAL 7001	27%
Red RAL 3001	43%
Light Grey RAL 7035	51%
Cream White RAL 9010	72%
White RAL 9001	84%

grey will reflect only about 50% of the energy. But a pure while deck will reflect over 80% of the radiation. Red decks absorb more than four times as much solar energy as white decks.

The difference in deck steel temperature can be quite dramatic. When we bought the Hellespont Enterprise, she was laid up in Brunei Bay, latitude about 5°. She had a standard red deck. I regularly measured deck temperatures in the high 50^oC's occasionally low sixties. Early in the afternoon, the steel would burn your hand if you left it on the surface for more than a couple of seconds. When we switched our decks to light grey in the late 80's, peak deck temperatures dropped to the low fifties, not as much as I had hoped. But when we went with pure white on the V-Plus, the peak deck temperatures dropped dramatically. In ten ship-years of operation, we never measured a deck steel temperature over 44C on the V-Plus. On the hottest day in the Persian Gulf, the deck would be cool to the touch.

The steel temperature on the underside of the deck is essentially the same as the temperature on the top side. White decks and topsides ensure that the tank coating will always be below the Glass Transition Temperature. This also implies that the tank will almost never breath, avoiding atmospheric pollution, saving cargo, and inert gas, and reducing the chances of getting air into the tank.[21] Aside from the glare, working on deck during the day is much more comfortable. And, at night, it is much safer. Of course, it also means you must issue sun glasses to the entire crew.

White is the only right color for tankers.[22]

---

[21] Undercooling at night is also reduced. On a dark deck and a clear night, you can easily get 3C undercooling due to radiation. On a white deck, there is essentially no difference between the ambient air temperature and the deck temperature.

[22] Epoxy coatings exposed to the sun chalk and turn a light cream color. This produces

Touch Up

Even with the best of coatings, good cathodic protection, and good inerting, there will be an occasional requirement to repair the coating. There are two keys here.

UHP Water Blast   The last 20 years has seen the development of a magical new technology: Ultra High Pressure waterblast. UHP waterblast uses a 3,000 bar jet of water to remove the coating and any scale. Combined with distilled water, it is actually superior to grit blast on a surface that already has a profile. Without the mess. Hellespont installed these systems on the V-Plus class and they were quickly being used everywhere. Some training and some precautions are required, but the combination of productivity and quality is spectacular. A surface blasted with distilled water won't turn for several days, so there is plenty of time to dry the surface off, and coat.[23] UHP waterblast is the only way to go for touch-up.

Access   It is a safe bet that better than half of all touch-up work will be in top 2 meters of the double sides. Good access is required to this area both for inspection and touch up. The Tromedy does not provide this access. But it is easily effected by enlarging a stiffener on both the inboard and outboard sides of the double sides about 2 meters below the deck. This should be the standard newbuilding spec.

---

a surprising increase in deck temperature as Table A.1 indicates. On the V-Plus, we overcoated the epoxy on deck with polyurethane which retains the pure white much longer. (The deck undercoat should have been water-born zinc silicate, but that's another story.)

   [23] One must take precautions to avoid salty water splashing back from neighboring surfaces.

A.3   Cathodic Protection

A double hull VLCC has about 350,000 m^2 of coated tank area, more than 50 football fields/pitches. Try as we might, no coating can be perfect. There will be defects in this coating and the coating will get damaged. The fundamental problem with coating as a steel protection system is that the smallest defect is trouble, eventually big trouble. A coating which is 99.99% perfect isn't good enough. If left to its own evil devices, that 0.01% will eventually destroy the tank. We must backstop the coating, both when the tank is immersed and when it is empty. For the immersed portion of the tank's life the back up is cathodic protection.

Rust is an electrical process. Electrons are transferred from the anode (which oxidizes) to a cathode (which doesn't). The goal of cathodic protection is to make sure that all the immersed steel in the tank is a cathode. This is usually done with zinc anodes.[24]

Zinc oxidizes in seawater more readily than steel. If a block of zinc (the anode) is wired to some steel and then they are both immersed in salty water, the zinc will pump electrons into the steel, faster than the steel can lose them to the seawater. The anode sacrifices itself to save the steel. Properly done, the anode will corrode but not the steel. This process only works when both the steel and the anode are immersed. It depends on the salty water, the electrolyte, to complete the circuit between anode and cathode.

The standard newbuilding specification for anodes in a coated tank is a mean current of 6 mA/m^2, five year life, 50% ballast ratio. If the yard uses 32 kg zinc anodes, this will result in about 1200 anodes for double hull VLCC ballast tanks, an inter-anode spacing of about 10 m.

For a well-coated tank this is OK. But the anodes must be maintained. Usual tanker practice is to periodically inspect the tank, look at the anodes, and guess how much zinc is left. This doesn't work. I've watched this process in action hundreds of times. The first inspector will come along,

---

[24] Impressed current would be much better. In an impressed current system, the electrons to be pumped into the steel are provided by the ship's generators. There is no need for sacrificial anodes, eating up the world's supply of zinc. And the amount of current can be precisely metered to the requirements. Impressed current is used to protect the external hull.

So why do we use anodes? Thank the Tromedy. The Tromedy has decided that impressed current in tanks is dangerous because hydrogen gas in created at the cathode. But this becomes a non-issue if the tank is inerted. More basically, any cathodic system including zinc creates hydrogen at the cathode. It has to if it is going to protect the steel. A properly metered impressed current system will produce less hydrogen than a zinc based system.

kick an anode, and pronounced it 30% wasted. The second inspector will do the same and call it 50% gone. Then I'll come along and write down something else.

The only way to check cathodic protection is to measure it.[25] Fortunately, this is a simple process. All that is required is a reference voltage and a voltmeter. The reference voltage is provide by a half-cell. The half-cell is dropped into the tank and the potential between the half-cell and the steel is measured. If that voltage is high enough, we can be sure that the zinc has pumped sufficient electrons into the steel, so that there will be no immersed corrosion in the tank, even where the coating is defective.

For double hull ballast tanks, it is not feasible to drop the half-cell into the tank for each reading. On the Hellespont newbuildings, we permanently installed three half cells in each ballast tank, low, mid-level, high, as far away from the nearest anode as possible. The leads from the half-cells were routed to a watertight gland on the tanklid. To take the measurements, the crew merely grounds a volt meter on the deck steel, and touches each of the three leads in succession.

The requirement is that the potential at each of the three half-cells be at least 800 mV within 24 hours of the tank being ballasted.[26] If this is not the case, then it is time to replace some anodes.

If and only if an owner follows this Spec, then there will be no wastage from immersed steel even in way of coating breakdown. If you go into a tank which is properly anoded, you will see white deposits on the steel where ever the paint is damaged. This is calcium. The anode/cathode chemistry is such that calcium precipitates out at the cathode. If and only if all the exposed steel is covered with a white calcareous deposit, then all that steel is cathodic. The anodes are doing their job.

Pitguard Postscript

The cathodic system outline above is not quite complete. In a double bottom ballast tank, it is impossible to get all the seawater out when the the tank

---

[25] A problem with anodes in well coated tanks is that the zinc can become deactivated. If the anode sacrifices too slowly, corrosion products build up on the zinc surface, insulating the zinc from the seawater, whereupon the anode becomes useless. You can't check this by kicking the anode.

[26] After each ballasting, it takes a while for the tank to become polarized, for the electrons and the protection to build up. We want to make that period quite short.

Hellespont uses a silver-silver chloride half-cell. If a different half-cell is used, the required voltage has to be adjusted according to the half-cell's position in the electromotive series.

is emptied or *stripped*. Even with a well-maintained piping system and a good crew, there will always be a centimeter or two of seawater laying on the bottom after the tank is stripped for the loaded passage.

The normal anodes can do nothing about this layer of water, since they will not be immersed. To protect the bottom of the ballast tank we need a special kind of anode called a *pitguard*. Figure A.1 shows the system Hellespont uses. The key is to get the bottom of the pitguard right on the

Figure A.1: Installation of Tsevas Pitguard

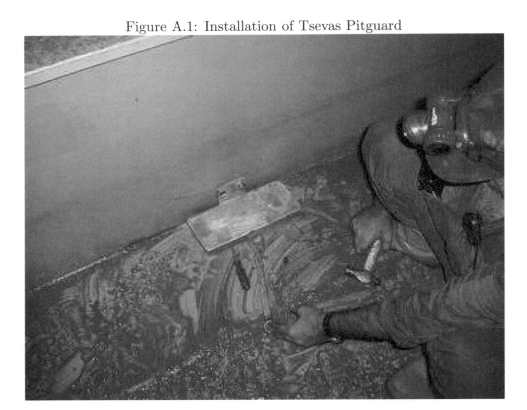

bottom of the tank, so that at least some of the zinc is always immersed.

But this means the pitguards cannot be installed by the yard. The yard prefers to install anodes before painting, tape them up, and then spray. This is a good system, since it avoids the coating damage associated with installing the anodes. But it can't be used for pitguards. The pitguard would interfere with coating the bottom.

The solution is to have the yard cut only the mounting holes in the bottom stiffener webs (without edge treatment). Plugs are placed in the holes to protect the hole inner surface from the coating. After delivery, we have our own crew actually install the pitguards, pulling the plugs, making sure the hole surface is clean, expanding a soft stainless steel sleeve against the interior of the hole and then bolting in the pitguards to insure good electrical contact.[27] On the V-Plus, Hellespont put one 12 kg in each flat bottom bay. This was probably overkill. One in each aft bay plus sort of checkerboard pattern elsewhere would have been plenty. But it is important to protect the ballast tank flat bottom. The flat bottom, usually covered with some muddy water, is hard to inspect and the coating hard to repair. The flat bottom tends to get damaged during valve/piping work. It is subject to coating erosion near the strums. Unless protected, any coating defect in the flat bottom quickly turns into a major pit. Proper pitguards are necessary.

---

[27] It is an open question whether it would have been better to use ordinary steel, rather than stainless to avoid the stainless/normal potential. All I can say is that the stainless system worked fine for at least two years.

A.4   Inerting

Cathodic protection will backstop the coating when the steel is immersed.
But anodes can do nothing for the steel that is out of the water. An empty
ballast tank or worse the empty space above the water in a partially full ballast tank represents ideal conditions for atmospheric corrosion. It's very wet
and very salty. Exposed steel in such conditions can rust away remarkably
quickly. The Tanker Structure Cooperative Forum (TSCF) uses 1.2 mm per
year.[78, page 243]

This TSCF number is far from the maximum corrosion rate. Here's the
Chief Ship Surveyor of Lloyds in an unguarded moment:

> In tanks which have been coated but, because of poor mainte-
> nance, the coating has been allowed to deteriorate, the rates of
> corrosion can be extremely rapid, perhaps approaching 6 mm
> per year locally in way of the coating breakdown. The greater
> part of ballast tank corrosion occurs when the tank is empty.[7,
> p 9]

People who are surprised by this kind of wastage like to call it "super-
rust".

The solution, as we have seen in Section 6.4, is inerting with double
scrubbed inert gas. Done properly, this will produce a reducing environment
in the tank and halt any atmospheric corrosion where the coating is defective.
There is no need to repeat Section 6.4 here, but I do need to fill in a few
implementation details.

Maintaining Positive Pressure

The biggest problem with inerting is to ensure that the very top of the
tank, the highest point, is always properly inerted. The forwardmost tanks
and nearly full tanks are particularly sensitive in this regard. Since tankers
normally have some trim by the stern, this is usually the forward, inboard
corner of the tank. The P/V valve should be fitted at this corner. If there
is any sign of incomplete inerting, this valve can be released momentarily to
flush out any pocket of air trapped in the top of the tank.

The second requirement is to ensure that the tank pressure never goes
negative which would suck in air, through the inevitable small leaks in the
P/V valves and elsewhere. Hellespont continually monitored and recorded
the IG pressure in both the cargo and ballast tank IG mains. The rule was
two level:

1. If the pressure dropped below 0.05 bar gage, then the IG would have to be topped off at the next 0200 local.

2. If the pressure dropped below 0.02 bar gage, then the IG is topped off immediately.

On the V-Plus, with white decks and stainless steel seated P/V valves we found that, on average, we had to top off about once a week. With white decks, the P/V valves will never open due to diurnal breathing. The key here is to minimize leakage, mainly by insuring that the P/V valves are in good shape. A 750 m^3/hr Inert Gas Generator was more than enough for this purpose. Periodically, the ships emailed their IG pressure readings and IG fuel consumption to the office for the superintendent's review.[28]

Monitoring O_2

We also continuously monitored the O_2 and SO_2 levels in the cargo and ballast inert gas mains. The O_2 level should never be over 5%. We were almost always able to keep it under 4%. In order to achieve this at low boiler loads, we speced dual throat burners. SO_2 levels should be less than 3 ppm at full cargo discharge volumes and less than 0.5 ppm at deballast volumes. The latter will require IG fans with a good turn-down ratio or a small fan.

Hellespont also fitted sniffers in the V-Plus ballast tanks. The main purpose of this system was to check for hydrocarbons (i.e. cargo tanks leaks); but the system also had the capability of measuring tank 0_2. The system we installed proved flaky and unreliable, so we also installed glands in the tank lid that allowed us to sample the tank atmosphere with portable O_2 and hydrocarbon analyzers. The ships regularly reported these numbers back to the office. We were still working toward a reliable, efficient tank sampling system when the V-Plus were sold. But I'm sure such a system is possible. But the key is to watch the O_2 in the very topmost portion of the tank.

Safety

As mention in Section 6.4, double scrubbed inert gas is clear as a bell and — at least to my insensitive nose — odorless. It is extremely dangerous. The Tromedy allows the P/V valve outlets to be only 2 m above deck. When a

---

[28] It is possible that air can be sucked into the tank by the sloshing of the liquid in the tank, but we never developed a reliable means of checking for this. Another reason for avoiding sloshing resonance.

tank is being loaded/ballasted, we are pushing a lot of inert gas out on the deck. I'm amazed we haven't suffocated anybody to date.

Anyway with double scrubbed inert gas, we need to two things:

1. Insure that the mast riser vents for both the cargo and ballast sides are large enough so that under all standard loading/ballasting scenarios, the P/V valves don't have to open. And these vents must be very high and nowhere near the accommodations.

2. Move the P/V valves outlets upward. I'd increase the current 2 m limit to at least 3 meters.[29]

Black and White

If a tank is anoded and inerted to the above specifications, then you will never see any color at all in the tank. All the exposed steel should be black (magnetite) or white (cathodic). Any brown or red at all means something has gone wrong. In ballast tanks, I like to purposely damage the coating under the deck somewhere near the tank lid. Whenever I enter a tank, I glance at that hole in the coating. If there's no color, then I already know I have little to worry about. If there is any color, somebody's in trouble.[30]

---

[29] A still better solution would be to eliminate the P/V valves entirely by properly beefing up the steel in the top of the tanks. This would get rid of P/V valve leakage and we could use vacuum to hold cargo in bottom damaged tanks. See Section C.9.2.

[30] Obviously, it is important that the inspection take place quickly after the tank is purged. It only takes an hour or two for the steel to start to turn. Inspection of inerted tanks should be infrequent — once a year is about right – and expeditious. Get in quickly, check everything out in at most two hours, and immediately re-inert.

A.5 Summary

That's it, folks. Follow the prescriptions of this Appendix, and your tanks will look the same whether they are 1 month old, 1 year old, 20 years old, or 40 years old. There will be no deterioration of the steel.

Now I know what the tankermen out there are thinking, for I know what goes on in your evil little minds. The dozen or so synapses therein have formed the "you're dreaming" pattern. There's no way the yards will accept these specifications.

Not so, little fellows. There is nothing unrealistic about this Spec. In fact, it is little more than common sense. In 1999, Hellespont, hardly the biggest owner, was able to get Korean yards to accept everything in this steel protection system except:

1. SA 3. I conceded SA 2.5 but the only difference between Sa 3 and Sa 2.5 is a little more care, a little more time. After some initial tribulation, we received a very high quality SA2.5 blast from both yards. The yards did not want to give us any excuse for requiring a reblast. The blast was for all practical purposes SA3.
2. 25 mg/m2 salt at the erection stage. I stupidly conceded 50 mg/m2 salt at the erection stage, which I now know was unnecessary. With the continued development of water blast, a 25 mg spec for the erection seams is easily achievable. In fact, the salt spec could be and should be dropped below 10 mg. Just needs a little pre-wash.
3. Erection Seam treatment. I conceded wire-brushing and grinding because I believed the yards when they claimed that blasting outside the paint sheds was illegal. But wire-brushing/grinding is terribly slow and man-hour intensive if the standard (St 3) is actually enforced. So when Daewoo got behind schedule, they started grit blasting the erection seams. I never found out whether or not this was illegal, but both the yard and the owner won by getting rid of hand treatment.
4. Final tank cleaning. Simply an amateurish oversight on my part.

All it took was a shipbuilding slump and a owner who was prepared to not order unless he got his way. The yards hated the Spec but they hated a hole in their orderbook even more.

Nonetheless I have considerable sympathy with your sceptical synapses. It is very difficult for an individual owner to change established practice. He needs help. He will not get it from Class. Class is part of the problem; Class is the problem. Conceivably the owners could voluntarily band together behind a common specification, but history is not encouraging.[31] But if the port states start rejecting tankers with tanks whose steel is not like new, then owners will have no choice but to go to a Spec like this. As soon as the owners have no choice, the yards will have no choice.

---

[31] Most independent tanker owners belong to an industry lobbying outfit called Intertanko. In 1987, in the middle of The Tanker War, Basil Papachristidis (then Chairman of Intertanko) and I went to the Intertanko meeting in Oslo and made a plea to the owners there to publicly threaten, as a group, to no longer go into the Persian Gulf unless our ships received naval protection. These guys' tankers were being blown up, their crews were being killed, and they looked at us like we were crazy. The motion was never brought to vote.

Intertanko has make other more prosaic attempts at collective action, such as standard charter party terms. They've all been flops.

Appendix B

Implementation of Twin Screw

The key requirements of a twin screw system are:

1. The ability to maneuver with the loss of one engine room including rudder.
2. No single failure can result in the loss of more than 50% power.
3. No interdependencies. Unless failures are truly independent, then the redundancy is a mirage.
4. Don't screw up normal operations. The crew is part of the system. If you complicate their lives, then they become the interdependency.

(1) is more or less adequately addressed by the current Class twin screw rules such as ABS R2-S+ rating or DNV RPS. The maneuverability requirement implies (or at least should imply) that a twin screw ship must have considerably more power than current large, single screw tankers, more than 30% more power. This will be at least partly repaid during boom periods by the additional 1 to 2 knots extra speed.[1]

---

[1] Operation at the other end of the spectrum, very low speeds, must receive attention. Many existing single screw tankers cannot operate stably below about 5 or 6 knots. Operators try to compensate by stopping and re-starting the engine, a dangerous, hard to control process. When we told Sulzer in 1999, we must have stable operation down to 3 knots for lightering and maneuvering in restricted waters, they looked at us like we were crazy. Why would anyone want to make the crew's life easier? They said their engine could not operate below about 20 RPM for any length of time. That was good enough. Hellespont had a brilliant engineering superintendent, Manoulis Kafouros. Kafouros took a look at the problem and came up with a simple modification of the fuel dump valve which we took to Sulzer. Sulzer incorporated this cylinder cutout system on the Hellespont ships. It worked great, allowing us to go down to 12 RPM without problems. These highly powered ships could operate at less than 3 knots for extended periods. Sulzer

The problems are (2), (3) and (4). Single failure here includes an engine room flooding or fire. In the Class Rules, the latter is addressed by requiring a watertight, A60 bulkhead between the engine rooms.[2] But there is an inconsistency in that only an A0 bulkhead is required between the engine rooms and the pump room. The aft pump room bulkhead should also be A60. Otherwise a fire in one engine room has an easy path to the other thru the pump room. Or a fire in the pump room, could take out both engine rooms.

One obvious implication of (2) and (3) should be that an at-sea black-out in one engine room must not take down the other engine room, even momentarily. ***However, current Class twin screw rules allow this gross interdependency.*** The only thing worse than trying to bring back one blacked out engine room is trying to bring back two. (2) and (3) require sufficient generating capacity on-line in both engine rooms, so that the generator on each side can handle its engine room plus all essential common loads with a generous margin.[3] This requirement will push the design toward shaft generators.

Eliminating interdependencies requires some careful thinking. In 1998, the MORUY lost steering and went aground in the St. Lawrence River. The cause was that the deck above the emergency switchboard leaked shorting out the emergency switchboard, and power to the steering gear was lost. I doubt if any of the recent twin screw tankers could maintain power to at least one steering gear in the face of an emergency switchboard failure. Obviously, we need two totally independent fuel systems as the BRAER proved.

(4) requires that we need good access between the engine rooms. Otherwise we make maintenance more difficult and that's exactly the wrong way to go. I'd accept the risk of large, normally closed doors in the centerline bulkhead at each flat rather than force the crew to climb out of one engine room to get to the other. And I'd accept the risk of a normally open when

---

happily appropriated the Kafouros design, calling it their Super Dead Slow system.

In any event, a properly designed twin screw tanker must be able to operate continuously down to at least three knots without resorting to kicking engines off and on. This requirement has important implications for the propulsion shaft bearing design.

[2] An A60 bulkhead will withstand most fires for a hour. An A0 bulkhead has no fire retardant requirements.

[3] The Class definition of essential should not be used. To Class, an emergency fire pump is a non-essential load. And the Class load factors are a joke. Typically, the real installed power required is 25% or more larger than that calculated using the Class load factors, especially when an engine room is under stress. See Section 5.13. A load shedding system will be needed for the truly non-essential loads, and to make sure that power is not drained back to the blacked out engine room.

manned door between the two engine control rooms, with the combined engine control room A60 insulated from both engine rooms. 99.99% of the ship's life the two engine rooms will be operated as a single entity. Separating the control functions is clearly unattractive. Nor do I like a Master/Slave pair of control rooms. There's far two many possible interdependencies, and, since the Slave system will almost never be used by itself, it will be rarely tested and never completely.[4] If the combined engine room is wiped out by a rapid intra-control room fire while the intra-control room door is still open, I'd fall back on local control.

Currently, the Class twin screw rules – at least by my reading – allow neither a combined control room nor decent access. In an attempting to be bureaucratically pure, they are producing overly complex, hard to operate engine rooms. I think this should be changed.

Most importantly, twin screw must not be used as an excuse for still less robust machinery. Any further reduction in current paper-thin machinery design margins will produce a gargantuan jump in failure rates, and obviate the value of twin screw. Quite the opposite, we must design machinery more conservatively. At a bare minimum, we must apply the 15% derating rule to current machinery.[5] Only then will we reap the full value of twin screw.

---

[4] The testing itself could take down both engine rooms.

[5] And we must collect (and force the vendors to produce) reliable Mean Time between Failure (MTBF) and Mean Time to Repair (MTTR) numbers for all essential machinery, so that we can perform a reasonable failure analysis of the system. Under current Class Rules and confidentiality agreements, this is a total black hole.

Appendix C

The Physics of Tank Spillage

C.1 Disclaimer

The physics of how a breached tank spills oil is an interesting subject on at least four grounds:

1. The results can be counter-intuitive and quite surprising in certain cases.

2. A tanker crew who truly understands the process can in many damage situations significantly reduce or even eliminate spillage by properly listing and trimming the ship. Conversely, a crew or responders who do not have this understanding can materially increase the spillage by improper cargo and ballast transfers. This has happened far more often than it should. An example is the TAMANO spill discussed in Section C.6

3. Tanker designers need to understand how tanks lose oil in order to develop ships with attractive spillage characteristics and avoid designs with poor spillage characteristics.

4. Regulators need to understand these physics in order to draft legislation which promotes ships with good spillage characteristics and discourages ships with poor spillage characteristics. In the past, poor understanding of tanker spillage has resulted in legislation that inadvertently promoted designs with very poor spillage behavior. The Marpol single hulls are an obvious example.

Having said this, it is essential to recognize that what happens after a tank is breached can have only the most marginal impact on overall tanker spillage. As we saw in Chapter 3, low to medium impact groundings in which the ship survives produce less than 9% of all the oil spilled by tankers. And low and

319

medium impact collisions are responsible for less than 3% of total tanker spillage. Differences in tank arrangement (pre-Marpol, Marpol, double side, double bottom, double hull, etc) and crew response can affect only a fraction of these small percentages. In general, in past tanker regulation, there has been far too much focus on attempting to reduce spillage after a grounding or collision has already occurred and much too little emphasis on preventing the grounding or collision in the first place. For example, far more spillage would be prevented by mandating twin screw than could ever be obtained by various tank arrangement alternatives.

Moreover, by far the single most importance cause of tanker spill volume and crew deaths is structural failure. And the most important cause of structural failure is segregated ballast tank corrosion. (See Section 3.2.) Tanker designers and tanker regulators must be careful to avoid increasing the probability of structural failure in an attempt to make a small reduction in spillage in certain groundings and collisions.

Still more basically, the central problem in tankers is not how tanks are arranged but a regulatory system in which the key regulator, the Classification Society, is beholden to the regulatee for his existence.

In short, the contents of this Appendix are not central to the core issues in tanker regulation.

Despite this, an enormous amount of effort, and even more hot air, has been expended on analyzing the pros and cons of a particular tank arrangement on the amount of oil spilled after a grounding or collision has occurred. Much of this discussion has been ridiculously politicized. In this highly charged debate, the simple, if sometimes surprising, physics of tank oil spillage has become obscured. Worse, an understanding of this process has not filtered down to either tanker operators or spill responders, despite the fact that that knowledge would do more to reduce spillage than all the paper studies of various tanker designs.

This Appendix is aimed primarily at those operators and responders. But it may also prove useful to tanker designers and regulators.

C.2 Hydrostatic Balance

In order to understand how a damaged tank spills oil, we need to understand *hydrostatic balance.* The physics is quite simple, even if the results are sometimes a little counter-intuitive.[1] Hydrostatic balance can be understood by any one who has balanced a large block of wood on a balance scale with a much smaller iron disk. It's not the volume that counts; it's the weight.

Crude oil is almost always less dense than water. An extremely dense crude oil such as Tia Juana Heavy from Venezuela has a specific gravity of 0.93; that is, a liter or gallon of this liquid weighs 93% as much as a liter or gallon of fresh water. A very light crude oil such as Zuetina from Algeria has a specific gravity of 0.80. A liter/gallon/whatever of this stuff weighs 80% as much as the same volume of water. The great majority of crudes have specific gravities which are between 0.82 and 0.87. Sea water has a specific gravity of about 1.02. It is about 2% denser than fresh water thanks to the dissolved salts it contains. More importantly, for present purposes, sea water is about 20% heavier than a typical crude oil.

With this background, let's start with the simplest situation: single bottom with the damage confined to the bottom. Figure C.1 is a sketch of an old style, pre-Marpol, single hull ULCC, fully loaded. The solid line sloping downward and to the right shows the internal pressure in the tank as we move vertically downward in the tank. In Figure C.1, we have assumed that the cargo has a specific gravity of 0.85, a middling density for crude oil. That is, a cubic meter of this oil weighs 85% as much as a cubic meter of fresh water. Inside the tank, the pressure head increases by 0.85 meters for each meter we move down in the tank. Thus the slope of the solid line is 0.85.

The dashed line shows the external pressure in the sea outside the tank. The seawater pressure head increases by 1.02 meters for each meter of depth. Seawater is heavier than oil; so as we move vertically downward the seawater pressure outside the tank increases more rapidly than the internal pressure in the tank. However, the pressure inside the tank has a head start since the top of the oil in a fully loaded tank is well above sea level. At some point the seawater pressure will catch up to the tank pressure.

The cross-over point is known as the *Neutral Level.* At any depth above the Neutral Level, the internal tank pressure is higher than the external sea pressure. Damage above the Neutral Level will result in a hydrostatic

---

[1] Equations will be confined to footnotes. They are not really needed anyway. What is important is the sketches. All the sketches in this document are to scale. They are anatomically correct.

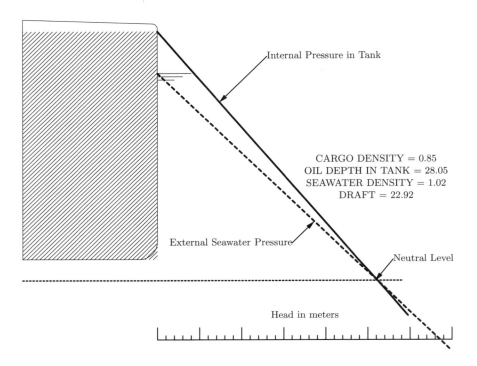

Internal Pressure in Tank

CARGO DENSITY = 0.85
OIL DEPTH IN TANK = 28.05
SEAWATER DENSITY = 1.02
DRAFT = 22.92

External Seawater Pressure

Neutral Level

Head in meters

NEUTRAL LEVEL IS 2.7 M BELOW KEEL
Hydrostatic outflow from damage anywhere in the tank including flat bottom

Figure C.1: Neutral Level, Fully Loaded Pre-MARPOL ULCC

outflow of oil into the sea. At any depth below the Neutral Level the external sea pressure is higher than the internal tank pressure. *Damage below the Neutral Level will result in a hydrostatic inflow of seawater* **into** *the tank.*

In Figure C.1, the Neutral Level is 2.7 meters *below* the keel. This means that even at the very bottom of the tank the internal oil pressure is higher than the external seawater pressure. Damage anywhere in the tank, even at the very bottom, will result in a spill. Oil will flow out of the tank until the internal and external pressures at the top of the damage have equalized.

Now suppose we draw down the initial level of cargo in this tank 2 meters. Figure C.2 shows the new situation, assuming the ship remains at the same draft. The oil has lost a considerable portion of its head start; and the

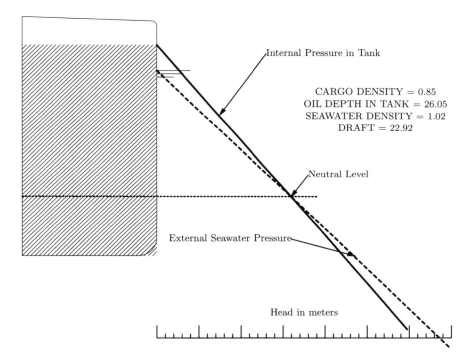

NEUTRAL LEVEL IS 7.3 M ABOVE KEEL
No hydrostatic outflow from damage below Neutral Level

Figure C.2: Neutral Level for same ULCC, Tank Drawn Down 2 M

Neutral Level, the depth at which the internal and external pressures are equal, is now 7.3 Meters *above* the keel. Drawing down the tank 2 meters has lifted the Neutral Level a surprising 10 meters.[2]

In this case, we have a multiplier of five, every meter change in the initial cargo depth changes the Neutral Level by five meters. This multiplier results from the fact that the solid and dotted lines in Figures C.1 and C.2 are nearly parallel. So a slight shift upward or downward in either of these lines, makes a big difference in the cross-over point.

In Figure C.2, if we have damage which is confined to the flat bottom, sea water will push into the tank lifting the oil in the tank until the internal pressure and the external pressure are equalized. When you do the calculations, you find that this will occur when the oil-water interface is 1.2 meters above the bottom. Figure C.3 shows this final situation and compares it with that which would have occured if the ship had initially been loaded as in Figure C.1.

The top half of Figure C.3 tells us that *as long as the damage is confined to the bottom*, a fully loaded pre-Marpol tanker will spill less than a few percent of the oil in each tank that was breached. Notice that the equilibrium level of oil in the tank is still well above sea level after the oil has stopped flowing out. One of the clains for double bottoms is that they are much better than the crummy old Marpol single bottoms in bottom damage. Well, the fact is that the old Marpol single hulls were pretty damn good at limiting outflow in bottom damage.

I need to make an extremely important qualification here. Figure C.3 assumes the ship is at the same draft before damage and after. As long as only one or two tanks are damaged, this will be nearly true. If a lot of cargo tanks are damaged, the ship will rise in the water during the outflow and this can materially increase the outflow. The multiplier is a two-edge sword. Conversely, if some ballast tanks are damaged and flooded or a quick thinking crew ballasts the ship down, the leakage can be markedly reduced.[3]

---

[2] For the geeks, the equation for the Neutral Level is

$$H_{NL} = \frac{\rho_{sea}D - \rho_{oil}H_{oil}}{\rho_{sea} - \rho_{oil}}$$

where H_{NL} is the height of the Neutral Level, ρ_{sea} is the sea water density, ρ_{oil} is the cargo density, D is the ship's draft, and H_{oil} is the initial level in the tank. The fact that the denominator is generally less than 0.2 gives rise to the multiplier. Heavier cargoes have higher multipliers and vice versa.

[3] Another less important, but still very significant qualification. All tanker cargo tanks are normally inerted. That is, they are pressurized with low O_2 gas from the ship's boilers. This prevents explosions. But it also increases the pressure in the top of the tank. Typically, this increase in pressure is equivalent to about a half-meter of sea water. The solid line in Figures C.1 and C.2 actually starts off about a half-meter higher than I have

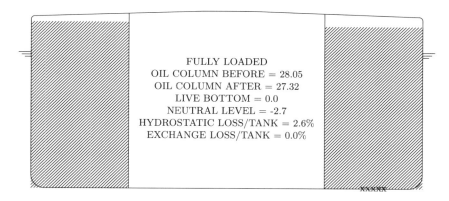

FULLY LOADED
OIL COLUMN BEFORE = 28.05
OIL COLUMN AFTER = 27.32
LIVE BOTTOM = 0.0
NEUTRAL LEVEL = -2.7
HYDROSTATIC LOSS/TANK = 2.6%
EXCHANGE LOSS/TANK = 0.0%

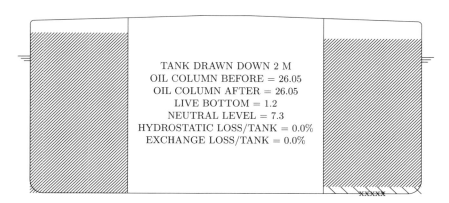

TANK DRAWN DOWN 2 M
OIL COLUMN BEFORE = 26.05
OIL COLUMN AFTER = 26.05
LIVE BOTTOM = 1.2
NEUTRAL LEVEL = 7.3
HYDROSTATIC LOSS/TANK = 0.0%
EXCHANGE LOSS/TANK = 0.0%

Figure C.3: Final situation, Full load vs Tank Drawn Down 2 M

The bottom half of Figure C.3 says we only had to underload such ships by about 7%, and they would have spilled nil oil if the damage is limited to the bottom. (Once again I'm assuming the underloading was accompanied by sufficient ballast to keep the ship at the same draft.)

The bottom half of Figure C.3 also says we must be careful to distinguish the Neutral Level from the equilibrium oil-water interface. In this situation, the Neutral Level is 7.3 meters above the bottom of the tank, but the oil-water interface after the sea water flows into the tank is only 1.2 m above the bottom of the tank. This equilibrium oil-water interface is called the *Live Bottom*.[4]

Most people have no problem accepting the fact that, if the level of oil in the tank is below that of the surrounding seawater, and we puncture the bottom of the tank, sea water will flow into the tank rather than oil flowing out.

But there are two aspects of hydrostatic balance that are much harder to swallow:

(A) One is that the water will flow in rather than oil flowing out even if the initial level of oil in the tank is above the surrounding seawater, as long as the weight of the column of oil is less than the weight of the column of sea water.[5] For a light crude and a pre-Marpol ULCC at deep draft, the level in the tank could be 4 meters higher than the sea level outside, and yet water would flow in from bottom damage rather than oil flowing. Water is heavier than oil. Think of that balance beam.

(B) The fact that a small change in the initial level of oil in the tank can

---

shown.

It is even a little more complicated than this. If there is outflow, the pressure in the ullage space will be drawn down, possibly as far as the P/V valves allow. If there is inflow, the pressure in the ullage space will be pushed up, possibly as far as the P/V valves allow. These effects can have a major impact on actual outflows. We will make the necessary adjustments in Section C.9.3.

[4] Assuming that there is a Live Bottom, the equation for the Live Bottom is

$$H_{LB} = \frac{\rho_{sea}D - \rho_{oil}H_{oil}}{\rho_{sea}}$$

where H_{LB} is the height of the Live Bottom. Notice there is no multiplier. In both the H_{NL} and H_{LB} equations, the seawater depth D at the damage is critical. It determines the external pressure. Change that depth and you change all the spillage numbers.

[5] It is not just laymen that have a problem with this. Many spill responders don't understand it. The report of the DIAMOND GRACE spill in Tokyo Bay by the response commander has a sketch which shows he believes that the equilibrium level in a breached tank is the seawater level.

make a far larger change in the position of the Neutral Level. As we have seen, thanks to the relatively small difference in density between seawater and oil, changing the initial level in the tank by 1 meter, typically changes the Neutral Level by 5 or 6 meters.

In our everyday life we don't have a lot of experience with different density liquids. If we fill up a U-tube with water, we know the level in the two ends of the tube will end up being the same. We sort of expect the same thing to happen, even if the liquids are not the same. If you have a U-tube, fill up one side with olive oil and the other with vinegar. You will see the difference. Anyway the physics couldn't be simpler or more irrefutable; and points (A) and (B) have been experimentally verified many times. I have to ask you to study Figures C.1, C.2 and C.3 until they really make sense to you.

The term *hydrostatic balance* is used in two different contexts:

1. To refer to the equilibrium situation after the the oil water-interface has stabilized, as in "the tank had reached hydrostatic balance".

2. To refer to a tank in which the initial, undamaged cargo level is low enough so that the Neutral Level is above the bottom of the tank, as in "the tank was hydrostaticly balanced loaded". This horribly awkward phrase is usually shortened to HBL. An HBL tank in calm water will not spill oil ***if the damage is confined to the flat bottom***.[6]

---

[6] In a similar fashion, we will sometimes used the phrases *hydrostatically over/under-balanced* to refer to a tank in which the cargo level is above/below the HBL level.

C.3   Marpol versus Pre-Marpol

For our first application of hydrostatic balance, let's compare Marpol single hulls with pre-Marpol single hulls. On the right side of Figure C.4 is a 215,000 ton Marpol VLCC which looks suspiciously like the EXXON VALDEZ On the left side is a standard 275,000 ton pre-Marpol VLCC which has been scaled to 215,000 ton deadweight. The Marpol VLCC is a slightly bigger ship, about 2 m taller, because none of the cargo tank volume can be re-used as ballast tank volume.

Both ships are fully loaded with a 0.85 specific gravity crude. For the pre-Marpol ship loaded down to her marks, this means using up only about 94% of the available cargo cubic.[7] But for the Marpol tanker, we must use all the available cubic leaving 2 to 3% for cargo expansion. The result is that the initial oil column in the Marpol tanker is more than 2 meters taller than that for the pre-Marpol ship. But the initial drafts are almost the same.

The visual difference between the ships in Figure C.4 is not all that striking. But when the tank on the right in the pre-Marpol ship is bottom damaged, a little less than 0.5 m of oil flows out before hydrostatic balance is reached. When the same tank in the Marpol tanker is bottom damaged over 2.5 m of oil flows out. **In percentage terms, the Marpol tanker spills five times as much oil. Applied to the Exxon Valdez which ruptured 8 of 11 cargo tanks, the extra 2 meters of outflow is about 10 million liters.**

This analysis is far from complete:

1. We have not adjusted for differences in tank arrangement. The pre-Marpol VLCC will typically have 24 tanks of which two are segregated ballast. The Marpol VLCC will have something like 15 tanks of which four are segregated ballast. Normally, the Marpol tank will be considerably bigger than the pre-Marpol tank. On the other hand, the Marpol ship has a higher probability of damaging a non-cargo tank than the pre-Marpol ship.

2. We have not adjusted for change in draft, trim, and heel. As we shall see, this adjustment is critically important. In the situation in Figure C.4 if the tank on the right is the only breached tank, then both ships will list away from the damage which will exacerbate spillage.

---

[7] A smart move in pre-Marpol days was to use up all the cubic in the center tanks in which case for most crudes the wing tanks are hydrostatically under-balanced when the ship is loaded down to her marks. This is precisely how IMO Reg 13(G) was implemented on our old ships, usually with no loss in carrying capacity. In the left side of Figure C.4, this was not done.

However, the Marpol ship will list more (and rise more) increasing spillage more.

3. We have not adjusted for tide (if stranded), IG pressure, nor the vacuum that is created in the top of the tanks with outflow.

We will get into all these matters. However, it is obvious that the Marpol single hulls are hydrostatically challenged. In fact, in the Marpol single hulls, the Tromedy after protracted deliberation came up with about the worst spilling tanker one can reasonably imagine.

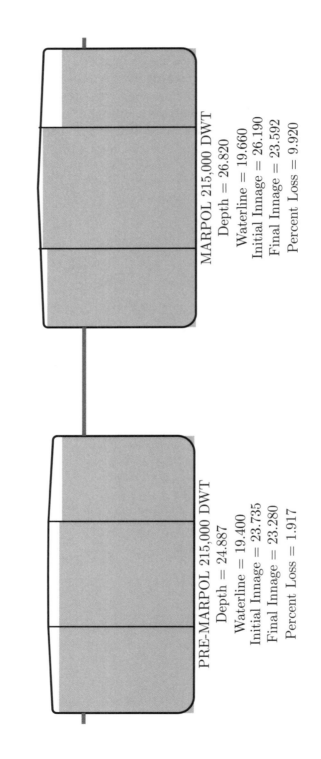

Figure C.4: Marpol vs pre-Marpol Spillage

BOTTOM DAMAGE TO TANK ON THE RIGHT

MARPOL 215,000 DWT
Depth = 26.820
Waterline = 19.660
Initial Innage = 26.190
Final Innage = 23.592
Percent Loss = 9.920

PRE-MARPOL 215,000 DWT
Depth = 24.887
Waterline = 19.400
Initial Innage = 23.735
Final Innage = 23.280
Percent Loss = 1.917

C.4 Yeah, but Where's the Seal

Another problem people have with hydrostatic balance is the efficacy of the seal. The Live Bottom is not really a bottom. In many situations, the oil-water interface will be quite close to the real bottom or equivalently the top of the damage. There's no barrier there; no membrane or anything similar keeping the oil in the tank. How good a seal can it be?

If the damage is confined to the ship's bottom, the ship is floating, and nobody does anything stupid, it turns out that a Live Bottom is a pretty effective seal. Almost all crude oils hate to mix with water. The molecules repel each other. This accounts for the spreading and persistence of oil slicks, even in fairly rough water. If you do manage to mix some of the oil into the water, it will immediately tend to separate.[8]

For a floating ship, there are two natural phenomena that can generate spillage after a Live Bottom is established: current and waves. After the EXXON VALDEZ, the US Coast Guard had decided it would be politically unwise to oppose double bottoms. This was a major change. In the 1979 post-Amoco Cadiz debate, the Coast Guard had argued for limits on tank size and against double bottoms. The main alternative to double bottoms was hydrostatic balance.

The Coast Guard knew they could not attack the basic physics of hydrostatic balance. They decided to go after the seal. In 1992, the USCG funded a series of 1/30th and 1/15th scale experiments at the David Taylor Research Center (DTRC).[37] These tests were an intriguing combination of crude but very interesting experimental science and blatant politics on the part of the sponsor.[22] But the key result is summarized in Figure C.5.[9] This figure shows the Live Bottom height required to effectively halt current entrainment according to these model tests. If the Live Bottom is right at the ship's bottom, current under the ship produces a wave at the oil/water interface. When a trough in the wave reaches the down current end of the damage, the oil in the trough is clipped off and lost into the sea. As the Live Bottom rises in the tank, the amplitude of the interface wave decreases;

---

[8] All the witnesses to the EXXON VALDEZ were struck by how violently the oil emerged from the water.[39][p 45] The velocity that the oil had attained in its 15 to 20 m climb to the surface generated little geysers. USCG Warrant Officer Delozier, who reached the ship three hours after she grounded testified

> The oil was coming out of vessel at a very intense rate .... bubbling up into the air, sometimes up to sixteen, eighteen, twenty inches high.

[9] The DTRC experiments were actually a follow on to work done at the Tsukuba Institute in Japan which produced similar results.

and, for a high enough Live Bottom, even the trough in the wave is above
the ship bottom, at which point current loss effectively halts. As Figure
C.5 indicates for a three knot current, the Live Bottom has to be about 0.7
meters above the real bottom.[10] For a 5 knot current, we need about a 2.2
m Live Bottom height. The required Live Bottom height goes as the square
of the current velocity as would be expected from Bernoulli's Law.

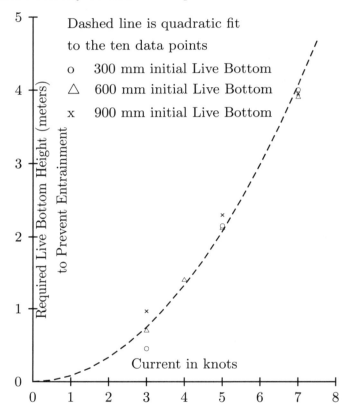

Figure C.5: Required Live Bottom Height versus Current Speed

I would not make too much of Figure C.5 for two reasons:

1. There is good reason to doubt the accuracy of the extrapolation of the
   model results to full scale. The difference between the DTRC results
   at 1/30th scale and 1/15th scale showed that the straightforward extrapolation used in the DTRC report and Figure C.5 was of limited

---

[10] Figure C.5 is not in the DTRC report. It is my interpretation of the results in Figure
9 of that report. It is the level of the Live Bottom in the tank 2 hours (ship time) after
the start of the experiment at which point the oil loss rate is nil.

accuracy. DTRC was careful to point this out and call for more research; but this has never been done. The results in Figure C.5 should be taken as indicative only.

2. The test procedure was to place the model tank in a circulating water tunnel and then open a hole in the bottom of the tank. This is OK experimental science but does not model a stranding.[11] Most severe groundings are strandings. In a stranding, the area around the damage is partially blocked by the sea bottom. Moveover, even if the surface current is say 3 knots, the current next to the sea bottom will be much smaller.

In any event, currents much in excess of 3 knots are reasonably rare and Figure C.5 gives us considerable comfort that, as long as the Live Bottom is a meter or more above the top of the damage, current will almost never be a factor. In extraordinarily high current environments, you may need as much as a 2 m Live Bottom height.

A real world example of the power of hydrostatic balance in the face of large current was the OCEANIC GRANDEUR spill. On March 3rd, 1970, the OCEANIC GRANDEUR hit an uncharted rock in the Torres Strait. The 61,000 tonner was nearly fully loaded with 55,000 tons of crude. When she hit the rock, 8 of 15 cargo tanks were breached. However, the ship flooded in a manner that resulted in her sinking 2 or 3 meters with a slight list to port, putting the port gunnel just underwater, Figure C.6. This sinkage improved the hydrostatic balance considerably. The ship lost considerably less than 1% of her cargo as a result of the initial damage.

The weather was calm throughout but the currents in the Torres Strait can be extremely strong. Despite this, the Australian investigation report explicitly says nil oil was lost during the subsequent three days *despite tidal currents of up to 6 knots* [emphasis mine].[4] This was not a stranding; the ship was at anchor during this period. Most of the 1100 kiloliters spilled was lost on the 7th day of lightering as the ship rose out of the water, reducing the external hydrostatic pressure. If they had done a really careful job of lightering and ballasting, this latter spillage could have been prevented; but

---

[11] Nor does it model the initial grounding process. Some have argued that during impact the damaged tanks are momentarily exposed to the very high "current" produced by the ship's forward motion, and attempted to apply the DTRC results to this process. But they are forgetting that not only will the damage be largely blocked by the sea bottom during that period, but sea bottom material will be penetrating into the tank volume. This was dramatically illustrated in the EXXON VALDEZ where the crew reported that the P/V valves of the damaged tanks vented violently as the ship rode onto the rocks. The first thing that happens is the liquid in the tank is forced upward.

probably, at the cost of a longer lightering, which would have entailed its own risks. Even so the OCEANIC GRANDEUR, with over half her cargo tanks breached, lost just 2% of her cargo. And we can be sure that the damage was not confined to just the flat bottom. In the real world, there is no such thing as a flat bottom only grounding.[12]

A more effective way of breaking a Live Bottom seal is wave pumping. Waves can disturb the Live Bottom two ways:

1. If the waves are small relative to the ship, almost always the case for big tankers near shore, or the ship is hard aground, we can ignore ship motion. In this case the local wave height in way of the damage becomes the key. In this situation, a conservative upper bound on oil lost to wave pumping is to assume the "real" sea level is the calm water sea level less one-half the wave height. In practice, wave pumping becomes quite slow as the Live Bottom rises to this "equilibrium" level. In the THUNTANK 5 grounding, the Swedes found that several days of 4 to 5 meter waves was equivalent to an effective calm water sea level, about 1.4 meters below the actual water level.[13]

2. If the ship is afloat and the waves are large enough to produce significant pitch, heave or roll, then the tank will continue to leak until the oil-water interface is in equilibrium when the tank at its highest point in the ship motion.

Groundings usually occur in protected or semi-protected waters. They never occur in the open sea. The sad fact is that, if a grounding occurs in a situation where the waves are so large that wave pumping is really important to spillage, the ship is unlikely to survive. Witness TORREY CANYON, ARGO MERCHANT, AMOCO CADIZ, (and just about all the other groundings on the coast of Brittany), BRAER, TASMAN SPIRIT and many others.

If current and wave pumping are not all that good at breaking the Live Bottom seal, there are two very effective ways of clobbering hydrostatic balance.

---

[12] A critically important factor in this casualty was the strength of the ship. The OCEANIC GRANDEUR, was able to withstand the over-design sagging moment associated with flooding the midships segregated ballast tanks while loaded *with her bottom all torn up*. The fact that this 61,000 tonner was built in 1965 meant that she had more strength than the later 1970's built pre-Marpol ships, not to mention far more strength than the tankers built in the 1980's and later. If the hull had failed — and a modern hull probably would have — the Grandeur would have spilled the better part of 50,000 kiloliters on the Great Barrier Reef, making this one of the most famous spills of all time. As it was, you almost certainly have never heard of this ship. (In 1980, the OCEANIC GRANDEUR(2) blew up due to cargo leaking into the Forepeak tank, killing two crew.)

[13] In this spill, the quick thinking master used vacuum to his advantage.

1. Pumping out intact tanks before pumping out damaged tanks. This lifts the ship out of the water and turns the multiplier against us. Since responders either don't really understand hydrostatic balance or are responding to other pressures, this is not that uncommon. It happened in the OCEANIC GRANDEUR, and in at least two other major spills, that I know about (the TAMANO and the IMPERIAL SARNIA. In each case, more than doubling the size of the spill. More on this later.

2. Put your ship aground at high tide, and then have the tide go out 2 or 3 meters, dropping the Neutral Level by 10 to 15 meters. This is what happened to the EXXON VALDEZ. Tidal height is crucial to grounded spillage, and must be allowed for in any realistic analysis of groundings. But before we address this issue (Section C.9.2), we need to worry about side damage.

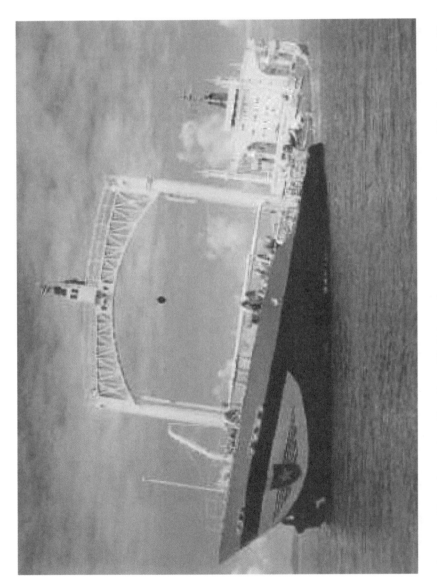

Figure C.6: Oceanic Grandeur after flooding. Hull is under extreme sagging moment but survived. No new tanker would. Note the extremely strong kingposts and the rare forward crowsnest, signs of an unusually well-speced ship. Source: Australian Maritime Safety Authority.

C.5 Side Damage and Exchange Flow

So far we have talked only about bottom damage. If the damage extends up the side of the tank and any real world damage will, the situation becomes a bit more complicated.

If we have side shell damage which is entirely below the waterline, two things happen:

1. First, we will have a hydrostatic outflow of oil or inflow of sea water depending on whether or not the Neutral Level is below or above the topmost point of the damage. This is the same as for the bottom damage case and follows exactly the same rules. As long as the top of the damage is below the waterline, the key point is the vertical height of the top of the damage. For damage that is entirely below the waterline, the topmost point of the damage plays almost exactly the same role at the lowest point in damage that is entirely above the waterline. You have to think upside down.

2. Second, if the resulting oil water interface after the hydrostatic flows have taken place is below the top of the damage, the lighter density oil will flow out the top of the damage while the heavier seawater flows in thru the bottom of the damage. When you do this at lab scale, the outflowing oil looks almost like a snake or a rope, emanating from the top of the damage. This *exchange flow* will continue until the oil water interface in the tank rises to the top of the damage.

Exchange flow is quite different from hydrostatic flow:

1. It is an order of magnitude slower. Since the outgoing oil has to be replaced by incoming water, the effective flow area is halved. When the flow area is halved, the flow velocity is reduced by more than half because of viscous effects around the perimeter of the flow. More importantly, the forces driving exchange flow tend to be much weaker than the forces driving hydrostatic flow. A typical hydrostatic flow will start out with a net driving head of 2 or 3 meters of oil. If the layer of oil below the top of the damage after hydrostatic flow is say 3 meters deep, the driving head is about 0.15 (the difference in the densities between oil and water) times this depth.[14]

---

[14] To my knowledge, there has been no real quantitative study of exchange flow, neither experimental nor theoretical. Playing around at lab scale, it is obvious that exchange flow is far slower than hydrostatic. Embiricos[25] talks about a grounding of an unidentified 90,000 tonner in the Suez Canal, in which the master noted that after 42 minutes, the spillage rate was greatly reduced. The log data indicates the tank emptied at 0.40 ft/min prior to that time and 0.05 ft/min after that time. Embiricos associates the earlier period

The "fact" that exchange flow is much slower than hydrostatic flow is the reason we can assume that hydrostatic flow happens first, then exchange flow. In reality, exchange flow begins before hydrostatic flow is finished. But, in most real world cases, the hydrostatic flow is so much faster that this assumption is close enough.

2. The pressure drop across the hole is in your favor. Once you get into exchange flow, below the very top of the hole, there is more pressure on the outside than on the inside.   Therefore it is much easier to make some sort of repair. If you can cover the hole with almost anything from the outside, even some kind of canvas it will tend to stay there. In hydrostatic flow, the flow pushes any attempt to plug the hole away from the hole.

3. The tube of outflowing oil climbs upward immediately. In the case of a double sided tanker, this means that all the oil will climb into the top of the double sides; and, if the double sides are still intact down to a little below the waterline, it will be captured there by hydrostatic balance. Much the same thing happens with hydrostatic flow but in this case, the outflow velocity can be large enough so that a good bit of the oil is carried outside the outer shell, before it turns vertically upward. You don't want either; but if you are faced with a choice of 100 cubic meters of hydrostatic flow or a 100 cubic meters of exchange flow, you would much prefer the latter.

This most definitely does not mean that side damage is preferred to bottom damage. Figure C.7 makes the point that side damage is much worse than bottom damage, and, if you must have underwater side damage, you want it as low as possible.

In Figure C.7, we start out with the same situation as in Figure C.1, a fully loaded pre-Marpol ULCC. We then damage the side shell with the highest point of damage 4 meters above the keel. Since the Live Bottom is well below the keel, the first thing that happens is hydrostatic outflow. We lose 5.3% of the tanks contents before hydrostatic flow stops.[15] In the top half of Figure C.1, when the damage was confined to the bottom, we lost only 2.6% of the tank to hydrostatic flow.

---

with hydrostatic flow and the latter with exchange flow. This is plausible but not proven. To say more, we would need the ship draft, the cargo density, the initial level in the tank, and the location of the top of the damage.

[15] The problem is that oil will flow out until the external pressure at the top of the damage is the same as the internal pressure at this point. For every meter the damage extends up the side shell, the outside head drops by ρ_{sea} but the inside pressure drops only by ρ_{oil}.

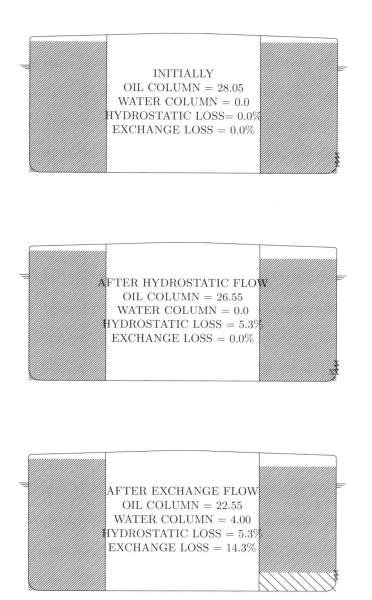

Figure C.7: Fully Loaded, Pre-MARPOL, Side damage up 4 M

And our troubles are not over. The situation after hydrostatic flow looks like the middle sketch in Figure C.7. The oil in the bottom 4 meters of the tank is below the top of the damage. This situation is unstable. The seawater pressure at the bottom of the damage is higher than the pressure inside the tank at the bottom of the damage. Sea water will pushes its way into the bottom of the damage forcing oil out the top. Unless we do something, this exchange flow will continue until we have lost all the oil in the bottom 4 meters of the tank, over 14% of the original cargo, for a total loss of about 20%.

If we initially underload the tank, so that the Live Bottom is 4 m above the keel, — this requires an initial oil column of 26.7 m or about 5% underloading, we will have no hydrostatic loss but we will still face a 14% loss in exchange flow.

In order to stop the exchange flow via hydrostatic balance, we would have to underload the tank to the point where the incoming hydrostatic flow of sea water will push all the oil in the tank above the top of the damage. This would require an initial oil column of 22.5 m or 20% underloading. The further up the tank the damage extends, the worse it gets. **The real problem with hydrostatic balance is that it is not very effective against side damage.** Of course, the same thing is true of double bottoms.

In general, you want to keep side shell damage as far away from the waterline as possible. If the damage is completely above the water line, you would prefer the bottom of the damage to be as high as possible, for in this case the low point of the damage determines how much of the tanks contents will drain out. But if the damage in entirely below the waterline, you want the highest point of the damage to be as low as possible, for in this case the high point of the damage determines how much outflow there will be. Worst of all is damage that straddles the waterline.[16] Collisions usually result in this kind of damage to the hittee. In this case, if we do nothing, we will eventually lose all the cargo in the tank.

---

[16] Despite the fact, that the single most important number for damage below the waterline is the highest point of the damage, it is almost never recorded in the spill investigations. You will see something like "6 foot gash in forward starboard tank". But unless we know the highest point of the gash (lowest if damage is all above the waterline), we can't do anything with this information.

C.6 Ballasting Down: the Tamano Spill

Hydrostatic balance has a number of implications, some of which people find surprising at first glance.

C.6.1 Ballast Down

If you have damage low in the ship, it almost always pays to sink the ship lower in the water. A little study of Figures C.1 and C.2 will reveal that, if we were in the full load situation, Figure C.1, and we sank the ship 2 meters lower, it would have more or less the same effect as having drawn the tank down 2 meters. In fact, it will have a bit more effect. For a medium density crude with a specific gravity of 0.85 and sea water with a density of 1.02, the equation for the height of the Neutral Level, H_{NL} is

$$H_{NL} = \frac{1.02D - 0.85H_{oil}}{1.02 - 0.85}$$

where H_{oil} is the height of the oil in the tank, and D is the ship's draft in way of the damage. Pressing the ship down into the water an extra meter is worth more than removing a meter of oil from the tank because a meter of seawater weighs more than a meter of cargo.

Figure C.8 shows the Figure C.1 situation if we are able to get the ship 2 meters deeper in the water. The Neutral Level has gone from 2.7 meters below the keel to 9.3 meters above. Generally, the most effective thing a crew can do if the ship has bottom damage is to get the damaged tank(s) lower in the water.[17] One of the good things about a double bottom is that, when it is damaged, it automatically ballasts the ship down. The same thing is true of an HBL-loaded single hull, but, unless a segregated ballast tank is breached as in the OCEANIC GRANDEUR, the amount of automatic ballasting down will be much less. Unfortunately, the way we build ships these days, it also automatically over-stresses the ship.

C.6.2 Do not discharge non-damaged tanks

Conversely, the dumbest thing you can do is to lighten the ship and bring it further out of the water.

I should know. The first spill I ever attended was the TAMANO in July of 1970 in Casco Bay outside Portland, Maine. At that time, there was a

---

[17] In doing so, we must be careful not to exceed the ship's structural limits. This is the subject of Section C.7.

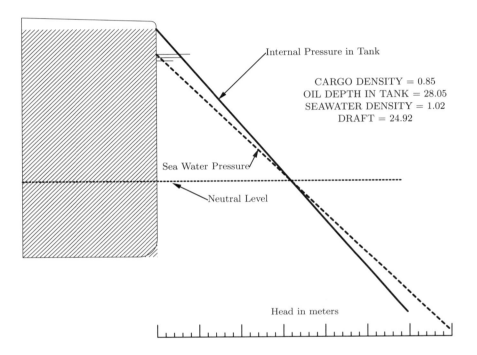

CARGO DENSITY = 0.85
OIL DEPTH IN TANK = 28.05
SEAWATER DENSITY = 1.02
DRAFT = 24.92

NEUTRAL LEVEL IS 9.3 M ABOVE KEEL

Figure C.8: Full load but ballasted down 2 M

pipeline from Portland to Eastern Canada. The TAMANO, a 100,000 ton, four year old, pre-Marpol single hull, fully loaded with heavy fuel oil, hit a ledge in-bound to the pipeline at about 0120 in the morning. The weather was clear. She had just picked up a pilot. This was probably a navigation error, although the ship alleged that a buoy was out of position. The ship proceeded to the terminal, where it was discovered she was leaking.

I was a junior faculty member at MIT at the time, and had made a very modest name for myself in New England by pontificating on the impact of oil drilling on Georges Bank. But I had never actually seen a real world oil spill of any size. The locals invited me and some of my students to see for ourselves. I jumped at the chance.

By the time we got there, the leakage had stopped. No one was quite sure why including me, although after the fact it was clear that the damaged tanks had gone to hydrostatic balance. (Later it was learned that only 1S was damaged, a 20 foot gash 8" wide — but the all important highest point of the damage was not reported — it was somewhere low in the tank).

The decision was made to off-load the cargo so that the ship could go to the yard for repairs. (Besides the Canadian charterers were desperate for the oil.) But the damaged tank could not be pumped out with the ship's pumps since the oil-water interface in this tank was above the tank suctions. Pumping this tank out would merely pump out sea water which would be replaced by more seawater. This is the normal situation when a tank is breached. The suctions for the ship's pumps are at the very bottom of each tank. Otherwise, you would never be able to completely empty the tank. But this means that as soon as the oil water interface in a seriously damaged tank is above the bottom, the ship's pumps can't pump cargo out of that tank.

So they started pumping out the intact cargo tanks. Immediately the ship began leaking again. Before we stopped we had more than doubled the size of the overall spill. At the time, neither I nor apparently anyone else had thought through the hydrostatic balance thing. In retrospect the situation could not have been handled any worse. By pumping out the intact cargo tanks, we lifted the ship out of the water and destroyed the hydrostatic balance. The damaged tank probably had a plan area of about 300 m^2. The heavy fuel oil cargo had a density of around 0.95. For every centimeter we raised that tank, we spilled roughly an extra 3,200 liters. The final spill volume was put at 378,000 liters. It took only a half meter reduction in draft to double the spill.

As soon as the spill was discovered, the ship should have been moved into deeper water and ballasted down as far as possible, listing and trimming the ship in the direction of the damage. At that point, we should have put submersible salvage pumps on-board and pumped out the damaged tank from the top down.[18] Only after we had removed the oil from the damaged tank should we even have thought about discharging the other cargo tanks. Preposterously stupid.[19]

Many years later, a Coast Guard veteran told me that the same thing had happened at the IMPERIAL SARNIA spill in the St.Lawrence Seaway in 1974 but I was never able to get any details. The TAMANO is the only major spill at which I have been physically present. One wonders how often this silly mistake is made.

The power of Hydrostatic Balance is a two-edged sword. Here are two obvious things NOT to do to avoid lowering the Neutral Level.

1. **Don't discharge intact tanks** which will raise the ship in the water massively increasing hydrostatic flow from the breached tanks.
2. Similarly, **Don't deballast the ship.**

The only exception to these two rules is: you have grounded at high tide and by deballasting/discharging/jettisoning you may be able to get the ship off before the tide goes out with horrible effect on hydrostatic balance — this is what happened to the EXXON VALDEZ — and/or the ship's structural integrity — see the SEA EMPRESS spill below.[20] Conversely, if you have grounded on soft, flat bottom at low tide and the situation is safe and stable, ballast down, stay put, and let the rising tide improve your Neutral Level markedly.

As soon as you get in trouble, call for submersible pumps.[21]

---

[18] These pumps can be lowered into the tank to a point above the oil water interface.

[19] I have not found any reference to the hydrostatic screw up nor the secondary spill in any of the official TAMANO documentation. It shows up only obliquely as a sudden "failure" of the containment equipment well after the initial leak had stopped. I don't know whether this omission was intentional, or simply due to complete ignorance of what was happening.

[20] The common salvage process of overpressuring, "blowing a tank", is an obvious example of Hydrostatic Balance in reverse. It should be employed only if the benefits outweigh the additional oil outflow and there is no feasible alternative.

[21] One can make a strong argument that all tankers should be required to carry a submersible pump and a means for driving it. Further the successful use of the system should be periodically demonstrated to port state inspectors.

C.7 The Right Response

Hopefully by now you are convinced that the right response in terms of ballasting and cargo transfers can be crucial in determining the final amount spilled. The question on the table is: how do you get the right response?

The answer that the Tromedy has come up with is something called an *emergency response service*. This is effectively written into both the USCG and IMO regulations.

The idea is that you have a bunch of experts at some shoreside location. They have data on the ship. They have the necessary software. They are given data on the casualty and the condition of the ship; and they decide what to do. The main purveyors of this service are our old friends, the Classification Societies. In fact for all practical purposes, the Classification Societies have a monopoly on the business of providing an emergency response service. The fees for enrolling a ship are quite reasonable: a one time charge of about $5,000 and then maybe $500 per year, highly negotiable. Owners are happy to pay this sum in order to check off the corresponding regulatory box. They can then conveniently forget about devising any response themselves.

There's only one problem with this system. It doesn't work. The system is trebly crippled:

1. It's way too slow. There is no guaranteed response time. The best that you will get from Class is something-like "the team can be fully operational normally within an hour of the client call out". In practice, this means you can count on something like two hours to get the experts out of bed, and into their chairs in a London or Houston office. What the ship does in the first hour is critical; the first 15 minutes more so. In most spills, if you wait a couple of hours before you even start responding, you might as well have stayed in bed.

2. It's way too far away. The so-called experts are unfamiliar with the ship, the specifics of the casualty, and the conditions on-site. It will take at least another hour while they gather the data, correct obvious errors, get a very rough, filtered idea of what's happening, and can start running numbers. And they never know what's really happening. The only people who have any idea what's really happening are the guys on-board. They are too busy to be filling out forms for somebody who may be 6000 miles away.

3. There's a good chance that there's something wrong with the data the experts are using. The problem is that the experts' software is rarely thoroughly exercised on a particular ship until a crisis is at

hand. No complicated software/data combination really works the first time. The middle of a big spill is not the time to discover and correct these problems. We made a random check of the Lloyds Register response service which is called SERS with the Hellespont Grand. SERS claimed the Grand had 18 cm of trim in a situation where she had no trim. Exxon had similar unhappy results when it tested the ABS service, which is wishfully called ABS RR (Rapid Response).[22]

The obvious solution is to provide the guys on-board: crew, coast guard, etc with the requisite tools.[23] This can be accomplished by a straightforward enhancement to the ship's *Loading Instrument*.

Every tanker has software on-board which takes as input an actual or potential tank loading pattern, and computes the corresponding draft and trim, estimates the stresses imposed on the ship by this loading pattern, and checks that these stresses are within legally allowable values. This program is called the Loading Instrument.[24]

It is not difficult to endow the Loading Instrument with the capabilities of handling damage and spillage, basically replicating the software that the response services supposedly have. My firm, Martingale, has developed such a program. It's called MLOAD. Martingale has given MLOAD to the Center for Tankship Excellence. CTX is rewriting the code to a much more maintainable and reusable form and will distribute it (including the Source Code) under the Gnu Public License. The rewritten version will be called CTX_MATE.

MLOAD/CTX_MATE serves three purposes:

1. It's a normal loading program in every day use. This is crucial. It means that the program has been thoroughly tested on this particular ship for a wide range of loading conditions. It means the crew is

---

[22] The software that the response services use is suspect or at least opaque. Whenever we have probed into this area we've received confused and sometimes evasive answers from the response services, with lots of phrases like "semi-manual" or "combined with judgment" etc. The truth is that the response services don't know exactly how the software they are using works, because they can't inspect it. They are using a combination of proprietary packages whose inner workings (the source code) are uninspectable by anybody but the vendors themselves. I don't trust any such software and neither should the public. Any software that claims to benefit the public should be subject to public review and inspection. It must be Open Source.

[23] Shoreside response teams are not entirely a bad idea. They can be useful in really big spills involving multi-day response, and spills in which the crew is incapacitated or has abandoned the ship. Sluggish shoreside response is complementary to the immediate shipboard response that I am advocating.

[24] Despite the fact that these programs can be critically important to vessel safety and the environment, they are almost invariably closed source.

intimately familiar with the program's operation and facile in its use. Turning to basically untested, rarely used, unfamiliar software in the middle of a crisis is a prescription for disaster. Finally, it means that the tank loading pattern at the time of the casualty is already in the program. With MLOAD, if a ship experiences damage, the crew can flip the program to Damage Mode with a single click, and type in six numbers for each damaged tank. (The six numbers tell MLOAD the location of the damage in that tank.) Click again and all the damage calculations are done. No multi-hour delay in getting up and running.

2. It's a salvage program capable of computing flooding, damage stability, and strength for any given loading pattern. The crew will immediately know if the ship is in danger of sinking, capsizing, or being over-stressed. In most middle sized spills, this will not be the case; but, if they are in danger of losing the ship, the crew needs to know right away.

3. It's a spill reduction tool. In order to properly compute the equilibrium draft, trim and heel for a damaged tanker, you must compute how much cargo is lost from the damaged tanks, and the extent of seawater flooding in all the damaged compartments. In other words, do all the hydrostatic balance calculations for each damaged tank, both the hydrostatic outflow/inflow and the exchange flow, properly accounting for the change in draft, trim, and heel as a result of the outflow and flooding.

And this bring us to the neat part. As soon as the crew determines that they are not in danger of losing the ship, they can start trying out possible ways to minimize spillage. If the damage is low on the hull, as is often the case, you want to get the damaged area as deep into the water as possible, in other words you want to trim and heel the ship toward the damage.[25]

Figure C.9 is a simplified screenshot of MLOAD in which a fully loaded pre-Marpol VLCC has experienced damage in the forward port cargo tank, 1P. The damage extends from the bottom up 5 meters on the side shell 140 meters forward of midships. In Figure C.9, the crew does nothing but watch. This is the normal response. Perhaps they are waiting for advice from an emergency response service. In this case, MLOAD tell us we will have a hydrostatic outflow of 2536 cubic meters (the number labeled HYDROLOSS) and then an exchange flow of 2008 cubic meters (the number labeled EXCHGLOSS), a very big spill. It also tells us the ship is in no danger of capsizing (See GM_corr) or further structural damage (MAX %SHEAR and

---

[25] There are a few unusual situations where this is not true. See Section D.1.

MAX %BEND). Pop-ups are available which go into more detail in these areas.

But our MLOAD equipped crew is on the ball. They realize they need to get the forward port side of the ship as deep in the water as possible. The Chief Mate asks MLOAD what will happen if he fully ballasts the Forepeak tank and the port ballast tank. Figure C.10 shows the result. If he can do this quickly enough, MLOAD tells him there will be no hydrostatic flow and the exchange flow will be reduced to 1018 m3.

He can turn a 4500 m3 spill into a 1000 m3 spill simply by trimming and listing the ship. How much of this reduction he will actually achieve will be determined by how rapidly he can ballast the ship relative to the outflow rate. But if the size of the hole(s) is not too large and he reacts quickly, he will get most of this reduction.[26]

The program also immediately tells the crew that ship strength and stability will not be a problem despite the large trim and heel and despite the fact that the ship is "over-loaded" by some 22,000 tons. I repeat all the crew had to do to get all this information is to enter the six numbers in the rightmost columns in Figure C.10 (the location of the damage) and click on REDO. And then enter two numbers (%FULL for FP and 3P) and click on REDO.

This little vignette hints at the fourth role of a program like MLOAD: a training tool. Most crews, owners, coast guards (and, I think, response services) are unaware of the power of properly trimming and listing the ship. The calculations are far too complicated to do by hand, so nobody does them. Whenever I show something like Figures C.9 and C.10 to even experienced tankermen or governmental authorities, I invariably get a "Wow!" or at least an "I don't believe it!". By running through a series of drills with a program like MLOAD, everybody learns about the true power of hy-

---

[26] If you are really with me, you are asking yourself how can ballasting down affect exchange flow. There are two ways. First, remember that hydrostatic flow takes place before exchange flow (more or less). Ballasting down can increase the hydrostatic inflow pushing a portion of the oil in the tank that was below the top of the damage above the top of the damage where it is no longer subject to exchange flow. Second, trim and heel can lower the volume of the tank that is below the top of the damage. You can see by taking the bottom picture in Figure C.3 and rotating it clockwise. Put a ruler across the sketch at the top point of the damage, but keep the ruler level (un-rotated). Note that the area below the ruler is a triangle (or at least a trapezoid) which is smaller than the original rectangle. In Figure C.10, this is happening in both the transverse and longitudinal directions. With heel and trim, we can play this game in both dimensions. In this case, the top of the damage (labeled KEYLEVEL in the screenshot), went from 16.4 m below sea level (Do nothing.) to 23.2 m below sea level with the ballasting.

drostatic balance in a very concrete context. For the first time, they really understand that in many cases by simply trimming and listing the ship, they can cut the spillage in half or more, or in some cases eliminate it entirely.[27]

The Loading Instruments on all tankers should have MLOAD-like or better capabilities.[28]

---

[27] The column labeled HBL shows how far each tank would have to be drawn down in order to become hydrostatically balanced. A negative number means that the tank is already under-balanced. These tanks cannot be leaking from a bottom pit. This can be very useful information when a ship has a bottom leak but doesn't know which tank it is.

[28] MLOAD is far from perfect. Big improvements can and should be made in at least the following areas:

1. MLOAD gives the crew no information on how rapidly spillage will occur.
2. MLOAD has only a limited grounding capability.
3. MLOAD does not model the capture of oil in double sides or double bottoms. See Section C.8 for work around.
4. MLOAD does not model the vacuum which can develop in the top of the tank with outflow.
5. MLOAD has no visualization capability. Pedagogically, we really need this.
6. The method by which MLOAD and all the salvage programs of which I am aware estimate the residual strength of a badly damaged hull is so error-prone that one can argue that it more misleading than useful. This method should be replaced by Finite Element.

Figure C.9: Damage 1P up 5 m. Crew does nothing

MLOAD Version 1.87. 2005-03-16T14:10:08Z GMT.   Ship is HELLESPONT ORPHEUM.   Load pattern is load.AL.dam1P.no.
USING BBLS/F, AT SEA ALLOWABLES,
Full load, Arab Light, arrival cond, damage 1P up 5 m from bot at 140
crew does nothing

TANK	O	PT	CGO	API	TEMP	DENSTY	ULLAGE	INNAGE	%FULL	VOLUME	WEIGHT	IGS_mm	HBL_m	TANK_WL	INTRFACE	HYDROOUT	EXCHGOUT	KEYLEVEL	xs_high	ys_high	zs_high	xs_low	ys_low	zs_low
1C	P	DU	AL	34.00	94.8	0.8391	2.587	28.874	96.00	164276	21915.9	510	2.799										
2C	P	DU	AL	34.00	94.8	0.8391	2.289	28.197	96.00	160840	21457.6	510	1.966										
3C	P	DU	AL	34.00	94.8	0.8391	2.303	28.188	96.00	120619	16091.8	510	1.829										
4C	P	DU	AL	34.00	94.8	0.8391	2.317	28.185	96.00	120547	16082.1	510	1.710										
5C	P	DU	AL	34.00	94.8	0.8391	2.286	28.205	96.00	160840	21457.6	510	1.567										
6C	P	DU	AL	34.00	94.8	0.8391	2.294	28.198	96.00	140721	18773.5	510	1.419										
7C	P	DU	AL	34.00	94.8	0.8391	2.489	28.002	96.00	99347	13253.8	510	1.120										
8C	P	DU	AL	34.00	94.8	0.8391	7.011	23.479	80.00	50193	6696.2	510	-3.452										
1P	D	DU	AL	34.00	94.8	0.8686	6.228	24.695	98.00	79652	10999.6	510	0.000	3.026	-16.402	2536.1	2007.9	-16.402	140.000	-16.402	5.000	140.000	-28.160	0.000
1S	P	DU	AL	34.00	94.8	0.8391	1.910	29.013	98.00	95604	12754.5	510	2.757										
2P	P	DU	AL	34.00	94.8	0.8391	2.080	27.762	96.00	126742	16908.6	510	1.737										
2S	P	DU	AL	34.00	94.8	0.8391	2.231	27.611	96.00	126742	16908.6	510	1.187										
3P	P	DU	sw			1.0250	29.872	-0.025	0.00	0	0.0	0	-22.476										
3S	P	DU	sw			1.0250	29.999	-0.156	0.00	0	0.0	0	-22.921										
4P	P	DU	AL	34.00	94.8	0.8391	2.441	27.419	96.00	94589	12619.0	510	1.152										
4S	P	DU	AL	34.00	94.8	0.8391	2.586	27.269	96.00	94589	12619.0	510	0.602										
5P	P	DU	AL	34.00	94.8	0.8391	2.079	27.762	96.00	126742	16908.6	510	1.331										
5S	P	DU	AL	34.00	94.8	0.8391	2.230	27.612	96.00	126742	16908.6	510	0.787										
6P	P	DU	AL	34.00	94.8	0.8391	2.061	27.781	96.00	107831	14385.6	510	1.209										
6S	P	DU	AL	34.00	94.8	0.8391	2.212	27.630	96.00	107831	14385.6	510	0.683										
7P	P	DU	AL	34.00	94.8	0.8391	1.966	27.891	96.00	67465	9000.5	510	1.217										
7S	P	DU	AL	34.00	94.8	0.8391	2.119	27.738	96.00	67465	9000.5	510	0.705										
8P	P	DU	AL	34.00	94.8	0.8391	1.764	28.071	96.00	31546	4208.5	510	1.339										
8S	P	DU	AL	34.00	94.8	0.8391	1.909	27.927	96.00	31546	4208.5	510	0.836										
FP	P	DU	sw			1.0250	23.979	-0.077	0.00	0	0.0	0	-22.304										
AP	P	DU	sw			1.0250	2.005	21.567	70.00	6145	1001.4	0	-1.098										
FOP	P	DU	fo			0.9500	8.590	13.032	47.00	12711	1919.9	0	-2.260										
FOS	P	DU	fo			0.9500	7.921	13.701	51.80	14009	2115.9	0	-1.917										
DO	V	DU	do			0.9000	1.427	8.743	94.62	2033	290.9	0	5.559										
LOTNKS	W		fi								123.0												
LOSUMP	W		fi								29.0												
DW1	W		fi								68.0												
DW2	W		fi								65.0												
FW	W		fi								168.0												
CSP	W		fi								50.0												

DWT	313375	2325 LT Sdwt	DRAFTMID	22.168	AL	2289839 TOV	2252514 GSV	305486 MT	HYDROLOSS	2536	GRNDxs	0.000	LOWxs	-156.701
CARGO	305486	TPC 175.4	DRAFT_AP	22.694	AM	0 TOV	0 GSV	0 MT	EXCHGLOSS	2008	GRNDys	0.000	LOWys	-22.657
BLLST	3059	MTC 4147	DRAFT_FP	21.642	AH	0 TOV	0 GSV	0 MT	GRND FORCE	0	LCB	9.088	LCG	9.097
BFO	4036	WETTED 29644	TRIM	1.052	AB	0 TOV	0 GSV	0 MT	DISPLCMENT	355082	TCB	0.137	TCG	0.103
OTHER	794	SEA_SG 1.0250	HEEL	0.668	LM	0 TOV			MAX_SHEAR	12480	VCB	11.468	VCG	14.353
MAX %SHEAR	-72.4% at FR164		PROP_IMM	12.140					MAX_BEND	-490181	LOW_PT	-22.66	DEPTH	999.99
MAX %BEND	-69.5% at FR177		GM_corr	7.839					MAX HOG	-0.185	MIN FLOOD	7.26 @ AP_TNK_VENT		

Figure C.10: Damage 1P up 5 m. Crew ballast 3P and Forepeak

```
MLOAD Version 1.87.   2005-03-16T14:11:35Z GMT.    Ship is HELLESPONT ORPHEUM.   Load pattern is load.AL.dam1P.yes.
USING BBLS/F,   AT SEA ALLOWABLES,
arab light, arrival, damage 1p 0 to 5 m above baseline at 140
crew ballasts 3p and fp, keeps IG
```

TANK	O	PT	CGO	API	TEMP	DENSTY	ULLAGE	INNAGE	%FULL	VOLUME	WEIGHT	IGS_mm	HBL m	TANK_WL	INTRFACE	HYDROOUT	EXCHGOUT	KEYLEVEL	xs_high	ys_high	zs_high	xs_low	ys_low	zs_low
1C	P	DU	AL	34.00		94.8	0.8391	2.883	28.741	96.00	164276	21915.9	510	-1.761										
2C	P	DU	AL	34.00		94.8	0.8391	2.570	28.074	96.00	160840	21457.6	510	-1.782										
3C	P	DU	AL	34.00		94.8	0.8391	2.534	28.114	96.00	120619	16091.8	510	-1.163										
4C	P	DU	AL	34.00		94.8	0.8391	2.522	28.137	96.00	120547	16082.1	510	-0.646										
5C	P	DU	AL	34.00		94.8	0.8391	2.584	28.065	96.00	160840	21457.6	510	-0.051										
6C	P	DU	AL	34.00		94.8	0.8391	2.545	28.104	96.00	140721	18773.5	510	0.606										
7C	P	DU	AL	34.00		94.8	0.8391	2.749	27.899	96.00	99347	13253.8	510	0.871										
8C	P	DU	AL	34.00		94.8	0.8391	7.060	23.587	80.00	50193	6696.2	510	-3.160										
1P	D	DU	AL	34.00		94.8	0.8550	-0.013	31.094	98.00	97557	13262.0	510	0.000	4.525	-23.173	0.0	1017.7	-23.173	140.000	-28.160	5.000	140.000	-28.160	0.000
1S	P	DU	AL	34.00		94.8	0.8391	1.612	29.469	98.00	95604	12754.5	510	0.734										
2P	P	DU	AL	34.00		94.8	0.8391	3.087	26.909	96.00	126742	16908.6	510	-4.540										
2S	P	DU	AL	34.00		94.8	0.8391	1.783	28.212	96.00	126742	16908.6	510	0.757										
3P	P	DU	sw			1.0250	3.686	26.315	95.00	93562	15247.0	0	0.757										
3S	P	DU	sw			1.0250	30.318	-0.322	0.00	0	0.0	0	-23.834										
4P	P	DU	AL	34.00		94.8	0.8391	3.375	26.639	96.00	94589	12619.0	510	-3.803										
4S	P	DU	AL	34.00		94.8	0.8391	2.059	27.950	96.00	94589	12619.0	510	0.969										
5P	P	DU	AL	34.00		94.8	0.8391	3.099	26.897	96.00	126742	16908.6	510	-2.878										
5S	P	DU	AL	34.00		94.8	0.8391	1.797	28.198	96.00	126742	16908.6	510	1.885										
6P	P	DU	AL	34.00		94.8	0.8391	3.036	26.959	96.00	107831	14385.6	510	-2.152										
6S	P	DU	AL	34.00		94.8	0.8391	1.735	28.261	96.00	107831	14385.6	510	2.566										
7P	P	DU	AL	34.00		94.8	0.8391	2.878	27.133	96.00	67465	9000.5	510	-1.342										
7S	P	DU	AL	34.00		94.8	0.8391	1.575	28.436	96.00	67465	9000.5	510	3.210										
8P	P	DU	AL	34.00		94.8	0.8391	2.514	27.475	96.00	31546	4208.5	510	-0.582										
8S	P	DU	AL	34.00		94.8	0.8391	1.303	28.686	96.00	31546	4208.5	510	3.739										
FP	P	DU	sw			1.0250	-0.278	24.304	95.00	45628	7435.6	0	-1.465										
AP	P	DU	sw			1.0250	1.976	21.718	70.00	6145	1001.4	0	0.151										
FOP	P	DU	fo			0.9500	8.814	12.919	47.00	12711	1919.9	0	-3.517										
FOS	P	DU	fo			0.9500	7.296	14.437	51.80	14009	2115.9	0	0.853										
DO	V	DU	do			0.9000	1.789	8.435	94.62	2033	290.9	0	4.524										
LOTNKS	W		fi								123.0													
LOSUMP	W		fi								29.0													
DW1	W		fi								68.0													
DW2	W		fi								65.0													
FW	W		fi								168.0													
CSP	W		fi								50.0													

```
DWT    338320              22620 MT Sdwt     DRAFTMID  23.558    AL  2312019 TOV  2274333 GSV  308445 MT
CARGO  308445     TPC        176.0           DRAFT_AP  21.298    AM        0 TOV        0 GSV       0 MT
BLLST   25045     MTC         4151           DRAFT_FP  25.819    AH        0 TOV        0 GSV       0 MT
BFO      4036     WETTED     30578           TRIM      -4.521    AB        0 TOV        0 GSV       0 MT
OTHER     794     SEA_SG    1.0250           HEEL      -5.800    LM        0 TOV        0 GSV       0 MT
                                             PROP_IMM  10.784
MAX %SHEAR  -60.1% at FR164                   GM_corr   8.445
MAX %BEND   -46.7% at FR175

HYDROLOSS        0        GRNDxs     0.000        LOWxs      94.500
EXCHGLOSS     1018        GRNDys     0.000        LOWys     -27.417
GRND FORCE       0        LCB       14.589        LCG        14.561
DISPLCMENT  380027        TCB       -1.115        TCG        -0.906
MAX_SHEAR    -8048        VCB       12.303        VCG        14.369
MAX_BEND   -328944        LOW_PT   -27.29         DEPTH     999.99
MAX_HOG     -0.096        MIN FLOOD  2.93 @ VENT_3P_AFT
```

C.8   Double Hull Bottom Damage

With the help of MLOAD, we are now in a position to analyze what happens when a double hull tanker incurs damage low in the hull. In Figure C.11 a fully loaded modern VLCC has received damage which just penetrates the inner bottom at the lower hopper corner.[29] The dashed line shows the assumed extent of damage. To make things a bit simpler, I have assumed that the damage is to a midships tank, so that we don't have to worry (much) about change in trim.

As Figure C.11 indicates, the ship sinks about 0.3 m due to the flooding of the ballast tank outboard of 3P. More importantly, it will list about 3.6 degrees toward the damage. The damaged cargo tank was originally over-balanced and has a hydrostatic outflow of 2811 cubic meters.[30]

Because of the list, a portion of the oil outflow will be captured in the double bottom. In this case, the volume in the double bottom above the top of the damage is just under 700 m³. However, the great bulk of the outflow will end up flowing up the outside of the inner side and be captured in the top of the double side.[31] The only thing that is required for the side capture to take place is that the side shell be intact down to bottom of the captured oil column, which will almost always be the case in any grounding in which the ship survives.

The situation in Figure C.11 is actually the best that can happen as far as double bottom capture is concerned. As the damage extends further inboard, the area of the triangle in the top of the double bottom drops sharply. *But the side capture is unaffected.* If the ship is stranded and

---

[29] Figure C.12 shows the MLOAD run with the assumed damage. MLOAD currently does not model the capture of oil in the double bottom or double side. The work around is to flood any damaged ballast tanks outboard of the damaged cargo tank(s). This will produce a nearly correct damaged draft, trim and heel, and corresponding outflow from the damaged cargo tanks. The capture of this outflow must them be computed by another program and can depend on how the ballast tanks are damaged.

Fortunately for MLOAD the weight of the oil/water column in the double side will be the same whether the column is all oil, all seawater, or some combination. (Balance beam again.) However, the center of gravity of this column will change slightly. MLOAD makes another small error by treating the oil captured in the double bottom as if were denser seawater.

[30] Since the assumed damage extends just above the lower hopper corner, there is also a small amount of exchange flow.

[31] As Figure C.11 shows, the top of the column in the double side will not be high as the top of the oil in the damaged tank because (normally) a larger portion of the double side column will be made up of seawater. However, the top of both columns will be above the sea-level.

Figure C.11: Damage at hopper corner. Light gray is cargo. Dark gray is seawater.

BEFORE DAMAGE

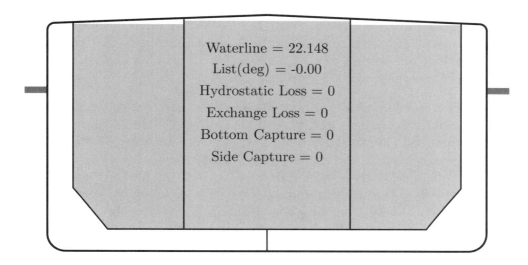

EQUILIBRIUM AFTER DAMAGE

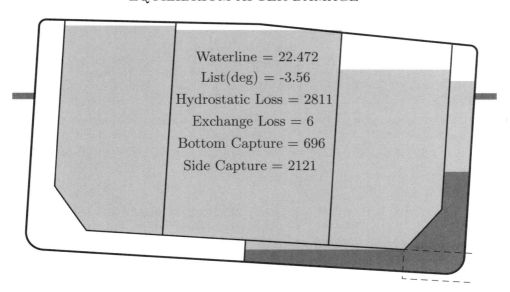

prevented from listing, the normal case in a major grounding, then there will
be no capture in the double bottom. The Exxon Valdez is an example.[32]
But the side capture is unaffected.

A cornerstone of IMO's evaluation of double hull spillage is the assumption that a double bottom will capture 50% of the outflow from the cargo
tank above it. The only justification I have found for this is a statement
made by IMO's Marine Environment Protection Committee (MEPC)

> If both outer and inner bottoms are breached simultaneously and
> the extend of both ruptures is the same, it is probable that the
> amount of seawater and oil flowing into the double hull space
> would be the same.[17, page 195]

The MEPC is *the* key body within IMO when it comes to tanker regulation.
This statement is nonsense and the experts on the MEPC must have known
it was nonsense. The statement is not true and, even if it were, what happens
in the double bottom immediately after the damage is irrelevant. What
counts is the equilibrium situation such as Figure C.11. And as Figure C.11
shows, the inner bottom will almost never capture anything like half the
outflow. In most cases, including a stranding in which the ship is prevented
from listing toward the damage, the double bottom will capture none or
almost none of the outflow.[33]

On the other hand, the double sides will usually capture a lot, quite
often all, the outflow.[34] For some unfathomable reason, the MEPC and

---

[32] The Valdez grounded at close to high tide on her starboard side. The port side was
still floating. As the tide went out, the port side dropped so the ship was listing away
from the high point of the damage. In such a situation, there would have been no double
bottom capture at all. But a tremendous amount of oil would have been caught in the
double sides.

[33] The MEPC seems to specialize in nonsense. The David Taylor Research Center
(DTRC) model tests outlined in Section C.4 indicated that 14% of the outflow would be
captured in the double bottom. This produced the following tromedic statement from the
MEPC.

> The results of the DTRC tests showed that the percentage of oil contained in
> the double hull space after simultaneous rupture of the shell plating and the
> inner bottom was less than 50% of the volume of the double hull space[sic].
> In the light of this, the Steering Committee agreed to retain the figure of
> 50% as originally assumed.[15][page 11]

Carroll, Orwell, eat your heart out.

[34] This was demonstrated exactly three months after the Valdez in the
Presidente Rivera Delaware Bay grounding. In this spill, the breached center tanks
lost 5.7 million liters. However, the pre-Marpol, single hull Rivera ended up spilling just
over 1.0 million liters. The rest was captured in segregated ballast and empty cargo wing

IMO ignores this.

Figure C.11 makes a still more basic point: in assessing outflow, you must account for the change in draft, trim and heel associated with the damage. The actual outflow is very sensitive to the local draft at the damage. This is why a crew can often change outflow by a factor of three or more simply by intelligent ballasting. Any method which purports to evaluate a design's spillage characteristics but ignores changes in draft, trim and heel will almost certainly be misleading.

---

tanks. The Marpol single hull DIAMOND GRACE spill in Tokyo Bay ended up being one-tenth the original estimate. This ship breached 1S (full cargo), 2S (empty ballast), and 3S (full cargo). Much of the oil from 1S and 3S flowed into the empty 2S, establishing hydrostatic balance far sooner that it otherwise would. Neither of these ships had anywhere near complete double side coverage.

Figure C.12: Double hull VLCC. Damage to 3P lower hopper corner.

```
MLOAD Version 1.87.  2005-07-27T12:57:26Z GMT.   Ship is SAMSUNG 1321.  Load pattern is load.10.evenkeel.d3p.
USING BBLS/F, AT SEA ALLOWABLES,
full load dep adjusted to zero trim and heel     (MINOR TANKS AND FIXED LOADS NOT SHOWN)
damage to 3P in lower hopper corner, crew does nothing
```

TANK	O	PT	CGO	API	TEMP	DENSTY	ULLAGE	INNAGE	%FULL	VOLUME	WEIGHT	IGS_mm	HBL m	TANK_WL	INTRFACE	HYDROOUT	EXCHGOUT	KEYLEVEL	xs_high	ys_high	zs_high	xs_low	ys_low	zs_low
1C	P	UL	L1	35.23	54.7	0.8489	2.072	28.750	98.00	182370	24612.1	510	5.449	9.055										
1P	P	UL	L1	35.23	54.7	0.8489	1.515	27.948	98.00	103801	14008.7	510	3.873	7.601										
1S	P	UL	L1	35.23	54.7	0.8489	1.526	27.936	98.00	103801	14008.7	510	6.142	9.559										
2C	P	UL	L1	35.23	54.7	0.8489	1.801	27.661	98.00	199520	26926.5	510	5.424	9.023										
2P	P	UL	L1	35.23	54.7	0.8489	2.673	26.790	98.00	126584	17083.4	510	3.713	7.436										
2S	P	UL	L1	35.23	54.7	0.8489	1.931	27.532	98.00	126584	17083.4	510	6.281	9.608										
3C	P	UL	L1	35.23	54.7	0.8489	1.801	27.661	98.00	199520	26926.5	510	5.489	9.076										
3P	D	UL	L1	35.23	54.7	0.8489	6.481	22.982	98.00	108903	14698.3	510	0.000	3.682	-20.640	2811.0	6.2	-20.640	5.000	-21.000	3.100	5.000	-21.000	3.010
3S	P	UL	L1	35.23	54.7	0.8489	1.931	27.532	98.00	126584	17083.4	510	6.346	9.662										
4C	P	UL	L1	35.23	54.7	0.8489	1.802	28.662	98.00	199520	26926.5	510	5.553	9.130										
4P	P	UL	L1	35.23	54.7	0.8489	2.673	26.790	98.00	126584	17083.4	510	3.843	7.544										
4S	P	UL	L1	35.23	54.7	0.8489	1.931	27.532	98.00	126584	17083.4	510	6.411	9.716										
5C	P	UL	L1	35.23	54.7	0.8489	9.107	21.357	73.00	131374	17729.8	510	-1.692	1.874										
5P	P	UL	L1	35.23	54.7	0.8489	2.616	27.848	98.00	81950	11059.7	510	3.948	7.638										
5S	P	UL	L1	35.23	54.7	0.8489	1.881	28.583	98.00	81950	11059.7	510	6.509	9.803										
SLOP_P	P	UL	L1	35.23	54.7	0.8489	2.283	28.181	98.00	35121	4739.9	510	4.384	7.969										
SLOP_S	P	UL	L1	35.23	54.7	0.8489	1.793	28.671	98.00	35121	4739.9	510	6.601	9.930										
FP	P	UL	sw			1.0250	26.738	-0.090	0.00	0	0.0	510	-22.879	-22.819										
1BP	P	UL	sw			1.0250	33.010	-1.654	0.00	0	0.0	510	-24.068	-23.978										
1BS	P	UL	sw			1.0250	34.920	-3.565	0.00	0	0.0	510	-24.687	-22.631										
2BP	P	UL	sw			1.0250	33.364	-3.901	0.00	0	0.0	510	-24.222	-24.128										
2BS	P	UL	sw			1.0250	34.990	-5.527	0.00	0	0.0	510	-22.631	-22.577										
3BP	F	UL	sw			1.0250	9.295	20.167	0.00	53922	8787.2	510	0.000	0.000	-999.999	0.0	0.0	0.000						
3BS	F	UL	sw			1.0250	34.984	-5.521	0.00	0	0.0	510	-22.576	-22.523										
4BP	P	UL	sw			1.0250	33.400	-3.937	0.00	0	0.0	510	-24.148	-24.057										
4BS	P	UL	sw			1.0250	34.990	-5.527	0.00	0	0.0	510	-22.521	-22.469										
5BP	P	UL	sw			1.0250	32.915	0.555	0.00	0	0.0	510	-23.645	-23.565										
5BS	P	UL	sw			1.0250	34.942	-1.473	0.00	0	0.0	510	-22.466	-22.416										
AP	P	UL	sw			1.0250	19.944	-0.910	0.00	0	0.0	510	-13.135	-13.312										
DIST_W_P	P	UL	fw			1.0000	0.912	7.673	100.00	1777	282.5	510	8.440	7.937										
FWS	P	UL	fw			1.0000	0.586	8.000	100.00	1777	282.5	510	9.798	9.257										
1FOP	P	UL	fo			0.9800	1.943	20.347	98.00	19031	2965.2	510	7.574	7.723										
1FOS	P	UL	fo			0.9800	1.579	20.710	95.00	15447	2406.8	510	9.660	9.734										
2FOP	P	UL	fo			0.9800	1.930	20.160	98.00	13974	2177.2	510	7.697	7.743										
2FOS	P	UL	fo			0.9800	1.620	20.470	98.00	10482	1633.2	510	9.729	9.700										
1FOSETT	P	UL	fo			0.9800	0.465	7.299	98.00	1001	156.0	510	-0.037	-0.034										
2FOSETT	P	UL	fo			0.9800	0.465	7.299	98.00	1001	156.0	510	0.151	0.147										
FOSERV	P	UL	fo			0.9800	0.475	7.289	98.00	1094	170.5	510	0.145	0.145										
DO	P	UL	lo			0.9000	1.248	16.048	98.00	3148	450.4	510	9.837	10.091										

```
DWT    303002          302 MT Sdwt    DRAFTMID 22.516    AL  0 TOV  0 MT  0 GSV    HYDROLOSS   2811     0 MT    GRNDxs  0.000    LOWxs  64.770
CARGO  282847  TPC     173.6          DRAFT_AP 22.348    AM  0 TOV  0 MT  0 GSV    EXCHGLOSS      6     0 MT    GRNDys  0.000    LOWys -24.216
BLLST    8794  MTC     3994           DRAFT_FP 22.685    AH  0 TOV  0 MT  0 GSV    GRND FORCE     0     0 MT    LCB    11.470    LCG   11.465
BFO      9665  WETTED  28889          TRIM    -0.337     AB  0 TOV  0 MT  0 GSV    DISPLCMENT 351152   0 MT    TCB    -0.749    TCG   -0.437
OTHER    1697  SEA_SG  1.0250         HEEL    -3.421     L1  2095834 TOV  2101074 GSV  282847 MT  MAX_SHEAR  -8889   MT   VCB   11.780    VCG   17.003
                                      PROP IMM 11.234    L2  0 TOV  0 GSV  0 MT         MAX_BEND -534983         LOW_PT -24.16    DEPTH 999.99
MAX %SHEAR -22.2% at FR071            GM_corr   6.810                                   MAX_HOG   -0.171         MIN FLOOD 7.88 @ 1BP_AFT
MAX %BEND  -84.9% at FR086
```

C.9 The Full Vacuum Tanker

C.9.1 Introduction

By now it has probably occurred to you that hydrostatic balance is a little like the old parlor trick of covering a glass of water with a piece of cardboard carefully turning the glass upside down, and demonstrating that the water does not run out. You'd be mostly right. In the case of the upturned glass of water, as long as you flip the glass in a way that preserves the vacuum above the water, the pressure head at the (new) bottom of the glass is simply the height of the column of water in the glass, about 0.1 meters for a normal glass. The pressure head outside is the weight of the column of air rising 70 miles or so to the stratosphere. This weight is equivalent to about 10 meters of water. The hydrostatic balance at the upturned top of the glass is extremely favorable.

But there is an important difference. If you break the seal between the glass and the cardboard ever so slightly, you will get exchange flow with the water running out the bottom of the crack and the air coming in the top. This air rises to the top of the glass, destroys the vacuum and the entire glass empties almost immediately. In the case of a damaged tank the incoming fluid in exchange flow goes to the bottom where it has no effect on the hydrostatic balance above the top of the damage. As long as the damage is entirely underwater, the tank situation is far more stable.[35]

Anyway, if you are still with me, you are probably saying to yourself, maybe there is some way we can use vacuum to prevent or reduce spillage. The answer is: if we were intelligent, we could.

A large number of vacuum variants have been suggested, but there are just two basic alternatives:

1. Passive systems.
2. Active systems.

---

[35] A closer analogy is the old trick of sucking water up a straw, and then quickly putting your finger over the end of the straw. The liquid in the straw will be well above the liquid in the glass. You can stir the straw, do just about anything you want, and the water in the straw will stay there.

C.9.2   Passive Vacuum Systems

In a passive system, the tank is simply sealed. If it is breached below the top of the liquid in the tank and there is outflow, the increase in ullage volume above the oil will automatically pull a vacuum on the top of the tank. It is pretty amazing how quickly this effect cuts in. If we go back to the situation in Figure C.1, a fully loaded pre-Marpol ULCC but seal the tank, the equilibrium oil column height after spillage is 27.98 m, meaning a loss of 7 cm of oil or 0.25% of the cargo before hydrostatic balance stops.[36] A passive vacuum system will halt almost all (but not quite all) the hydrostatic outflow in even a fully loaded tank if the damage is low in the tank.

However, the real value of vacuum is its ability to resist loss of hydrostatic balance due to tide and other effects. Suppose we have the situation in Figure C.1 but the ship is stranded at high tide and the tide goes out 3 m. This is roughly what happened to the EXXON VALDEZ. If the top of the tank is open to the atmosphere, this will drop the oil column in the tank 3.6 m or an additional loss of 13% of the tank. Our original loss of less than 3% has quadrupled. However, if the top of the tank is sealed, the equilibrium oil column height only drops 0.7 m as the tide goes out to 27.23 m. Even with the tide clobbering the outside external pressure, the loss is limited to 2.9% of the tank. *If the Exxon Valdez, had had a passive vacuum system she would have spilled about 4,000 tons rather than 40,000 tons, far less than even the most optimistic double bottom estimate.*[37]

---

[36] The equation for equilibrium is

$$H_{ig}\frac{z_u}{z_t - H_{oil}} + H_{vp} + \rho_{oil}H_{oil} = \rho_{sea}D + H_A$$

where H_{ig} is the initial inert gas partial pressure (called 7 m for now), H_{pv} is the cargo's vapor pressure (say 3 m), H_A is the ambient atmospheric head (about 10 m), z_u is the initial ullage height, z_t is the (average) tank height, and the other variables are as before. The left hand side is the absolute internal tank pressure, the right hand side is the absolute external pressure. Solving this equation generates a quadratic term in H_{oil} which resists the outflow. The initial effect of this term is zero, but it builds rapidly with any outflow.

This equation assumes perfect gases, which is close enough for our purposes. When oil is loaded into a tank, some of the oil will evaporate. This evaporation will continue until the number of oil molecules leaving the liquid is matched by the number of molecules reentering the liquid. The pressure exerted by the oil molecules in the top of the tank at that point is called the *cargo vapor pressure*. The rest of the pressure in the top of the tank is produced by the inert gas molecules. This pressure is called the *inert gas partial pressure*. Under the perfect gas assumption, the two pressures sum to the total pressure in the top of the tank.

[37] The most useful move that Hazelwood and his crew could have made would have been to try and jam the P/V valves shut.

So why don't we implement this simple system? There are a number of valid questions a vacuum system must face.

1. Structure in the top of the tanks In theory, tanker decks are designed to take 2 meters of water over the deck which is equivalent to 2 meters of vacuum. Although as far as I could tell from my time in Korean newbuilding yards, this is never checked, in practice tanker decks are almost certainly stronger than this.

Stenstrom points out that, whenever a cargo tank has a large breach, there will be a momentary vacuum pulled on the top of the tank because the flow thru the P/V valve cannot keep up with the oil outflow.[76] Yet in many such cases, there has been no structural damage to the top of the tank. A practical example was the THUNTANK 5 grounding in 1986 in which the quick thinking master refused to survey the breached tanks because he would have had to break the vacuum.[38] Unlike OBO's (see DERBYSHIRE), there is no history of tanker decks being stove in by plunging waves. My own experience from over-pressuring tanks is that the bulkheads go before the deck.

In any event, in order to implement vacuum, the structure must be designed to take the vacuum. In my view, the criteria should be that the tank should be able to handle a full vacuum (-1.0 bar gage). This means we don't have to worry about under-pressuring the tank. In fact, thanks to cargo vapor pressure, this will give us a nice safety margin, and allow us to eliminate at least the vacuum side of the troublesome P/V valves.

To my knowledge, there has been no truly public, complete structural analysis of this issue. Mansour has done an unpublished finite element study which indicates that stresses in the top of a VLCC tank would be increased by 9.4% by a -0.4 bar vacuum.[48] A Japanese submittal to IMO claims that a tanker deck can take an underpressure of -1.37 bar before failure.[3] But with a good finite element model, it could easily be and should be done. I've done some back of the envelope calculations and I'm quite confident that the increase in steel required will be less than 5% of total lightweight, most of it going to the upper bulkheads.[39] The structural issue can be easily analyzed and handled. The overall result will be a more robust and safer ship.

---

[38] This was a small coastal tanker, not fitted with inert gas. The Swedish Maritime Administration estimates that the Master's action cut the spillage by 60%. On a modern tanker, it is not necessary to open the tank to measure the cargo volume.

[39] It will certainly be less than the extra steel required by a double bottom.

3. Depends on Cargo Vapor Pressure The cargo's vapor pressure plays a critical role in any vacuum system. Crude oil vapor pressure can vary over a wide range and depends critically on temperature. 75% of the common crudes have a vapor pressure equivalent to less than 4 m water at 38C, a fairly warm loading temperature. But there are some oddballs with loading temperature vapor pressures as high as 7 m water. For these cargos, a vacuum system will not be as effective as for less volatile crudes. On the other hand, it takes only a little bit of vacuum to produce most of the benefit.

3. Maintaining vacuum To implement the passive system, we will need isolation valves on each tank's IG line. These valves will normally be closed whenever the tank contains cargo. But these valves will have to be open when the tank is being discharged and loaded, and when the inert gas requires topping off. During these periods the tank will not be protected by the vacuum system. However, we are talking at most a percent or two of a tank's life.

We also have to ensure that the tank can hold a vacuum at least long enough for enough cargo to be transferred so that the tank won't leak cargo when the vacuum is relieved. This is not difficult.

Hellespont had a policy of maintaining a positive 0.5 m IG pressure in the top of the tanks of the V-Plus class. This ship had a total cargo tank volume of 514,000 m^3. To do this we found we had to run a 750 m^3/hr IG generator about 3 hours per week. This points to a leakage rate of 0.4% per week. If the beefed up structure allows us to eliminate the P/V valves, the source of most of the leakage, then even this leakage rate will be cut drastically.

In any event, if the system is leaking, it will show up in excessive and expensive inert gas topping off. However, any passive vacuum system will need to monitor and record tank pressure and 0_2 for each individual tank.

4. Transferring cargo. As we saw in Section C.6, often it is necessary to drop salvage pumps into the damaged tank in order to transfer cargo out. With current technology, this will require breaking the vacuum. But by then we will have had a chance to plug the damage. And devising a salvage pump system that doesn't have to break the vacuum would not be difficult. A simple pressure lock is all that's required.

5. Crew Errors Vacuum systems have been criticized on the grounds that they depend on the crew not screwing up. In the case of a full vacuum tanker, the only new responsibility is that the tank isolation valves must be open during load/discharge/topping off IG and closed the rest of the time. The only dangerous error is the valve is closed during loading. If the isolation valve is incorrectly closed during discharge we will draw a big vacuum on the tank, but this is precisely what the tank is designed to take in case of damage. If the valve is incorrectly closed during topping off, the only effect is the IG pressure won't come up which will immediately show up in the tank pressure readings. In any event, topping off will be much rarer in an isolated P/V valve-less tank than it is now. If the valve is closed during loading and nothing is done, then the tank will be damaged by the over-pressure. This is nothing new. Crews have been over-loading tanks for a long time. I've had two cases of tank damage due to overloading of tanks with P/V valves.[40] There is no way a P/V valve can keep up with a cargo pump once liquid not gas is in the valves.

Nonetheless, it would be a good idea to have alarms on the individual tank pressure gauges which would alert the crew to the problem and allow then to divert the cargo elsewhere and call for the terminal to shut down. This is exactly the situation we have now with high level alarms.[41] I would also design the structure so that the bulkheads fail before the deck. Then even in the worst case scenario, the cargo will usually stay on-board.

If the crew left the isolation valves open when they should be closed, we would be no worse off than we are now. Even a totally unprofessional, horribly lazy crew is not going to do this. It would increase IG topping off frequency which is lot more work than closing the valves. Besides the open valves would show up in the tank pressure recordings which would be – or at least should be – available to Port State inspectors.

In short, the additional crew responsibilities are quite modest, nothing compared to their current responsibilities. It burns me when ideas are rejected because they require the crew to open and close a few valves. Yet a concept which trebles or quadruples the segregated ballast tank area which the crew must maintain is accepted on the grounds that it requires no crew interaction.

---

[40] In both cases, a bulkhead was damaged but there was no spillage.
[41] You could also have an interlock which would open the isolation valve whenever the tank suction valves are open, but this is probably overkill.

The only real reason for not implementing a passive vacuum system is that we are unwilling to put a little extra steel in the top of the tanks.

C.9.3   Correcting for IG Pressure/Vacuum

We are now in a position to correct an inaccurate assumption I have made in just about all our hydrostatic calculations up to now. In these computations, I assumed that the top of the tank was open to the atmosphere. In reality, the top of the tank will be inerted, usually with a positive pressure head of about 0.5 m, and protected by P/V valve(s) which are normally set to open at -0.4 m on the vacuum side. *In effect, every standard tank uses a passive vacuum system, but the vacuum is limited to -0.4 m.*

Applying the modified equation of Section C.9.2 but limiting the vacuum to no more than -0.4 m and using an initial over-pressure of 0.5m and assuming a crude with a vapor pressure of 3 m, to the situation in the top half of Figure C.3, we find that the equilibrium oil column height is 27.90 m for a loss of 0.3% of the cargo. The effect of the vacuum is much more important than the initial inert gas over-pressure.

But when we apply this equation to the hydrostatically under-balanced situation in the bottom half of Figure C.3, the sea water only pushes the oil column up 0.17 m, putting the Live Bottom at less than 0.2 m above the ship bottom rather than 1.2 m above we computed earlier. Sealing the top of the tank hurts us in hydrostatically underbalanced situations. Of course, this is still better than having a spill, and it is an easy matter for a crew, alerted by an HBL aware loading program, to release (some of) the pressure from such tanks.

C.9.4 Active Vacuum Systems

In active vacuum systems, after loading, the pressure in the top of the tank is mechanically lowered by pumping out a portion of the tank atmosphere. There are any number of variants of this system. The American UnderPressure System (AUPS) has probably received the most work.[26] This system maintains a modest 1 to 2 m vacuum by a blower. Under normal operating conditions, it is a closed cycle system adjusting the ullage gas temperature to keep the ullage pressure constant, cooling the gas when the pressure gets too high and heating it when the pressure gets too low. It does this by continually extracting gas and running it thru a heat exchanger. The system was given a full scale test on one tank of a 35,000 ton tanker in 2001. The control system reportedly worked fine, but the test was artificial in that water instead of oil was used as the simulated cargo. The tank took the negative pressure without any problem, but of course there were no seaway or other stresses imposed on the ship at the same time.

The AUPS system and most vacuum systems were primarily aimed at retrofitting existing pre-Marpol ships. Hence they adopted very mild vacuums and had to reliably release the vacuum when it became too high. My own view is that it is better to build the ship to take full vacuum, and not have to worry about structural failure from too much vacuum. This avoids all kinds of control systems and tricks such as controlling ullage gas temperature to keep the pressure within narrow bounds.

Anyway suppose we had a tanker built to take full vacuum. Currently, all tanker cargo tanks must be inerted, that is the empty space at the top of the tank is filled with low oxygen gas produced by the ship's boilers. There is a network of piping on deck that distributes this gas to the top of each tank. Now suppose after loading we pull a 5 meter vacuum on this system. Figure C.13 shows the hydrostatic balance in an individual tank. The external pressure is higher than the internal pressure at all levels, even at the waterline. Now consider what happens if one of the tanks is damaged near the bottom.

You are right. ***The damaged tank will automatically pump itself out to the undamaged tanks.*** This transfer will begin immediately upon damage with absolutely no intervention from anybody. Please re-read the last two sentences. The increase in pressure at the bottom of the damaged tank — indicated by the double arrow in Figure C.13 — will push cargo thru the IG lines to the other tanks. In the situation shown in Figure C.13, seawater will push an amazing 17 meters into the tank as long as there is

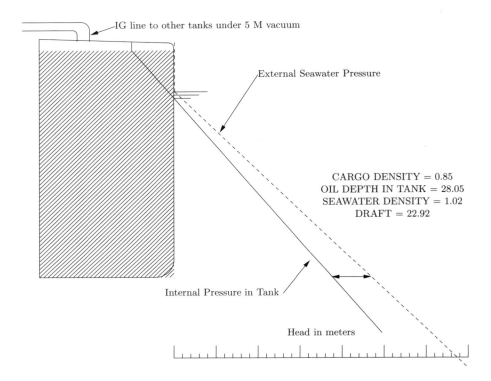

IG line to other tanks under 5 M vacuum

External Seawater Pressure

CARGO DENSITY = 0.85
OIL DEPTH IN TANK = 28.05
SEAWATER DENSITY = 1.02
DRAFT = 22.92

Internal Pressure in Tank

Head in meters

NEUTRAL LEVEL IS ABOVE THE TOP OF THE TANK
Internal pressure is lower than external pressure at all levels

Figure C.13: Active Full Vacuum(5M) Tanker, Full Tank

room in the other tanks.[42]

The Active Full Vacuum Tanker has a number of other important advantages.

1. As in the Passive Full Vacuum Tanker, we eliminate structural failures due to tank underpressure.

2. We can eliminate the P/V valves. Since the structure can take zero absolute pressure there's no way of pulling too much vacuum. Existing tankers suffer from being very sensitive to overfilling or a P/V valve failing closed. There is no way that an active FVT can be damaged by underpressure (i.e. P/V valve fails during discharge) and it's much less sensitive to overfilling (the overfilled cargo simply goes to the wrong tank). Moreover, since there will be much less tank breathing (normally none), by leading the vacuum pump exhaust up the stack, we can create the same kind of deck we have on the LPG ships, a totally closed system. This means we can have pumps on deck, electric valve actuators, etc, etc.

3. Eliminating the PV valves eliminates the normal cargo evaporation that is taking place daily due to either the P/V valves opening to relieve excessive pressure during the hot part of the day or simply by leaking. Some people claim that far more cargo is lost to the atmosphere than is spilled to the sea. I think the amount of cargo evaporative losses are less than sometimes claimed, but still they represent both a substantial source of pollution and an economic loss. And there is no doubt that most P/V valves leak most of the time. The only question is how much.

4. Since there will be no tank breathing, we no longer have to treat the deck as a gas dangerous area. We can have pumps on deck, electric valve actuators, electric motor driven winches, etc as we do on the

---

[42] Assuming there is sufficient volume elsewhere in the system and the vessel draft doesn't change, the equation for equilibrium is

$$H_{ull} + \rho_{oil}H_{oil} + \rho_{sea}(Z - H_{oil}) = \rho_{sea}D + H_A$$

where H_{ull} is the absolute pressure in the evacuated ullage space, Z is the height of the cross-over line above the keel, and the other variables are as before. In reality an active full vacuum tanker will sink as it floods which will help matters assuming it's not overdone. Obviously, it is essential that the damage doesn't break the vacuum, i.e., the damage is entirely below the waterline. I've also assumed the vacuum doesn't decrease which requires either a lot of unfilled volume or the vacuum pump being still operational.

Conversely, if the vacuum pump is operational and it is possible to pull an additional 1 meter of vacuum on the IG lines, then the sea water will push another 5 to 6 meters into the damaged tank.

LNG and LPG ships. And the dangers associated with releasing inert gas just above the deck are eliminated. Inert gas is deadly to any crew member who happens to breath it.

This remarkable capability does not come for free. In additional to the extra steel high in the hull (a boon for a whole lot of reasons), the active FVT will have to address the following problems.

1. Unlike the pre-Marpol ships, in a fully loaded double hull tanker, there normally is little excess volume in the other cargo tanks. The unused volume is all in the ballast tanks. This implies that either we build in excess cargo volume, or pull a vacuum on the ballast tanks as well. The latter option suggests a varient in which the vacuum is drawn only on the ballast tanks, the connection to these tanks being opened by the crew upon damage. Since there will be a slight delay in this opening, this varient accepts a small amount of spillage in some cases in return for a far simpler system overall.

2. Pulling the vacuum and maintaining it will require vacuum pumps and a system for reliquifying the extracted vapor. This is all standard technology, but the key will be to keep the leakage to a small value. The fact that the P/V valves are gone will be a big help here.

3. Leakage into the tanks is a major safety concern. A leak in the vacuum piping could expose the tanks to an explosive atmosphere. It will take a big leak to move the tank out of the too-rich zone but, at a minimum, this will require careful pressure monitoring. At a maximum, it will require a double pipe system in which the annulus is inerted.[43] This is a legitimate concern and we need careful, conservative design here.

4. Similarly, a collision in which the tank is breached above the waterline could result in the tank vapors and outside air mixing, creating an explosive mixture. The same thing is true now, but with the active FVT we'd have to be still more careful. On the other hand, the situation is actually better than it is now for LPG and LNG carriers. If the double sides are inerted, as they should be for other reasons, the gas escaping from these tanks would form at least a momentary blanket. Needs some study.

5. Damaged stability could be compromised by flow thru the IG/vacuum lines to the low side. This also needs competent study. In most cases, the damaged side will be the low side in which case transfer out of

---

[43] The pull-vacuum-on-ballast-tanks-only varient avoids this problem as well as cargo vapor pressure and reliquifaction concerns. However, the ballast tanks will have to be individually valved; and the crew must open only the valves to the non-damaged ballast tanks. The damaged ballast tanks should be vented.

the damaged tank is not a stability concern. At worst, it implies slightly more compartmentalized tanks to meet the same floodable length requirement.[44] Interestingly, if the inert gas lines are the same height as they are now, the situation will be little different than what we have now. Currently, if a tanker takes on enough heel, oil will flow from the high tanks to the low thru the IG lines. **Yet this is not accounted for in any damage stability analysis that I know about.** With the active FVT, the only difference is that this flow will take place a little sooner.

6. The self-transfer capability depends critically on the density and vapor pressure of the cargo. High vapor pressure and high density hurt. For a ULCC in which the IG/vacuum line is 8 meters above sea level, the worst cargos I've looked at so far are Saharan Blend (very high vapor pressure but light) and Mayan (heavy with a surprisingly high vapor pressure). In both these cases, equilibrium occurs after the water has pushed about 5 meters into the tank. Of course, this is already much better than a double bottom; and the situation can be improved drastically by lowering the IG line slightly at a cost of possibly exacerbating objection (4).

7. Sooner or later during salvage you are going to have to break the vacuum. True, but by then much if not most of the oil will have already have transferred itself out of the damaged tank, you can have salvage pumps in place ready to go, containment and collection equipment deployed, etc. You also will have had a chance to plug the damage in a zero or negative pressure differential situation.

8. The system doesn't work well during discharge. During discharge the ship will come out of the water. For a VLCC, this rise is over 10 meters, even if the crew does its best to keep the ship as low as possible by ballasting as soon as possible. You will lose the self-transfer capability during the latter part of discharge (and the early part of loading). There's no getting around this but we are talking about a very small portion of the ship's loaded life, a portion in which the ship is at low risk of grounding or collision (unless it is lightering). The active FVT works best when the ship is fully loaded, which is exactly when you want it to work.

9. What happens when the vacuum pumps or reliquification plant is non-operational? The ship converts to a passive FVT by closing some

---

[44] Another possible fix is list actuated one-way valves. These could be simple, pendulum flapper valves.

valves.

Any vacuum system does nothing for you if the tank is damaged above the waterline. But even here the ship will be better than a double bottom ship. In the FVT the double sides will be about 1.8 times the width of double hull double sides. The FVT will take nearly twice the side shell penetration before a cargo tank is breached. And the amount of ballast tank coated area will be nearly halved.

C.9.5   Vacuum Summary

The active full vacuum tanker has two advantages over the passive FVT:

1. in many situations, it eliminates the initial spillage, and
2. it has the amazing self-transfer capability.

However, the active FVT has some mechanical complexity, will be moderately costly, and needs considerable research. The passive system needs only a little steel and some valves. If I were king of the world, I'd immediately require passive full vacuum on all new tankers. The passive system is dead simple, would result in a more robust ship, and obtain 90% plus of the active system's spill reduction. In general, far too much emphasis has been placed on zero outflow versus volume reduction. Once we had a fleet of passive FVT's out there, we could experiment with active FVT's at our leisure.

C.9.6 Postscript

Our little tour of tank spillage physics is over. This physics of course is independent of any tanker design alternative. But I can't resist adding one gratuitous political comment.

The argument for a passive full vacuum tanker is so strong that you would think that the environmentalists would be clammering for it. In 1989 after the Valdez spill, the National Academy of Science created a National Research Council (NRC) committee to explore alternatives ways of reducing spillage. The committee consisted of academicians, professional environmentalists, federal bureaucrats, and two oil company executives. It's fair to say it was environmentally oriented. I went to this committee and presented the case for a passive full vacuum tanker. The result was two paragraphs in a 350 page book.

> This concept [passive vacuum] has several inherent disadvantages It poses the same difficulties as the mechanical vacuum in terms of interface with the ship's structure and existing safety systems. Secondly, without instantaneous identification of the damaged tank(s), and closure of all vent lines and piping to the tank(s), the system would not react quickly enough the attain anywhere near the vacuum required.
>
> In other words, the structure has to be built to take the vacuum.
>
> Total nonsense. The tanks are already isolated.
>
> If a passive vacuum system depends on automatic closure of all tank vents from a remote location or on pressure and/or liquid/level sensors in the tank, malfunction of this system could cause a catastrophe. With the ship discharging at full rate, the vents absolutely must remain open, or the IGS must be operating. Otherwise a major collapse of the deck and/or other structure would ensue, with a strong liklihood of explosion and fire — all occurring in a port. Finally, the allowance for initial cargo outflow negates the limited advantages of this concept over a mechanically driven vacuum system. The concept will not be considered further here, but it deserves further research and development.[16][p 130]
>
> FVT does not nor do most passive vacuum systems. A transparent strawman.
>
> But structure can take full vacuum!

The passive full vacuum tanker was so badly misconstrued that it is impossible to believe that it was done innocently. But I still don't know why. Why would a bunch of intelligent, environmentally concerned people, most of whom had no selfish stake in the issue, go out of their way to diss an environmentally attractive system in an intellectually dishonest manner.

This is a part of the Tromedy, even I won't attempt to explain.[45]

Anyway, the NRC report sealed the doom for tankers that would have been much safer than and environmentally superior to double bottoms, at least in the United States.[46] A big opportunity lost.

---

[45] The NRC committee like others before and after focused exclusively on reducing spillage after a collision or grounding has already occurred. It never looked at what caused the collision or grounding nor means for eliminating the collision and grounding in the first place. ***Machinery redundancy and twin screw are mentioned nowhere in the 350 page book.*** The book barely mentioned corrosion and hull structural failure by far the single biggest cause of oil spills. It never squarely addressed the increase in ballast tank coated area associated with double sides and double bottoms. Truly tromedic.

[46] Which means everywhere. No owner can invest in a tanker which cannot trade to the United States.

Appendix D

The Politics of Tank Spillage

D.1   The Mid-Deck Tanker

Once you understand the nature of tanker casualties and the physics of tank spillage, it is child's play to come up with alternatives to double bottom which are superior in terms of spill volume, and at the same time have less ballast tank coated area, and much less chance of a ballast tank explosion. We've already seen the power of vacuum. Another possibility is dividing the cargo tanks vertically. We will take a brief look at just one of the many variants on this concept which have been suggested, the Mid-Deck Tanker.

In this concept, a deck is fitted across the cargo tanks, usually at about 45% of the depth of the ship as shown in Figure D.1. Vent pipes or trunks are fitted from the lower pipe to the main deck. The ship has double sides and a single bottom.

As the top half of Figure D.1 shows the hydrostatic balance for the lower tanks is highly favorable. For a VLCC, the external sea water pressure at the bottom of the ship will be about 10 m head higher than the internal oil pressure at the bottom of the lower tanks. There will be no hydrostatic outflow at all from any damage below the Mid-Deck. There will of course be exchange flow from side damage but in many cases the double sides will capture most if not all of that flow. And these double sides are about 1.8 times as wide as the double sides on a double bottom ship. For any given side shell damage, there is about 80% more side capture volume.[1]

---

[1] Double sided, single-bottom tankers are the one case where it can sometimes pay a crew to list a ship away from bottom damage. If such a ship is hydrostatically over-balanced and damaged on the bottom, then list away from the damage (which the ship will usually do of its own accord) will direct the outflow to the damaged double side where it can be captured. List toward the damage will direct some of the outflow along the

Figure D.1: Mid-Deck, Damage up 3 m. Light gray is oil, dark gray is seawater

BEFORE DAMAGE

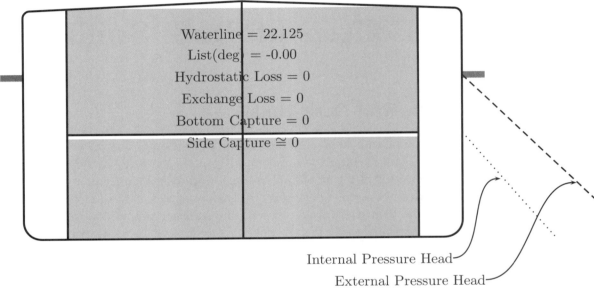

Waterline = 22.125
List(deg) = -0.00
Hydrostatic Loss = 0
Exchange Loss = 0
Bottom Capture = 0
Side Capture $\cong$ 0

Internal Pressure Head

External Pressure Head

EQUILIBRIUM AFTER DAMAGE

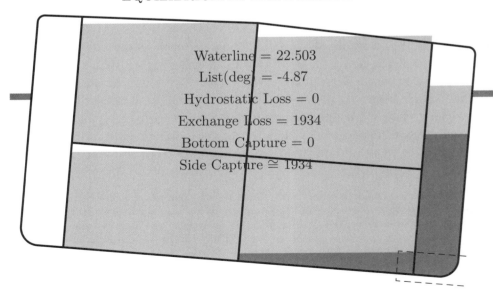

Waterline = 22.503
List(deg) = -4.87
Hydrostatic Loss = 0
Exchange Loss = 1934
Bottom Capture = 0
Side Capture $\cong$ 1934

The concept has excellent ability to withstand an ebb tide. Even after a 3 m drop in the tide, such as that experienced by the EXXON VALDEZ, the hydrostatic balance is still 7 meters in our favor. ***If the Exxon Valdez, had been a Mid-Deck ship, she would have spilled very little oil.***
The other good points about the Mid-Deck are:

1. Slightly better collision resistance than a double hull. It takes a deeper penetration to damage the inner sides than on a double hull. For the reasons given in Section 3.11, I would not make much of this. Any serious collision will penetrate the inner sides of both the double hull and Mid-Deck.

2. More efficient use of ballast tank volume. Ballast that is underwater is almost an oxymoron. The sea water weight in the submerged portion of a ballast tank is matched by the buoyancy of the submerged volume. It is only ballast that is above the waterline that actually sinks the ship. Since more of the Mid-Deck's ballast volume is above the waterline than a double hull's ballast, we need less ballast volume, resulting in a smaller, cheaper ship for the same cargo capacity.

3. ***The Mid-Deck has considerably less ballast tank coated area to maintain.*** A double hull VLCC will have a coated area of about $225,000 \text{ m}^2$. A Mid-Deck, VLCC will have around $140,000 \text{ m}^2$.

4. ***Cargo tank bottom pits will not leak into ballast tanks.*** One major source of ballast tank explosions is eliminated. The interface area between the cargo tanks and the ballast tanks is about 60% that of a double hull.

When you run a Mid-Deck thru the IMO hypothetical damage scenarios, you find that the ship has an average spill volume three to four times less than a double hull. So here we have ship that is slightly cheaper to build than the double hull, easier to maintain, less chance of a ballast tank explosion, and in terms of volume is much more resistant to spillage than the double hull. A no-brainer, you say.

Not for the Tromedy. The Tromedy, mainly through the unrelenting efforts of the US Coast Guard, has effectively outlawed the Mid-Deck not to mention a whole range of other alternatives that are still better than the Mid-Deck.[2]

---

bottom to the undamaged side where it will escape side capture.

[2] My favorite is the unfortunately named Coulombi Egg. The Mid-Deck does a poor job of using its favorable hydrostatic balance to move the oil away from the damage. The small vertically oriented ventilation pipes take only a small amount of oil before the equilibrium will be established. This puts the Live Bottom interface close to the real bottom where it could be subject to current, wave-pumping, vessel motion, and the like.

Figure D.2: Coulombi Egg, Damage up 3 m. Light gray is oil, dark gray is seawater

BEFORE DAMAGE

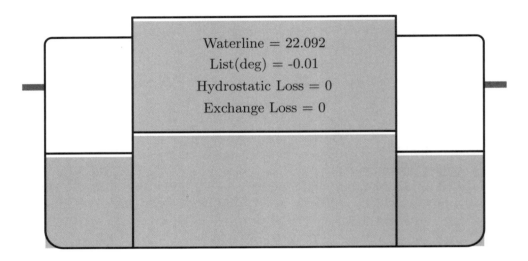

EQUILIBRIUM AFTER DAMAGE

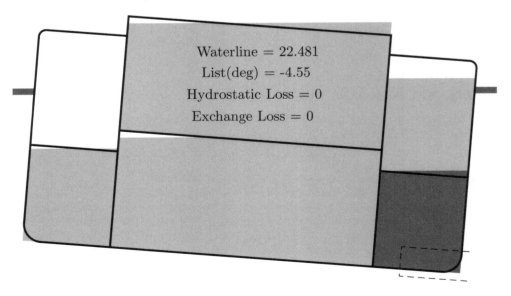

This means that, if we have another EXXON VALDEZ, the ship will spill 20 million to 30 million liters as opposed to less than 2 million liters. And, unless we inert the ballast tanks, it means we will have a slew of ballast tank failures and explosions, killing people and putting oil in the water.

The Coulombi Egg is a mid-deck design, but the ballast tanks are set above the outboard cargo tanks as shown in Figure D.2. The lower tanks are connected to these ballast tanks by non-return valves. When a lower tank is damaged, the incoming sea water pushes the oil in the damaged tank up into the ballast tank. There is an automatic transfer out of the damaged tank much like the active full vacuum ship. If the damage is near the bottom of a lower cargo tank, the Live Bottom will end up about 9 m above the ship bottom well protected from current, wave action and ship motion. But what I really like about the Egg is that **a VLCC built to this design will have only 66,000 m² of ballast tank coated area, and less than 20,000 m² of cargo tank/ballast tank interface area.** Ballast tanks properly inerted, the Egg is about as good as it gets in terms of minimizing ballast tank explosions on a segregated ballast tanker. Notice also that you can use air to blow out the damaged tank without putting any oil in the water. This can be a big help in refloating the ship. (This description of the Egg is not quite up-to-date. IMO in its wisdom required some changes to the original design which in my opinion degraded the performance of the concept.)

The transfer process is totally automatic. There are no sensing systems, no control systems. Just simple non-return valves. A leaking non-return valve will put some seawater in a cargo tank. But on a CTX standard tanker the bottom half-meter of all cargo tanks is properly coated and anoded. The leak will show up in the ullages, and the non-return valves in the ballast tanks are in a location where maintenance is easy. Of course, under IMO rules, this intelligent connection between the cargo and ballast tanks is completely illegal.

Others including Embiricos have suggested very similar concepts.[25] The Coulombi Egg in its current form has some faults. The tanks are too long; and for a VLCC the center tanks are too wide. We need more sub-division. The roll behavior in ballast is quite unattractive. But as long as all tankers are twin screw with very beamy hulls — they will be, won't they? – we can live with this.

D.2   The Defense of the Double Skin

For once I can't blame the Classification Societies. The culprits here are
the professional environmental community, tanker owners, Conoco, and the
US Coast Guard. Twin skin is such an obvious response to a big spill for
anyone who does not understand the physics of tank spillage nor the ballast
tank maintenance problem and the real danger associated with cargo leaking
into ballast tanks. Prior to the Valdez this included everybody outside the
tanker industry (and many people inside).

When the EXXON VALDEZ occurred, the environmental community was
understandably ignorant on these matters. It saw an honest chance to make
a difference for the environment and immediately called for double hulls.
The industry response was interesting.

The shipyards jumped at the idea. They could care less about the environment or killing tankermen. But they loved the new business.

Tanker owners were split. Few cared much about the environment or
killing tankermen. The calculus was based on how the new regulation would
trim tanker supply and push rates up. If an owner felt he would come out
ahead in the phase out process — an owner who had a young fleet — he
supported it. If not — an owner who had lots of old ships — he opposed it.
The divided owners had nil impact on the political process.

The only momentary questioning of double hulls came from the oil companies' marine departments. At the time, the marine departments still had
enough technical smarts and professionalism to realize there were safer alternatives, which would spill less oil. They mounted a campaign to put those
alternatives before the US Congress, asking for less prescriptive legislation.
But the oil company marketing types realized this was a loser. It would
just piss off the customer, at a time when the public were already ranking
oil companies below lawyers. When Conoco broke ranks with the "clap-
ping seal" ad, showing all manner of animals happily applauding Conoco's
new double hull VLCC, the marine departments knew they were dead. Oil
company opposition to mandating double hulls evaporated. In fact, the oil
companies jumped on the double hull bandwagon.

There was nobody left to defend the environment or tankermen.   In
theory, the US Coast Guard had the technical knowledge and the safety
concern. But the USCG, which had argued against double hull after the
AMOCO CADIZ on spillage and safety grounds, suddenly decided that double
hull safety issues were unimportant and spill-wise the double hull was the
only way to go. It became the most vociferous, single minded proponent of
double hull on the planet. I really don't know why, but initially I suspect it

was related to the appropriations process. The Coast Guard always has an uphill fight for the taxpayer's money, and to espouse a politically incorrect cause — the TV programs were still showing dying birds and otters during the congressional hearings — to the same people who controlled your budget would have been bureaucratic suicide. Whatever the reason, the USCG became the leader of the double hull band.

Meanwhile, various individuals had begun pointing out the physics of tank spillage and developing alternatives to double hulls. (Double hull safety issues, which should have been at the core of the discussion, were rarely brought up, largely because it was impolitic to admit that tankers had safety problems.) I took a crack at this myself, talking to Congressional staffers and environmental activists. My experience was that both were quick studies. But even when the professional environmentalists understood the physics of the problem and the alternatives, they were unwilling to attempt to deflect the double hull momentum. This was the first truly major "victory" for the environmental movement and to risk this victory with confusing technical details was unthinkable. It seemed to me that these people were more interested in their jobs than the environment. The staffers pointed out the obvious. Unless the environmental spokesmen supported the alternatives, it would be political suicide for their bosses to not mandate double hulls. I already knew that Congressmen were more interested in their jobs than the environment.

The only result of this effort was a requirement in OPA 90 that the USCG study alternatives to double hulls and recommend approval of any design which the USCG deemed equal to or better than the double hull. Similar wording crept into the IMO 1992 double hull amendments. It did not take long for proponents of various alternatives to the double hull to point out that some of these concepts such as vacuum and Mid-Deck spilled one-third or less oil on average than a double hull in a wide range of damage scenarios, and therefore according to these clauses should be approved.

Here's where things get weird. Instead of welcoming these environmentally superior concepts, a large portion of the professional environmental community and the USCG decide to fight them. I don't know why. Anyway once the defenders of the double hull realized that the double hull could not compete on spill volume, they decided to concentrate on spill number.

The tactic was to focus on the the probability of zero outflow. As we saw in Section 3.1, almost all spills are very small. A double hull is relatively ineffective on big spills but it's quite good at reducing the number of little spills. Earlier IMO design evaluation schemes were based on average spillage under a range of hypothetical damage scenarios. Now a design was to be evaluated on a combination of average spill volume, "extreme" spill volume, and the probability of no spill at all.

The design evaluation process became:

1. Run the hull thru a range of damage scenarios.
2. For each such scenario compute the spill volume. If no cargo tank was penetrated in the damage, count this scenario toward the probability of zero outflow.[3]
3. Compute the Pollution Prevention Index, E, via

$$E = k_1 \frac{P_O}{P_{OR}} + k_2 \frac{0.01 + O_{MR}}{0.01 + O_M} + k_3 \frac{0.025 + O_{ER}}{0.025 + O_E}$$

where P_O and P_{OR} are the probability of zero oil outflow for the design being evaluated and a reference IMO double hull respectively, O_M and O_{MR} is the mean outflow parameter for the candidate design and the IMO double hull, and O_E and O_{ER} is the extreme outflow parameter for the candidate design and the IMO double hull.[4] If a candidate design's E is greater than or equal to 1, then the ship is regarded to be as good as a double hull.

The IMO coefficients of the three terms (k_1, k_2, k_3) are (0.5,0.4,0.1). This was based on arbitrarily picking coefficients so that double hull and the Mid-Deck would end up with about the same E. (I swear I'm not making this up.) To do this, they had to give more weight to the probability of zero spill than to the mean spill volume. The bugger factors 0.01 and 0.025

---

[3] Just to make sure there was no mistaking the intent, it was decreed that any non-double hull tank that is bottom penetrated spills at least 1% of the tank volume **regardless of how favorable the hydrostatic balance is or where the Live Bottom ends up**. This was done despite the fact that IMO's own model tests at Tsukaba and David Taylor Research Center (see Section C.4) showed that the location of the Live Bottom was crucial to whether or not there would be any dynamic losses. 1% in these calculations is a big number. The IMO reference double hull VLCC has a mean spillage of just 1.5% in the very mild IMO damage scenarios.

And just to make doubly certain of the outcome, we throw in a largely non-existent bottom capture (Section C.8) and ignore the side capture which is critical to non-double bottom designs such as the Mid-Deck.

[4] The mean/extreme outflow parameter is the mean/extreme spill volume per the IMO calculation divided by the ship's cubic capacity. The extreme outflow is roughly the spill volume that will be exceeded 5% of the time *in the hypothetical damage scenarios*. This "extreme" outflow is still very small compared to the loss of a ship, or even an EXXON VALDEZ type spill. All the IMO damage scenarios are quite mild by the standards of Chapter 3. At IMO no one worries about the brobdingnagian spill.

Double hulls, however bad their spillage characteristics, (for example, the one-acrossers of Section 5.2) are exempt from this process. Most actual double hulls do not have an E as good as the IMO reference double hulls.

also reduce the importance of spill volume. None of these numbers have any physical meaning.[5]

By now, you are asking yourself what in the world does all this have to with spill resistant tankers? The answer is very little. The goal here is not the reduction of spillage, but the defense of the double hull. But the end result is regulation that is strongly biased toward designs which are good against little spills and against designs that are effective in reducing big spills — the exact opposite of the philosophy I argue for in Section 3.1.

Suppose we had a magical VLCC design that always spilled just a little oil in every one of the hypothetical damage scenarios, but overall spilled on average four times less oil than the reference double hull and whose "extreme" spillage was also one fourth that of the double hull. The E of such a ship would be 0.945. Even though this ship would reduce oil on the water by a factor of four relative to a better than normal double hull when subjected to the same damage, it would be judged inferior to the double hull and unacceptable.

Remarkably some environmentalists think this is good, arguing in effect that repeated little spills are more damaging to the environment than a rare big spill whose volume is far, far larger than the combined volume of all the little spills.

> The difficulty here is that the double hull, as it currently exists, provides a certain level of protection, especially with respect to the probability of what they call zero discharge, as opposed to the probability [sic] of a extreme discharge or a mean discharge. And because the IMO standard does not meet that level of probability of zero discharge, the Coast Guard reserved its position on behalf of the U.S. with respect to that particular standard. If there were a new design on the scene that could achieve an equivalent level of protection as the double hull for zero discharge, then clearly the environmental community at least would be supportive of that. But so far we haven't seen any designs which meet the standard. [Sally Lentz, Ocean Advocates, Testimony to the House Subcommittee on Coast Guard and Maritime Transportation, 1998-07-15]

This is the philosophy that thinks it is better to drain a small leak into a double bottom where it could result in the loss of the ship and a brobding-nagian spill rather than drain it into the sea where it will be spotted and

---

[5] In the bureaucratese of the US Transportation Research Board,

> The fact that IMO's choice of weighting factors cannot be related to any real measures of environmental consequence in itself would appear to eliminate the method from consideration.[49][page 29]

fixed. The double hull has turned these defenders of the environment into apologists for the giant spill.

It gets worse. Despite the blatant biases towards double hull, naval architects kept coming up with designs, that not only reduced overall spillage by a factor of three or more relative to the double hull, but also had E's over 1.00. In 1997, IMO after all kinds of delays grudgingly approved one of these designs: the Coulombi Egg.[6] But the USCG has refused to approve any alternative to the double hull.

The United States Coast Guard's position is the probability of zero outflow is the only thing that counts — spill volume is irrelevant — and that this position is imposed on them by US law. Here's the Assistant Commandant before Congress in 1999

> Our interpretation is that the double hull requirements were mandated to prevent, as far as practical, any spills from occurring in US waters. That was based on the Federal Water Pollution Control Act, which states "The Congress hereby declares that it is the policy of the United States that there should be no discharges of oil or hazardous substances into or upon the navigable waters of the United States." Our 1992 report concluded that the double hull was unmatched in preventing the majority of oil spills when compared to the proposed alternatives at that time. None of these alternatives or the alternatives evaluated since can match the superior performance of the double hull regarding the key performance measurement of the probability of zero oil outflow for both collisions and groundings.[Admiral Robert North, Testimony to House Subcommittee on Coast Guard and Maritime Transportation, 1999-06-29][7]

The USCG is nothing if not consistent. In 1997, the developers of a system called the Central Ballast Tank jumped through the hoops of the IMO oil outflow evaluation method and came up with an E better than 1.0. They took the numbers to the Coast Guard. But the Coast Guard said "sorry, we don't accept the IMO weighting factors, (k_1, k_2, k_3)." Somewhat taken back, they asked the USCG what were the Coast Guard's weighting factors. They were told $(1.0, 0.0, 0.0)$.[Penn Johnson, Testimony to House Subcommittee on Coast Guard and Maritime Transportation, 1997-10-30] In other words, it is the United States Coast Guard's official position that

---

[6] The Mid-Deck was included in the IMO 1992 double hull amendments.

[7] Elsewhere in this testimony, North admits "The Herbert Engineering report [paid for by the USCG] confirmed the results of the Marine Board and IMO studies. The double hull design was most effective in low energy casualties, while the Mid-Deck design was most effective in high energy casualties".

there is no difference between a 1 liter spill and an EXXON VALDEZ.[8] Even for the Tromedy, that's impressive stupidity.

There is only one cure for this kind of bureaucratic irrationality. If the Coast Guard is misinterpreting Congress's position, Congress will have to tell the Coast Guard that that is the case. Unless they do so, we will never get anything better than double hulls.[9] No shipowner can build a big tanker that cannot trade to the United States.

And toss the IMO oil outflow method into the paper shredder. It's not an evaluation method; it's a setup.

D.3 Obligatory Warning Label

All this tank arrangement nonsense can be fascinating, both technically and from a political science point of view. And perhaps there is a lesson here about avoiding prescriptive, technology stunting regulation with unappreciated side effects, in favor of pollution cost based penalties. But from the point of view of tanker regulation, this is just a side show, a freakish side show to be sure, but still a side show. The core problem in tankers is not tank arrangement. The core problem is a system in which the regulatee controls the regulator.

---

[8] Among the many interesting corollaries of this position is that internal tank subdivision has no value. A ship that has 40 cargo tanks is no better than a ship with a single humongus cargo tank as long as both have the same outer boundaries. In general, concentrating on the probability of zero outflow denigrates the value of many, small tanks. The shipyards love this.

[9] Congress did take a half-hearted stab at doing this. The 1998 Coast Guard appropriations bill required an independent look at the tanker design evaluation issue. The result was a 2001 Transportation Research Board report.[49] This report correctly dismissed the IMO evaluation scheme as nonsense. But it then went through a complicated simulation process involving heroic assumption after heroic assumption to conclude that the societal consequence of a spill varies at about the 0.4 power of spill volume. In other words, a 40 million liter EXXON VALDEZ spill is only 1000 times worse than a 1 liter spill. If a spill the size of a Yuppie water bottle costs society one thousand dollars, then the EXXON VALDEZ cost society one million dollars, about 10% of the value of the lost cargo. Truly preposterous. (But a heck of a lot better than the USCG position which holds that the cost to society goes as the 0.0th power of spill volume.)

Per Congressional direction, this report looked only at groundings and collisions after they had occurred, ignored structural failures, explosions due to cargo leakage, and machinery failures. In treating groundings, it assumed that the ship was always stranded and then assumed that the only source of damage was the ship's kinetic energy. In fact the brobdingnagian stranding spills have almost always been associated with the ship's breaking up due to wave action, or the cargo exploding. Another totally misdirected effort. As far as I can tell, the TRB report has had no impact on either the USCG or IMO.

Appendix E

The Joint Tanker Project

The Joint Tanker Project (JTP) is an effort on the part of three of the most important tanker Classification Societies (ABS, DNV, and LR) to eliminate differences in their tanker construction Rules. The project's web site is at www.jtprules.org. The JTP was begun in 2001 in the wake of ERIKA and the CASTOR. The JTP Rules are now in their Third Draft and pretty much finalized.[65] These Rules have been adopted by IACS and will be the IACS tanker construction Rules beginning in April, 2006.

The Joint Tanker Project adopted the philosophy that the existing Class Rules were basically satisfactory. All we need to do is to eliminate the mostly minor differences in the three Rules, and to tighten up the corrosion margins a bit. The result is that, while some steel has been moved around, overall the ships will be little if any stronger. The Joint Tanker Project itself examined a number of existing tankers designs and redesigned them to the new Rules.[66] Table E.1 summarizes the results. For big tankers, the indicated increase in steel weight is about 3%, nothing like the 15% plus that Chapter 6 argues for. This is a product of adopting essentially the same

Table E.1: Increase in steel weight (tons) due to JTP Rules

TANKER TYPE	OLD RULES	JTP RULES	INCREASE
VLCC	28,403	29,203	2.8%
AFRAMAX	9,919	10,399	4.8%
PANAMAX	7,454	7,697	3.3%
PRODUCT	5,467	5,599	2.4%
PRODUCT	4,347	4,606	6.0%

loads — ignoring the advice of Paik and Faulkner[64] — and basically the same structural design philosophy as the old Rules. Moreover, even the three percent is illusory. Once the yard structural whizzes get their hands on the new Rules and start "optimising", the three percent will quickly disappear.

The JTP also missed a unique chance to move the Rules to a full hull finite element model basis. This is preposterous. I can only imagine the internal debates on this one, with the techies ending up being as astounded as I am and the commercial guys arguing that such a change would push owners and yards out of the three Classes completely. The final decision was almost certainly made at the top, that is the commercial, level. Perhaps they reminded the project team that the goal was harmonization, not improvement. However it happened, an enormous lost opportunity.

As just one result, the Rules in the forebody and the aftbody including the engine room remain a set of prescriptive formulae of dubious origin replete with all sort of calibration factors. (See Section 5.8.) Hull deflection in way of the shaft and engine, a critical issue, is not addressed at all.[1] There remains no real way of discovering weak points in the structural design outside the midbody, or even within the midbody under certain asymmetric loadings. The JTP does call for a welcome improvement in the finite element modelling in the middle of the ship; but this just makes the failure to extend the FE model outside this area all the more incomprehensible.

The one area where the JTP Rules do represent a significant improvement, at least on paper, is the treatment of corrosion. The corrosion allowance is in absolute terms and for the most part the allowed corrosion is consistent with the allowances. For cargo and ballast tanks the allowed wastage before renewal is required is between 2.0 and 3.5 mm depending on location. For a big tanker this is 10 to 20% of the initial thickness, a considerable improvement over the 20 to 30% allowed by the old Rules.

However, 10 to 20% is still a hell of a lot of rust, far too much. And we are still faced with the twin problems of measuring wastage discussed in Section 2.11.

1. The thickness measurements are automatically biased to the high side by the fact that it is more difficult to obtain a reading on a more wasted bit of steel than a less wasted. This phenomenon can easily push the measurements to the high side by 10% or more.

2. Still more importantly, the owners control the thickness measurement

---

[1] Other than in the form of unenforceable bromides which usually start with "Consideration shall be given ...". This is the JTP's way of saying "This is a big problem, but we decided not to do anything about it."

process both through their control of Class and by their choosing and hiring the thickness measurement firm. There is no limit to this particular bias.

Only a hopeless optimist would believe that the JTP Rules would have made any difference in the case of the ERIKA or the CASTOR or the scores of other structural failures we have examined. The only real solution is to allow nil wastage per Chapter 7 enforced by a non-owner controlled inspection regime. But that is not what the Joint Tanker Project is about.

The JTP Rules are wedded to the tromedic status quo. No where is this made more clear than in their assumption of single screw. The Joint Tanker Project is quite out front about this. The new Rules explicitly do not cover twin screw tankers.[2] Even the old Rules did not turn their back on twin screw. Fundamentally, the Joint Tanker Project is not about improving tanker safety and reliability. It's about maintaining the Tromedy.

---

[2] Nor do they limit tank size in any meaningful way.

Bibliography

[1] ABS. Investigation into the damage sustained by the m.v. castor on 30 december 2000, final report. Technical report, ABS, October 2001.

[2] B. Allenstrom. Design for next millenium. *SSPA Highlights*, 99(9), 1999. page 3.

[3] Anon. Ultimate strength analysis of deck structure of a crude oil tanker with an application of an underpressure method. Technical report, IMO, Subcommitte on Ship Design and Equipment, 1993. DE 37/Inf. 8, 23-Dec-1993.

[4] Australian Maritime Safety Authority. Oceanic grandeur oil pollution incident, torres strait, 3 march 1970. Technical report, AMSA. www.amsa.gov.au/Marine_Environment_Protection/ Major_Oil_Spills_in_Australia/Oceanic_Grandeur/index.asp.

[5] M. J. Baratt. Collision avoidance maneuvers in restricted visibility. *Journal Institute of Navigation*, 29(4), October 1976.

[6] Robert Bea, Rob Pollard, et al. Structural maintenance for new and existing ships. Technical report, SNAME, March 1991. Marine Structural Inspection, Maintenance, and Monitoring Symposium, Arlington 1991-03-18/19.

[7] J.G. Beaumont. Ship constuction and safety (with particular reference to oil tankers). Technical report, LR, March 1990. Beaumont was Chief Ship Surveyor for Lloyds.

[8] National Transportation Safety Board. Grounding of the u.s. tankship exxon valdez on bligh reef, prince willian sound, march 24, 1989. Technical report, NTSB, July 1990. NTIS PB90916405.

[9] B. Box. Clouds grow over dh leaks. *Seatrade Web*, 6, February 1999.

[10] D. Brodie. The kirki incident. In *1993 Oil Spill Conference Proceedings*, 1993.

[11] A. Brown et al. Structural design and response in collision and grounding. *SNAME Transactions*, 108:447–473, 2000.

[12] R. Cahill. *Collisions and their Causes*. The Nautical Institute, 2002.

[13] R. Cahill. *Strandings and their Causes*. The Nautical Institute, 2002.

[14] J. C. Card. Effectiveness of double bottoms in preventing outflow from bottom damage incidents. *Marine Technology*, 12(1):60–64, 1975.

[15] Marine Environment Protection Committee. Report of the imo comparative study on oil tanker design. Technical report, IMO, January 1992. MEPC 32/7/15, 17 January 1992.

[16] National Research Council. *Tanker Spills, Prevention by Design*. National Academy Press, 1991.

[17] National Research Council. *Double Hull Tanker Legislation*. National Academy Press, 1998.

[18] National Research Council. *Oil Spill Risks from Tank Vessel Lightering*. National Academy Press, 1998.

[19] CTX. *The CTX Model Tanker Newbuilding Specification*.

[20] J. Devanney, S. Protopopa, and R. Klock. Tanker spills, groundings, and collisions. Technical report, MIT Sea Grant Program, June 1979. MITSG 79-14.

[21] Jack Devanney. Cargo tank bottom pitting. Technical report, Center for Tankship Excellence, 2005.

[22] Jack Devanney. The imo tanker spillage evaluation methods. Technical report, Center for Tankship Excellence, 2005.

[23] Jack Devanney and Mike Kennedy. The down ratchet and the deterioration of tanker newbuilding standards. Technical report, Center for Tankship Excellence, 2005.

[24] Jansen E. Corrosive inerting gases reducing double hull life by half. *Maritime Reporter and Engineering News*, March 2001.

[25] P. Embiricos. The quest for the environmental ship. Technical report, Intertanko, May 1991.

[26] Husain M. et al. Completion of the test program of the american underpressure system (aups). Technical report, Office of Naval Research, March 2004. ONR Contractor Report A0002.

[27] D. S. Etkin. Worldwide analysis of marine oil spill cleanup cost factors. Technical report, Arctic and Marine Oil Spill Program Technical Center, June 2000.

[28] D. Faulkner. An analytical assessment of the sinking of the m.v. derbyshire. Technical report, Royal Institution of Naval Architects, 2001.

[29] E. Gold. *Handbook on Marine Pollution.* Gard, 1985.

[30] W. Gray. Port state control, where to now? Technical report, Port State Control, 2000, May 2000. Keynote address at Melbourne Conference.

[31] W. Gray. The first arctic tanker. *ABS Surveyor*, 2:18–22, 2005. Summer, 2005.

[32] S. Hertzog. Oil and water don't mix – keeping canada's west coast oil-free. Technical report, David Suzuki Foundation, March 2003.

[33] E. N. Hurley. *The Bridge to France.* J. P. Lippincott, 1927. http:/www.gwpda.org/wwi-www/Hurley/.

[34] IACS. What are classification societies? Technical report, International Association of Classification Societies, January 2004. www.iacs.org.uk.

[35] INTERCARGO. Bulk carrier casualty report. Technical report, INTERCARGO, 2001. published annually.

[36] Exxon Company International. Operational restrictions of double hull tankers without longitudinal bulkheads. Technical report, Exxon, November 1993.

[37] G. Karafiath. Accidental oil spill due to grounding: Summary of model test results. Technical report, USN David Taylor Research Center, June 1992. NTIS ADA-253677.

[38] K. Katoh et al. Study on localized corrosion on cargo oil tank bottom plate of oil tanker. Technical report, SNAME, World Maritime Technology Conference, 2003.

[39] John Keeble. *Out of the Channel.* Harper Collins, 1991.

[40] J. F. Kemp. The danger of collisions with merchant vessels. *Journal Institute of Navigation*, 30(3), September 1977.

[41] I. Kim. Opa 90 and the decision to own or charter tank vessels. *Journal of Maritime Law and Commerce*, 35(2):219, April 2004.

[42] J. Landels, A. Thorpe, and K. Takita. Tankers recalled as cracks found. *Lloyds List*, July 1990.

[43] R. A. Levine. The design and service experience of the polar endeavour class tankers. *Marine Technology*, pages 60–64, 2004.

[44] E. V. Lewis et al. *Principles of Naval Architecture, Volume III.* SNAME, 1989.

[45] Shell Tankers (U.K.) Limited. Crude oil cargo tank pitting. Technical report, BSRA, 1968. B.S.R.A/ Report NS. 234.

[46] SSY Consultancy & Research Ltd. The cost to users of substandard shipping. Technical report, OECD Maritime Transport Committee, January 2001.

[47] M. Lutzen and B. C. Simonsen. Grounding damage to conventional vessels. Technical report, SNAME World Maritime Technology Conference, 2003. San Francisco.

[48] A. E. Mansour. Effect of negative pressure on tanker structure. Technical report, Marad, 1996. part of MH Systems Concept Definition Documentation.

[49] Transportation Research Board Marine Board. *Environmental Performance of Tanker Designs in Collision and Grounding.* Natinal Academy Press, 2001. Special Report 259.

[50] F. McGarr. In the matter of the oil spill by the amoco cadiz off the coast of france on march, 16, 1978. Technical report, US Court of Appeals for the Seventh Circuit, January 1992.

[51] D. T. Melitz, E. J. Robertson, and N. J. Davison. Structural performance management of vlccs: An owner's approach. Technical report, BP Shipping Ltd, February 1992. paper presented to SNAME New York Metropolitan Section.

[52] W. Mitchell and L. Sawyer. *Sailing Ship to Supertanker*. Terence Dalton, 1987.

[53] C. G. Munger. *Corrosion Prevention by Protective Coatings*. National Association of Corrosion Engineers, Houston, 1984.

[54] C. G. Munger and L. D. Vincent. *Corrosion Prevention by Protective Coatings*. National Association of Corrosion Engineers, Houston, second edition, 1999.

[55] E. Naess. *Autobiography of a Shipping Man*. Seatrade Publications, 1977.

[56] M. X. Navias and E. R. Hooton. *Tanker Wars: The Assault on Merchant Shipping during the Iran-Iraq Crisis, 1980-1988*. Tauris, 1996.

[57] John Newton. *A Century of Tankers*. INTERTANKO, 2002.

[58] R. Niebuhr. *Moral Man and Immoral Society*. Scribners, 1933.

[59] OCIMF. Factors influencing accelerated corrosion of cargo oil tanks. Technical report, Oil Companies International Marine Forum, September 1997.

[60] Tribunal of Inquiry. *Disaster at Whiddy Island, Bantry, County Cork*. Irish Stationery Office, 1979. Prl. 8911.

[61] American Bureau of Shipping. Guide for inert gas system for ballast tanks. Technical report, ABS, June 2004. ABS Pub. 0131.

[62] Standing Committee on Transport. Ships of shame: Inquiry into ship safety. Technical report, Parliament of the Commonwealth of Australia, December 1992.

[63] J. K. Paik. A guide for the ultimate longitudinal strength assessment of ships. *Marine Technology*, 41(3):122–139, July 2004.

[64] J. K. Paik and D. Faulkner. Reassessment of the m.v. derbyshire sinking with the focus on hull-girder collapse. *Marine Technology*, 40(4):258–269, October 2003.

[65] Joint Tanker Project. Common structural rules for double hull tankers. Technical report, ABS, DNV, LR, October 2005. Third Draft.

[66] Joint Tanker Project. Consequence assessment (phase 2). Technical report, ABS, DNV, LR, July 2005.

[67] M. Ratcliffe. *Liquid Gold Ships, A History of the Tanker, 1859-1984.* Lloyds of London Press, 1985.

[68] J. Shields. *The Invisible Billionaire, Daniel Ludwig.* Houghton Mifflin, 1986.

[69] B Sodahl. Stena v-max: A total concept for safe oil transportation in confined waters. *Marine Technology*, 39(4):250–255, October 2002.

[70] J Soltz. The effects of substrate contaminants on the life of epoxy coatings submerged in sea water. Technical report, National Shipbuilding Research Program, March 1991.

[71] ABS Staff. Microbial generated corrosion of tank plating in crude oil carriers. *ABS Safenet Advisory*, 1(2), October 1997.

[72] Exxon Technical Staff. Large oil tanker structural survey experience. Technical report, Exxon Corporation, June 1982. Exxon position paper.

[73] Fairplay staff. Bermuda: Pollution danger threatens economic survival. *Fairplay*, 40(4):23–24, July 1990. 1990-07-05.

[74] Fairplay staff. Classification societies: Getting ready for a shorter life. *Fairplay*, 40:37, September 1990. 1990-09-20.

[75] OSIR staff. Castor article. *Oil Spill Intelligence Report*, February 2001. pages 3-4.

[76] B. Stenstrom. Measures on board ship to minimize the escape of pollutants in case of accidents. Technical report, Swedish Maritime Administration, June 1988. MEPC 26/18, 29 June 1988.

[77] D. Tolliver and S. Morton. Computer controlled robotic marine coatings applications system. *Journal of Ship Production*, 21(3), August 2005. pages 195-202.

[78] TSCF. *Guidance Manual for Tank Structures.* Witherby, 1997.

[79] I. Watanbe, T. Yao, and H. Ohtsubo. Analysis of the accident of the mv nakhodka. *Journal of Marine Science and Technology*, 3:171–193, 1998. translation of the Japanese original, in two parts.

[80] J. H. Wheatley. Circumstances of collisions and strandings. In *Marine Traffic Engineering*, 1972.

[81] D. T. Yasunaga et al. Study on cargo oil tank upper deck corrosion of oil tanker. Technical report, SNAME, World Maritime Technology Conference, 2003.

[82] D. Yergin. *The Prize, The Epic Quest for Oil, Money and Power*. Free Press, 1990.

[83] Z. Zannetos. *The Theory of Oil Tankship Rates*. MIT Press, 1966.